THE GREAT PATERNALIST

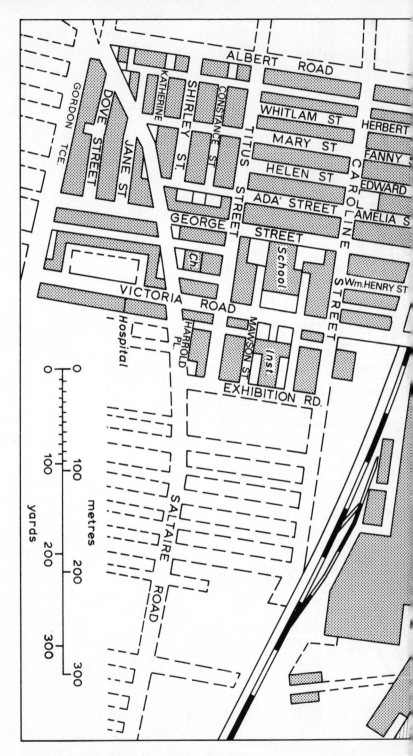

Street Plan of Saltaire

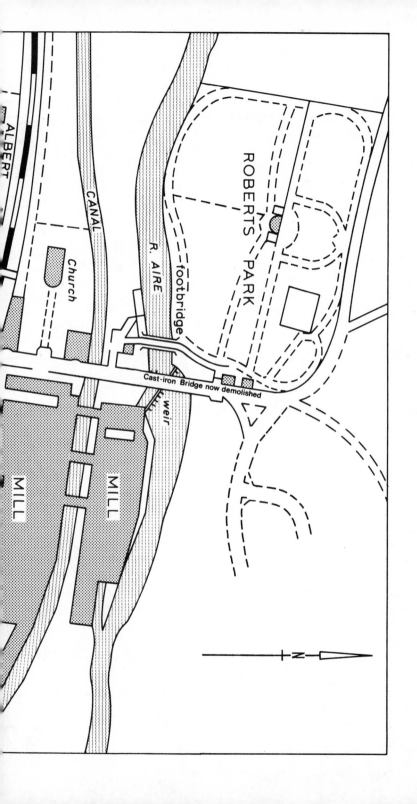

ALBERT

CANAL

Church

R. AIRE

footbridge

ROBERTS PARK

Cast-iron Bridge now demolished

weir

MILL

MILL

N

FOR EVELYN

THE GREAT PATERNALIST

TITUS SALT
AND THE GROWTH OF
NINETEENTH-CENTURY
BRADFORD

JACK REYNOLDS

MAURICE TEMPLE SMITH · LONDON
ST MARTIN'S PRESS · NEW YORK

in association with
THE UNIVERSITY OF BRADFORD

Reynolds, Jack
    The Great Paternalist.
    1. Salt, Titus   2. Saltaire (West Yorkshire)
    Biography
    I. title
    942.8'17'0924   DA690.S1/

ISBN 0 85117 230 X

First published in the United States of America in 1983
by St Martins Press Inc.
175 Fifth Avenue, New York, NY 10010. All rights reserved.
Library of Congress Card Catalog Number 83-40119
US ISBN 0-312-34638-7

Typeset by Tellgate Limited, Shaftesbury
Printed in Great Britain by
The Camelot Press Ltd., Southampton

CONTENTS

MAPS

TABLES

PREFACE

I have tried to address this book to an audience of general readers who may be interested in history as more than a simple celebration of the past. Naturally I also hope that professional teachers and students of history will find something of interest in it.

Titus Salt was one of a handful of men who directed the life of Bradford during the most important period of its history, the period during which an entirely new social complex was established which in turn became one of the great industrial centres in the world. Salt was the best-known of the group both as a highly successful entrepreneur who developed a new branch of the worsted textile industry and as the creator of the model village of Saltaire. When he died his fame was international and in England he was regarded as the epitome of all that was best in the enlightened Victorian capitalist.

It is impossible to write a biography of the man in the conventional sense of the term. Precise and intimate documentation of his private and public life, in letters and diaries, is not available. The record of his activities as a textile manufacturer is restricted to deeds of partnership, a small day book in which he recorded his experiments with alpaca in 1834 and 1835 and a few letters to other firms. By using the public record, however, it is possible to compose a useful history of the times of Titus Salt which deals with the absorption of the process of industrialisation into the local culture and brings out the part played by Titus Salt in it. This information leaves us with a number of tantalising hints about the man and his work, none of which in fairness can be pursued, but the main outlines of his career and impact are clear enough. He was not a dramatic leader of public opinion, for an inability to speak confidently in public prevented the development of a suitable platform manner. At times he seems to have been somewhat withdrawn, and it is perhaps characteristic that his most impressive contribution to history, Saltaire, was an individual and private gesture. But he was always an influential member of the community. At one time or another, he served in almost every important position in the town. As a native of the first rather than the last part of the century, he exercised the paternalist authority of the wealthy employer. By and large, it was directed to the reconciliation of men and women to the industrial world in which his fortune had been made. Thus he played a significant part in fashioning the mid-Victorian consensus. Both as entrepreneur and social engineer his career was part of the history of Bradford. I have tried to write a book which, without exaggerating or underrating the man's influence, holds the two themes of Salt and Bradford together in a coherent whole.

ACKNOWLEDGEMENTS

I should like to thank the University of Bradford for its help in publishing this book and for providing me with the opportunity to do some of the work. I thank the University of Leeds for permission to use material from my article, 'The General Election of 1859, Bradford', first published in *Bradford Centre Occasional Papers* No. 1, *Nineteenth Century Bradford Elections*, September 1979. I also thank the Bradford Central Library for the use of photographs of Titus Salt and of Bradford. I recall with great pleasure the interest taken and the aid given by students, undergraduate and in further education, who have taken my local history courses and the postgraduates whose researches I have supervised. The staffs of all the libraries I have used have been unfailingly helpful, and I should like to express my gratitude in particular for the help given by David Croft, Carol Greenwood, David James and Elvira Wilmot of the Bradford Central Library and Jennie Finder, John Horton, and Peter Kettley of the J.B. Priestley Library at the University of Bradford. I am also indebted to my friends and colleagues not only for the pleasure of their company but for direct help in many ways. Olwen Billcliffe and her family helped me to understand Saltaire; Paul Coles was always ready to discuss any of the problems I had in the writing; Nigel Copperthwaite took photographs, helped with the maps and on a number of expeditions gave me the benefit of his special geographical insights; he also helped me to take house measurements in Saltaire and Manningham; Derek Fraser's exhaustive knowledge of Victorian England was at my disposal; he also read the manuscript and suggested a number of improvements; Alan Farmer translated some of the German of Georg Weerth;

3

Stephen Holt first suggested the idea and pursued my interests indefatigably; for many years I have had the benefit of John Iredale's special knowledge of textile history and textile technology; Elisabeth Jennings gave me references to the Holden Papers; Keith Laybourn and I discussed the work regularly and he made very perceptive comments about the manuscript; Mike Leah took photographs and drew the maps; E. Russell provided me with internal measurements of Saltaire houses; the tenants of 13 River Avenue, Palmers Green, gave me hospitality when I worked at the British Library; Denys Salt gave me information about the Salt family and has allowed me to use the family records in his possession; Barbara Thompson has generously put at my disposal time, notes, statistics and her wide knowledge of Bradford sources. Sarah Yeadon has taken some of the photographs. My own family have helped me constantly. Janet, Jennifer and Catherine were ready to find urgently needed information and Janet also did some of the German translations. My wife, in addition to everything else, helped to collate the Census Enumerators' Returns and did the typing. I am very grateful indeed to all of them. The mistakes, however, are mine.

I

BRADFORD IN THE FIRST DECADES OF INDUSTRIALISATION

THE SETTING

In 1820, John Nicholson, a Bradford working man with ambitions as a poet, eulogised the industrial achievements of his fellow Bradfordians and the progress of the town in a poem – *the Commerce of Bradford*.

Hail, glorious Commerce! goddess of our isle!
Thou, who has rais'd her to the towering heights!
Where, throned she sits, the empress of the world, –
Britannia's glory, hail! of thee I sing;

Thou hast a daughter, whose industrious hands
Supply the earth with stuffs of richest hues,
In which are dress'd the sultan and the slave, –
Princes and Kings, Jews, Pagans, Turk, and Priest,
The Indian ladies and the Persian dames, –
Bradford her name, now known throughout the world.

Small was her fame, her trade and wealth were small,
When from a few thatched cottages she arose,
To form a street, the shadow of a town;
But view her now – behold her bursting forth
In far extending streets, majestic built,
Wherein the mould'ring bricks are seldom seen
While polish'd stones compose her rising walls,
And, speak in silent accents, through our land –
Where Commerce reigns, Old England's sons are bless'd![1]

Some thirty years later, Edwin Smith, an old Chartist who saw the period in a different light, published one issue of a working-class newspaper *The Voice of the People*. It included a humorous dialect article which saw the same period as the epitome of the 'good old days', a sort of golden age, when relations between master and man were friendly and close, before the grim spirit of industrial capitalism had captured the town and its activities.

I used to sit i't wool wi't meastur, an git my porridge, and after that smoke a pipe o' bacca wi' him, an he used to say, 'Na, Jack, lad! ha art ta gettin on? Ha is't wauf an barns? Is ther owt as I can du for thee? When ivver there's owt the matter wi' you, or't family tell me, and I'll help thee.' I used t' say, Nay, meastur, I's much obleeged to thee. We're aw reight; I kill'd a pig a forthnit sin, an sud be glad to bring thee a ham on't wen it's reddy, as interest for't brass tha lent me wen aar Bet gat her bed; besides that, we brewed two stroak o' rare guid drink t' last week, an we've a sek o' flaar i't haase so we no 'casion for onny help, thank thee aw't same. Then he said, 'Whoy lad, I sud be ashamed o' myself tu tak owt fur interest from a poor man. Tha's paid me honestly, an that's all I want. But I tell thee what, Jack, lad, I like a bit o' real honnest hoame-fed bakin, an not that Manchester muck that's made in a factory an sold wen it's three days cured. . .[2]

Both poet and journalist were looking at the scene through rosy-coloured spectacles, but together they establish the elements of the situation. Bradford was entering the final stages of a process of transformation. A relatively simple semi-rural world, somewhat detached from the mainstream of economic and political life, was becoming a completely organised industrial society, the international centre of the worsted textile industry. The old world had not as yet been obliterated. The culture, the social habits and the institutions of a new world had not been clearly established. Two worlds with their own distinctive characteristics were measuring up. Patterns of economic development were being laid down, the mobilisation of new social forces was started and the battlefields for the crucial social and political conflicts of the 1830s and 1840s were defined. In other words, the creation of an urban class-oriented society was under way; looking back, some saw the dawn of progress, brash and disruptive but beneficial, and others, the unhappy end of an ordered and kindly stability.

At the beginning of the century continuity with the past was still most obviously preserved in the topography of the area and

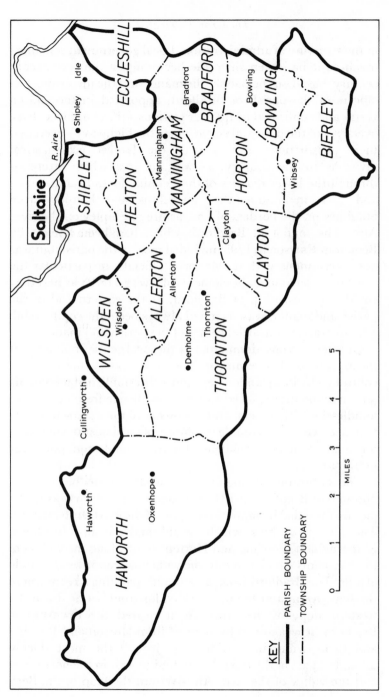

The Parish of Bradford

KEY
PARISH BOUNDARY
TOWNSHIP BOUNDARY

ECCLESHILL

BRADFORD

Idle

Shipley

Bowling

BOWLING

BIERLEY

R. Aire

Saltaire

SHIPLEY

HEATON

Manningham

MANNINGHAM

Bradford

HORTON

Wibsey

SHIPLEY

WILSDEN

Wilsden

ALLERTON

Allerton

Clayton

CLAYTON

Cullingworth

THORNTON

Thornton

Denholme

HAWORTH

Oxenhope

Haworth

0   1   2   3   4   5

MILES

in the structure of administration. Local government remained much as it had been since the beginning of the seventeenth century, based on the parish, the manor and the township. The officers of the parish of Bradford, appointed in the church vestry and confirmed by quarter sessions – the churchwardens, overseers of the poor and surveyors of the highways – exercised their jurisdiction over one of the largest ecclesiastical divisions in the country. It was an area which stretched through the lower reaches of the Pennine foothills and moors and took in innumerable townships and hamlets from Stanbury on the borders of Lancashire to Shipley on the river Aire. The manor of Bradford, which had been bought by Benjamin Rawson in 1795, included most of the parish but was not coterminous with it. Manorial officials, in particular the constables, sustained the elements of law and order as best they could. The township of Bradford, at the eastern end of the parish and manor, was, as it had always been, the commercial, administrative and social centre of the parish and manor.

Quarter sessions, dominated by the local gentry, remained at the apex of local government. The parish vestry, manned and controlled by local landowners and well-established merchants and manufacturers, faced as yet no challenge from aggressive middle-class Dissenters; and the owner of the manor was able to deflect with little trouble the efforts of local businessmen and other landowners to challenge his traditional monopoly over local markets.[3]

The geographical alignment of what was to become the borough of Bradford in 1847 still stood out as clearly as in the picture provided by manorial records of the fourteenth century. The four townships which would make it up, Bradford, Manningham, Bowling and Horton, stood along the valleys of three streams which ran into the wide bowl made by the circle of hills. The Bradford Beck, a clear and sparkling stream where the boys swam and the men tickled for trout, came down the western slope of the bowl. As it neared the township of Bradford, it was joined by streams from Horton and Bowling and then swung in a wide loop around the most thickly inhabited part of the township to find an exit in the north-east and the valley of the river Aire. Within the loop of the Beck domestic settlement and commercial activity concentrated in and around the medieval thoroughfares, Westgate, Ivegate and Kirkgate, an area beautified by ancient elm trees and cleansed by the scavenging of the ubiquitous pigs, kept as of right by the labouring poor. As a persistent reminder of the past, medieval burgage tenures along Kirkgate could still be defined clearly. The Bradford Fields, the medieval Biredolefield of the township, stretched across the eastern slopes of the hills. They were all enclosed, except for the Common, the Bradford Moor, which lay at the top of the hill; most of them had been enclosed by 1500 and almost all the rest by agreement in the seventeenth century. In this part of the township a well-used road now crossed the Common and provided a shorter route into Leeds than the old medieval way which still meandered through the hamlets of Undercliffe, Fagley and Farsley to link up with the Kirkstall–Leeds road. Bunker's Hill Colliery occupied most of the ancient Myrashay enclosure. But the fields were still thinly inhabited and used principally as pasture for the cattle and sheep of the local dairy farmers. John Reins, a wealthy villein living in Bradford in the fourteenth century, would have been bemused in the Bradford of the eighteenth century, but he could have found his way about, for building still followed the medieval lanes and paths. So few, in fact, had been the overt physical changes before the beginning of the nineteenth century that the Johnson Map of 1802 offers a perfectly adequate starting point for the reconstruction of the geography of medieval Bradford.[4]

The elements of the economy were also the same as they had been for centuries – a mixture of manufacturing and farming in which there was more than a suspicion of subsistence. Through time the proportions had changed very considerably – the textile manufacture had long been the principal source of wealth; yet it is easy to forget how much of rural life still persisted. A return made by the Vicar of Bradford in 1801 indicates that about 10 per cent of the total area of the parish was under arable production, and clearly a good deal more provided pasture of varying degrees of fertility for the stock-raising which was the principal activity of the local farmer. The chief products were dairy produce and meat for the growing

9

concentration of population and wool for the local industry. The most extensively cultivated food grain was – not unnaturally, given the poor agrarian potential of the region – oats, eaten as porridge or in the form of havercakes, for, as the Vicar of nearby Baildon noted in his return, 'the common bread used is oaten or havercake, except in families of the first class . . . and they only allow wheat bread at their [own] tables.'[5]

The textile industry preserved enough of its traditional structure and practice to sustain the fact of continuity. There had been an important change in the late seventeenth century when the worsted stuff manufacture was introduced from East Anglia to the western part of the West Riding to fill the gap left earlier in the century by the collapse of the woollen cloth manufacture there. Worsted stuff or pieces differed from woollen cloth as a result of using a different type of yarn. In making a woollen yarn the short fibres of the fleece were utilised and these were spun in a random arrangement into the yarn. In a worsted yarn the long fibres were used and these were spun together in parallel along the axis of the yarn. As a result, a worsted fabric was smooth, resistant to the touch and amenable to clear pattern definition, unlike a woollen fabric which was malleable and somewhat soft to handle. Production was still almost entirely domestic. The separation of the long fibres was done by the operation of woolcombing and this was destined to remain a hand process until well into the nineteenth century. Using a pair of heavy metallic combs which he heated and reheated in a charcoal fire, the hand comber separated what he called 'the tops' – the long fibres needed for worsted spinning – from 'the noils' – the short fibres which were a by-product sold off to the woollen manufacturer. There were no large concentrated units of woolcombing; work was done in small domestic premises or suitable outhouses by 'small masters' working with their families or with one or two journeymen. Weaving and spinning were still domestic-based activities. There were several factories in the parish of Bradford, but as yet none either in the township itself or in the group of townships which were to become the borough of Bradford several decades later. In fact, factory building in Bradford had encountered some physical resistance. Working conditions in domestic industry had their disadvantages but as yet nothing like the horrors uncovered in the 1840s in Bradford had been reached. At the very least, in what was still a rural environment, even the poorest cottages had reasonable access to the natural elements of light and sun and open air. John James, who was the first to write a history of Bradford, has left a sketch. The common sight, he wrote, on a fine day was that of women and children in the streets and lanes of the town, 'employed with the labour of spinning upon the one-thread wheel in which they greatly excelled'.[6]

But the old world had never been a static world. If it had been, the nineteenth century could not have witnessed such a dramatic transformation, for the creation of an industrial-capitalist society was a long process of evolution and development out of the constraints of feudalism. The eighteenth century had already seen a number of significant changes. Flourishing iron manufactories – destined for greatness in the nineteenth century – had been established in Bowling and at Wibsey Low Moor to exploit the valuable coal and iron ore deposits in which the south of Bradford was especially rich. Coal mining had become a profitable ancillary industry; the only significant industrial intrusion into the Bradford fields along the eastern slopes was the Bunker's Hill Colliery which occupied a considerable part of Boldshay and Myrashay. The Leeds–Liverpool and Bradford Canals and a number of improved turnpike roads relieved something of the town's geographical isolation. And, most important, the worsted textile industry had come to dominate the employment of capital and labour. The evidence, meagre as it is, suggests that, while at the beginning of the century perhaps 20–25 per cent of the population worked at the trade, by 1780 between 45 and 50 per cent were earning their living mainly through their connexion with it.[7]

The expansion of the worsted industry was accompanied by changes in the social structure of the industry. By the end of the century it was controlled by the rich woolstaplers and manufacturers who had the resources to exploit the opportunities of national and international markets. There had been a massive extension of the 'putting-out' system, so that

Bradford men had their spinning done over a wide area of northern England. 'In putting out wool to spin we sent a pack of tops . . . to Skipton by the canal. . . We had spinning done in Lancashire as far as Ormskirk; in Craven and at Kirkby Lonsdale: in Wensleydale, Swaledale, and other parts of North Yorkshire', Thomas Crossley, an important Bradford manufacturer at the end of the century, told John James when he came to write his *History of the Worsted Manufacture*. It is difficult to be precise about the relationship between the big entrepreneurs and the textile craftsmen – the weavers and the woolcombers – for in the state of flux which characterised the position every variety of involvement was displayed. Weavers and woolcombers, working in their own premises, able to determine the hours and pace of their work, claiming the right to take their own apprentices, sometimes with an element of security in a few fields or an allotment garden, were still called master manufacturers and had the appearance of independence. Woolcombers seem also to have organised small units of production headed by a 'basketeer' who supervised their activities and might collect work from a number of different sources. The woolstapler or large-scale manufacturer rarely had an interest in the industrial training of weavers and woolcombers. This was done by the craftsmen themselves who could claim therefore that the apprenticeship system was still alive. Most of the evidence, admittedly provided generally by the big merchants and manufacturers, gives the clear impression that the appearance of independence conceals at best a form of sub-contracting. There can be little doubt that in the years around the end of the century, as the number of journeymen increased rapidly and markets spread over wider and wider areas, the independence of the textile craftsman was becoming more apparent than real.[8] Even given the meagreness of the quantitative evidence, there are several indications of the pattern of development. On the one hand, trade union activity had increased among journeymen woolcombers by the 1790s. On the other hand, the directors of the Bradford Piece Hall, opened in 1773 and extended in 1780, provided only a limited number of selling outlets, far fewer than would have been necessary in the woollen branch of the industry, suggesting that only a comparatively small number of worsted cloth manufacturers were in contact with regional or wider markets. The establishment of the Worsted Committee in 1777 was the clearest indication of the way in which the industry had developed. The Committee was a union of large employers of labour which had been given statutory recognition despite antagonism to other forms of union associated with industry. Its principal purpose was to maintain industrial discipline in the admittedly difficult circumstances of a 'putting-out' system which had spread for beyond the immediate control of the individual master manufacturer. Its authority ran throughout the whole of the northern worsted area and Bradford manufacturers were its principal adherents.[9]

Economic expansion was accompanied by an increase in population brought about at this time more by improvements in human fertility than by migration from outside. The increase began in the 1740s and continued relatively slowly until the 1770s. Then between 1781 and 1801 the population of the township of Bradford increased by about 50 per cent from approximately 4,200 to 6,300, an annual increase of about 2 per cent. The population of the four contiguous townships, Bradford, Bowling, Horton and Manningham, which eventually became the borough, increased slightly faster from about 8,500 to 13,500, about 5 per cent.[10]

In these years, the population of Bradford should be seen first of all in terms of a division between the dependent and the independent: between those who sold their labour and their time and those who provided work for others or lived directly off the product of their own labour. It is in the traditions of this fundamental split that the element of deference – persistent through the greater part of the nineteenth century – is rooted. It is impossible to be exact about numbers or a precise dividing line. In so far as the payment of direct taxation offers help, James suggests that in 1781 there were 403 houses in the township of Bradford chargeable to the window tax, an indication perhaps that rather less than half the total population were above the level of the simple dependent cottager. Sir F.M. Eden, in a nationwide survey of the condition of the poor, reported of Bradford in 1795 that 470 houses paid the tax. As the number of houses had probably increased to about 1,200, it looks as if the number of dependent cottagers was going up as the population increased and the worsted textile manufacturers fastened their hold on employment opportunities.[11]

To look more closely, there was a sprinkling of well-established gentry families living around the periphery of Bradford and forming the apex of the social hierarchy. Sir Francis Lindley Wood, progenitor of the Earls of Halifax and the most distinguished of the Bradford gentry, still lived at Bolling Hall in Bowling, although he was transferring his Bowling property, at great personal profit, to the Bowling Iron Company. Sir Henry Tempest, a descendant of the original Bowling family, lived at Tong Hall. The Listers occupied Manningham Hall, the Rawson family, the Manor Hall in Kirkgate. The Sharp family had a representative in Little Horton, and the Wickhams were at Low Moor, where they had transferred their allegiance from the land to iron manufacturing. A handful of other local families also claimed armigerous status. Most of them had recently emerged from yeoman stock, like the Hodgsons of Manningham, or had recent or existing connexions with trade and industry – the Stansfields of Esholt, Francis Duffield of Town Hill in the township itself, and John Preston, one of the partners in the Low Moor Iron Works, were perhaps the most important.

A new middle-class élite was also beginning to take shape, within the township and the immediate vicinity. It was headed by what had been known for centuries as 'the principal inhabitants of the town' – well-to-do farmers, hovering on the verge of gentry, important manufacturers and merchants and the professional men, the lawyers, doctors and parsons. It is customary in discussing this group to give pride of place to John Hustler, a Quaker. He is said to have been the real driving force behind the improvements in the economic infrastructure of Bradford – the Piece Hall and the two canals – and he is the only eighteenth-century Bradfordian to have merited an entry in the *Dictionary of National Biography*. He was the son of a small yeoman farmer of Bolton, Bradford and took to the wool trade

14

about the middle of the century. This élite group included men like Abraham Balme, farmer, land agent and mine owner, who carried through the legal negotiations required for the Bradford Canal, an Anglican in religion; John Rand, a stuff manufacturer, a Norfolk man by origin and also an Anglican; James Garnett, who had made the first tentative experiment in worsted machine spinning in Bradford in 1794, a leading Methodist for some years and later a member of the Independent Chapel; Samuel Broadley, a woolstapler, Baptist by religion; John Aked, a timber merchant, Anglican; Richard Sclater, a woolstapler; and Richard Fawcett and Nathaniel Murgatroyd, two young worsted manufacturers. Their interests merged with those of the local 'gentry', to whose ranks some of them, as graduates, legally belonged and others eagerly aspired, while they created the investment opportunities – canals, turnpike trusts, and occasionally new factories – which the gentry as eagerly sought. Yet they remained a distinctive group, united in various forms of economic activity, though much diversified in religious allegiances and political attachments. Some of them were ready to challenge the residual manorial control over market tolls and the monopoly of corn milling, although they were as yet in no position to bid for the substance of local power which lay with the parish establishment manned by Anglicans, and local quarter sessions manned by the upper crust of the gentry.

Below them, in social hierarchy, there was a further 'middling' group of substantial artisan-traders and shopkeepers, the hatters, furniture maker, saddler, tallow chandlers, the grocers, butchers, innkeepers and pottery dealer, whose presence is indicated in the *Parish Registers*.[12] At some point, their lives touched the ranks of the aspiring journeymen whose way of life was shared by younger members of these families, and perhaps also that of the better paid of the textile craftsmen, most of whom by this time would nevertheless be regarded as 'dependent' rather than 'independent'. Beneath them came the humbler craftsmen and textile workers – the main body of an emergent working class – and at the bottom of the heap, the mass of the labouring poor, the labourers and the servants, all those men and women who lived from hand to mouth on the meagre wages offered by the carrying and fetching jobs of a labour-intensive economy.

Institutions reflected the shifts which were taking place in social structure. The creation of a Property Protection Society to fill the gaps in an inadequate policing system and the transformation of the Water Company into a profit-making organisation spoke of a well-to-do middle class with property to preserve and a desire to extend it. The existence of thirteen friendly societies with an average membership of about 130 testified to the existence of a substantial group of relatively well paid men, 'independent' or 'dependent', somewhere beneath them. The fact that woolcombers were known to belong to a trade association with national links indicated the way in which the Bradford trade, like its West Country counterpart, had accepted large-scale capitalist organisation and showed that the elements of working-class consciousness were there.[13]

It was in religion and religious organisation that changes were most easily recognised, for in a non-secular 'God's world' social change was bound to be reflected in this way. Changes which had started in the sixteenth century proceeded with great vigour through the seventeenth and eighteenth centuries. An archbishop's visitation return for 1743 suggested that only about one-fifth of the population of the parish were Dissenters. By 1793, it was said that at least half the population of the township of Bradford, the part of the parish where the Anglican Church was strongest, were in that category. It would be nonsense to think in terms of a simple division between a landed community of Anglican gentry and farmers, on the one hand, and a manufacturing and trading community of Dissenters on the other. A good many farmers in the West Riding were Dissenters, and there was always a strong Anglican element among Bradford manufacturers. Nonconformists and Dissenters predominated, numerically, if not in other ways.

The Quakers, though numerically small, were probably the most important of the sects in the eighteenth century. They had always had a strong following among the small yeoman farmers whose properties ringed Bradford, and by 1732 had erected a meeting house. In addition to the Hustlers, the banking family of Peckover had brought prestige to the sect and new enterprise capital to the town before the end of the century. Congregationalists had established themselves in a chapel in Horton Lane in 1782, and in the same year the Baptists had built one in Westgate, near the Beck. The Methodists had established themselves in the town early in the life of the new non-conformity and by 1767 had what Wesley called the largest Octagon chapel in the kingdom. They were to be by far the fastest-growing sect throughout the next century, although internal divisions were to fragment their membership.[14]

Change had also been accompanied by an increase in the wealth of the community. Gloomy prognostications at the end of the century suggested that there was no hope for a local banking venture and that grass would grow in the streets before long. But these were no more than subjective responses to short-term adversity. Indeed, the facts that so many people were out of work in such periods, and that the town was nevertheless able to support the great increase in poor rate, suggest that there was plenty of surplus capital and surplus labour available for profitable investment.

BEGINNINGS OF A FACTORY TOWN

Looking back in the mid-nineteenth century, old men emphasised the great changes which had taken place since the turn of the century, and recalled the eighteenth century in terms of its quiet scenes and ancient customs. One veteran recalled the days when 'the rooks were cawing in the grove in the Hall Ings; when Dicky Hodgson's hounds cast off in Manningham Fields . . . when Madam Rawson dwelt in the Manor House, and the last cast-off pair of her jester's red plush breeches swung over the wooden arms of an automaton placed at the entrance to Farrar's shop in Ivegate'.[15] Another remembered the opening of the Bradford Canal, and the gentry boating there on a summer's evening. He remembered the open market for the butchers at the bottom of Westgate, the market cross which stood there, the cock-fighting and bull-baiting, and a third remarked that when he had been a boy he had known everybody he met in a morning's walk through the town. Now he did not know the streets, where people lived. Whatever can be said about the evolutionary nature of the process of industrialisation, these men had no doubt that they had lived through a considerable revolution.[16]

At the beginning of the nineteenth century a great deal began to happen very quickly. In 1803, the leading inhabitants of the town headed by John Hustler and Edmund Peckover obtained an Act of Parliament 'for paving, lighting, watching and improving the town of Bradford and part of Little Horton. It was the first effective intrusion into the prerogatives of the old administration and aroused some opposition from Bradford Tories when first proposed. Francis Duffield, Richard Sclater, Richard Hodgson and several others called a town meeting at the Piece Hall to protest at the expense which would eventually fall on the shoulders of the inhabitants, and a number of important names, like those of John Rand and Matthew Thompson, were missing from the list of first subscribers to initial expenses for an Act. Benjamin Rawson, however, joined the reformers, though presumably to protect his own interests. The Act gave authority over an area which stretched from the Paper Hall in High Street, to Westgate just below Lumb Lane, across the Beck a short way up Great Horton Lane, from there to the end of Vicar Lane and back to the Paper Hall – the principal area of concentration at the bottom of the hills which surrounded the township. This geographical limitation was to prove a source of weakness, since it was impossible to control developments just outside the area named. The authority it conferred also clashed both with that of the parish vestry, and with that of the surveyors of the highway appointed by it. A board of fifty-eight commissioners was to exercise authority under its provisions. They had to be men of substantial position, possessing estates of at least £1,000, and were to be replaced, as necessary, by co-option.[17]

In 1800 in the area which eventually became the borough, there was only one factory. By 1830, there were thirty-four, some of them, like John Wood's at the bottom of Manchester Road, Rand's at the bottom of Horton Lane, Garnett's in Barkerend Road, J.G. Horsfall in North Wing, Illingworth and Murgatroyd in Union Street and W. Rouse and Son in Canal Side, large establishments with national reputations.[18] 'The first stages of the technical transformation of the Bradford worsted trade was more or less completed. The bulk of the spinning processes, except in very busy times, were carried out in factories, and engaged the activities of an industrial proletariat of women and children. The power loom had been introduced in 1824, though its use was as yet far from widespread; tentative experiments were being made with machine woolcombs. The wool market had moved from Wakefield to Bradford and the stuff market from Halifax and Leeds. The specifically Bradford innovations – mixed cotton and wool cloths, the Ripley dyeing techniques, the use of alpaca and other new fibres – which were to carry the Bradford trade to the heights of its industrial fortune, were still to come, but already the town had seen twenty years of extraordinary development. The leadership of the British worsted textile industry was now firmly in the hands of Bradford's manufacturers and merchants.

Circumstances in fact provided unique opportunities for textile entrepreneurs in Bradford in this period. Bradford had not been heavily committed to water power in the eighteenth century. Expansion had not been excessively rapid, thus, as steam power became more readily accessible after 1800, there was surplus capital and labour available for expansion and the benefits of cheap coal from the local coal mines could be reaped to the full. As elsewhere, there were few restraints on the activities of the entrepreneurs, beyond the physical limitations of geography. Few social demands were made on profit; Pitt's wartime income tax was abolished in 1816 and rates levied within the township of Bradford were a small proportion of expenditure. Public space, for example, could be appropriated with little cost. Factories accumulated along the watercourse, the Beck and the Canal, for the water which was essential, particularly in the early stages of the industrial process, and for use as sewers for the disposal of human and industrial waste. No regulations controlled hours of work, for the factory legislation as yet in existence did not apply to the worsted industry. Neither the parish vestry nor the new board of commissioners could have imposed much social or environmental discipline, for the entrepreneur was well

19

represented in both bodies and in any case both lacked effective power, even supposing they would have wished to use it. Thus the advantages of concentrating industry and commercial activity in the lower reaches of the Bradford dale could be claimed by the profit maker. The disadvantages were born by society in general.

Most important of all, the capital cost of expansion was, relatively speaking, low. For a number of reasons, the pace of technological change was such as to stimulate the growth of a mixed system of production. Factories were erected to carry out the initial processes connected with spinning. The more skilled work of weaving and woolcombing continued to be done in the homes of the workers or in premises provided by them. A considerable proportion of the fixed costs of both day-to-day activity and expansion was thus borne by the worker. The entrepreneur could maintain a suitable level of liquidity; his purchase of raw material for the broadening of his business interests was not impeded; and capital investment could be timed more conveniently. Entry to the industry was also eased. Although poor men, however able, were unlikely to make much progress as independent masters, a relatively modest amount of capital was sufficient to start a successful business. Bradford working men might look back on this period as a golden age. Undoubtedly, for the entrepreneur it was precisely this.

It would be unrealistic not to recognise the pitfalls and dangers which faced the entrepreneurs even in the most propitious general circumstances. In the absence of limited liability, failure could mean disaster, and the mortality rate among worsted firms was always high. Even Richard Fawcett ('King Dick'), who had dominated the Bradford trade in the first two decades of the century, was bankrupt in 1830. The international market on which real prosperity in the industry depended was subject to impediment through war, blockade, tariff. The supply of wool was already providing difficulties. Given the flexible condition of technological improvement and adjustment, investment decisions could be crucial in an uncertain market. Worsted textiles was always a business which demanded a great deal of technical expertise from the entrepreneur at all levels and stages of production. It could also demand strong nerves and sound local connexions, for terms of credit were long, markets widely scattered, and the cycle of demand not easily predictable. It could be reported of the Bradford trade in 1826 that 'it is an unthankful duty to record week after week the state of a market once flourishing now in a state of progressive decline'. Yet, given all the difficulties, the Bradford worsted manufacturers could assert in the 1820s that 'during the last eventful thirty years the manufacture of long wool [i.e. worsteds] had never languished; the operative hands had been fully employed; and the master manufacturer had been enabled to give a rate of wages sufficient to afford to the labourer the means of subsistence, even in times of scarcity'. In 1832, the *Leeds Mercury* confirmed the report: 'few towns were more prosperous than Bradford, no trade . . . so steady for many years'.[19]

Although the most dramatic stories of fame and fortune were to be told later in the century, men like John Wood, John Rand, Matthew Thompson, James Garnett, William Rouse, Swithin Anderton and Christopher Waud had little to grumble about. The rise of the Garnett enterprise, for instance, was as instructive as the more highly publicised ventures of later years, the Salt, Lister, Holden and Illingworth enterprises. James Garnett emerges in the record as a piece maker (i.e. a worsted manufacturer) in the 1760s. He lived at the Paper Hall, a substantial seventeenth-century house. It had lost some of its distinction since the days when it had first been erected and was not perhaps regarded as one of the houses of the well-to-do in Bradford. He ran his business from it. Unfortunately, there is no evidence of its extent in this period. About 1760, he was a member of the Methodist connexion and is recorded as having allowed the society to use his barn at the Paper Hall for meetings during the building of the first chapel, the Octagon in Great Horton Road. In 1780 he became a member of the Independent Congregation, just being reconstituted after a split in local Independency. In the following year he became one of the trustees of the new chapel which was erected for their use. It seems that his affairs were prospering. In 1777, he was one of Bradford's four representatives on the Worsted Committee at the foundation and continued in the office for

21

over twenty years. Local tradition has it that he was the first manufacturer to introduce spinning machinery into the town. In 1794, he is said to have installed a number of hand-driven spinning machines in the Paper Hall. In 1815, his sons began to build a steam-powered factory about half a mile further up the hill from the centre of the town; apart from the Bunker's Hill Colliery, the first industrial intrusion into the medieval townfield. By 1824 it was completed and as one of the largest in Bradford had a capital valuation of over £8,000. In 1854, W. Garnett bought the estate of the Hustler family which lay at the top of the hills above the works and from Undercliffe House, one of the most distinguished houses in Bradford, he was able to survey the activities below.[20]

Bradford had now become a magnet for people seeking work or business opportunities. An upsurge seems to have begun about 1803 and after 1810 the population of the town and parish began to grow at a staggering rate. The population of the 'borough' of Bradford grew by 130 per cent between 1811 and 1831, by 64 per cent between 1811 and 1821 and by 65 per cent between 1821 and 1831. A comparison with the figures for Great Britain (17 per cent between 1811 and 1821) and for the West Riding between 1821 and 1831 (22 per cent) indicates the magnitude of the increase. In addition, Bradford was outstripping its nearest local rivals. In the three decades, 1801 to 1831, the township of Halifax grew by 4, 40 and 29 per cent, while the township of Bradford was growing by 21, 68 and 78 per cent.

To some extent the increase was due to a birth rate which continued high even by the standards of the early nineteenth century, and which more than offset a persistently high death rate. By 1820, however, the greatest impulse came from the constant influx of new inhabitants, into the areas where new factories were being erected. The process of urban concentration dictated by the geographical inflexibility of steam as a source of power and the limitations of the means of transport and communication was under way. The townships of Bradford and Horton grew by about 250 per cent, Manningham by 190, Bowling by 170, while the parish in general was increasing by about 150 per cent between 1801 and

1831. Most of the new inhabitants came from the immediate neighbourhood. Of the more distinguished settlers, the Salt family, which moved from the Wakefield area in 1822, provided a characteristic example. George Ripley came from Halifax in 1805 and founded the famous dyeworks which bore his name. Thousands of more humble people who could not go much further than they could walk came from the nearby villages in Bradforddale itself and from Airedale, Wharfedale and the lower Pennines to take advantage of the opportunities which an expanding urban economy presented.[21]

At the same time important minorities were being attracted from further afield. Among those who were to join the new middle-class élite and who were therefore to share the domination of Bradford's affairs for the greater part of the nineteenth century, one comparatively small but highly significant group was already beginning to make its mark – the Scots, of whom Robert Milligan, later Mayor and Member of Parliament for the borough, was at this stage the most important. One or two Germans had already arrived, but the main body was to come a decade later. In addition there was by 1830 a significant and well-organised contingent of Irish people, mainly Roman Catholic, settled in the town. A few stood out as members of the professional and trading community. Victor Rochefort had taken advantage of the facility afforded Irish wool merchants by the Act of Union of 1801 of bringing Irish wool to the British market and set up in Bradford in 1813. He was in a prosperous way of business and was an active participant in Liberal-Radical politics; W. Egan was a respected hardware merchant and the principal gunsmith in the town; there was at least one Irish doctor. The majority, however, went to swell the ranks of the textile operatives. In 1834, the Reverend Father Murphy reported that six years earlier when he had been priest in Bradford there had been an Irish community of some four or five hundred who had come mainly from the Mount Mellick area to work as weavers and woolcombers. In fact mass had been celebrated in Bradford in 1824, for the first time since the Reformation, and a Catholic chapel was opened on Stott Hill behind the parish church in 1825. The newcomers had settled down in the huddle of streets, courts and yards which were springing up in the Wapping and Goitside districts near to the new factories where the children could find work and their parents employment as outworkers. They seem to have been accepted without enormous difficulty as part of the working-class community, although their separate identity was recognised and sometimes resented. The recital of mass in a public house before the chapel was built caused some consternation, as did a public debate between Catholic and Protestant ministers of religion in Eastbrook Chapel. The Orange Order thrived. On the other hand, the Catholic community played a part in the affairs of Bradford. It supported the Dispensary with collections made in church and collaborated in temperance demonstrations in the early thirties. Significantly, also, in the great strike of 1825 the workers' strike committee was quick to recognise the importance of Irish support and to enlist the formal aid of the community. Father Murphy reported that his flock had had good wages, lived comfortably and dressed like the English. There was little evidence of a serious clash of cultures in this period.[22]

Although the rest of the new population was principally of West Riding origin, a sizeable minority came from further afield. Scruton, describing the life of the Bradford woolcomber in this period, said: 'They came from Kendal, North Yorkshire, Leicester, Devonshire, and even from the Emerald Isles; so that to spend an hour in a public house (the comber's calling was a thirsty one), one might have heard a perfect babel of different dialects.' The vast majority came from rural areas and so faced, for the first time, a more complex pattern of life in the town. Scruton continues his description of the woolcomber: 'His attachment to rural life was evidenced by the fact that in hay-time and harvest he used to lay aside his woolcombs, take up his scythe . . . and go to his own country a harvesting. . .'[23] It was also a young population; more than 50 per cent were under twenty.

Changes of this magnitude in the pattern of production and in the physical concentration of people associated with it were inevitably the agencies of further transformation. A daily reminder of the social costs of industrialisation came from the pall of thick yellow smoke which had begun to lie across the valley (and with which Bradfordians were to have a sort of love/hate relationship for the next 160 years). Baines reported in 1822 in his *Directory*: 'In Bradford, as in almost every other manufacturing town in the West Riding, the inhabitants have of late years suffered considerable annoyance from the smoke emitted from steam engine furnaces and they look forward with some impatience to the removal of this increasing nuisance which may be so easily effected.' Formal complaints were made about Rand's Mill in 1814 and Horsfall's Mill in the following year. Whittaker's Brewery in Horton Road and the Iron Foundry in Tyrrel Street provoked a good deal of consternation, but in every case the Commissioners were satisfied that the chimneys were of 'sufficient height and constructed so as to consume smoke'.

A terrier taken in 1825 (on behalf of the Vicar Henry Heap) referred to ancient glebe lands which 'formerly consisted of three enclosures of meadow ground, lying contiguous in Goodmansend, (Bridge Street) within the township of Bradford aforesaid, commonly called the Old Vicarage Closes, containing together four acres; but as the smoke from the different mills has rendered the grass of herbage unfit for cattle, the half of this land has been sold for £1750 and the money placed in the three per cent consols'. But already 'where there was muck' there was money. A local poet expressed that resigned acceptance which became Bradford's response to this normality of their daily lives:

Hail, Bradford – in thy dark and smoky story,
What though the mid-day sun in vain may shine,
Let smoke be still the index of thy story,
And soot in place of sunbeams still be thine.

The Beck was becoming the open sewer of the town. By 1826 it was sufficiently polluted for the vestry to use recipients of poor relief to clean it out. The canal matched the Beck for filth. Slums were growing up around the factory areas – Wapping, the bottom of Manchester Road and the Goitside were already overcrowded and unhealthy. In 1832, the cholera epidemic 'made fearful ravages in the Wapping district'. In general, the building of houses was falling behind the needs of the community. While the population increased by four times between 1801 and 1831, the stock of housing went up by three times and the position deteriorated from an average of about five per house to one of six per house in 1831.[24]

As yet, however, there was no collapse of the environment such as was to occur twenty years later. The built-up area remained comparatively small. It was still easy to get out into something like a rural environment. The villages which made up the parish – indeed, those which were to make up the borough – were still separated sharply. The walk from Horton to Bradford took the pedestrian through two miles of meandering country lanes. Despite his strictures about the smoke, Baines could also write: 'the town is pleasantly situated at the junction of three beautiful and extensive valleys . . . the soil is dry, the air sharp and salubrious, the annual mortality in the town not exceeding one in fifty'.

While it was possible to discern in the eighteenth century the outlines of the social structure of nineteenth-century Bradford, the demographic changes which took place between 1800 and 1830 both sharpened the picture and made the pattern simpler. The influence of the upper gentry on Bradford affairs diminished; the last local representative of the Rawsons left the Manor House in 1804; Sir Francis Lindley Wood abandoned Bolling Hall and by 1816 had disposed of the whole of the Bolling property to the Bowling Iron Works. The Listers, who became the most conspicuous representatives of the gentry in Bradford, Fields, Hirds, Wickhams, Bousfields, Tempests and Ferrands continued to dominate quarter sessions and the local benches of magistrates. At the same time an urban middle class was developing which was to take control of the town.

Its members continued to be of diverse social background and varied geographical origin, and they straddled the full range of political and religious belief. Thus the local Tories, Anglicans and Wesleyan Methodists generally – Dr Outhwaite, a local landowner as well as a medical practitioner, Richard Fawcett, John Rand, John Wood and Matthew Thompson – were joined by the Rouse family, the bankers Alfred and Henry Harris, and the Rev. G. S. Bull. The Whig-Liberal element –

the Hustlers, Murgatroyds, Garnetts and Illingworths – were reinforced by Robert Milligan and his fellow Scotsman and partner Henry Forbes, by Salt, Ripley and the Quaker, John Priestman. Younger men, like Mr Beaumont, the Methodist surgeon, and Joseph Farrar, a local hatter, Henry Brown, the draper who eventually established the multiple-store of Brown Muff and Co. and E. Parratt, an ironmonger, were also beginning to come into the historical record.

By 1830, an élite and an 'alternative élite' could be easily identified. The alternative élite was composed to a considerable extent of newcomers to the town, men whose future was committed to the continuing progress of the worsted industry, who were making their fortunes and whose position needed the consolidation of great wealth and recognised political authority. They were generally Dissenters in religion. The legal disabilities under which they suffered provided the mainspring of their future political activities. An important section were Independents, members of the Horton Lane Congregational Chapel, from where an active and increasingly wealthy caucus had begun to provide the leadership of a growing Radical element in the Whig-Liberal camp.

The established élite of well-to-do manufacturers and landowners of long standing in the town and parish, predominantly Tories and Anglicans, found such men – new men on the make, as they saw them – uneasy bedfellows. Nevertheless, lines of political demarcation became a good deal more flexible in the years after the Napoleonic Wars, and indeed from time to time almost a conciliatory spirit seems to have prevailed. The social and economic developments of the period demanded political re-evaluations. Some Tories, Matthew Thompson and Swithin Anderton, for instance, saw the need for change in constitutional and economic policy; on the other hand, the extreme Radicalism which demanded democracy at once was too aggressive – too dangerous – for most of Bradford's new additions to the business and professional community.

In general, goodwill seems from time to time to have encouraged collaboration in areas where it became impossible in the later 1830s. Dr McTurk, a much respected Tory, was reported as having said that when he arrived in Bradford in 1824, ecclesiastical differences had not interfered with friendly intercourse. On the evenings of the dissenting chapels' anniversaries the parish church was closed and the friendly action was, he said, reciprocated when the parish church festival came round.[25] The Bradford Auxiliary Bible Society, whose aim was to distribute a Bible to every home in Bradford, had as its joint secretaries in 1819 W. Morgan, the curate of a new church, Christ Church, in Darley Street and later a bitter polemicist on behalf of the established church, and Dr. W. Stedman, the leading Baptist minister in the town. The Temperance Society, started in 1830 through the initiative of Henry Forbes, had an executive body which included McTurk and the Rands along with the goods Dissenters Illingworth, Murgatroyd and Ramsbotham. Tories shared the same platform with Whigs, Liberals and Radicals in the campaigns to condemn slavery in the British colonies, the monopoly position of the East India Company and the economic iniquities of the Corn Law. During the great debate about the Reform Bill (1830-1832) which re-ordered the parliamentary system, men like J. G. Horsfall, Matthew Thompson and the Harris brothers joined the new men, the Liberals and the Radicals, to ensure the creation of a new parliamentary borough in Bradford.[26]

Meanwhile, the position of the textile working classes was being redefined. A factory proletariat, mainly as yet of women and children engaged in the various processes of spinning, was being created. The small masters gradually disappeared as the factory owners began to employ large numbers of workmen directly, providing not only the materials but also the tools and equipment needed to do the work. The woolcombers and the weavers were degraded to the level of sweated outworkers. The final stages of the process were marked by a protracted and bitter strike which began in June 1825.[27] It lasted for four months and involved about 20,000 workers in the Bradford area. It offered a sharp contrast to festivities which had taken place earlier in the year. In the February, the Bishop Blaize holiday, a seven-yearly anniversary in honour of the patron saint of woolcombers, had been celebrated with unusual lavishness and generosity – a comment on the buoyancy of the trade in the previous months. Though the festival by now was little more than a celebration of the already remarkable successes of the Bradford worsted manufacturers, a good many journeymen woolcombers took part and most of the population took it as a public holiday. Thus it retained something of the flavour of an old tradition and seemed to indicate that a sense of common purpose and community persisted within the industry.

But other voices were being heard, voices which announced in unmistakable tones the arrival of nineteenth-century capitalist society. Balgarnie, the nineteenth-century biographer of Titus Salt, captured the mood well.

The disastrous strike was an unfortunate sequel to the Septennial Festival of Bishop Blaize, the patron saint of the woolcombers. In 1825, this festival was celebrated with greater pomp than ever and the streets had never before presented such a scene of dissipation and frivolity . . . the influence it exerted upon the minds of people must have been most demoralising indeed. It was a relic of semi-barbarous times and strangely out of character with the present. It was an anachronism which evidently ought to be brought to an end. So thought the intelligent part of the community; but how was it to be accomplished? Public meetings were held at which methods for the moral and intellectual improvement of the people were discussed. Lectures . . . were commenced to promote this end. What was the result? The Blaize ceremony was never celebrated again. Before the next September a new order of things was inaugurated.[28]

The strike and its outcome confirmed the new order of things.

As we have seen, the position of the worsted woolcombers and weavers already lacked in the eighteenth century the independence of the many small masters in the woollen cloth branch of the West Riding industry. In the first twenty-five years of the nineteenth century their position collapsed. Twenty-six factories, several of them very large by the standards of the day, now produced all the yarn used in the Bradford district and a good deal used in other parts of the country. They dominated the market for the product of the woolcomber's skill, the tops and noils from which the yarn was spun, and some of them, vertically integrated to produce finished materials, controlled the weavers' market as well.

29

Thus they were able to determine levels of wages and employment. In 1819, they met to fix a reduction in wages in anticipation of the deflationary effects of Robert Peel's measure for the resumption of cash payments.[29] At the same time, the general buoyancy of the yarn and stuff market and the improvements in mechanical spinning recently introduced increased the demand for woolcombers and hand-loom weavers and led to the swamping of the crafts and the disappearance of the small master.

Of course, elements of small-scale independence continued to exist. Factory production of yarn encouraged some growth of minor sub-contracting in woolcombing. Basketeers and 'pot-lords' emerged to make a parasitic type of living by collecting work from different warehouses and distributing it to woolcombers on their books. When the union of Bradford weavers and woolcombers was founded in 1825 two of its members were described as master weavers and one as a master comber. But there were few masters of this type left to respond to the invitation to join with the journeymen in their struggle. The evidence, such as it is, suggests that the dividing line between Capital and Labour was clearly defined.

It is frequently assumed that the principal motive behind the strike was the fear the handworker could be assumed to have about the introduction of machinery into the trade. It is an assumption which ought to be approached with some reservation. A power loom was available for worsted weaving and tentative efforts had been made to introduce several into the district shortly before, although not in Bradford itself. It is also true that the masters' association claimed during the course of the strike that power-loom weaving reduced the cost of production by 75 per cent, and promoted the view that the militancy of the workers was bound to stimulate capital investment in the new machinery. Some combing was also already done by machinery. But the apprehension created ought not to be exaggerated. The power loom was still clumsy and unreliable, and the machine comb had not passed out of an experimental stage. The opinion was freely expressed that the machine could never replace hand combing.

The comber next employs his ancient art,
Which no machinery can supersede.
In vain the ingenious stretch their utmost skill:
As oft as tried, the expensive schemes of art
Abortive prove; – the comber still employ'd,
Sings at his work, and triumphs o'er them all;
Then plans for ale; and when the quart goes round,
Talks of his travels, happier than a king.

– wrote John Nicholson in 1823.[30] Natural conservatism and the buoyancy of the market in the early years of the decade served to allay the anxieties of the weavers; in any case the masters' statement had a clear element of propaganda in it since their pricing took no account of the frequent stoppages still caused by the clumsiness of the power loom. It was one of the features of the case put forward by the strikers that they had no hostility to the introduction of machinery, neither did they object to factory production as such: indeed, during the strike they wanted to keep the children at work in the factories against whose owners they were striking. It was the masters who imposed a lock-out of children to diminish the financial resources of strikers whose children worked in the factories. It seems therefore that their perception of the situation in which a strike seemed necessary was a good deal more complex.[31]

The specific demand which the union put forward, and the rejection of which led to the strike, was for an increase in wages, partly because weavers' wages had fallen a long way behind the cost of living and partly because new and more difficult demands were being made on the woolcombers' skills through the introduction of new wools and more complicated types of cloth. As it progressed, the strike became a struggle for union recognition and the equalisation of wages throughout the district. The masters not only denied the wage increases but also challenged the principle of union organisation, which in turn had challenged the traditional paternalistic relationship between master and man. The strikers, on the other hand, understood clearly that the right to organise was necessary as a countervailing force against the organised strength of the factory owners, and equalisation of wages was also necessary in

31

order to reduce the dangers of a labour market, which was likely to embrace fewer and fewer buyers and more and more sellers. Of course, their appreciation of contemporary technical changes in the cotton industry and in some parts of the woollen and worsted industry contributed to their assessment of the situation, yet they were not specifically alarmed at the imminent or actual threat of new machinery in combing or in weaving. They were concerned with the changing social relationships of production. In the face of an industrial reorganisation which gave a small number of factory owners immense economic and social power, they were trying to maintain the strength and dignity of labour, to establish the right to some control over conditions of work and with it a claim to social respect. Working, for the most part, in their homes, they did not sell their time precisely; they were nevertheless selling their labour to work on materials provided by others, and as such were wage-earners dependent on the capacity or willingness of others to provide employment. Wage labour of this sort had always carried the stigma of dependence;[32] it was the function of the trade union to dispel that stigma and to capture for the group which had become wage-earners the dignity and something of the sense of independence which attached to the free artisan or craftsman who sold the product of his labour. The leaders of the Bradford strike knew that the right to bargain collectively and freely with those who wished to buy their labour was crucial in this battle.

There is a sense in which the strike called out a unified response from working men and women. The strikers appealed for national help and got it to the extent of £15,826 from unions all over the country, blacksmiths, joiners, cobblers, cabinet-makers, sawyers, tailors, hatters, tanners, miners, weavers, woolcombers and others. In the Bradford area sympathetic journeymen craftsmen contributed over £2,000 and the Operative Carpenters were particularly aggressive in their support of the strike. In the two iron-manufacturing centres at Low Moor and Bowling small concentrations of population – miners, the furnace men and foundry workers – collected £268. On the other hand, the response of the textile industry was less uniform. The woolsorters, the true aristocrats of the industry, well paid and often independent artisans not threatened by changing conditions, and the mill mechanics, the beneficiaries of industrial change, gave little support and thus revealed areas of disagreement which were to bedevil the world of textiles through the century and beyond.[33] Capital also had its defaulters. One or two of the large firms broke ranks in mid-July and either refused to take part in the proposed general lock-out or paid the increase requested. But for them it was a matter of expediency – they could afford the temporary disapproval of their peers more easily than losses in trade and profit. For the rest, the textile employers, backed by the ironmasters and other employers outside the immediate area of the strike, maintained their hostility to it.[34]

Defeat, which came in November, was something from which the textile workers were very slow to recover. Some sort of textile organisation remained in being for a short time. There were Bradford connexions with the Leeds Union of Clothworkers and Bradford woolcombers were active in 1827 and 1832. But as far as can be estimated the numbers of participants in these activities were very small. Despite the recognition accorded to the union to bring the strike to an end, textile employers remained hostile to unions among their weavers and woolcombers. Such textile unions as persisted merged with the Chartism of the thirties. From time to time a woolcombers' protective society appeared, but there was no continuous union organisation until the end of the century.

In the aftermath of the strike the prosperity of which local commentators had frequently boasted was temporarily shattered. The slump of 1826 hit the Bradford trade with particular ferocity; unemployment and distress reached the levels which were to become familiar in the late thirties. One bank in the town could not survive the holocaust and went bankrupt. The working-class response was as intimidating as the despair from which it arose. The dignified and rational opposition which the trade union had offered in the previous year gave way, understandably, to uncoordinated mob resistance to attempts to introduce the power loom into the town. J. G. Horsfall had set up a number of power looms in his mill (which still stands) behind the parish church in North

Wing. In April, there was news that anti-machinery rioting had taken place in Lancashire, and towards the end of the month mills in Addingham and Gargrave were attacked. There followed in Bradford scenes which were to become familiar during the next twenty years or so. At the beginning of May, the weavers and combers were holding huge demonstrations to draw attention to the distressed condition of themselves and their families. The magistrates, alarmed at the news from other parts of the North, had collected a force of special constables, and the military were called into the town. The meetings held on the 1st and 3rd of May both ended with the spectacle of the hungry and ill-clad work-people on the march through the town intent on storming Horsfall's Mill. Without leaders and without any constructive plan, the hostility of the crowd, though frightening for Horsfall and his small defence force of woolsorters and mechanics, amounted to little more than menaces and stone throwing. The second occasion had ended when the Yorkshire Yeomanry intervened. At the end of the day two of the rioters had been killed and a number injured. Two were in prison, and detachments of the Yorkshire Yeomanry and the Leeds Rifles occupied the town.[35]

There were, however, other areas of 'working-class' experience where the record was not so melancholy. The elements of a sub-culture which had its own values could be discerned. Joiners, carpenters, stone-masons and printers all had their organisations, and within the textile industry overlookers and woolsorters. They tended to claim publicly the role of friendly society rather than trade union or club, but they drew their strength from the continuing sense of collaboration within the community which must always have existed in a pre-industrial Christian society. The printers, about whom we know little more than the mere fact of their existence, were following the normal practice of their trade. But it was not only the fact that printers' unions had existed for many years, in other places. Printers had also long organised themselves at the place of work. The long-established practice of 'chapel' organisation tended to make of each printing shop a little 'republic' which worked to rules based on the simple principle of 'fair shares for all', and less formal but comparable

34

arrangements may well have existed in other trades.[36] A branch of the Independent Order of Odd Fellows had been established and was soon to provide a hall which offered a platform to working-class opinion in the town. The history of early Co-operation is as shadowy in Bradford as elsewhere; we can say, at least, that a Bradford Co-operative Society was active in 1830.[37]

It is difficult to be dogmatic about the place of religion in working-class life, in these years. Attendance at a place of worship was probably always more of a middle-class habit than one of the working classes, and this became increasingly the case in the industrial cities. It may be assumed that, as was certainly the case later, working people were more assiduous in sending their children to Sunday school than in going to a service themselves. The number of seats available is some indication of the sparseness of regular attendance. We may say that the Roman Catholics, the Baptist Societies and the Methodists eventually attracted the largest numbers of working-class adherents and that, as far as it goes, it was the Primitive Methodists who drew most firmly on a specifically working-class experience. In Bradford, there were three Primitive Methodist chapels by 1830 – in Manchester Road, at Bowling and in Great Horton. It is from the latter that such evidence as we have is available. Numbers were small – but its existence as a religious organisation depended on the communal experience, translated into religious activity, of a small number of families geographically separated from, though not isolated from, the larger village. It is also worth noting the presence of a small number of secularists led by Squire Farrar, the Paineite lawyer, and Christopher Wilkinson, the radical printer.

The main influences on morals and religion were nevertheless middle-class-inspired. Rev. W. Morgan, denying, somewhat over-generously, the inadequacy of educational facilities in Bradford for poor children, said that a school of industry had been open for twenty years, the Quakers had a Lancastrian School and every place of worship had at least one Sunday school attached to it. There were probably a considerable number of private ventures – the Wesleyan

Methodist Sunday School in Bowling Old Lane was rented out for a day school during the week at a rent of 1s. In all of them the stock-in-trade was Reading, Writing and perhaps – sometimes – Arithmetic. A main purpose of most of them seems to have been the sort of moral exhortation suggested by Morgan's *Pastoral Visitor*:

To your employers you owe much; they have devoted their time, talents, and fortunes to business, and to *that* business you are indebted for your maintenance. If you labour for them, they labour for you; hence, the obligation is mutual. . .[38]

By 1832, there was also a Mechanics' Institute, supported principally by the Dissenters. An earlier venture of 1824, started by Squire Farrar and Christopher Wilkinson, was too independent to attract middle-class support. By 1834, the committee of the new institution was claiming:

Many of those who during the political turbulence of the period which preceded the formation of the institute were, through timidity or prejudice, led to believe that it would be a seminary for disaffection . . . a nursery for political demagogues and anarchists, have . . . opened their eyes to its usefulness.

Dangerous controversy was avoided by the exclusion of religion and politics as areas of discussion and by concentrating the institute's work in three neutral fields – the three Rs, lectures on general science and the provision of an innocuous library. Its place in the life of working-class Bradford had still to be assessed.[39]

Despite the excitement of three decades, changes in Bradford were by no means complete. Bradford remained nearer to 1700 than to 1900. As if to confirm a reluctance to enter the modern world, a proposal to link Leeds and Bradford by railway, supported by many of the businessmen, was defeated by the combined opposition of local gentry and the Canal Company.[40] Nevertheless, the stage was being set for a new era. Manufacturers were beginning to experiment with the new materials and techniques which were to make the town the international leader of the worsted textile trade. In the field of social reform, efforts to mitigate the harshest brutalities of industrialisation were gaining some success.

The factory posed new problems of human behaviour, particularly in the employment of children. The evidence is well known and it is perhaps enough to recall Tester's unchallenged assertion that in Bradford factories young children worked from 6 a.m. to 7/8 p.m. (with half an hour for dinner) and William Cobbett's ironic comment that British prosperity seemed to depend on 30,000 little girls in Lancashire.[41] There is little in the times to suggest that the problem would have been faced without the compulsion of parliamentary legislation. The Factory Act of 1833 prohibited the employment of children under 9 in cotton, worsted and woollen factories, limited to eight per day the hours which children of 9 to 13 worked and twelve per day for young people from 13 to 18. The Act also provided for the appointment of factory inspectors and so offered some assurance that it might eventually be effectively applied. It was the product of a movement in which Bradford men played a very important part. It had begun in the late twenties in isolated efforts by small groups, which included some of the wealthiest of Bradford's élite, to persuade the trade as a whole to cut the hours their factories worked. It took fire when John Wood, Bradford's wealthiest manufacturer, persuaded Richard Oastler to come into the fight. He became the acknowledged leader of a considerable movement which united well-to-do Tories with large sections of the poorer classes: in Bradford men like John Hall, an overlooker in the Wood factory, John Douthwaite, a young school-teacher, Peter Bussey, who had emerged as a working-class leader during the strike and who brought a considerable following behind him, and trade clubs like the Operative Carpenters. 'Short-time' committees, organised locally, publicised the issue very effectively – their most dramatic venture, the massive demonstration of enthusiasm and determination in the huge open-air rally of West Riding support at York. The well-to-do carried the fight to Parliament. The campaign took on a strong socio-political flavour as the demand for factory legislation became a permanent part of the Tory programme and resistance to it a feature of the Liberal case. It looked as if the traditional forces of a humane paternalism had at last confronted the new and callous economism of the industrial capitalists. The polemics were savage. Before long, Oastler was angrily denouncing 'those Sunday saints and week-day devils, the sleek, pious, holy, and devout dissenters, Messrs Get-all, Keep-all and Work-all'. The evangelical Tory businessmen and Anglican parsons who supported the movement for reform were accused of the most despicable hypocrisy – their interest, opponents claimed, had nothing to do with humanity and charity, but was purely in the party battle. But there *was* cruelty and exploitation, and whatever the motives which went to make up the movement the outcome was humanitarian. Moreover, the dispute was not polarised to the extent it became later. There were Tories like Swithin Anderton who disapproved of legislative interference, some Liberal Radicals like the young W. E. Forster supported it, and some on both sides – Miles Illingworth and William Rouse, for instance – accepted the need for some compulsion and would have settled for an eleven-hour day. But the campaigners were bitterly disappointed at their failure to get a ten-hour day for the women and young people and the fight became part of the continuing struggle of the next twenty years.[42]

The field of battle had also been defined. The Reform Act of 1832, which had reconstructed the parliamentary system, made a parliamentary borough out of the townships of Bradford, Bowling, Horton and Manningham, the area in the parish where industrial capital was most heavily concentrated. Thus a new unit came into existence which had no legal relationship to the ancient institutions of parish and manor. It was to become the base of future social development and the focus of political conflict. Bradford was to elect two Members of Parliament. Voting was restricted – for democracy was still many years away – to men who occupied property of an annual value of £10 or more. Members were to be elected, in other words, almost exclusively by the middle and upper classes. The Bradford register of voters compiled for the end of 1832 listed 1,137 names, about 5 per cent of the population, and included no more than about 5 per cent of that total who might be classified as working men, albeit better off than the average of the class. There were no permanent party organisations; elections were fought by *ad hoc* committees made up of 'friends of the candidate'. These men helped to meet electoral expenses, though the candidate himself was usually expected to make a generous contribution. Voting was open. Where there were two MPs, as in Bradford, the voter had two votes but could vote once only. He could act in one of three ways. He could vote for one man only using one vote. This was known as a plumper. He could use both votes for two men of the same party or alliance – a double vote – or he could vote for two men of opposing parties – a split vote or a cross vote. The elector climbed on to the hustings (in Bradford generally outside the Court House in Hall Ings) and announced his voting intentions to the returning officer seated there in the centre of his officials, the candidates and their most powerful supporters – in front of a large crowd of vociferous and often agitated spectators. There was talk of the need for a secret ballot, but open voting was still seen as expressing a perfectly reasonable demand for honesty and courage in the expression of opinion.

This was not democracy, establishing the right of every adult simply as an adult to the dignity of full citizenship. It was an adjustment of the limited constitutionalism which attached the vote to the 'responsibilities of property'. Wealth and social authority continued to dominate, and the imposition of extra-political pressure on the voter remained a relatively easy matter. Still, because of its very openness the system did not exclude non-voters from all influence. If they were properly organised, they could bring a good deal of pressure to bear on the voters, if only through a system of mild intimidation.

The first Bradford election was not exciting. Three men presented themselves to the electorate: E. C. Lister, of whom the *Halifax Guardian* remarked that 'his residence in the immediate neighbourhood of Bradford seems his *only* qualification'; John Hardy, the Recorder of Leeds, a partner in the Low Moor Iron Works, living in the old Manor House in Kirkgate, identified with some asperity as 'once a thorough paced Tory but now a most gallant reformer'; and George Banks, a Leeds businessman, whose political position seems to have been difficult to define. He was in fact an enlightened Tory of moderate reforming views. Lister and Banks were both firm Anglicans, Hardy a Methodist. On the platform, there was little to differentiate them. Hardy spoke for the secret ballot, Banks was strong for factory reform, Lister's specific views could not be established since he was too ill to take part in the electioneering. All were presented as reformers of one type or another. Lister and Hardy took the seats. The election suggested above all that party division within the new industrial order was not yet clearly established. The list of Banks's supporters, in particular, offered proof. It included every shade of opinion, the Vicar Henry Heap and the Baptist minister B. Godwin, the good Tory manufacturers John Wood and Matthew Thompson, the old-fashioned Whig Samuel Hailstone and the firm Dissenters Robert Milligan, Henry Forbes and James Garnett.[43]

For the rest, the election demonstrated as much as anything the continuing strength of the old establishment. Lister, who had been elected with little effort, was now the senior representative of the gentry in Bradford, and Hardy stood for well-established local influence. In 1832, the alternative elite – either as Dissenters or a powerful business interest – were not yet confident enough to stand on their own feet. There were, however, other indications. During the agitation about the Reform Act, the Bradford Political Union, an association of working men led by one of the leaders of the strike, Peter Bussey, had emerged. It had given its support to the middle-class reformers, and had made a significant intervention in the election.[44] This was the first of a succession of working-class associations – some of them very militant – which throughout the century harnessed working-class opinion behind the democratic cause intended to make the working man a full citizen of the society he lived in. In 1833, another instrument of battle emerged. The handful of manufacturers and merchants who led the Liberal-Dissenters invited William Byles to Bradford to start publication of a new paper 'devoted to the principles of civic and religious liberty'. In February 1834, the first issue of the *Bradford Observer* appeared. In general the process of adaptation to new demands was going forward at all levels, and the area of conflict was broadening. The next twenty years were not only the years which saw the most important changes in the economy of the town; they were also the years of most threatening social crisis.

ARRIVAL OF THE SALT FAMILY

In the early months of 1822, Daniel Salt came to settle in Bradford. He was forty-one and already a man of considerable business experience. He had tried his hand with varying degrees of success as ironfounder, drysalter and white cloth merchant, and since 1811 as a farmer. Attracted now by the opportunities of Bradford's expanding economy, and disappointed, as many farmers must have been, by the difficulties of contemporary farming, he proposed to invest the capital raised by the sale of his farm in some section of the wool industry.[45] There is a little evidence that he explored the possibilities of a business connexion with the Garnetts, the worsted spinners of Barkerend Road. Like him they were Independents. Their factory was being expanded and they might have welcomed additional capital, but nothing came of it. In the event, he took an office in Market Street and started business as a woolstapler. In 1823 he bought land in Cheapside with the assistance of his brother, an ironfounder in Leeds, from the heirs of John Preston, who had recently died, and from the Lord of the Manor, Benjamin Rawson, and built a warehouse in Cross Street. Later, he built a second warehouse in Piccadilly, and this became the headquarters of his activities.

Unlike a number of the many newcomers to Bradford with whom he was to be closely associated, in business and in social life, he did not come as a stranger to the town. He was a West Riding man with useful connexions already established both in the commercial world and in the Dissenting community of which he was a member. He was born in 1781 at Hunslet near Leeds, he had been educated at Heath Grammar School and had worked in the family business as an ironfounder until shortly after his marriage. He married Grace Smithies, the daughter of Isaac Smithies, in 1802, and went to live in her family home, the Old Manor House, Morley (a few miles from Bradford) to take over the business of white cloth merchant and drysalter to which she had succeeded on her father's death a short time before. In 1811 he took the lease of a hundred-acre farm at Crofton, near Wakefield, and stayed a farmer for eleven years. Thus he was a familiar figure on the West Riding wool and grain markets. Both the house at Morley and the Crofton farmhouse were licensed for 'Independent' public worship. Thus the Salts were also well-known members of the West Riding dissenting community, belonging to a circle of friends and associates which included a considerable number of the well-to-do West Riding business community. It is clear, as well, that he was already well-known in Bradford dissenting circles before he settled in the town. Legal documents compiled very shortly after his arrival in Bradford named him as one of the trustees to the estate left by Thomas Trout, the Bradford postmaster.[46]

His rapid immersion in the life of the town confirms the impression. In 1824 he held vestry office as an overseer of the poor and in 1825 he was named as a commissioner under the Act of 1803, along with Dr Outhwaite, for many years the leading representative of the professional gentry in Bradford. Salt was an ardent reformer, active, like most Dissenters, in the cause of Catholic Emancipation, the anti-slavery movement and the demand for free trade. In 1831, he was elected one of the Constables of the Manor, and so took the chair at a number of the town's Reform meetings. As a result, in 1832 he was hailed by the euphoric crowd celebrating the passing of the Reform Act, as Bradford's 'Father of Reform'. He was a prominent member of the Horton Lane Congregational Chapel and one of the trustees of the new Salem Chapel built between 1834 and 1836, after the Horton Lane Chapel congregation had outgrown the accommodation there. This was very much a Salt family venture – his son, son-in-law, and he had undertaken most of the administrative and legal work associated with it.[47]

He remained prominent in the political and social life of the town until shortly before his death in 1843 – being elected to the first Board of Guardians in 1837, and playing a prominent part in the various Radical organisations which were developed between 1835 and 1841.

When he first came to Bradford, he lived in a house on North

Parade a few yards from his warehouse and about the same distance from the Salem Chapel. When he retired in 1834 he had a house built further along Manningham Lane, which was the continuation of North Parade. Sufficient of the house was standing until recently to show that it had been a good, well-sized dwelling, characteristic of the early nineteenth century. Of the interior, there was just enough left to show an excellent staircase with a delightful wrought-iron hand rail, suggestive of a well-appointed and tastefully decorated home. It was erected on the boundary between the townships of Bradford and Manningham in the area which was to become the principal middle-class zone of nineteenth-century Bradford. Already, some upper-middle and middle-class houses stood nearby, but meadow and pasture still predominated. Thus, the house, though by no means isolated, stood in one of the more attractive parts of the district. Only one mill, Lilycroft Mill owned by the Lister family, about a mile and a half away, could pollute the atmosphere, and this was not in fact built until four years after the house went up. The house had open field on three sides. There is virtually no evidence to indicate the sort of life which Salt and his wife provided for the children, of whom there were five living – Titus, nineteen when the family came to Bradford, three girls, Sarah, eighteen, Ann, fourteen, Grace, ten, and another boy, Edward, aged eight.[48] Daniel Salt himself was a tall, well-made man with a reputation for intelligence and wit. He was by no means a rigid Puritan; he liked to spend his evenings with his friends in the George Inn in Market Street. When he died he left a substantial cellar, and he was not noticeably connected with the Bradford Temperance Society. Although he had been a prominent member of the Horton Lane and Salem congregations he had (much to Balgarnie's regret) never affirmed his faith by taking communion in the congregation. The *Bradford Observer* remarked of him that he was a man of plain commonsense and sound intelligence, his business and political acumen respected by his associates, but that he had come to find the fierce competitive pace of industry in the nineteenth century distasteful and had therefore retired in his early fifties. Apart from that, we know that he had a pronounced stammer.[49]

Grace Salt, his wife, is a very shadowy figure indeed. According to Balgarnie, she was a devout member of the Independent connexion – it was through her, apparently, that the children received their religious education. Balgarnie also suggests that she suffered a good deal of ill-health and that it was on this account that a preaching licence had been obtained for the Crofton farm, since frequently she was unable to make the three-mile journey to Wakefield to the nearest Independent chapel. Balgarnie adds that she suffered from nervous depression. She outlived her husband by eleven years, dying at the age of seventy-five.

The Salt family belonged to the comfortably-off yeoman-manufacturing world which provided one of the main ingredients of Bradford's nineteenth-century middle class. As with details of personal life, however, it is impossible to give more than an impression of the family's wealth. The house on Manningham Lane was a substantial two-storeyed house with three bays, gardens and outhouses. The woolstapling business was successful – the warehouse which housed it was one of the largest in Bradford at the time, and Daniel had been able to retire in comfort at the age of fifty-two. In his will, he left £3,000 in trust for his wife and £850 to his daughter Sarah, since he had given his other children that amount more than the sum he had already given to Sarah. For the rest, his estate was to be divided equally among the five children, still alive.[50]

The three girls all married in the close circle in which they had grown up. Sarah married William Atkinson, the son of an apothecary whose premises were in Kirkgate, a short distance from her home. He is variously described as druggist, book-keeper and, towards the end of his life when he had started to live on his income, as gentleman. After Daniel's death and the sale of the house in Manningham, Mrs Salt went to live with Sarah at Mirfield, a little village near Morley. Ann married a Mr John Smith, a worsted spinner, connected by marriage with the Crossleys of Halifax, Independents like the Salts, and worsted manufacturers. The only firm information we have on them is that they retired to the island of Jersey where they lived in a house called Undercliffe Lodge (Undercliffe was a small hamlet on the outskirts of the Bradford of the day, and then one of the more romantic spots of the area). Grace married her cousin, Charles Smithies. She emerges occasionally in the record to provide a hint that she was separated from her husband. In 1841, on the night of the census, she was at the Manningham house with her two children. About the same time, her father advanced her £200 in addition to an unknown sum she had already had. In 1855, she was living at Mirfield with her oldest sister and her mother, and her husband is described as ' . . . late of Leeds . . . now being, (if living), a resident at or near Antwerp'.

Edward, the youngest child, took over the family firm shortly after his father's retirement and continued to run it for several years, though apparently with little success. In the forties he was in partnership with a Mr Smith (perhaps his brother-in-law), as a worsted spinner working in rooms hired in the Lilycroft Mill. In 1854, he was in Australia, and does not appear in Bradford directories after that,[51] although his wife Anne and after her death his daughter Ann are both listed. Whatever the situation here, both Anne and her daughter were part of the Salt circle, attending the various functions and entertainments which Titus provided from time to time. They are both buried in a small and simple plot in Undercliffe Cemetery – the only Salt grave in Bradford, now that the Salem graveyard, where Daniel and Grace were buried, has been demolished.

Of the early life of Titus, as well, we have no more than the highly selective evidence of Balgarnie. He was born on 20 September 1803 and was nineteen when he came to Bradford. He had had a reasonable education of the kind readily available at the time for boys of his social position. After a short time at a dame school in Morley he had attended Batley Grammar School until the family moved to Crofton. He then went to a school in Wakefield conducted by Mr Enoch Harrison. It was one of the many proprietary schools which had sprung up in the West Riding to provide the 'plain Commercial education' which boys of this sort were likely to need. An acquaintance described Titus as 'tall and proportionately stout and of somewhat heavy appearance . . . he was generally of studious turn of mind . . . rarely mixing with his school-fellows'. He added that he spoke so little that it was impossible to recall anything particularly that he had ever said. Several sketches which he did as a schoolboy survive. Two – of village scenes – show qualities of draughtmanship and perception, and, of their kind, are good. One – a conventional shipwreck – is a good deal less well executed. No more than schoolboy exercises; nevertheless, they seem to indicate some artistic ability.[52]

What principally emerges from the meagre record of his youth is that he was somewhat introverted, perhaps even withdrawn. This was an aspect of his personality which presented difficulties throughout the whole of his life. Even as a successful businessman and leading public figure he was reputed to have great difficulty in making up his mind to a decision. His inability to speak confidently and coherently in public was one of his most widely recognised characteristics. He was – clearly – a man with a highly developed sense of responsibility, but he exercised it most easily in a private capacity. His most famous contribution to history, the model industrial village of Saltaire, which he created between 1853 and 1875, was for all its flamboyance a private gesture. It has been suggested from time to time that his inability or unwillingness to speak in public grew out of sensitivity about his pronounced Yorkshire accent, but there was more in it than that. However, as with almost everything of close personal importance, we are in the field of speculation. Nervous depression in the mother and a father who stammered badly offer very little, except tantalising hints, as indications of the sort of youthful influence which went to build his difficult personality. There was an unusual combination here of great determination and sense of responsibility offset against personal diffidence which could cause acute embarrassment both to him and to his associates.

Titus Salt was apprenticed when he was seventeen to a Mr Jackson, a woolstapler of Wakefield, and apparently spent a disappointing two years, acquiring very little knowledge of the trade in that time. When he came to Bradford he spent two years with William Rouse and Sons, and under the instruction of John Hammond obtained a more comprehensive insight into the trade. In 1824, he joined his father in the firm which was henceforward known as Daniel Salt and Son, Woolstaplers, and remained in business with him for the next ten years. It was a firm which was not afraid of new ideas. In addition to the staple business in English wools, it specialised in the sale of *Donskio* wools, materials which came from Eastern Europe and which previously had been regarded as unsuitable for the worsted industry. There is some evidence that the firm went into yarn spinning about 1829 in order to demonstrate to conservative customers the suitability of the material.

He took part in the public life of Bradford alongside his father, as a Liberal-Radical and a Dissenter. His local importance was not, as yet, great enough for him to get more than occasional mention as attending a meeting on Catholic emancipation, or parliamentary reform. For the rest, he was enrolled as a special constable during the rioting at Horsfall's Mill in 1826. He also served for a time as superintendent of the Horton Lane Chapel Sunday School where, characteristically, he proved a capable administrator, but too timid about speaking in public to lead the children in their prayers.

In 1829, he married Caroline Whitlam of Grimsby. She was the youngest daughter of George Whitlam, a wealthy sheep farmer, who is generally supposed to have had business connexions with the Salt firm. Two more of the Whitlam girls married Bradford woolmen. Amelia, the oldest child, had married George Haigh in 1820, and Lucy, two years older than Caroline, married Charles Timothy Turner in 1833. The Salt–Whitlam Bradford connexion appears to have constituted a close-knit family group; Salt's first girl was named after her aunt, Amelia, and for a number of years they all lived within walking distance of each other, in the middle-class enclave on Manningham Lane. Titus had a house in North Parade, a continuation of Manor Row, quite near to his father's house; the Haighs and Turners lived next door to each other in Manor Row, and Edward Salt also lived in Manor Row after his marriage in the late thirties.[53]

Between 1836 and 1843, Titus lived about five minutes' walk further away at a house at the junction of Thornton Road and Little Horton Lane. His affairs had prospered and he had taken over the Union Street Mills as the headquarters of a thriving empire. Thus he went to live close to the works, in a part of the town where at one time only the well-to-do had lived, but which was now beginning to deteriorate under the effects of industrialisation. On the one side his closest neighbour was the wealthy Miss Balme, who had inherited much of the Sharp property. On the other was Samuel Bower, known everywhere as a prominent Socialist, and not far away there were Nelson Court and Fawcett Court in the heart of some of the worst slum property in Bradford. The oldest of his children spent some of their earliest years living very close to some of the more inhospitable parts of the town. The children born were William Henry (1831), George (1833), Amelia (1836), Edward (1837), Herbert (1840), Fanny (1841), and Titus (1843). By 1843 he had had enormous success, and following an already well-established pattern he left Bradford and went to live with his growing family in a handsome mansion called Crow Nest at Lightcliffe, some ten miles away.[54]

II

THE ECONOMY AND THE ENTREPRENEUR

THE ECONOMY

When Titus Salt began to trade on his own account in 1834, Bradford already dominated the worsted textile trade in the United Kingdom. As yet, however, Bradford manufacturers had not developed any specifically Bradford innovations; their success had been based on the adaptation of devices and of machinery invented and proved in other places and in other branches of the textile trade. In the next thirty years they were to exploit innovations and inventions developed in the Bradford district, and these were to carry them to international supremacy in the worsted trade. Perhaps the most important of these developments were those which extended the range of raw materials used in the industry. In the years after 1836 the basic trade of Bradford developed into the production of mixed, rather than pure woollen, fabrics, in which cotton was used with wool, alpaca, mohair or silk.[1]

This helped to overcome difficulties in the supply of long-fibre wools caused by the expansion of the industry. John Wood, writing to G. R. Porter at the Board of Trade in 1834, expressed his fears: 'This district I fear will shortly suffer severely from a deficiency of wool occasioned by a very high price of British grown long or combing wool, the material that furnishes employment to many thousands of this vastly populated district.[2] After the slump of the late twenties, wool prices rose steadily through the thirties with only one brief setback in 1837.

In the local wool markets there was a good deal of discord between farmers and manufacturers. In June 1835, the *Bradford Observer* reported that if there was no improvement, 'a conflict must ensue between growers and consumers' for a number of

49

farmers 'were with-holding wool in anticipation of further advances'. The use of materials other than wool was stimulated, and at the same time the manufacturers created a demand for lighter and more elegant fabrics, for the new primary materials greatly extended the quality and range of goods available. They also cheapened costs of production since any increase in the supply of the raw materials was bound in some way to influence the level of prices. According to James, the contemporary historian of the worsted trade, a Manchester man, Joseph Barratt could claim to have been the first man successfully to combine a cotton warp with a worsted weft to produce what became known as Orleans cloth. He was said to have done this in 1826 and as a result to have built up a limited though successful export trade to the USA. However, there were difficulties about dyeing the new product and it was not until 1837 that, with these resolved, the product began to make a great impression in the Bradford markets. One Bradford manufacturer gave James an account of his start in this branch of the trade:

Twenty years since, we were manufacturers of goods made entirely of worsted, our fabrics being known as 'merinoes' made exclusively of sheep's wool. . . The style and design of these goods then so much approved, would now be considered vulgar and unsaleable. . . .

We continued to make exclusively this class of goods, until the close of 1837 when our attention was directed to cotton, as a substitute for worsted warps. . . We claim to be among the earliest manufacturers who successfully used cotton warps in Bradford goods for women's wear. Our first goods were cotton warp double twills but there was much difficulty in dyeing these satisfactorily, and it was not until September, 1838, that we made a fair start with cotton warps in goods designated by the name of 'orleans cloth'. . . .

As proof of the attention excited by our orleans cloth, it was the usual thing to find two or three merchants awaiting the opening of our room doors at Bradford on market day and Mondays, and on one occasion a very amusing scene or rather struggle occurred between two merchants in the steps leading up to our rooms, one a well-known Quaker buyer, the other a younger merchant determined to be first in.[3]

Even more important was the introduction of alpaca, for this was the source of what was virtually a new branch of the industry, as important in its own day as the introduction of man-made fibres has been in ours in opening up a new area of exploitation. The alpaca, imported from Peru, was a long-fibred wool, with a shininess which made it look like silk and a softness and elasticity which made it suitable for the production of excellent cloths with an attractive sheen or lustre on them. It became known in the United Kingdom in the early years of the nineteenth century when new trading connexions were being developed with Latin America. Although several amateur innovators experimented with the new material, it was not until the thirties that its commercial possibilities were tested. A Mr Benjamin Outram of Halifax is named by James as the first manufacturer to market alpaca cloth, but his costs of production were high and the cloth he made did not have the fine lustre which became the characteristic of this material. A number of other firms also produced experimental materials, including J. G. Horsfall, Messrs Wood and Walker and Wauds of Bradford, the latter of whom always claimed to have been the true initiators of this lucrative trade. But there is general agreement that Titus Salt must be regarded as the real pioneer in this field as the man whose persistence and ingenuity resolved the problems, which had defeated all others, of combing and spinning the raw material to provide cloths of high quality and attractive appearance.[4]

Salt was no stranger to experimentation, for as wool buyer to his father's firm he had followed his father's lead in pushing the little used *Donskoi* wool which came from Eastern Europe. The story which Charles Dickens related in *Household Words* of the manner in which Salt first came across alpaca wool may be true, for all we know. The story goes that on a business trip to Liverpool in 1834, he found some bales of alpaca abandoned and rotting on the dock-side. After a few preliminary tests with a small quantity he had extracted from the rotting pile, he bought up the whole consignment at the give-away price of eightpence a pound and so began the industry which was to bring him fame and fortune, and great prosperity to the Bradford district. Unfortunately, its veracity has to be suspected. Much the same story was told about Samuel Cunliffe Lister's introduction to silk waste and in any case it falls too aptly into the pattern of the Victorian business parable for total credibility.[5] However Salt was certainly experimenting with alpaca by June 1835. The only piece of documentary evidence there is about his business activities is a small day book which he kept between 1834 and 1837. It seems to have been a book in which he kept a personal note of special transactions and experiments, since it does not contain enough to cover three years' entire work. It contains the following entry, 'Peruvian wool' being alpaca:

27 June 1835. 1 bag *Peruvian* Wool weighed off June 15th. 1 cwt 1 qrs 10 lbs

Cwt	qrs	lbs					
	1	7	best sortings at	1/6d	£2	12s	6d
	1	17	2nd	1/-	£2	5s	0d
		23	3rd	8d		15s	4d
	1	13	Combing	1/4d	£2	14s	8d
		4	Grey	10d		3s	4d
		2	Fribs	4d			8d
1	1	10	average	1/2d	£8	11s	6d

Salt obviously treasured the page since at some time he had added his signature at the top. Some months later another entry specifically used the name alpaca and gave a breakdown of costs of combing the wool (it is worth noting that the sale of the noils very nearly covered all the combing costs):[6]

October 1836. 2 packs of *Alpaca* 4s black and broken

480	lbs	at 16d	£32		
56	lbs soap	4d		18s	8d
8	pints oil	9d		6s	
287	lbs tops and combings	4d	£ 4	15s	8d
			£38	0s	4d
140	lbs noils at 10d		£ 5	16s	8d
	2/3 per 1b		£32	3s	8d

Robert Milligan, years later, told James that he had first dealt in alpaca goods in the spring of 1839.

The economy and the entrepreneur

It was during the spring of the year 1839, that Titus Salt, Esq., with whom we had done business in worsted yarns, introduced to our notice Alpaca yarns. Several attempts had been made by manufacturers to use this article in combination with worsted warp, or as warp, but the manufacture did not prove successful, until the production of what we termed 'Alpaca orleans', formed of cotton warp and Alpaca weft. The first entry of these goods in our books is an invoice to Mr Salt, in June 1839, of two pieces of Alpaca at seventy-six shillings per piece. The first considerable order which we undertook for 'Alpaca orleans' was on the 19th June 1839, for five hundred and sixty pieces, 27 inches wide, at forty-two shillings per piece, proving, at this date, that our practical difficulties had been successfully overcome. Then became established the Alpaca trade which has since risen to so much importance. At this time, Mr Salt was the only spinner of Alpaca weft in Bradford.[7]

Along with a small team of trusted assistants, Salt had been working in great secrecy for about eighteen months on the problems which alpaca presented. By adapting the machinery available, they had between them overcome the difficulties of spinning the material into a true and even thread. The weaving of alpaca with a worsted warp had also produced a cloth with little interest and no market appeal except that of novelty. Salt and his team had the idea of binding alpaca weft with cotton or silk warps; and this gave the characteristic lustre which made it an attractive cloth, and produced at the same time a durable, relatively light and reasonably priced cloth which could be easily adapted to the fashions of the day. Salt and others also made greater and greater use of mohair – imported from the Levant – and some small amounts of Australian wool were already beginning to appear in the market by this time.

One further innovation was needed before the production of all kinds of mixed cloth could be achieved. The combination of a vegetable with an animal material presented difficulties for the dyer; and indeed when wool and cotton were first combined it was the practice to dye them separately, since cotton was not as amenable to permanent dyes as wool. The techniques of dyeing them together were mastered by Edward Ripley and Son, and taken up by other firms in the town. The results far surpassed the expectations of most people, for the problem had generally been regarded as insoluble. One of the leading

53

manufacturers in the town summed up the achievement for James's history:

Infinite credit is due to the dyers of Bradford goods for the extraordinary and rapid improvement in their art. The manufacturers are indebted beyond all computation to the efforts at improvement continually put forth by the dyers. By the joint aid then of the dyer and manufacturer, such goods as figured orleans, produced at prices from eight shillings and threepence to about twenty-five shillings the thirty-six yards in the grey, are made to assume a lustre and brilliancy of colour which could not have been dreamed of a few years ago.[8]

The years between 1830 and 1860 were also the years during which the industry was almost completely mechanised. In spinning, which was already a factory-based part of the trade, there were great increases both in productive outlets and in productivity. In 1839 there were seventy-one spinning firms in the townships of Bradford, Manningham, Bowling and Horton. Between them they used 1,720 spinning frames – a total of 165,120 spindles. In 1850, there were 87 firms employing 268,653 spindles and in 1856, 88 firms using 336,618 spindles. Spinning machinery was also becoming more efficient, and more efficiently operated. The development of the 'dead' spindle and the invention of the 'screw gill' made for greater output per spindle and also led to the production of finer and stronger yarns. The speed of the spindle was increased quite substantially from 1,400 revolutions per minute in 1825 to 1,800 per minute in 1850, and productivity was further increased in the 1850s when the system was generally adopted of one girl looking after both sides of a frame instead of one side as formerly, and when the cap frame came into general use in the Bradford trade.[9]

Although some hand-loom weaving was still done in outlying villages like Baildon and Allerton, weaving was almost completely mechanised by 1850. In 1825, the power loom was still a clumsy and unreliable machine against which the good hand-loom weaver had a reasonable chance of competing, particularly if trade was good. In the thirties it became increasingly reliable and after 1837 the introduction of alpaca orleans which demanded great and regular tension in the weaving process encouraged its more rapid modification and introduction into the trade. By 1850 there were some 17,642 power looms in the parish of Bradford and as seven years later there had been no increase we can assume that the transformation of the process was pretty well completed. It had, however, taken the miseries of a whole generation of hand-loom weavers to complete. Most firms operated a mixed system for years. Salt was using power looms in 1836, but still had hand-loom weavers in his employ for some years after the Saltaire Mill had been opened. In 1838, Willet, Oxley and Co. had 100 power looms and 100 hand weavers; Willet and Co 100 power looms and 500 hand weavers. But the future was clear to all. Robert Leach, a manufacturer in Thornton, had no power-loom weavers in 1838, employed about 500 hand-loom weavers but knew quite well that sooner or later 'the power-loom manufacturers would be able to drive us out of the market'; as Rev. G. S. Bull commented, it was a 'race between capital mounted on a railway steam engine and labour on crutches',[9] a view confirmed by the introduction of a system which enabled the weaver to look after two looms instead of one. As with spinning, not only had capacity been increased: productivity had also been augmented. The speed of the power loom was raised by at least 100 per cent between 1839 and 1850, and improvements and adaptations made possible operations on the power loom which for years had seemed destined to remain the field of the good hand-loom weaver, a development summed up by the *Bradford Observer* as removing all the limits to the extension of the fancy department of the Bradford trade.[10]

The most intractable problem of technological innovation was woolcombing. Hand-loom weavers were still employed in the fifties, but it was a problem of relative costs rather than the technical efficiency of the hand loom which held back the total elimination of the hand weaver. Combing was a different matter. Although Cartwright had developed a combing machine as early as 1792, and the Collier machine was in use by the 1820s, Samuel Cunliffe Lister could write that fifty years after Cartwright's invention no one had really succeeded and there had been no reason to think that anyone would. Lister, of course, was preparing the way for the praise of his own inventions. Nevertheless, there was still no satisfactory machine on the market. The standard against which combing was measured was hand combing and so it remained until the fifties. Salt did a comparison of hand-combing and machine-combing costs and recorded his results in the day book already mentioned. Machine combing had the advantage only for the first six grades of wool. For the six better grades, into which the woolsorters were expected to separate the raw material, the hand comber still had the advantage. Comparative costing carried out in 1837 showed that while hand combing was about 9 per cent dearer than machine combing, the yield was better, so that the use of the machine depended on the type of work to be done. In the forties renewed interest brought a number of inventors into the field, the most important of whom were Josue Heilmann, a Frenchman, E. G. Donisthorpe, a Leeds engineer, and the two Bradford manufacturers Isaac Holden and Samuel Cunliffe Lister. From the various models produced were developed the Lister Nip comb, in which were incorporated some of the Heilmann ideas, the Holden square motion comb, and the Noble comb, in the development of which Donisthorpe played a considerable part. These destroyed such advantages as the hand comber had had. By 1853 Lister, determined to recoup his vast investment, had bought up all the important combing patents and was charging £1,000 as patent right for the one machine, the Lister Nip, he was prepared to put on the market. Even at that price it was a profitable machine to the buyer, the cost of the standard product, the 'top', was reduced from about two shillings a pound to fourpence a pound, and it was said to replace the work of 100 men. The final mechanisation of combing took place in two stages. The first, taking advantage of both Lister's comb and earlier versions, took place between about 1848 and 1857, and as far as Bradford was concerned eliminated about four-fifths of the hand labour required at that time. The second phase occurred after 1862, when Lister's patents had expired, and it became possible to make use of the Holden square motion and the Noble comb, which some men preferred and others needed since, as Holden was ready to point out, no single comb was totally efficient for every kind of wool.[11]

By mid-century, the parish of Bradford had almost half the productive capacity of the British worsted textile industry and the borough alone had well over a third. Industrial building on a lavish scale accommodated a great deal of new capacity or provided superior accommodation to old establishments. Between 1852 and 1874, there were 1,045 new mills and warehouses built in the borough alone, including all the most famous and largest mills which now attract the admiration of the industrial archaeologist. Salt's mill at Saltaire was comfortably first – completed and occupied by 1853: Black Dyke Mills were extensively enlarged in 1868. Manningham Mills went up in 1873. Daniel Illingworth built new premises in Thornton Road in 1861. Isaac Holden's new establishment at Princeville was built in 1862. A vast range of worsted fabrics was produced. These included all-wool materials, though the orleans mixed fabric became the principal product of the industry. Three large firms dominated the alpaca and mohair business – Salts, Fosters' Black Dyke Mills at Queensbury, and G. & J. Turner of Great Horton – and took most of the alpaca imported from Peru for their own use. They were able to produce mixed cloths with standards of beauty which could not be bettered in any fabric. The main product of the Bradford industry was a relatively cheap black orleans which became almost standard wear for women in many parts of the world.[12]

At the Great Exhibition of 1851, which Bradford manufacturers supported with great enthusiasm, all the most important manufacturers obtained awards. J. G. Horsfall and Co. of North Wing were praised for the quality of a variety of fabrics, outside the day-to-day range of the Bradford trade:

The Jury have noticed as particularly deserving of commendation the article denominated 'Saxony cloth' for ladies' dresses. The weft is made from the finest Saxony wool and the warp from the finest Australian wool, both combed by hand. The Coburgs in cotton warp, wefted with worsted are admirable and manifest a high degree of regularity, obtained by the excellence of the yarn employed and the talent of the weaver. The 'henrietta' cloths are made from spun silk warps and weft of finest Saxony wool and are distinguished by a softness combined with a firmness of texture that has never been surpassed.

Walter Milligan, one of the earliest to experiment with alpaca, was praised for

a series of embroidered alpaca goods produced by a process which they have patented; a style of manufacture noticeable for its elegance and novelty. The patterns are printed on white silk and the greatest possible accuracy is necessary in the weaving, in order that the printing blocks may fit; . . . the goods shown by this firm are highly creditable to their ingenuity and skill.

There was also a very considerable trade in worsted yarns, which were supplied not only to the home market but to a considerable export market as well, and this also received the commendations of the Exhibition Jury, Salt and Foster being especially mentioned. Salt undoubtedly stood high among worsted manufacturers at the Great Exhibition. The commendation which accompanied his awards reads:

For a complete series of alpaca and mohair manufactures, (a branch of business carried on almost exclusively in England), which illustrates very strikingly the great capabilities of these materials. The articles are of great variety, including fabrics composed of alpaca with cotton warps, and with silk warps, yarn dyed, and dyed in the piece; they are plain, twilled, figured, Chines, or made with printed warps. There are also goods composed of mohair with similar combinations. All are characterised by peculiar lustre and brilliancy, equal in many cases to silk; they are remarkable for regularity of texture, softness and fineness. It may be confidently stated that similar goods have never before been produced, and the great increase in the consumption of articles of this description among all classes of the community, renders the display an interesting and important one. Mr Salt was one of the first to introduce alpaca wool into the Bradford trade and by his enterprise and skill has mainly contributed to the extent and perfection which this department of industry had attained. In addition to the articles already mentioned, Mr Salt exhibits an assortment of moreens used for furniture hangings; one series being made from English wool, and the other from the Russian Donskoi fleece wool. The latter especially so, considering the difficulty in the way of working up so coarse a material, which had never been combed prior to Mr Salt having effected that object.[13]

Handling the greatly augmented volume of trade in worsted pieces and yarns was a mercantile community which had grown from 12 in 1834 to 252 in 1873. With the development of dyeing and finishing facilities in Bradford and the completion of the first railway link to Leeds in 1846, Bradford became the obvious commercial centre for the whole of the West Riding worsted textile area, as well as the principal location for worsted manufacturing. Thus Bradford merchants were able to play a significant part in the evolution as well as the marketing of Bradford cloth, for it was generally as much a part of the merchant's function to take responsibility for the dyeing and finishing of those commodities which he handled, as it was to help in channelling them to meet the tastes of the consumer. A number of men made comfortable fortunes out of this activity. From comparatively humble beginnings, Robert Milligan created the largest mercantile enterprise in the town. He had started commercial life as a travelling draper and concentrating on the home market the firm was lucrative enough by 1853 to be housed in the 'neo-Italian Renaissance' structure next to St George's Hall – a building which affirmed very boldly the substantial prestige of the firm. Three of Bradford's mayors between 1847 and 1866 – Milligan himself, Henry Forbes and J. V. Godwin – were senior partners in this enterprise.[14] Among other forceful characters who made their reputations in the mercantile field were James Law, like Milligan a Scotsman, energetic and determined, and Henry Mitchell, eventually managing director of the Bradford branch of the Manchester firm of A. S. Henry, a man with an international reputation as a fine judge of textiles.

A great deal of the export trade, particularly but not exclusively that in worsted yarns to the Continent, was in the hands of German merchants resident in Bradford, for the German houses, reading the signs of the times, had started to move from Leeds in the mid-thirties. By 1860 there were about sixty in Bradford, about a third of the total number of merchants in the town. Among them were a number of very distinguished men. Charles Semon was mayor in 1864-5, and always a philanthropist of great generosity. Jacob (later Sir Jacob) Behrens was one of the principal members of the business community – ready to formulate ideas and policies, and able to support his views with well-researched statistical evidence. The Germans formed a distinctive community in Bradford. Few of them were naturalised until late in the century, and they continued to regard themselves as German, most of their sons going to fight in the Franco-Prussian War.[15]

Commercial developments led to changes both in the system of production and in the system of marketing. Relatively speaking, the competitive market contracted. The late fifties and sixties saw the beginnings of some specialisation. Now it was generally only the largest firms which carried out all the processes of cloth manufacture from wool buying to the sale of finished cloth. Most of the manufacturers bought their yarn from specialist woolcombers and spinners, for the capital outlay of machine combing was high, and the production of a variety of yarns beyond the range of most manufacturers. They restricted the range of their cloths so that although a very great variety was produced in Bradford, many small firms only produced a few of them themselves. Thus in practice competition was restricted for such firms had only to concern themselves with those who produced the same cloths. Stuff merchants also abandoned, as they grew in size, the traditional display of goods in an open and visible market and traded directly from their warehouses.

The entrepreneurs also undertook the modernisation of the economic infrastructure. Bradford was linked by rail to the towns of Yorkshire and the West Riding and to the great metropolitan centres of the kingdom. The railway had come late to Bradford and many of the fortunes made out of industrialisation were founded in an economy which depended on a combination of local water and road transport and such railway networks as could be reached by these means. In 1837 one firm was offering both freight and passenger transport from Bradford to London in two days, by way of Hull and making use of both railway and steamship facilities. Until 1849 passengers coming from Manchester by train completed the journey to Bradford by horse-bus from Brighouse. The cost of bringing wool from Leeds to Bradford – eight miles – was greater than the cost from Hull to Leeds – sixty miles. Bradford men complained fairly regularly that Leeds merchants would always have the advantage until Bradford also had a direct link with Manchester. However, after the failure of the 1830 proposal for a Leeds–Bradford railway there were no initiatives until the great railway boom of the mid-forties. In 1846, a track was opened following the line of the canal as far as Shipley and then along the valley of the Aire, a long route selected because of the difficulties presented by the sharp climb over the hills to Leeds on the shortest possible route. It was incorporated into the Midland Railway system at great profit to its Bradford protagonists. There was, however, a continuous railway link with London and the extension of the line to Keighley and Skipton in the following year made a railway journey to Manchester possible, although by a roundabout route. By 1854, a shorter line over the hills to Leeds had been completed and the railway links to the south of Bradford established railway contact with Halifax, Wakefield, Manchester and a number of smaller centres in the West Riding; a miscellany of lines shared between the Lancashire and Yorkshire and the Great Northern companies thus provided alternative routes to the South and West. By the mid-fifties the basic structure of the Bradford railway system had been laid down and by 1867 in all its essentials it was complete.[16]

The common policies and activities of the employers were also given coherence and authority through the Chamber of Commerce founded in 1851, the honour of its inauguration being claimed both by William Rand and Henry Ripley at different times. It was the representative of the manufacturing and commercial capital of the international trade in worsted cloth and covered all the interests of its members as producers, merchants and employers. Its code of by-laws for the settlement of commercial disputes was unchallenged. It was the pressure it could use that brought about substantial improvements in postal and telegraphic communication to Bradford in the early fifties. Under its auspices, Jacob Behrens, during the negotiations for a commercial treaty with France, provided Richard Cobden with the massive statistical and other evidence which gained advantages for the worsted industry in the French markets not shared by the Lancashire cotton industry. One of its major concerns was the development of raw wool resources – particularly in Australia but also in other parts of the world. By

1867, after Bradford manufacturers had taken a few knocks at the French International Exhibition of that year, it began, through its more intelligent and progressive members, to take an interest in technical education. It also acted as an employers' association in the conventional sense of the term, providing a forum for the determination of policy on factory legislation, negotiating with governments about such matters as the control of factory machinery, and offering a common front against any challenge of importance.[17] The Bradford Wool Exchange, a characteristic 'Lockwood and Mawson' pseudo-Gothic building, erected in one of the principal thoroughfares of the town, was opened by a small company headed by Henry Ripley, and quickly became the most important of the markets available to the international trade. At the same time a more attractive commercial centre was developed as evidence of a prosperous and soundly based economy. Industrial establishments began to move further out. The bankers had built new and more fashionable quarters and some of the new warehouses put up for the merchants between High Street and Leeds Road reached artistic levels which continue to delight those who find cultural satisfactions in the physical evidence of Victorian art.[18]

THE ENTREPRENEURS

The years between 1834 and 1873, almost exactly the years spanned by Salt's career, were the years of greatest achievement in the Bradford worsted textile trade. A great deal of money was still to be made after 1873, and the industry would continue to be of international importance for nearly a hundred years, but after 1873 it would never be possible to boast of an undisputed sway which had seemed to place it – almost, but not quite – beyond competition, through the excellence of its techniques and the enterprise of its merchants. Between 1834 and 1873, Bradford men continued to reap the benefits of the technical changes they had pioneered and at the same time to enjoy, at least until the sixties, the managerial advantages which partial mechanisation provided. Although there were sharp and unpleasant crises in 1854, 1857 and 1867, world trading conditions were, in general, highly favourable to Great Britain. A period of inflation and rising prices caused by the gold discoveries in the United States and Australia and the wasteful expenditure of the many wars in the third quarter of the century, created the background for the booms of 1852-7, 1861-6, and 1869-73. A European-wide relaxation of tariffs, the opening up of free trade markets in China and Turkey and continuing expansion in America and the colonies offered unprecedented opportunities to an industry which at this stage could afford to face any type of competition with equanimity.

The men who presided over Bradford's industrial fortunes were at the same time a remarkable group well equipped to exploit these circumstances. Their dedication to the 'great art of getting on' unleashed John Ruskin's critical vocabulary, but for them it was proof of an ability to come to terms with life. Some of the men he had in mind were men of very considerable talent. They had their share of peculiarities and oddities. Salt had his strange reluctance for public speech and private letter writing and that habitual dislike of making up his mind which irritated his junior partners. S. C. Lister had a paranoiac aggressiveness, which made him the victim of imagined exploitations and led him to at least one bitter but unnecessary quarrel. Holden had something of a fad about food, health and the causes of longevity. In Jacob Behrens there seems to have been a streak of contrariness which led him to unexpected failures in generosity, as, for instance, when he gave no more than £100 to the proposed Technical College though he had been one of its most capable advocates. It goes without saying that all liked their own way. Salt's treatment of his weavers when they started a strike in 1868 was uncompromising. He refused to deal with them until they returned to work. Henry Forbes provoked the easy-going Daniel Salt to anger by his determination to be first on every occasion. James Law was reported to be 'very able but too much addicted to his own point of view', and Ripley was, to say the least, a militant publicist in pursuit of his own ends.

But their more positive qualities were worth taking note of. Among them the four great Bradford innovators, Salt, Lister, Holden and Ripley, stood out as men of true imagination.

Forbes and Behrens showed something of the same quality in their own less technical but complicated field. They had all mastered the complexities of a difficult trade which constantly required careful technical as well as business judgement, and were the leaders in a trade which took pride in the achievement of excellence – to be considered a good textiles man still carried its own peculiar distinction. Some of them were widely travelled men. They also had their share of conventional culture. The German community is generally given the credit for importing 'culture' into Bradford social life, and there is no doubt about the contribution of some of them – W. D. Hertz and his wife, among others, played a significant part in the organisation of Bradford's musical and educational facilities. But we should not accept too readily Behrens's condemnation of Bradford as an intellectual and artistic wasteland before the arrival of the Germans. The Exhibition, held on behalf of the Mechanics' Institute in 1840, two years after Behrens came to the town, revealed quite unexpected standards of artistic taste. It was the vicar, Scoresby, who revitalised the Philosophical Society in 1846. There was also a long-established tradition of choral singing in the West Riding. Samuel Smith's St George's Hall, a fine building opened in 1853, was intended to house top-rate musical performances. Another Smith, like his namesake also in the textile trade, had an excellent and voluminous library which eventually became the nucleus of the Public Library stock started in 1868. Of those who were dissenters – their chapel-going deserved more than the sniff which Matthew Arnold accorded it in *Culture and Anarchy*, for it could make great intellectual and moral demands. And for better or worse they were the representatives in Bradford of those men whose interests and activities refashioned the social and political bases of the country in the nineteenth century.[19]

In 1851, Henry Forbes estimated the value of the British worsted trade at £12,500,000 of which the West Riding accounted for £8,000,000. James gave higher figures for 1857, £18,000,000 for the country and £10,000,000 for the West Riding, and Jacob Behrens provided an estimate for 1864 of £33,600,000.[20] These figures, if they do nothing else, provide evidence of great and rapid expansion, and among the upper and middle classes there was widespread agreement that it was an expansion which had brought prosperity and enormously improved opportunities to the working classes in general. It is, however, doubtful whether this was reflected in much improvement in their real purchasing power, at least until towards the end of the sixties, although the period may well have seen greater security of employment than was usual in the nineteenth century and some improvement in conditions of work, following the Factory Act of 1850. But children still went to work between the ages of eight and nine and half-timers were not – as is sometimes supposed – being eliminated.

The evidence of financial success and new social opportunity is more easily observed towards the other end of the social scale. Such evidence as there is indicates that only 5,968 out of an adult population of about 80,000 and an adult male population of 38,000 paid income tax in 1871; of these about 2,000 earned between £100 and £150 a year. The average earnings of the remaining 3,846 came to approximately £406 per annum, in a town where it was a very good and very healthy workman who could average an annual income of £86. Economic prosperity provided the basis from which a number of considerable family fortunes were created for a new upper class – the new industrial gentry – and handsome competences for the relatively small successful middle class. (In Bradford, as elsewhere, however, there were very few 'rags to riches' sagas.[21]

Of course, not all who came into business in Bradford in these years were highly successful. J. W. Turner, a local historian, suggested in a lecture in 1877 to the newly established Historical and Antiquarian Society that, out of 227 wool firms in business in 1830, 146 had gone bankrupt or otherwise out of business in 1877. The career of William Marten puts the enormous success of a handful into perspective. He had come to Bradford from Sussex in 1820, two years before Daniel Salt and his family. Like Titus Salt he had worked for W. Rouse and Sons for two years and then became a woolstapler, a business he carried on successfully but not dramatically so for a number of years. His business was badly hit by the depression of 1857 and he retired, living modestly but comfortably in Manningham until his death in 1874.[22]

Few of the textile fortunes reached the highest levels. Of those whose main activities fall within the period of effective industrialisation in Bradford, only one local man was listed as a millionaire when he died – William Foster of Black Dyke Mills.[23] But there were a number of Bradford textile manufacturers who by any standards were wealthy men. Some of them joined the ranks of the aristocracy and the titled gentry and a number confirmed their success in industry by converting their resources into landed estates, a reversal of the process which had been an important source of capital during industrial mechanisation. Samuel Cunliffe Lister 'out of his considerable profits had been able to spend £800,000 within four years and think little of it'. He bought the Masham and Jervaulx estates in North Yorkshire as suitable background to the title he hoped to obtain, and some years later became Lord Masham.[24] Salt, Holden and Ripley were all created baronets, and Jacob Behrens and Henry Mitchell were knighted. Of these only Ripley bought any land; Holden had a lavish extravaganza of a mansion built at Oakworth in Keighley; Salt's public memorial to the future, the village of Saltaire, had, *inter alia*, the virtues of some originality at least for Bradford. Among the non-titled, Matthew Thompson bought an estate in Kent in 1834, John Wood had many acres of land in Hampshire, George Hodgson, the textile engineer, an estate in Norfolk. The Mitchells of Bowling took to farming and horse-breeding in Ireland.

Of this new industrial gentry, Isaac Holden was in some ways the most interesting. He is generally assumed to have come from a working-class background and this is more or less true. His father had been a colliery overseer or manager but he had known hard times occasionally and Isaac had had to supplement the family income by earning as a weaver. He was a Scot with the advantages of an early nineteenth-century Scottish education. Emigrating to England, he followed a variety of occupations including that of schoolmaster until, in 1830, he came to Cullingworth near Bradford to be book-keeper to the local firm. He had already shown something of his inventive genius – he has some claim to have invented the Lucifer match – and he now directed his attention to the most intractable problem of the worsted industry – the machine comb. As his employers took little interest in his ideas he set up in business for himself in Bradford in 1842. He lacked the capital to ride out the depression which started in 1846, for the development of the machine comb was an expensive business, and in 1848 he entered a partnership with Lister which lasted until 1857. During these years they were developing the machine comb and at the same time Holden ran the firm's successful enterprises in France. Several years after the partnership ended, Holden started what became an equally successful combing business in Bradford, exploiting the now greatly increased demand for the services of the specialist machine comber. He was a devout Methodist and remained a Gladstonian Radical all his life. He sat in Parliament for the Northern Division of the West Riding and later for Keighley, and was generally to be found active in most of the 'good causes' of the day. He died in 1897, leaving a personal estate of £317,635. He had also given his children some £2 million before he died.[25]

Samuel Cunliffe Lister also was a man of great technical ingenuity and enormous drive. He began in the textile trade in one of the factories built by his father, Ellis Cunliffe Lister – the Lilycroft Mill, in 1838 – and built up a firm which probably made more money than any other in the nineteenth century in Bradford. He claimed to have started three new industries in Bradford, by his own inventions, machine combing, velvet and plush power-loom weaving and the utilisation of silk waste. During his working life he had taken out more patents than any other man in Europe, and had spent over £600,000 in the development of his ideas. He was the only one of the textile manufacturers to come directly from the ranks of the landed gentry. Politically he came from a Whig family, classed himself as a Liberal Moderate for many years, but by the late sixties was moving to the Conservative camp. He was among the first of the Bradford men to abandon the free trade policy and personally financed much of the fair trade movement in the 1880s. He is probably best known as the principal director of the firm which fought the Manningham Mills strike of 1890-91, the strike which served as the catalyst of the Independent

Labour movement in the West Riding.[26]

Henry William Ripley's career shows a number of the clearly defined characteristics of the new men. His grandfather, George Edward, had moved from Halifax at the beginning of the century and had started a small dyeing business in Bowling. Henry William went to school with Alfred and Henry Illingworth and Charles Stead (later a director of Salts) at Joseph Hinchcliffe's Academy in Little Horton, a highly prized 'modern' school whose curriculum was designed to meet the needs of the commercial and industrial middle class. In 1830 he joined his father in the dyeing business. He played an important part in solving the problems of dyeing mixed fabrics, in particular alpaca, though his father seems to have regarded the experiments he conducted as a waste of time and raw materials. He married the adopted daughter of Robert Milligan, who supervised the first marketing of the new cloth, and lived for a long time at Lightcliffe where he was more or less next-door neighbour to Titus Salt. Personal friendship with the Salt family seems to have survived the vicissitudes of political and industrial fortune, for the Salt family were among the chief guests at Ann Ripley's wedding and gave a number of handsome presents.

Ripley had been brought up as a Dissenter and, like Salt, had attended the influential Horton Lane chapel. In his early days, also, he was regarded as an advanced Liberal though he never played a very active part in the main Radical organisations in the town. By 1858 he was worshipping in the established church, and by 1874, when he sat with W. E. Forster as one of the two Bradford MPs, he was as good as a member of the Conservative Party which was taking on a new lease of life both nationally and locally.

He was never a popular man in Bradford. He had an irritating capacity for self advertisement, and an offensively authoritarian approach to his position as an industrialist. He played, nevertheless, a large part in the public life of Bradford, though with varying fortune. He was an alderman for a number of years, representing Bowling. He sat as MP for Bradford during the Disraeli Administration of 1874 to 1880, after an inglorious rejection in 1868 on a successful petition of electoral corruption. He had been president of the Chamber of Commerce during its formative years in the fifties. He was also chairman of the Wool Exchange Company and evoked the wrath of Bradford's organised working class by inviting Lord Palmerston to lay the foundation stone in 1864. His most successful contributions to Bradford life were in the field of education. He was one of the most generous supporters of the highly successful Borough West School, and one of the chief benefactors of the Mechanics' Institute. Salt and he, between them, provided most of the money for its new building in 1872. He was also among the chief advocates of a technical college. He had a number of philanthropic ventures to his charge, the almshouses in Bowling and the Woodlands Convalescent Home in Rawdon being the most important, and built a small industrial colony, Ripleyville, in Bowling. He was also a great dyer, his protégés, the apprentices trained in his firm, being eagerly sought by other dyers in Britain and in Europe. He was made a baronet in 1881 and died in 1882. He left a personal fortune of £321,429.4s.10d. His eldest son, who had been educated at Rugby and Oxford, inherited the title and the property in Shropshire, Rawdon and Lightcliffe. The second son took the firm, still one of the largest in Europe.[27]

Most of Bradford's nineteenth-century entrepreneurs have had their critics, contemporary and historical. Titus Salt was always presented by contemporary literature and journalism as the epitome of the very best in Victorian capitalism. Among contemporary Bradfordians, also, criticism was muted; such as it was, it left the essentials of his career and life unmarked. There is no doubt that he was easily the most generally respected of Bradford's Victorian employers.[28]

In this aspect of his career, however, as elsewhere, we have to be content with the bits and pieces which can be put together from directories, newspapers and occasional references in the letters and papers of others, to add something to Balgarnie's rather facile hagiography. Salt and his father had started a spinning department of their stapler's firm in rooms in Thompson's Mill at the Goitside, where they shared power and other facilities with two other firms, Jowett and Smith and Robert Waud. They were joined by Edward, the youngest son, and shortly afterwards, in 1834, the father retired. Within a few months, Titus also had left the firm and started to work on his own account, the family partnership being officially dissolved in 1835. It is generally accepted that he started his new venture at Hollings Mill in the Goitside and he quickly acquired other premises in or near Hope Street. By 1836, he had taken over the large mill in Union Street, previously occupied by Daniel Illingworth and Nathaniel Murgatroyd and standing just inside the boundary of Horton Township. It became the headquarters of a rapidly increasing alpaca empire, to which were added three other mills before 1850. He also employed large numbers of hand woolcombers who lived in the Manchester Road area, near the Union Street mill, and hand weavers who lived for the most part in the villages of Allerton, Clayton and Baildon.[29] His success in these years was aided by the provision of new capital. In 1843 he inherited his one-fifth share of his father's estate. But his specialities, the mixed alpacas, were the specialities of the age. He had helped to create a new demand for a type of cloth in a wide range of variations, which fitted precisely the requirements of the new fashions in women's garments. Lustre cloths, in other words, look their best on the crinoline. Demand for Salt's products in these lines rarely failed badly for many years. In the slump of 1845-8, he claimed that until the revolutions on the Continent disrupted communications he had been able at least to keep all his men – combers, sorters and mechanics – at work. He added that the revolutions had cost him £10,000 a month in lost trade.[30]

We have few details of the way in which he conducted operations in these years in Bradford. He seems to have concentrated the work of the various mills by process or by product. It is fairly clear that preliminary processes, including sorting and machine and hand combing, were controlled from Union Street where administration and financial matters were also seen to. Like others, he enjoyed the benefits which the mixed system of production gave, and like others he had to face the social and moral problems it presented. His attitude towards factory reform, wage remuneration and the introduction of machinery was the standard one for men of his class and time. Wages found their own level and mechanisation could not be artificially controlled. He was not in favour of factory legislation limiting hours of work. Indeed, throughout the 1840s he was the chairman of the manufacturers' opposition committee.[31]

Occasionally there are glimpses of him as an employer. In 1847 he celebrated the Liberal electoral victory with a couple of factory parties for his workpeople at the 'weaving establishment' in Silsbridge Lane. The first took the form of a dinner for his fifty overlookers, craftsmen and mechanics. The second was a tea party and dance at the Odd Fellows Hall for the 350 woman weavers and their escorts. Some six years earlier a newspaper report had shown him in a different aspect – ready to use the facilities of the Worsted Committee to bring to trial two woolcombers suspected of stealing charcoal from him. Two men not in Salt's employment had been seen carrying sacks of charcoal from his warehouse in Union Street and on investigation claimed that they were collecting charcoal for a group of woolcombers who worked together. It is as likely that the men were collecting on the tickets which Salt's firm issued to their employees since woolcombers used them as a form of money during the week and bought the equivalent amount of charcoal back at a premium when their wages were paid. The case was dismissed. It is one of several incidents which show Salt as an employer applying the discipline of the trade as all did, and there is no reason to suppose that Salt was anything other than a strong disciplinarian in matters which concerned the work of the firm.[32] Salt, however, emerged from these difficult years of transition a wealthy man and with his reputation as a good employer unsullied. The building of Saltaire, begun in 1850, fifteen years after he had begun in business on his own, confirmed the economic success of his enterprise and established a legend that is very difficult to penetrate.

Saltaire was created for reasons which transcended the needs of business. Nevertheless, the efficient organisation of the firm was of primary importance.[33] As a committed Liberal, Salt expected prosperity to follow the establishment of free trade and he wanted to be ready for further expansion. In addition, the recent developments in the wool-combing machine meant

71

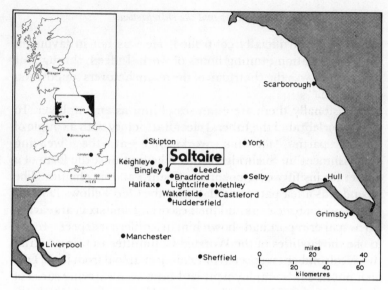

Saltaire and the West Riding of Yorkshire

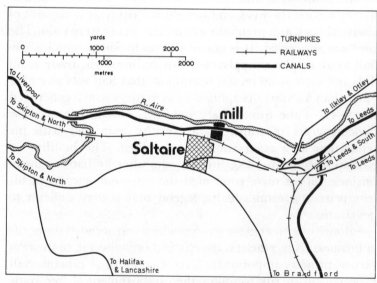

Saltaire – communications

that he could now think in terms of total factory production; but if he was to buy new machinery he needed more space and a greater supply of water than he could command on his existing sites. At the same time, to concentrate all his activities in one large mill instead of the five smaller units he used in Bradford was bound to cut out a great deal of waste and make administration easier. As it would have been impossible to find a suitable site in Bradford, the business reasons for building a large mill instead of the six smaller units he used in Bradford

The site he selected – four miles from Bradford – was on commercial grounds alone one of the best which could be found in the North of England. It stood between the river Aire and the Midland Railway line which ran from Leeds through Shipley to the North, and through its centre ran the Leeds–Liverpool Canal. Thus it stood on the crossroads of the principal lines of communication, north–south and east–west, in a position which ensured cheap transport costs for coal, raw materials and finished goods. The mill was built in a fifteenth-century Renaissance style characteristic of Tuscany and was designed by the Bradford architects, Lockwood and Mawson. William Fairbairn, one of the great engineers of the day, designed the lay-out and constructed the engineering facilities. The mill's productive capacity indicated the magnitude of the design – 30,000 yards of cloth every working day, and employment at full capacity for over 3,000 people. The building was completed in all essentials in 1853 but a smaller establishment was added in 1868 on the site of an old water mill at the river bank. The opening on 26 September 1853, Salt's fiftieth birthday, was the occasion of the most lavish hospitality.[34]

We catch occasional glimpses of him in these later years in operation as an entrepreneur. There is no doubt about his astuteness as a businessman. He was one of the only two men to get the better of Samuel Lister in the struggle about monopoly rights over the machine-combing patents. Edward Akroyd, the Halifax worsted manufacturer, and he combined to buy the Heilmann patents which they knew Lister had to have if he was to establish a complete monopoly of the manufacture of machine combs. In Lister's own rather petulant words:

Colonel Akroyd of Halifax, and [Sir] Titus Salt, being full of money, speculated and bought Heilmann's patent, feeling sure that I must have it or fight. This made matters still more serious, as their combined purses, and great influence in the trade, made them very formidable opponents. They agreed to give Schlomberger thirty-three thousand pounds for it, and offered it to me on the same terms, but subject to their having, free of patent rights, as many machines as they required for their own business. Hard terms for me, but I had either to accept that or fight. Another law-suit involving such serious sums of money was too great a risk, so I agreed to their terms, and paid the money to Schlomberger. They were thus never anything out of pocket – rather a good 'spec' for them, as I was then charging a thousand pounds patent right for each machine. How many they had I don't know, but a considerable number were necessary for such large concerns.[35]

Salt was able to stock the woolcombing shed at his new mill at a cost of £200 per machine instead of the £1,200 which was Lister's market price at the time. There are also occasional references to Salt's activities as a businessman, in the Black Dyke Mills' papers, used so successfully by Eric Sigsworth in his book *Black Dyke Mills*. On one occasion Foster complained quite bitterly of the intensity of competition which Salt had always offered the Black Dyke firm. On another occasion, the two firms combined with Turners of Horton in what seems to have been 'conspiracy in restraint of trade' to keep the import price of alpaca down, and later we see Salt peremptorily breaking off such an agreement when he thought his interests were no longer served by it.

The business remained a family firm throughout Salt's lifetime. Salt brought in as junior partners two very able men from his senior staff in 1854, Charles Stead and W. E. Glyde, the brother of Jonathan Glyde, the Horton Lane pastor. The other partners were the members of his own family. William Henry and George entered the firm at the same time as Stead and Glyde and Titus and Edward probably in 1865 when Glyde decided to retire. Titus himself remained senior partner all his life, his position very carefully delineated by the articles of association. After 1861, however, he lived in semi-retirement, relinquishing day-to-day control of the business to his partners, and intervening usually only in times of crisis. He could afford to take life more easily. The wealth which the firm had brought and which it continued to bring enabled him to enjoy the luxurious life-style of an English gentleman, to indulge his family in their somewhat extravagant pursuits, and to pursue himself the vast range of charitable activities with which his name was now associated. When he died his personal estate was valued at just short of £400,000.[36]

The charitable and benevolent activities which this wealth supported were a continuing obligation. There is no evidence that, like Isaac Holden, who put aside 10 per cent of his profits for charity, he made a fixed allocation of his income, but he gave constantly and generously all his life. He began to figure in the subscription lists at the modest level which befitted his status in the late twenties. By the forties he was regularly among the principal contributors, standing alongside people like the Rands and Priestmans, but giving pride of place still to men like Robert Milligan. By the sixties he was usually the chief contributor, though sometimes he shared the honour with Arthur Harris, the banker.

Apart from the charitable trust of £30,000 set up for the poor of Shipley, the most notable of his benefactions were the Bradford Town Mission, the Bradford Tradesmen's Homes, the Hull Seamen's Children's Orphanage, the Bradford Grammar Schools and the Leeds Road Fever Hospital. He gave lavishly to the Congregational cause – Scarborough Congregational Church was largely financed by him – and he gave constantly to the Liberation Society. He was also a major source of income for the Liberal Party both nationally and locally.

The wealth which the firm provided also supported his active public career. Titus at one time and another occupied every local public office, except that of Poor Law Guardian, open to a member of a dissenting community. He was elected High Constable of the Manor in 1841-2, an office roughly equivalent in esteem to that of Mayor later, but carrying few duties except that of organising and presiding at all town meetings properly requisitioned by the required number of rate-paying inhabitants. From 1847 to 1854 he was the senior alderman in

Table 1 List of some charitable and other contributions

Bradford Boys' Grammar School	£6,000
Bradford Girls' Grammar School	£5,500
Hull Seamen's Orphanage Home	£5,000
Bradford Fever Hospital	£5,000
Northern Counties Lunatic Asylum, Lancaster	£5,000
Liberation Society	£5,000
Bradford Tradesmen's Homes	£2,100
Scarborough Congregational Church	£2,600
Fund for Aged Ministers	£1,800
Bradford Mechanics' Institute	£1,200
Peel Park, Bradford	£1,000
Lightcliffe Congregational Chapel	£1,000
Royal Albert Hall	£1,000
Yorkshire College of Science	£1,000
West Riding Congregational Union	£1,000
Bradford Ladies' Educational Association	£ 100
Distress Relief Fund for Lancashire	£ 500
Sick and wounded on both sides in the Franco-Prussian War	£ 250
Bradford Blind Institute	£ 500
Halifax Crossley Orphanage Home	£ 100
Turkish Atrocities Relief Fund	£ 100
Parish Restoration Fund	£ 50
Bingley Boiler Explosion	£ 50

the new Bradford Corporation, sitting for the South Ward, where the Union Street Mill was located. In 1848-9 he was elected Mayor of the town after Robert Milligan, the Scotsman, had seen the infant corporation through the worst of its teething pains. As alderman, his primary concern seems to have been with the question of smoke pollution. As mayor he devoted a good deal of time to questions of moral and social depravity. Like most of the aldermen, he did not attend meetings assiduously, even in the early days of the Corporation. He presided at almost all the full council meetings held during his term of office, but rarely found the time, as he said on account of his many business commitments, to attend the meetings of committees of which he was *ex officio* a member. By 1853 he was a regular absentee from most of the meetings he was entitled to attend, and let it be known in that year that he did not wish to be re-elected as an alderman.[37]

During the same period he sat regularly on the bench of the Bradford court and seems to have acted generally with the sympathy which his contemporaries expected from him. Like most of his fellow-employers, he seems to have had no doubts about applying the rigour of the Worsted Act to the recalcitrant textile workers who were a regular component of the daily list. On the other hand, he was known to offer personal help to men and women who came in front of him, if their histories suggested a particularly harrowing series of misfortunes. After 1854, however, here as with municipal affairs, either his interest waned or he was satisfied that local affairs were in safe hands. In fact, after the initial battles for control of the town had been fought, Salt, like most of the leading figures in the town, did not take a continuing part in its administration.

By this time also, quite apart from his growing business and the development of Saltaire, he was an active member of the Chamber of Commerce and acted as president in 1855-6. He served for two years as president but does not seem to have played a leading role in the Chamber afterwards, although he remained a very important member and sat ex-officio on the Council. As president, he made the longest public speech he ever made – on the occasion of a Grand Demonstration in favour of the reduction of import duties on wines and other commodities, held at the Crystal Palace and organised by the Anglo-French Free Trade Association and Wool Duties Committee.

The speech is a conventional statement of the free-trade case cogently and specifically argued to the circumstances of the Anglo-French worsted trade and illustrating very clearly Salt's ready acquiescence in the optimism of the free traders. Bradford's prosperity, he thought, had been based on free-trade principles. French and English worsted trade were reciprocal rather than competitive, for England was eager to buy all wool merinos, which the French could produce much better than anyone else, and merely wanted an open field for its own specialities – alpacas, lustres and moreens. Thus neatly dividing the market up in favour of the Bradford men – for it was in the latter field that the greatest volume of trade could be expected – he thought that the French had nothing to fear. The experience of Germany and Belgium where some liberalisation of trade had been achieved showed that the introduction of the new cloths stimulated native ingenuity to emulative competition and economic expansion.[38]

He was always a member of the inner circle of well-to-do Radical Dissenters who played a leading role in the reformation of Bradford's public life. In the forties and fifties, Forbes, Milligan and he provided the effective leadership of the group. His precise function is difficult to establish. The total absence of private correspondence leaves us to rely on the few speeches which are reported and a number of bald and simple interventions in committees in which he was generally making a practical suggestion about the application of a principle. In public he never took the lead in formulating political ideas or the strategy of a campaign, his role on public occasions almost always being either as chairman of a meeting or a supportive function to the main speakers. A casual impression from reading contemporary newspapers is that he was formal seconder to more resolutions at public meetings than any other leading man in Bradford. Yet it is difficult to believe that his value in political circles stopped with his reputation as an employer and his wealth. It is of course quite possible that he played an active part in Bradford politics simply because he liked to be in the centre of things. There was no compulsive obligation, and indeed one or two big employers kept quite aloof from politics, the Drummond family being the most notable of the absentees. I think that he was more considerable than his public utterance implies. Men deferred to him for his great reputation and his wealth, certainly. But he was an able man. The Rev. R. Cowan, the Saltaire pastor, thought he stood head and shoulders above his contemporaries for his quickness of perception and his intelligent assessment of a situation.[39] The evidence suggests that Salt's opinions counted, but they were brought out in committee or in private conversation rather than in public discussion. His interventions in council discussions were generally of a practical nature – not concerned to analyse problems, but putting forward practical suggestions for their resolution.

Through the forties and fifties he was particularly active in politics. He supported the cause of the Anti-Corn Law League with great enthusiasm and the various concerns of the Dissenter interest with equal fervour. He also showed a great deal of sympathy with the ideals of 'moral force' Chartism and contributed enormously to the fashioning of a political consensus which included the 'better disposed' of the working classes, and which began to take a solid form towards the end of the 1850s. He was ready to stand for Parliament in 1857, took a seat in 1859 and remained in Parliament for two years.

In 1861, at the age of fifty-six, he resigned his seat and went into semi-retirement; he had found parliamentary life something of a burden, and he was beginning as well to be troubled with the gout, which plagued him for the rest of his life. He was seen more rarely on public occasions. For some years he was to be principally occupied with his philanthropic activities and the completion of Saltaire, and he did not take any active part in the political life of the town until after 1867. By that time most of his early associates were dead and he had become the Grand Old Man of Bradford Liberalism, president of both the Bradford Liberal Association and the West Riding (Northern Division) organisation. He made a dramatic assault on W. E. Forster's education policies in the election of 1874, but he was now very much the venerated figurehead. His prestige locally and nationally was enormous; he was one of the folk heroes of Victorian capitalism; in Bradford he was almost beyond criticism. When Bradford's wool men wanted to decorate their Wool Exchange with busts of those who had made the nation great, it was inevitable that they should choose him as one of the two representatives of Bradford. The other was S. C. Lister.

The details of Salt's private and family life are even more obscure than his business activities. Perhaps the most important fact which emerges from the record available is that he lived all his life with the disadvantage of having great difficulty in speaking in public. Clearly he had a very highly developed sense of social as well as private responsibility and equally clearly he took a good deal of pride in the achievements this led him into. At the same time his business and personal interests (which included Saltaire) came before his public obligations. He was a friendly and approachable man and perhaps, owing to his basic diffidence, a little naive in personal relationships. He was devout, a regular worshipper and a generous supporter of religious and charitable causes. Of those in which he took a direct and personal interest perhaps the most important to him were the Orphans' Home at Hull, and in Bradford two missionary ventures, the Bradford Bible Women and the Town Mission which he helped to found. He was not a bigot in religion and characteristically never contributed to the funds of the anti-Catholic Protestant Association.

The evidence also suggests that he enjoyed the close life of the family circle. They lived in four houses at different times during his lifetime, the two in Bradford, Crow Nest, Lightcliffe from 1843 to 1859 and again from 1867 to 1877 and Methley Hall near Leeds between 1859 and 1867. Salt spent a good deal of money on the last two. Methley Hall was said to be 'furnished with all the elegance and luxurious taste wealth can command'. Crow Nest was apparently regarded as the true family home, since it was here that the children had spent the greater part of their childhood and youth. They left unwillingly in 1859 and returned with great pleasure when Salt was able to buy the house outright in 1867. Balgarnie describes it:

The mansion is of hewn stone, and consists of the centre portion with a large wing on either side, connected by a suite of smaller buildings, in the form of a curve . . . the south side presents a landscape of secluded beauty, in which wood and lake, lawns and terraces, flower gardens and statuary, delight the eye. The conservatories are also situated on the south side, in a line with the mansion, and are so lofty and extensive, as almost to dwarf its appearance. The central conservatory is more spacious than the others, and contains, in a recess, an elaborate rockery and cascade of French workmanship, which were objects of great attraction at the Paris Exhibition. The lake was constructed after Mr Salt's return, and affords another illustration of his fine eye for the beautiful and picturesque in nature. It is of uniform depth, well stocked with fish and aquatic birds, the latter finding shelter on the island in the middle. The vineries, pineries, and banana house are situated at a considerable distance from the mansion. . . Mr Salt took great delight in the cultivation of fruits and flowers, but the banana was his special favourite at Crow Nest, and it attained dimensions rarely met with in this country. Its luxuriant foliage, immense height, and gigantic clusters of bread fruit more resemble those of a tropical than of a temperate clime.[40]

He entertained regularly at Methley and at Lightcliffe. In the main his guests were drawn from personal and family friends in the locality and the political and business acquaintances he had in Bradford and the West Riding. Among them were Lightcliffe men like A. McLaurin, in the wool business in Bradford, and George Portway, the inventor of a type of automatic loom which, like other local inventions of the later nineteenth century, never found a backer, and others like James Law, Robert Milligan and the Crossleys of Halifax whose names figure more prominently in the local record. The firm's Turkish connexion occasionally provided an exotic visitor like Mr Petrokokinós, a business associate. While the family were at Methley, the Rev. P. Y. Saville, the local vicar and son of the Earl of Mexborough, came regularly to the house – a matter which caused some consternation in good Congregational circles. The commanding officer of the local Volunteer Rifle Battalion was entertained at Crow Nest – and caused stern Radical eyebrows to rise – but these visitors probably reflected the interests of two of the sons who were neither Liberal nor Dissenter. Miss Peachey, a young Leeds woman in the forefront of the fight for women's medical education, came on one occasion, probably as the guest of Titus junior and his wife. The conventionally distinguished were also to be found regularly among the guests in the Salt household. Samuel Morley, wealthy manufacturer, a powerful member of the Congregational Church and MP for Nottingham, important pastors and theologians like the Rev. Thomas Binnie and the Rev. Dr Guthrie, and the engineer William Fairbairn came from time to time and the two missionaries David Livingstone and Robert Moffat stayed at Crow Nest while they were in the district to give lectures at Bradford.[41]

From the time the family went to Crow Nest they were able to live the life of the wealthy upper class in luxurious surroundings and in contact with important people of the day. Salt did not, however, surrender entirely to the claims of his status. He was now a 'crested and carriage gentleman', but in the matter of education he remained faithful to the tradition of the Dissenters. Eight of the eleven children survived, Whitlam and Mary having died of scarlet fever in infancy and Fanny of tuberculosis at the age of twenty. William Henry, Amelia, George, Edward, Herbert and Titus junior were born in Bradford at the house in Little Horton Lane, near to the Union Street headquarters of their father's firm; Helen and Ada were born at Crow Nest. The two oldest boys first went to school at Huddersfield College, a new school established in 1838. The Principal was a scholar of Trinity College, Cambridge but the school was intended to serve Dissenters in the West Riding who wanted some education for business or had not succumbed to the lure of the public school. Although the classics were taught, the prospectus emphasised that particular attention would be paid to modern languages, writing, commercial arithmetic and book-keeping.[42] However, in 1847 when Edward was ten, he and his two older brothers William Henry and George went to Mill Hill School in London, an establishment which was intended to provide the facilities of a public school for the sons of well-to-do Dissenters. Its curriculum corresponded much more than that at Huddersfield to the conventions of what constituted the education of a gentleman's son. The other two boys, Herbert and Titus, went to the school when they were nine. Altogether William Henry stayed for one year, George two years, Edward six to seven, Herbert six and Titus only two years. Titus left at the same time as his older brother, in 1855, when there was a serious outbreak of scarlet fever in the school which had to be temporarily evacuated, and did not return.[43] None had any formal education after the age of sixteen to seventeen, and scholastically none of them made much impression in the establishments they attended, though two at least showed evidence later of considerable ability. The girls were educated privately, and it is just possible that Amelia went for a time to a school for young ladies run by Miss Scott, the sister of the Congregational pastor of College Chapel.

All the boys probably worked in the factory, learning the business from the age of sixteen to seventeen, and all except Herbert were taken into partnership. William Henry retired comparatively early from the firm. In 1855, he married Emma

Dove Octaviana Harris, the daughter of J. Dove Harris, Mayor of Leicester in 1856 and MP for the town 1865-74. In 1865 he bought an estate of 250 acres at Mapplewell in Leicestershire along with a handsome mansion and began to devote himself to the life of a country gentleman. On his father's death he inherited the title, £100,000 for its upkeep and a personal fortune of £80,000. He is buried outside the church at Woodhouse Eaves near Mapplewell in a modest grave, quite unlike the family tomb in Saltaire. A short obituary in the local press referred to him as quiet and unostentatious and with little taste for the practical life of business. Edward married Emma Harris's cousin, Mary Jane Susan Elgood, and after her death in 1870, Sarah Amelia Rouse, the granddaughter of the William Rouse with whom Titus Salt had had his early training in the wool trade. Edward worked in the firm until the Salt interest in it was sold out in 1892 and devoted himself to local politics in Shipley. He lived within walking distance of Saltaire at Ferniehurst, a house in Baildon which he had built in 1862. In 1892 he moved to Bath, where he died in 1903.[44]

Edward and William both showed a leaning towards the life of the traditional gentry as young men, for they were the only members of the family to take out gun licences or to show much interest in any kind of field sport. In the sixties both became members of the Conservative Party and, like their wives, members of the Church of England. This influence in the Salt family caused some people to suspect that Titus himself was contemplating a similar move. Again we simply do not know what the situation was. Titus was attending services in the parish church at Methley and was a close friend of the Vicar. Perhaps there was something in the rumour, for Balgarnie was at great pains to explain the matter away, pointing out that there was no Congregational church near Methley and suggesting that all that had really been demonstrated was Titus Salt's great virtue of open-mindedness.

If he was wavering and if he was likely to be influenced by family pressures, however, there were others to consider. The most important of them was Titus junior, a vehement – and, unlike his father, a vocal – Radical and Dissenter. He came into the firm when he was just turned twenty-one and was the most able of the directors and partners, although it was said of him that 'the world of business was not the most congenial world to him but he devoted himself to business and denied himself many pleasures because they were incompatible with that devotion'. In addition to responsibilities at the Saltaire factory he also took over responsibility for the Dayton Coal and Iron Company, USA, which had passed into Salt hands in 1870. He also supervised the administration of Saltaire village. In 1866, he married Katherine Crossley, daughter of John Crossley and niece of Sir Francis Crossley MP, of the Halifax textile firm and close personal friends of the Salt family. Together they dominated the life of the village for a number of years after the death of Sir Titus. Titus junior was always an active politician and – although, like most of the Salts, a reserved man – an able public speaker. After 1865, he took over most of the active duties of local political life, which his father had tended to give up after he left Parliament, but to which he had devoted much of his time as a young man.[45]

Like his older brother he lived within walking distance of the mill, first at Baildon Lodge and after 1872 at Milner Field, a great Victorian extravagance, built for him on the other side of the river – the fourth of the mansions which the firm of Salt and Sons was able to support. A visitor described it as 'a gorgeous mansion within, large, massive and imposing without'. It was carpeted with thick Turkey carpets. There was oak panelling everywhere, and some of the windows were of stained glass. The hall was dominated by a large stone fireplace and a large organ in carved oak. In the library and the drawing-room, there were huge carved alabaster chimney-pieces and in the dining-room, mural paintings. Numerous costly ornaments in china, carvings and paintings, decorated the rooms.[46] *The Builder* described the house as being

placed almost due north and south, the entrance being on the north side, through a massive gateway into an enclosed courtyard. The principal rooms face the south and open on to a wide terrace with flights of steps leading down to the park. The house is built of local stone with brick linings, forming hollow walls. The roofs are covered with Whitland Abbey green slating. Some of the rooms have moulded open ceilings of oak, and the woodwork of the principal rooms is either wainscot oak or chestnut. Burt and Pott's casements are fitted to the opening windows. The entrance hall and corridor are faced with stone in party colour. The old English type of plan adapted to the present requirements has been adopted, and the whole treatment of the work has been kept in harmony, much of the fittings and furniture having been made from special designs.[47]

It was a measure of their wealth, the importance of their local position and the reputation of the village of Saltaire that between 1882 and 1887 Mr and Mrs Salt were to entertain members of the royal family twice. In 1882, Edward then Prince of Wales and Princess Alexandra came to Bradford to open the new technical college and stayed overnight at Milner Field, and in 1887 when the Royal Yorkshire Jubilee Exhibition was held at Saltaire, Princess Beatrice, Duchess of Battenberg, and her husband also stayed there. Entertaining lavishly for some years, the Salts made Milner Field and Saltaire the centre of local 'society'.

Titus's private interests lay in floriculture and the exercise of a considerable talent for mechanics and handicrafts. He planned and constructed the heating system of his very large conservatories in the grounds of Milner Field. He organised experiments with the new telephone, linking up Saltaire Mills, Crossley's Mills, Halifax and Milner Field for a series of trials. He delighted in giving lantern shows of his fairly frequent travels abroad. His principal hobbies, however, were as a skilled wood and metal turner and as an ivory carver, in which capacity he produced a number of ceremonial tools for local occasions such as the laying of the foundation stone of the Bradford Town Hall.

He died in November 1887, at the age of forty-five, not entirely unexpectedly since a heart weakness had been diagnosed two years earlier. Mrs Salt and her four children, Gordon, Harold, Lawrence and Isobel, continued to play an active part in the life of the village and the locality until they left Milner Field in 1904. Mrs Salt kept some contact with the village until she died in 1930. She was buried alongside her husband in the family mausoleum at Saltaire.

Of the other children, very little indeed is known. Until 1886, George worked in the firm and gained a reputation as a clever amateur mechanical engineer. His most extravagant personal gesture seems to have been a luxury yacht which he kept moored at Scarborough. He did not marry until he was turned forty, and until then lived the conventional and comfortable life of the wealthy Victorian bachelor. For some years he was one of the organisers of the annual Bradford Bachelors' Ball and it was probably he who caused Holden eyebrows to be raised at the Royal Yorkshire Exhibition in 1887:

If the exhibition should prove a financial success it is believed by many that it will be very damaging to the morals of the people. Last Sunday, Mr Salt visited the Exhibition in company with some play actresses from the theatre at Bradford and I heard today that they had lunch in the Exhibition together.

Herbert rejected the business life altogether, and by his early twenties was established as a gentleman farmer at Bell Busk in the Yorkshire Dales. He married late in life and was converted to the Catholicism of his wife.[48] Amelia, the oldest girl, acted for some years as her father's private secretary and concerned herself along with her mother with the charitable visiting required in Saltaire and with the day and Sunday schools at Lightcliffe Congregational Church. In 1873, at the age of thirty-nine, she married a very wealthy railway engineer and a leading London Congregationalist, Henry Knight of Wimbledon. The press descriptions of her marriage are an interesting comment on Victorian social relations, and the position the Salts occupied in the district:

The village [of Lightcliffe] presented a most gay and festive appearance, numerous flags, Union, Jacks and pennants being suspended from the top of the railway station, the Congregational Church, the Parsonage, and other buildings. Mr S. Baarsdorf and several other gentlemen resident in the locality shewed the interest they took in the ceremony in a similar manner. The church was filled with visitors and there were great crowds outside. The police were on duty to keep order.

The scholars of the day and Sunday schools were given tea and buns at 4 p.m. At 6 p.m. the young people of the Congregational church were given 'a substantial tea' and Titus junior entertained them afterwards with one of his lantern slide shows.

After a honeymoon at Scarborough, Salt's favourite holiday resort, the couple went to live in Philimore Gardens, Kensington.[49]

Salt died in 1876 and sixteen years later the firm and the village were sold to a consortium of local businessmen. The connexion with the village became very tenuous, for the family was scattered and only Katherine Salt and her children remained in the locality. After her husband's death, Lady Salt sold Crow Nest and, with an unmarried daughter, went to live in London. She died in 1893 and the local paper reporting her funeral said that she was now a shadowy figure from the past, remembered only by older workers in the mill.[50] By 1902, except for Katherine Salt, the family's contact with Saltaire was almost ended – being confined to occasional visits for charitable and social purposes. Even before the end of the century the seat of the baronetcy had been established at Crickhowell in Wales.

III

YEARS OF CRISIS:
1834–1850

In an article published in the *Neue Rheinschen Zeitung*, Georg
Weerth, a young German poet living in Bradford for several
years during the mid-nineteenth century, gave an account of a
coach journey from Brighouse, still in the heart of rural West
Yorkshire, to Bradford six miles away. He contrasted his
pleasure at the 'beautiful gardens . . . the meadows succulently
green as Alpine flowers where the most handsome cattle roam
. . . and the magnificent wheatfields' through which the first
part of his journey took him, with his stupefied amazement at
the sudden appearance of a place where the mills, the steam
engines and the mean homes of industrial workers were
crowded on top of one another, where 'suddenly, on a bright
day, it became evening', where 'we stop in the dark alley of an
evil smelling town. We are in Bradford.'[1]

He was describing the cultural shock – the sense of alien
intrusion – which the mere sight of a nineteenth-century
industrial town gave to many of its contemporaries. The
population of Bradford and its environs had continued its
massive expansion as the wealth and economic importance of
the area continued to grow. The population of the
parliamentary borough was 43,527 in 1831, 66,713 in 1841, an
increase of 53 per cent, and 103,771 in 1851, an increase of 55
per cent. The unprecedented nature of this expansion, along
with the corresponding rise in the number of mills from 67 to
129 between 1841 and 1851, created enormous problems. The
town became a crucible of social experiment, for in such places
the most serious social problems of the age were located.[2]

This was most obvious in the sudden and savage desecration
of the environment. In twenty years the green and pleasant

valley of the Bradforddale had been transformed into a hideous battleground of industry. It would be impossible to establish, from the mass of evidence testifying to the facts of spoliation, a league table of merits and demerits among the various industrial agglomerations of Great Britain. Georg Weerth's view was that Bradford took precedence over Manchester, Birmingham and Leeds, and other visitors passed similar judgements. Charles Dickens, who must have been something of a connoisseur, thought that it was the beastliest of places. One government commissioner said that it was the dirtiest town he had ever seen. No one would pretend that pre-industrial Bradford was without misery, hunger and hardship, but this was a new phenomenon, which men lacked either time, inclination or capacity to control. All who worked in the town suffered from the pollution of its natural resources of fresh air and fresh flowing water and there were whole areas where life could hardly be maintained at any level of decency. Foul-smelling streams, miserable and unsanitary houses huddled around the many factories that belched out their black smoke for six days in the week, unpaved and uncleansed streets and thoroughfares used as the common tip for every kind of excrement and waste and a yellow, sulphureous smog which frequently hung over the low-lying centre of the town and rasped the lungs and barred the sun and light – these formed the physical background of life in the new industrial society.

Yet the questions posed went beyond the facts of the environment, important as they were. The rapid collection of an industrial workforce had created a population with special characteristics. It was a population which had been on the move. Many of them were first-generation town dwellers and first-generation factory workers. Predominantly, the town was a 'world of strangers', and although family patterns of migration eased some of the difficulties, it was a society in which the inhabitants needed to establish the *mores* of a way of life in new and different circumstances. It was a population which also contained the possibilities of cultural antagonisms, for by 1851 about 10 per cent were Irish, sometimes non-English-speaking and usually Catholic.

The central issue therefore concerned the social relations of men and women living in a new order of society. The problem posed was that of re-establishing a decent order in the way in which people behaved towards each other. Of course, as elsewhere, men and women living in Bradford developed a common experience which sprang from the facts of geography and common habitation as well as from the circumstances of work. There were also elements of stability which could be exploited. Despite the massive influx of new faces, the old townships were never completely eradicated from local affection, for if the population was 50 per cent immigrant, it was 50 per cent native. The most heavily infiltrated township, Bradford, was swamped by the urban concentration, but Horton, Bowling and Manningham retained their conscious separateness and continued to provide special focuses of community long after the municipal corporation had been established. There was thus a framework within which simple and informal neighbourhood groups, and more formal trade clubs, friendly societies and semi-official insurance clubs, the churches, chapels, mechanics' institutes and improvement societies, broke down the anonymity of the urban sprawl and provided the sinews of social order and discipline.

At the same time, the question of where authority lay had to be settled. The problem posed was – Whose order was to prevail? The conflict which had been predicted by the events of the 1820s had to be resolved in the late thirties and forties. Great fortunes were being built up and the alternative élite had consolidated its economic position. Its members were now to challenge the old Anglican establishment for a political authority which matched the economic influence they exercised in the town. At the other end of the social scale working men were stepping up their demand for political citizenship – the right to the vote which would give them some control of the circumstances in which they lived. All working men were witnesses of the miseries of hand-loom weavers and hand woolcombers, committed to slow obliteration, and almost all of them faced the threats and disasters of massive unemployment in the dark years between 1837 and 1842 and again between 1845 and 1848. It is very clear why Bradford was a centre of near-revolutionary activity for some years.

In the unfolding of events, the two basic issues – redistribution of power within the middle class, and the response, both middle-class and working-class, to working-class aspirations – were interwoven into a complex pattern which makes the history of Bradford very confused in these years. The question of religious equality entered the middle-class conflict in the form of the church rates controversy. Should Nonconformists be forced to continue paying the traditional subventions to the Anglican Church which all property owners legally owed, even when they made no use of its ministrations? The cessation of the levy in Bradford was a triumph for local Liberal–Dissent, though real equality was still a long way off. The establishment of something like political equality within the middle classes in 1832 was followed some fifteen years later by a general victory for Liberal economic policy with the repeal of the Corn Laws and in Bradford specifically a Liberal victory on the question of town government and control of the bench of magistrates. Thus, the way was clear for a re-stabilisation of political life in the ranks of the élite.

Anti-Poor-Law agitation was exhausted by 1837; the passing of the Factory Act of 1847 and its amendment in 1850 effectively ended the factory reform movement; Chartism, the working-class movement for revolutionary changes in the parliamentary system, was defeated by 1848. Working-class opinion was deflected to less fundamental political solutions and the conditions were created for the emergence of a general consensus. It was based on a broad Liberalism, the idealogical mainstay of early industrial capitalism, but of course it rested on the willingness of some members of the working classes to accept the tutelage of their supposed 'betters'. The ideological colour of the new society was confirmed, and at the same time the position of the new social classes of industrial revolution clarified.

THE FIRST ENCOUNTERS

Before this, there were nearly twenty years of discord and turmoil. Feeling ran high during 1833 as the factory reformers defended their position against the threats of a government inquiry and party division began to congeal. In 1834, the Bradford Liberal—Dissenters started to publish the *Bradford Observer* and joined the national agitation about the payment of church rates. In the following year they were defeated ignominiously in the general election. In an effort to displace one of the sitting members, the Methodist John Hardy, they brought from Manchester George Hadfield, an outstanding advocate of the cause of civil and religious liberty and a man with a national reputation. Hadfield was defeated comfortably by an alliance of Methodists and Anglicans.[3]

The election was quickly followed by attempts at more permanent political organisation than the *ad hoc* committees which had traditionally run elections. Encouragement from the Carlton Club, *de facto* headquarters of the Tory Party, led local Tories to establish the Bradford Constitutional Association to organise the proper registration of voters and secure the return of Tory members.[4] In the same week, the Bradford Reformers (as many of the Liberal—Dissenters preferred to call themselves) started the Bradford Reform Society to fight elections efficiently and to keep the Reform issue in the public eye. The subscription to the Society was 2s 6d and it was to be run by a president, two vice-presidents, a treasurer, four secretaries and sixty-two directors. Among them were Daniel Salt, in whose warehouse, the largest in Bradford, the inaugural meeting had been held, Titus and his brother-in-law George Haigh, and after 1841 his youngest son, Edward. The list of directors also included Robert Milligan and his associate Henry Forbes, now among the principal cloth merchants in the town; James Rennie, a successful draper; William Murgatroyd, Miles and Daniel Illingworth, and Richard and James Garnett, leading worsted manufacturers; Edward and Henry Ripley from the largest firm of dyers in the town; Henry Brown, eventually founder of Bradford's largest department store; E. H. Parratt, an ironmonger; Victor Rocheford, an Irish woolstapler; and George Oxley. All belonged to religious denominations other than the Anglican Church.[5]

The political organisation of the non-voters followed a more difficult course. By 1835 the Bradford Political Union was showing signs of the sort of strain which bedevilled working-class political life through the century. The multiplicity of causes which had to be fought, the differing aspirations of different sections of the working classes, the suffering caused – though not to all in the same degree – by changes in the structure of industry and the economic slump, made it difficult to establish a common front. The Bradford Political Union had backed the middle-class reform movement as a first step towards civic freedom for working men. Disillusion followed the Act of 1832 as quickly here as elsewhere – the publication of the Poor Law Amendment Act in 1834 had quickly demonstrated the temper of a new and reformed Parliament. Owenite Socialism attracted a good deal of support, for a time. The local trade clubs joined Owen's general union, the Grand National Consolidated, and the Rev. G. S. Bull, already prominent in the factory reform agitation, chaired several meetings of Owen's National Regeneration Society.[6] In 1835, however, further attempts were being made at more conventional political organisation. In January, a group of non-electors met at the schoolroom of William Hill, later the editor of the *Northern Star*, and formed the Bradford Radical Association. Its principal members were the better paid among the non-electors: the craftsmen, artisans, small retailers and minor professional men, some of whom had been members of the Political Union. There were a few textile workers in its ranks. Its leaders were men like Christopher Wilkinson, shortly to become a master printer; John Douthwaite, like William Hill a schoolteacher; the old Paineite and lawyer's clerk, Squire Farrar; and John Jackson, who had been a woolcomber but was now a nurseryman and gardener. It was perhaps the first concerted activity of Bradford's 'aristocracy of labour'.

The Association acted as host to the future Chartist leader Fergus O'Connor on at least two occasions, once in 1835 and again in January 1837 when he was guest at a 'Radical' dinner given at the Roebuck with John Douthwaite in the chair. O'Connor was in fine form. Urging on his audience the need to act alone, he reminded them that

the Whig-Radical was a creature of ambition who made himself the willing tool of a certain party that he might drive others out of power to get into possession of it himself. The Tory-Radical was a creature of wealth, the advocate of primogeniture and the pension list. The Democratic-Radical was he who looked to an equal distribution of law and justice to all classes of the community.

Several weeks later the message was underlined. Squire Farrar, Christopher Wilkinson and Samuel Bower went as a delegation from the Radical Association to meet the committee of the Reform Society. Their request for support for a petition in favour of household suffrage was rejected, the committee deeming it inexpedient to make any resolution on the subject.[7] In September Chartism came to Bradford. With John Jackson in the chair, the Association held a meeting at the Hope and Anchor to hear Henry Vincent address them as a missionary from the London Working Men's Association about the discussions taking place among London working men. Speaking to the toast, 'the People, the legitimate source of all power', he discussed the six principles which were to form the 'People's Charter', and to provide the context of the democratic debate through the century. They were universal manhood suffrage, the secret ballot, payment of MPs, abolition of property qualification for MPs, equal electoral districts and annual parliaments. By 1837 Conservative working men had also been organised into the 'Loyal and Constitutional Society of Working Men' – the Operative Conservatives.[8]

But the question which first stimulated sharp political antagonisms after 1835 was the question of ecclesiastical privilege. This was to be expected. The privileges which attached to membership of the established church were a deep offence to a dissenting community which had a long history of achievement in the intellectual as much as in the commercial and manufacturing field. Their position was precisely that taken by members of the Radical Association. They were responsible men. They demanded the rights of responsible citizens. In their case, however, economic power and social position gave them access to institutions through which their demands could be pursued. In 1834, Bradford Dissenters played their part in a national campaign by petitioning Parliament for the total abolition of church rates. In the same year, two Quakers, J. Priestman and J. E. Ellis, were summoned for non-payment, and in subsequent years all attempts to fix a rate were defeated by crowding vestry meetings with Dissenters who refused to accept any proposals.[9]

Towards the end of 1838 the Anglican authorities made a determined effort to get a rate fixed and collected. The meeting arranged turned out to be extremely turbulent. So many attended that it had to be held in the churchyard. After a great deal of bitter wrangling, the meeting was once again adjourned. Henry Heap, the Vicar, was taken ill at the meeting and within two months had died. Vicar of Bradford since 1815, he had lived through a period in which the various denominations had lived for the most part amicably side by side – when the Bradford branch of the British and Foreign Bible Society had been run by the 'union of all denominations of Christians . . . without the least sacrifice of principle'. He had little stomach for the rigour of the new order in Bradford and had acquiesced generally in the tactics adopted in avoiding the church rate. He was now succeeded by the Reverend W. Scoresby, a man of very different temper.

Scoresby came to Bradford with an international reputation as scientist and sailor, for he had been ordained into the Church after years of success in these fields. He threw himself into his priestly duties with the same vigour he had shown as a sailor. Intellectually, he was the equal of the eminent Dissenters who came to Bradford in the same era, Dr Stedman and Dr Godwin, the leading Baptist ministers, and Rev. Jonathan Glyde, the pastor of the Horton Lane Congregational Chapel. After he arrived in Bradford, the fight was engaged fiercely and several years of extremely sharp polemic followed until the matter of church rates was settled. However, although the question remained important both as a day-to-day issue and in terms of its impact on the future, it was overshadowed by the problems presented by working-class agitation.[10]

In 1837, the Bradford Liberals had had the electoral success which they thought their work with the Reform Society had merited. George Hadfield had been dropped – his intransigent anti-State Church stance was recognised as an electoral liability in a town like Bradford where the old establishment still remained powerful. He was replaced by W. Busfeild, a member of the Bingley family of gentry and like Lister an innocuous Whig-Liberal, who pushed the Tory, John Hardy, into third place and took over the seat. Political opinion was now sharply crystallised. In 1835, over 18 per cent of the electorate split their two votes between the two parties. Now only about 4 per cent did so.

The election itself was fought with great vigour; Bradford was rapidly learning the conventional techniques of the Victorian election. A great deal of 'undue influence' was exercised by both parties; polling day was associated with scenes of violence of which the highlight was a massive brawl between ironworkers and miners employed by the Tory ironfounders of Bowling and Low Moor and the Radical hand-loom weavers of Great Horton. The *Bradford Observer* commented:

Another such contested election in Bradford, as that which has just terminated in the triumph of the Reformers, and the town will be, we fear, past all reformation. More injury has been done to the morals of our inhabitants within the two or three past weeks, than all the sermons preached . . . will repair in as many years.[11]

The victory of the Reformers also owed something to the support of the Radical Association, though such support showed as much as anything the complexities of non-elector politics. Since the Poor Law Amendment Act had been passed in 1834 there had been conflict over its provisions. Though sometimes administered at local level less harshly, its intention was to reduce poor relief to a bare minimum and to make its distribution through the workhouse system as inflexible as possible in order to reduce the bargaining power of Labour in the labour market. It horrified almost all working men and women and established a view of upper-class callousness which remained alive at least until the system disappeared. At first most Tories disapproved of it, though, naturally, Whigs and Liberals, whose government had introduced it, backed it more or less consistently. Alignments generally were much the same as those of the factory agitation, which it consequently embraced through 1837, for it was seen as part of the same struggle against a brutal economism.

At the beginning of that year, arrangements were put in hand for the introduction of the Act to Bradford. The Bradford Poor Law Union, which included the parliamentary borough and the surrounding district, was set up and on 10 February a Board of Guardians was elected to administer it. Since a number of Tories had boycotted the election, the six Bradford men elected to the Board were all Liberals – William Hardcastle, John Hill, James Rennie, Thomas Buck, Christopher Waud and Daniel Salt. The operation took place against a background of hostile meetings. At the end of January a very large open-air meeting of working men had condemned the law. In February, a large middle-class audience heard the Rev. G. S. Bull denounce the Act with his characteristically powerful eloquence: 'I hear the suppressed but powerful and Heaven rending moan of the widow and the fatherless, of the friendless saying "Lord, how long!"' At the beginning of March a town meeting heard Matthew Thompson and the Rev. W. Morgan call for the repeal or at least the amendment of the Act. At the first meeting of the Guardians, there was a scuffle outside the Court House in Hall Ings where the meeting was held and at the second meeting troops had to be called in to restore order in the crowded streets. But by the end of the year the local front against the law had been broken, when a number of Bradford Tories led by Thompson dropped their opposition. They had, he said, been converted by the sense and reason of the law.[12]

In addition, the election took place against a background of growing economic distress as the grimmest period in the nineteenth century began. In April 1837, the *Bradford Observer* reported that markets were stagnant and prices falling. Of the yarn market it was said that 'we never remember a worse market than we have had today [25 April] . . . the little business that has been transacted was only effected by a reduction in prices'. In June the principal inhabitants held a public meeting to consider the 'distress among the working classes', the outcome of which was a public subscription list. In bringing the meeting to an end, J. G. Horsfall, a leading Tory manufacturer, moved, with that condescension which we find hard to comprehend today, that 'the thanks of this meeting be given to the working classes for the patient manner in which they had borne their suffering'.[13] Meanwhile the condition of the hand-loom weavers was deteriorating rapidly. Cyclical pressures were added to the impact of structural changes and, as we have already seen, hand-loom weaving was to be eliminated as a major element in the industry between 1835 and 1845. In April 1835 the hand-loom weavers had held a meeting in front of the Court House to consider a petition to Parliament complaining of the 'unequal competition between power loom and hand loom'. The *Bradford Observer* sprang to the defence of the new technology with a panegyric on the development of Bradford:

There are those who recollect the time when spinning was all done by hand – when the building of the first mill was protested at as a public nuisance – when the steam engine was going to ruin all the old women at a stroke. Look at Bradford – doubling its population in some dozen years – wealthy beyond any town in the kingdom for its size, with scarcely a horse power, or a warehouse, or even a private house to be had. Was our trade ever so large or our prospects so good as at the present days? And how many old women have been ruined? Fluctuations have been and will come again, but was there ever a time at any period. . . . When wages were so good, or living lower or machinery so extensive as at present?[14]

But 1836 saw the end of several years of buoyant conditions. By November 1836, the *Bradford Observer* was reporting that the price of manufactured goods was falling and markets were stagnant; at the end of 1837 it reported: 'we gladly dismiss the last month of 1837 with the hope of being able to give a very different picture at the close of 1838'.

There was plenty of information available about the condition of the hand-loom weavers, quite apart from the evidence of the eyes. Reports appeared regularly in the local press of the inquiry held by H. S. Chapman in September and October 1838. Elizabeth Dracup's evidence was revealing. She was a widow with three children. The total family income, including that of one of the children, came to 10s. 6d. a week out of which she had to pay fixed charges of 4s. 8d. rent and 1s. 8d. for heat and light and the preparation of the weft and warp she was to use during the week. Understandably, she could make no provision for the future, belonging neither to sick club nor funeral society. Altogether there were about 20,000 living in and around Bradford in conditions of abject and increasing penury.[15]

Tories and working-class Radicals had collaborated in the past on the question of factory reform and more recently on the Poor Law issue, and might have found some common line of action to help the hand-loom weavers. But in Bradford, a Tory–Radical alliance was really a matter of convenience. The Radical Association, O'Connor's Democratic Radicals, preferred to march at this point with O'Connor's Whig-Radicals. A strong minority led by Chris Wilkinson and Squire Farrar had always thought the Poor Law Amendment Act a sensible reform; and for all of them the overriding consideration was the question of civic liberty and the destruction of privilege. Some Liberals stood, sooner or later, for changes in the franchise. Despite the rebuff which the Radical Association was given in February, as interest in the question of the vote revived, the Association threw its influence behind the Liberals in the general election.

After the election, the affirmation of democracy which working men had made in Chartism took the debate into new areas of experience.[16] The People's Charter was published in May 1838 and quickly became the inspiration of a nation-wide working-class demand for the revolutionary changes in government which it had put forward. The movement which voiced its ideals was never a homogeneous one, however. The aspirations of different sections of what contemporaries called 'the operative classes' and the needs of men in different parts of the country differed, and these were reflected in Chartist opinion. Most important was the difference between the 'moral force' and 'physical force' men – between those who were prepared to await the deliberations of Parliament and those who talked the language of revolution. In the north, the Great Northern Union, led by Fergus O'Connor, co-ordinated activity and Bradford men formed a branch of this, the Bradford Northern Union, in September.[17] It included at first some members of the Radical Association, moral-force men primarily concerned with the extension of the franchise. It had the men who followed Peter Bussey in his more violent and more wide-sweeping attacks on what he saw as an 'unjust system' and the majority were weavers and woolcombers alerted to the need for political activism by the horrors of their situation. Bradford Chartism released the bitterness of men forced into despair by the economic system and the gloomy science of economism which sustained it.

The language of violence quickly began to dominate the discussion, both in the form of simple incitement to machine breaking – 'We must go to the places where the power looms are, for they are the greatest evils we have; we must burn 'em and break 'em up, and pay no respect of persons' – and at more sophisticated levels of military preparation. Moral-force men – the Chris Wilkinsons – began to dissociate themselves from the wilder flights of imagination.

Sympathy with the Chartists had been quite widespread at first, particularly among churchmen. Scoresby held a special service for them at the parish church in August, and Bull preached for them on the same evening at Bowling St John's. Both mentioned the dangers of violent courses, the evidence of which had been mounting through the year. Bussey in one speech had advised his audience to arm themselves: 'those who cannot get a musket let them buy a brace of pistols and those who cannot get pistols let them buy a pike – aye a pike with a shaft eight feet long, and a spear fifteen inches long at the end of it'. Reports from the Bradford magistrates to the Home Office in the summer of 1839 claimed that drilling had been going on for the greater part of the year, that arms were widely distributed and huge meetings openly asserted both a determination to revolt and the legality of such actions. The *Bradford Observer* issued a warning:

Chartist intolerance and violence has done much to make Whigs conservative and Tories tolerant of Whiggery. Hence Liberty and the progress of right principles have been sacrificed by a forced union of opposites.

At the end of August a small body of the Eighth Hussars arrived in Bradford and were quartered in inns in the town centre. A number of special constables had been enrolled, and the Chartist movement was penetrated by police spies.

Nationally, the Chartists had agreed to call a convention of delegates to organise the presentation of the People's Charter in the form of a petition to Parliament. Peter Bussey was the

Bradford representative. It was an unhappy experience. The convention broke up in disagreement on the physical v. moral force issue. Eventually the petition was also rejected, and the organisation of the movement was disrupted by the arrest of most of the leaders. Peter Bussey was a member of an insurrectionary committee prepared, along with John Frost and several others, to plan a general revolt. Bussey, unfortunately, lost his nerve as the time for action came nearer, and went into hiding from where he later went to the USA. The Bradford men failed to turn out at the first general signal, a rising in Newport led by Frost to rescue Henry Vincent, imprisoned there. A second plan for a Yorkshire/Lancashire rising failed in early January 1840 and another attempt centred this time on Bradford itself also failed towards the end of the month. The rising which took place on Sunday, 26 January, came as the climax to the excitements of nearly a year. The *Observer* reported:

During the whole of Monday, the town continued in a state of feverish excitement . . . the Court House presented the appearance of a place in a state of siege. Soldiers on guard, a six-pounder in front and a large posse of special constables in and about the place.[18]

Inside, a number of men who had been arrested for their part in the projected rising were committed for trial on charges of high treason and conspiracy and riot. Meanwhile a large crowd assembled outside and showed their sympathy by throwing mud on the 'clothing of every person who from their dress [had] any claim to respectability'. Ten were tried at York and, the charge of high treason having been abandoned, were given sentenced ranging from three years hard labour to one year. The rising was reported as the desperate but foolhardy sacrifice of a handful of ill-prepared quasi-revolutionaries, and this is the record which has gone into most of the published accounts. A. J. Peacock in his monograph on *Bradford Chartism* has shown that it was much more serious than this, but it cannot be suggested that there was ever a chance of success. Bradford was a 'physical force' town but there was always a quality of despair in its defiance of the 'forces of law and order': ' . . . sooner than eke out a miserable existence in the manner they do at present, death, in whatever shape he may level his shafts, shall terminate the struggle, for it is more honourable to die by the sword than of hunger'.[19] Yet the movement was not by any means exhausted. By the end of 1840, the National Charter Association was in being; although not large, it gave a framework of activity to the most determined of the Chartists everywhere. A branch was organised in Bradford by mid-1841.

Meanwhile, the Socialists had recovered from the debacle of 1834, and were active once again. A number of men who had supported the Radical Association in pursuit of franchise reforms – notably Sam Bower and John Douthwaite – abandoned the society and turned their attention exclusively to Socialism. Bower wrote several pamphlets between 1837 and 1838 in which he discussed a future programme. He shared the disillusion of the Chartists with Whig Reformers:

The illusions of Whig Reform have one by one melted into thin air. The promised shaking of the tree deferred so long that the working classes, tired of waiting, with aching eyes and watering mouths, the descent of the golden shower, have long ago forsaken it.

He argued for a committed and consistent experiment in the co-operative community, for it was only in the conditions of equality which they provided that men could find the way to a good life. He feared that the pursuit of universal suffrage might prove something of an irrelevance. 'Meanwhile it is a matter of no inconsiderable importance that the working classes . . . should be disabused of the idea that universal suffrage is a necessary preliminary to [a just] system being brought into operation.[20]

By 1840, the Socialists could afford their own Hall where from time to time Robert Owen and Fergus O'Connor – the two great inspirations of working-class life – could be heard. Despite the impediments offered by the local Gas Company which refused to light the hall, lecture programmes attracted audiences of between seven and eight hundred. Often they included a number of Chartists, for there was always an affinity between Socialists and at least what we may call left-wing Chartism. Chartist speeches in Bradford revealed more than a concern for an extension of the franchise. They shared with

Socialism a common disdain for the 'Whig-reformer' and a common regard for an order of society based on principles not offered by the dogmas of Liberalism or Conservatism. Scoresby and Glyde went to a number of meetings to do battle with Anti-Christ; they were alarmed at the large number of women there.[21]

The Rev. F. Clownes, one of the tutors at Horton Baptist College, saw great danger in the relationship and urged middle-class electors to break the Chartist–Socialist alliance in the name, as he saw it, of their Christian duty. He asked the middle classes to 'give the Charter a cool and dispassionate reading' for it was clear that 'the charter must sooner or later have the attention of the Liberal party, and the sooner the better'.[22] Sentiments like these played their part in the formation of the United Reform Club, a formal amalgamation between the Reform Society, the middle-class 'Whig Radicals' of O'Connor's speech and the Radical Association, that part of the working class which had apparently no dangerous elements like physical-force Chartists and Socialists now.

The United Reform Club was founded in September 1841 immediately after the Liberal electoral defeat.[23] John Hardy, in effect a Tory, though he claimed some Liberal connexion still, had finished triumphantly at the head of the poll, thus avenging his defeat of 1837. His victory was due in large measure to the positive nature of Peel's leadership of the national party. In Bradford it was confirmed by the co-operation of Tories and Chartists, in turn the result of the disasters to the local economy. The Chartists, who had their own electoral committee, put up William Marten who won on a show of hands. When his opponents demanded a ballot he withdrew, advising his supporters to transfer their support to the two Tory candidates.[24] With this defeat, the Liberals began to strengthen their organisation and so formulated the alliance of what was described by the *Observer* as the 'two principal reform bodies in the town'. The influence of the old members of the Radical Association was sufficient to bring about an important change in policy. The new society started with a declaration in favour of household suffrage, yet within months, the vote 'for all males over twenty-one' was written into the constitution as the society's principal aim. Not all members of the society were happy with it. Nevertheless a powerful section in the middle classes had accepted the principle of manhood suffrage, at least for the time being. It represented the first formal link between middle-class reformers and 'the better sort of working man' in joint pursuit of the working-class objective of the vote. Although its fortunes were mixed, it was in the line of the strategies adopted with great success in the fifties and sixties.

At the meeting held on 17 September to start the venture, the sponsors issued a statement to the effect that the times offered a favourable opportunity for forming 'an association to promote the great principles of FREEDOM for which all classes of Reformers are struggling, and the triumph of which will be ensured by *mutual concession* and co-operation'. 335 members were admitted, of whom 115 had the parliamentary vote. 106 paid 2s. 6d. a quarter and 229, 1s. a quarter. Several wealthy Radicals gave substantial donations, Henry Forbes and Titus Salt each paying a £10 subscription and a £25 donation. The *Bradford Observer* remarked that the 'working classes should regard disinterested generosity of this description, as evidence of a sincere wish for their elevation in the scale of society'. But of course the Radical Association could not really be regarded as representing the vast majority of working people in Bradford in these years, that is, the labouring masses. Seen in its best light it represented those who had rejected the most outright demands of Chartism, the possibilities of violent action, and the social philosophy which lay underneath. But the social division was there. Appropriately, Chris Wilkinson was among those who negotiated the amalgamation. The composition of the club management reflected the Victorian sense of deference to position and recognised the financial importance of the well-to-do. So – Henry Forbes was president. There were four vice-presidents, John Lupton Esq. and Titus Salt Esq. represented the Reform Society and Mr George Binns and Mr J. Richardson the Radical Association. The treasurer was Mr J. V. Godwin, only son of Rev. B. Godwin, at that time a partner with Milligan and Forbes. The secretaries were W. S. Nichol, clerk in a warehouse, and W. German, in a small way of business.

The fortunes of the United Reform Club are not easy to follow after the first two years. Public interest in the question of the franchise diminished in the years between 1842 and 1846. The club seems to have fallen quickly into the control of the well-to-do. By the end of 1842, William Byles, the editor of the *Bradford Observer*, had replaced W. S. Nichol as the principal secretary and its most urgent concerns were with the essentially middle-class agitations about legal electoral office, church rates, the Corn Law, and the question of incorporation.[25]

MOUNTING TENSION

The next ten years were to be critical for the development of what was now a highly politicised town, described by the *Leeds Intelligencer* as 'the stronghold of dissent, whiggism, socialism, chartism and infidelity'. This was to be a decade of fierce conflict and frightening violence. Tory-Conservative was locked in battle with Whig-Liberal for supremacy in the town so that every issue became a political conflict. Both were terrified by the threat of Chartist violence although prepared to accept Chartist help when violence was not threatened. As if to put a stamp on the decade, magistrates decided early in 1841 to strengthen the institutions of public order, by erecting a permanent military barracks at Bradford Moor, on the eastern outskirts of the town and about two miles from the centre. The six Bradford magistrates – E. C. Lister, Matthew Thompson, H. W. Hird, Charles Hardy, John Rand and J. G. Paley – writing to the Home Office to request financial help, since they had no funds which could be allocated to this purpose, explained that 'the population in this neighbourhood is so dense – so excitable and constantly changing and still increasing – that in our opinion military force is indispensably requisite to preserve the public order'. By the end of the year a troop of cavalry and several companies of infantry were in occupation of the new buildings.[26]

Their presence in the town was not universally popular. Chartists had obvious reasons for disliking the presence of the army. Many Radicals also saw the army as part of the privileged order they were concerned to destroy. The *Bradford*

Observer did not bother to conceal distaste when it carried reports of the incidents which occurred between the civilian population and the soldiers, 'the heroes of the thirty-second Regiment now quartered in our town for the preservation of public order'. The local yeomanry, which had recently been created, also came in for criticism. They were trying, said the paper, to intimidate the working classes to whom they offered a fine example of military preparation in defence of their own self-interest. The enemies they were learning to attack were neighbours, acquaintances, their own working men. One leader concluded:

Every unit of a yeomanry corps, as he walks or rides the streets, every company of them at drills and reviews, is a walking or riding or galloping signpost on which is written so intelligibly that he who runs may read – 'Working men, look here! the sword shall drink your heart's blood should you ever become troublesome.'

At the same time, a local clergyman, Archdeacon Musgrave, at the service consecrating the colours of the yeomanry, called upon the congregation to thank God for them to preserve law and order and protect the working classes from their own folly. Towards the end of 1842, after the serious rioting of that year, at a meeting of gentlemen connected with the town and trade of Bradford, G. T. Lister (Tory) and Titus Salt (Radical) moved and seconded a resolution to thank the magistrates, yeomanry and constables for the zeal, energy and discretion with which they carried out their duties.[27]

The increasing political tension of the decade was shown in the way elections for the Board of Guardians and all other elective offices of the township and vestry were fought as political issues. The office of High Constable of the manor had frequently been occupied by a Liberal–Dissenter through the thirties. For several years now it became almost their monopoly, for it was the most distinguished elective office available, and carried real power since, in the absence of a mayor, the Constable took control of all public meetings. Titus Salt, who was beginning to move into the front rank of Liberal leaders now – a senior member of the Reform Club, one of the two or three most generous supporters of the Anti-Corn Law

League – was elected High Constable in 1842.[28] By 1845, also, they were electing churchwardens from among their numbers. The temper of politics at the time was also shown in public meetings. Again in 1842, the Chartists took control of a town meeting called to give support to the Anti-Corn Law League. Salt as chairman cut a figure of acute embarrassment as vocal Chartists compelled the meeting to discuss Chartist rather than Anti-Corn Law resolutions, and as most of Salt's close associates there left the meeting.[29] A look at the elections of 1841 would confirm the impression. In the general election John Hardy had pushed W. Lister into second place. Thus the second Whig–Liberal candidate, W. Busfeild, lost the seat he had had since 1837. Lister died several weeks after his election and the subsequent by-election was fought between Busfeild and W. Wilberforce, the son of the anti-slavery reformer. It was one of the fiercest elections ever fought in Bradford. A good deal of brawling took place, there were accusations that voters had been kidnapped, and when Busfeild scraped home by four votes the wrath of the *Leeds Intelligencer* exploded: 'Mr Busfeild is the member for bludgeoning; not the member for Bradford. He is the representative of the baseness, the bloodiness, the brutality of the Whigs'.[30]

The church rates issue also flared up. There had been an unsuccessful attempt to levy a rate in 1840, but the church party had no intention of leaving the matter there. In February 1841, the churchwardens called a vestry meeting. It was again so massively attended that it could not be held in the church but once again took place in the churchyard. In the way which had become familiar, the meeting was adjourned on the motion of two Dissenters. The church wardens, however, produced an affirmation from the Archbishop of York, which gave them authority to make the levy despite the wishes of the majority. They called a meeting in May and when the levy was denied declared their intention of carrying through the terms of the Archbishop's document. The dissenting party had in fact offered to donate voluntary subscriptions as a way out of the dilemma, but the church party saw this as tantamount to accepting defeat, and rejected it on the grounds that it fell outside the terms of the Archbishop's affirmation. Tempers ran high on both sides. Over two hundred signed the minute book in opposition to the declaration of the rate, including three future Liberal mayors and a number of the men who were to become aldermen and councillors after a municipal borough had been established. The meeting broke up in disorder. In the event, the victory of the church party was a hollow one. The most powerful of the Dissenters resisted the collection of the rate. Titus Salt was reported as dismissing the collector from his door with the words, 'I tell you I will not pay', and other notable rebels included William Murgatroyd, Edward Kennion, Daniel Illingworth, Henry Forbes, Robert Milligan and the Garnett brothers.[31] The most decisive action was taken against the printer John Dale. Summoned to answer for his refusal to pay before the West Riding magistrates, all Anglicans except one, his case was taken to the High Court where it languished until 1846, when Dale's stand was vindicated by a verdict declaring illegal the levying of a rate on a minority vote.

In Bradford, however, the matter had been settled by default. The Dissenters showed that they could control the vestry meeting by calling for adjournment again in 1842 and by electing as churchwarden representing the parish John Dale himself. The suggestion made at the United Reform Club to elect Christopher Wilkinson – well-known for his secularist beliefs – was not pursued, but in later years E. H. Parratt and John Buck, a friend of the Salt family and executor of Daniel's will, were elected to the position. Although the Vicar's warden could move the levy himself, in practice the church party conceded that they had to wait for the 'Dale' decision, and no general church rate was called for in Bradford again.

The reformers now tried to shift the attack to the question of town government, but before the campaign could be started the town and indeed most of industrial Britain was thrown into turmoil by a second wave of widespread public disorder. By 1842 the deepening of the long depression was once again giving renewed bite and determination to Chartism. The National Chartist Association which had been formed in 1841 organised a second Chartist petition to Parliament in the spring of the year. Although rejected in Parliament once again, it was successful as a demonstration of working-class opinion, for the

Chartists were able to claim four million signatures. With this encouragement, Chartist leaders turned a series of industrial disputes in Lancashire into the beginnings of a general strike and an affirmation of Chartist strength. On 12 August a meeting of delegates from Lancashire and Yorkshire was held and passed one resolution demanding the end of 'class legislation' and the immediate implementation in law of the Charter and a second which called for a general strike.[32]

Bradford, like the rest of the West Riding, was as ripe as Lancashire for action of some sort. There had been 45,000 signatures to the Charter petition and by the middle of the year large regular meetings were being held. Once again the economy was in bad shape, prices were low, the demand for yarns, in particular, almost non-existent, and unemployment very high. Edward Akroyd of Halifax, leading a delegation of West Riding manufacturers to the Prime Minister, was reported as telling him:

The only trade left which was possessed of life and vitality was that consisting of mixed goods of cotton and worsted printed and fancy wovens, figured and embroidered. . . . The fancy trade employs fewer and requires more capital. . . . Many operatives are out of work; those suffering the most are the hand-combers and the weavers.[33]

Unlike the hand-weavers, the combers were not yet feeling the consequences of expendability. But the existence of a vast labour supply, the employment of which did not require great capital outlay, added to the miseries of demand depression. A contemporary report illustrated the situation:

On a recent Saturday a comber weighed out the first portion of 54 lbs of fine Australian wool; he wrought hard upon it with his wife and a child until the Tuesday next but one following when he delivered his work – 18 lbs of tops at 7d a lb; ten shillings and sixpence for eight days' labour of three persons, from which 3d was deducted for washing the wool, leaving 7s 8½d for one week's supply. He of course carried in a much larger weight of noils, for which he received no remuneration, though by his labour rendered more valuable.

He finished his report with the statement that while in 1838 the wages of three persons for six days had been £1. 18s. 8d., a sum which covered the purchase of 206 lb of flour, in 1842 the wages for three persons for eight days was 10s. 3d., the equivalent of 55 lb of flour. Another observer, a moral-force Chartist, warned the middle classes of the dangers which society faced, referring to the intense bitterness he discerned, particularly in the manufacturing districts, between middle and working class. 'They distrust each other,' he said, 'perhaps, they hate each other!' He suggested that the middle classes were to blame. Unlike the working classes, who in 1832 had threatened to revolt in order to help the middle classes to the vote, the middle classes had stood aside while Chartist leaders were arrested during the Chartist campaign for the vote in 1839. Working men and women were alienated from society, and alienated would remain until they also had their due as citizens, their enfranchisement.[34]

For the moment, despite such pleas, there was to be only confrontation. In Bradford, the magistrates swore in 1,000 special constables and called for military reinforcements from Leeds. The Bradford Chartists held a meeting on 18 August and voted to join the protest movement on the resolution of Henry Hodgson, the veteran of 1840.

The People's Charter ought to become the law of the land as it contains the elements of justice and prosperity and we pledge ourselves never to relinquish our demands until that document becomes a legislative enactment.

The meeting formed up in procession and marched off up Manchester Road to join strikers in Halifax, stopping most of the mills along the route, either going or coming back, by putting the boiler systems out of action. On the following day an attack on Lister's mill at Manningham was diverted to Frizinghall and the Keighley Road by a troop of cavalry which blocked the Toller Lane approach to the mill. Instead, the Bradford contingent marched along the Keighley Road helping to stop most of the mills in Shipley, Bingley, Baildon and Wilsden. In Bradford itself, another contingent attacked several mills without much success. Rands' mill at the bottom of Little Horton Lane was defended with great vigour by the overlookers, woolsorters and engine men. Rouse's mill on Canal Road was saved by a company of the Seventeenth Lancers, and Horsfall's mill in North Wing was saved by one of the magistrates, Joshua Pollard, who road his horse into the crowd and delayed it long enough for the overlookers and mechanics to close the mill gates. On the third day, the strikers concentrated with some success on the mills to the east of Bradford towards Pudsey and Stanningley. But the day culminated in a fight between them and the combined specials and cavalry in Dudley Hill, in which the strikers were dispersed and a number of arrests made. From then on the troops imposed harsh and vigorous controls on the streets and within a week the town was reasonably quiet. About a hundred of the strikers had been arrested and some sixty were sent to stand trial at York. The special constables remained on duty and the Yorkshire Hussars were billeted in the town. A company of the Seventeenth Lancers and 700 of the Seventy-third Foot occupied the barracks. Nationally, most of the Chartist leaders had also been arrested.

There is a suggestion of discrimination in the selection of the mills attacked. Of those named in the press, the three mentioned in Bradford itself all had histories of disturbed labour relations. On the other hand, many of the large mills in Bradford remained untouched because they stood in narrow streets where the tactical possibilities of attack were limited and Lister's mill, which had only been in operation four years, stood on the line of what was clearly the agreed route of march for the day. The mills which were attacked in a sense picked themselves partly from reputation, partly from the access which their position gave. There is some confusion about the Chartist commitment to the disorders. Most of the national leaders spoke out against violence when mills were forced to stop. In Bradford, the *Bradford Herald*, a short-lived Tory paper, accused the local Chartists of fomenting trouble and then leaving others to bear the brunt of conflict: 'Throughout the whole proceedings we have noticed that the cowardly agitators belonging to this deluded body of men [i.e. the Chartists] have taken no part in the riots.' In fact, a number of well-known physical-force Chartists played their part; perhaps the paper's venom was directed on this occasion at the old moral-force men who as members of the United Reform Club attracted political mud-slinging from the local Tory press.[35]

MUNICIPAL CORPORATION

The fight for control of local government began in earnest in 1843 after the church rates controversy had been engulfed in the slow complexities of the law.[36] It centred around proposals to obtain municipal borough status for the parliamentary borough. The first shot in the campaign took the form of a proposal, moved by the Liberal members, for an Improvement Bill to extend the powers of the Board. On the same day the Reform Club held a special general meeting of members and others to promote the cause of incorporation. About 250 people, 'mainly of the middle classes', attended and agreed that the condition of the town warranted fundamental changes and formulated the resolution:

The principle of representative government is the one most in accordance with the habits and predilections of the English people, that experience has proved that although not without defects it has been the means of procuring a larger amount of good than could have been obtained under any other system and that it is as expedient to place the affairs of small communities under vigilant popular control as those of a nation, and for these general reasons as well as for others of a subordinate character, it is the opinion of this meeting that prompt and energetic measures be adopted to procure for the Borough of Bradford a Charter of Incorporation.[37]

Salt became a prominent member of the sub-committee of thirty, which was appointed to carry the resolution into effect.

The meeting, held four days later in the Temperance Hall, created some confusion. Some of the Commissioners put forward their proposals for an extension of powers. They were defeated. So were the proposals in favour of incorporation sponsored by Salt and his companions. The *Bradford Observer* was furious. It claimed that the meeting had not represented informed and intelligent opinion but had been packed by three groups whose sole interest was the ill-informed and prejudiced intention of preventing any sort of change. The groups referred to were the small farmers of Horton, the Operative Conservatives and the Imperial Chartists, led by John Smith, a

112

well-known local Chartist of conservative and pacific views and Squire Auty, a right-wing populist and an aggressive Orangeman.

All persons who are interested in house breaking, all admirers of dirt and smoke will be quite content that Bradford should remain as it is. . . A narrow short sighted self-interest explains the opposition of certain classes in the town. . . . Operative Conservatives . . . the most despicable of all nondescripts oppose all reform except the repeal of the Malt Tax. As for the Imperial Chartists led by Messrs Smith and Auty, their conduct sets all reasoning, all calculation at defiance.[38]

There was more to it than that. Of course, the Ladies of the Manor, the Canal Company and the Bowling Iron Works opposed changes which were against their interests. But, however clearly a logical outcome of contemporary development, the borough of Bradford was as much an artificial creation as the metropolitan authority was many years later. It defied local sentiment and long-established practice. It was to be many years before natives of the district thought of themselves as citizens of the Borough of Bradford. They remained men and women of Horton, Bowling and Manningham or of the township of Bradford, distinct from each other, and referred to themselves in that way in official documents. In fact, most of the most influential protagonists of incorporation were immigrants who had none of the habitual loyalty to a local township which natives had. At a more practical level, as the Board of Guardians had demonstrated, the out-townships objected to helping to pay the expenses of a voracious central area. Horton farmers saw little immediate benefit in paying rates for cleansing and lighting an area they might use once a month. Nor did they see the system as being necessarily as democratic as William Byles had claimed. John Smith in fact pointed out that the franchise would be positively undemocratic, for few working men would have the ratepayer qualification required. The opponents of reform also played on the fear of a borough police force which might threaten the independence of Chartist political expression.

But, whether incorporation was the right answer or not,

something needed to be done. While the particular course taken by the Liberal-Radicals expressed the determination of wealthy men to be masters in their own house, the fact was that industrialisation had now reached the point at which its social consequences could no longer be ignored. Most of the township of Bradford and parts of Horton, Bowling, and Manningham were simply unfit for human habitation. A town had sprung up in which the means of establishing something like order in the use of natural space either did not exist or the appropriate provisions could not be or were not applied by the legal authority. Report after report was to portray starkly the consequences of such lack of regulation. They described the inchoate pattern of building in working-class areas developed by the speculators; the narrow streets of small back-to-back houses with neither lavatory nor washing facilities, the many closed courts and alleys, the total lack of provision for their cleaning and the widespread use of ill-ventilated and ill-drained cellar dwellings, the frequent flooding in the lower part of the town whenever the stinking refuse in the Beck prevented the flow of heavy rainfall through a water-course narrowed by overcrowded buildings on its banks, all compounded by the lack of general drainage, sewerage and an adequate supply of water.[39] The Report of the Board of Surveyors made to the Commissioners for inquiring into the Sanitary Condition of Populous Towns (dated 22 March 1844) gives the most precise description of administrative difficulties. Although the General Highways Act of 1835 had improved the situation in the sense that instead of the two parochial officers appointed since the sixteenth century to act as surveyors of the township, thirteen elected representatives could divide the responsibility on a geographical basis, anomalies remained. There was confusion between the Board of Commissioners and Surveyors as to the exact duties and obligations of each. More important, the obligations of private property to the public good were rarely acknowledged. Great confusion existed about the control of causeways and footpaths. Responsibility for their maintenance lay somewhere in the limbo between the two bodies and the habit had developed of regarding them as private property. Thus in the previous winter an attempt to improve a causeway had been forcibly resisted – 'the owners of the property adjoining [the causeway] drove the workmen off by main force' – and the causeway had remained all winter in an unfinished state, highly dangerous to the public. Nobody had any power to clean up nuisances on private property as such. Around the Shambles, 'in the most public part of the town . . . [there were piles of] refuse, offal etc. from the butchers' shops, necessaries, ash-places and urinaries'. Part of the area was also unpaved and in wet weather was ankle-deep in mud. The Bradford fairs, relics of manorial privilege and thus beyond the available controls, contributed twice a year to the confusion, and the canal and beck, the only public sewers in the town, were a permanent and obscene reminder of the urgency of the problems of urban engineering.

Opponents of incorporation could argue that the problems of industrial society could easily be solved if men accepted responsibility for their own actions and businessmen paid the social costs of their activities as a direct charge on business profits, a type of 'if only men were good' argument. Few intelligent people doubted that matters could not be allowed to continue in the same way. This was the decade when any political veteran could raise a laugh from a public platform by recalling the days of his youth before the smog came and when the Beck was a clean and wholesome stream and the young men of Bradford could play their games of football on Hall Ings. The Health of Towns Commission provided powerful reinforcement when it showed that Bradford had a lower expectation of life than other parts of the West Riding: twenty years three months against twenty-three years one month for Leeds, twenty-seven years four months for Halifax, and a massive thirty-six years three months for Pateley Bridge, thirty miles away in the Dales.

There were other matters to take into account. Some – and generally the more influential among the old establishment – lived in circumstances which did not provide a daily reminder of the need for change. But for those who needed to use the centre of the town, there was no escaping the fact that a new context of social life was needed. There was, to begin with, a serious problem of criminal activity. The edition of the *Bradford*

Observer which reported the defeat of the first moves towards reform carried reports of a number of 'daring and violent robberies'. £3,000 had been stolen from a counting house in the centre of the city in broad daylight. In one of the busiest thoroughfares burglars had broken into a merchant's office in the centre of the city and dynamited their way into the safe. Others had forced their way into the premises of Messrs Peckover and Ellis despite the fact that they were 'barricaded like a castle'. At a more personal level there were important questions of social habit to be resolved. A large population of people who were unlikely to know more than a handful of the people they would meet in a journey across the centre of the city needed a framework of practices and conventions appropriate to the situation. It was, for instance, difficult for a woman to avoid the attentions of the inebriated. It might be prudish to object to the constant spectacle of men urinating outside the public houses in Kirkgate, but the implications went further than this. In the centre of the city all sorts and conditions of men and women met and the problem was to establish simple criteria of conduct which would allow all to go about their affairs safely and comfortably. In this connexion, it is significant that among those Tories who supported municipalisation, there was a high proportion of shopkeepers and others who had interests in the town centre. A police force would not stop burglary and by-laws would not of themselves change social habit, but both seemed a necessary condition of improvement.[40]

However, while such considerations moulded the discussion, it has to be emphasised that for the principal actors the issue remained primarily political. Most Tories considered that, without changing the structural power, improvements in the Board of Commissioners and the creation of a more effective police force under the provisions of the 1835 Police Act would be sufficient. Most Liberals argued that only a complete revision of local institutions through a municipal corporation would suffice. For them it was a question of substituting for the authority of an establishment based on the privileges of Anglicanism, one based on the authority of a voting system which they hoped to dominate. Of course motivations were as mixed as they are in any political situation. Self-interest worked alongside genuine moral fervour. Anglicans could not easily surrender what they saw as a part of a composite spiritual authority. Dissenters felt an obligation to elevate the values by which they lived and worshipped into the sphere of public affairs.

The municipal reformers were not to be restrained by the initial setback. They presented a petition to the Privy Council and in the middle of 1844 were expressing confidence in the outcome. But, unhappily for the *Bradford Observer* and the Reform Club, the mid-forties were years in which the fortunes of Toryism ran high in Bradford as elsewhere. Fiscal policies which introduced free trade and substituted direct for indirect taxation met with approval. Several years of prosperity, punctuated only by the seasonal dislocations which could always upset the textile trade, took some of the steam out of Chartism. Tory social policy was progressive enough to offer hope of further improvement. A Factory Act, which the Bradford employers' committee, chaired by Titus Salt, viewed with great suspicion, limited the working hours of women and adolescents to 12 a day and of those under 13 to 6½, though it lowered the minimum age to 8. The Chartist land scheme found echoes in the allotments system fostered by paternal Tories like William Ferrand, Squire of Bingley. Scoresby, still maintaining stoutly the principle of his right to the cure of souls through the parish, opened several schools for the instruction of the poor and lent his influence to a number of working-class causes. He supported the woolcombers in their agitation about home-working conditions. He also ran a campaign about the working conditions of women in factories – a campaign inspired by what he had seen of the textile factory town, Lowell, during a holiday spent in the USA. The alliance of wealthy traditional Tory with Horton farmer and working-class Chartist proved unbeatable. The Commissioner appointed by the Privy Council to investigate found that a majority of 2,000 rate-payers had indicated their opposition to municipalisation. 10,716 had signed the anti-corporation counter-petition, 8,715 the one in favour of a corporation.[41]

By 1846, however, the political situation both locally and

nationally was changing. The economic indicators forecast a gloomy future. Peel was out of office, defeated by his own party after he had repealed the Corn Laws, and the prospects of a general election had sharpened once again the interest of Chartists in the franchise, and broken the Tory-Chartist alliance. With a Liberal Government in office, fortune favoured the municipalisation lobby, and in April 1847 a Charter of incorporation was granted to the town. In 1846, Lord Morpeth, the Whig-Liberal MP for the West Riding, visited Bradford. He attended a *soirée* at the Mechanics' Institute, and is thought to have suggested in private conversation with leading Liberals that the new government would be sympathetic to a fresh proposal. He confirmed this at an open meeting the following day. Henry Brown took charge of the organisation of a new petition, and kept details quiet until preparations for the campaign were completed. Thus, when the Commissioner, Major Jebb, arrived in Bradford to start a new inquiry, the Tories were unprepared. A number of leading Tories had already accepted defeat, and those who remained obdurate were left with little in the way of defence. Joshua Pollard, the managing director of Bowling Iron Works, quickly patched together a new counter-petition, but claimed that the one used previously ought to be allowed to stand. J. G. Horsfall, trying to frighten the laggards, said that Leeds was sinking under the burden of rates imposed by the Corporation there. Squire Auty raised a laugh when he affirmed that Manchester Road in Horton where he was Constable of the township was as quiet as any place in the district. The issue was not in doubt at this stage, Jebb ruled in favour of incorporation, and on 18 August 1847, at the Court House on Hall Ings, the incorporated municipal borough of Bradford had its first meeting. Its boundaries were those of the parliamentary borough. It therefore took in the area of maximum urban concentration in the district. The town was to be divided into eight wards, North, South, East and West, Bowling, Little Horton, Great Horton and Manningham, and the Council was to consist of the mayor, fourteen aldermen and forty-two councillors. A member of the Council had to be possessed of either personal capital to the value of £1,000 or a tenement rated at not less than £30 per annum. All male householders could vote, provided they had paid their rates, had not received help from the Poor Law authorities in the previous year and had lived in the town for three years. In the event, 5,457 men out of a possible total of 12,792 had the vote in the first instance. The limitations weighed heavily against working men – particularly since until 1854 small cottages in which the rent was less than £4 a year were not assessed for rates.[42]

The distribution of office in the new Council reflected faithfully both the purpose of the battle and its outcome. Robert Milligan became Mayor and alderman and the thirteen other aldermen elected by the councillors were Titus Salt who took the largest number of votes, Joshua Lupton, James Garnett, William Rand, Edward Ripley, S. Smith, Henry Forbes, Thomas Beaumont, John Smith, George Rogers, William Cheeseborough, Henry Brown and Christopher Waud. All except Cheeseborough were Liberals, although neither Beaumont nor Waud was of as pure descent as most of the others. Milligan, Salt, Brown, Ripley, Forbes and Garnett were also members of the Horton Lane Congregational Chapel – the power house of Bradford Liberal Dissent – and only one was an Anglican – William Rand, who was poised politically half-way between Liberalism and Toryism. It was clear that the list of aldermen had been drawn up in the Horton Chapel vestry before the council meeting, for by some accident of organisation, it was circulated in the council meeting. Not only Tories were angry. At least one Liberal councillor from one of the townships complained that having been invited to the meeting in the Chapel vestry for 8.15, he had arrived to find that it had actually begun at 6 p.m. and that the business had already been concluded. The first election held in the August also produced a strongly Liberal Council and more comprehensive Radical representation. At a second election, held in November in order to establish the electoral calendar in accordance with general practice, Conservatives managed to establish a balance.

More important than the aldermanic bench, however, was the bench of borough magistrates, for the office of magistrate carried great status and great personal authority. The section of the West Riding bench which had dealt with Bradford affairs had been composed of members of the local 'county' families: Colonel Tempest of Tong Hall, W. P. Stansfield of Esholt Hall and W. B. Ferrand of Bingley, for instance, members of the two 'iron' dynasties of Bowling and Low Moor and one or two wealthy manufacturers from long-established families, like John Rand and Matthew Thompson. Most of them lived some distance from the ᵗown and all were Tories, except Ellis Cunliffe Lister, a Whig. Tories tried without success to impede the appointment of borough magistrates and in the event twelve were named. They were Titus Salt, William Rand, Samuel Smith, James Garnett, Samuel Cunliffe Lister, Henry W. Ripley, Joshua Lupton and Robert Milligan (as mayor) – all Liberals and all connected with the worsted trade either as merchants or manufacturers – William Cheeseborough, a Tory wool-merchant, Alfred Harris and Samuel Laycock, Tory bankers and Dr McTurk, the distinguished medical practitioner, a Tory and the brother-in-law of John Rand. It was less partisan than the previous West Riding bench had been, and could be said to represent the 'principal inhabitants' of the town, rather than a political party. Yet it was predominantly Liberal. Its composition underlined the success of Liberal – Dissent in the battle within the middle classes for position and authority.[43]

By the end of 1847 the Liberals had two further triumphs which they had celebrated; one, a national issue – Peel's Repeal of the Corn Laws in response to the turmoil of the Irish Famine and the Europe-wide trade depression, the other, local – victory in the general election of 1847. In Bradford as elsewhere the Corn Law agitation had been directed and mainly supported by middle-class Liberals. There was some working-class support; Christopher Wilkinson, John Jackson, Edward Parratt, William Metcalf and their Radical associates in the Reform Club formed the Working Men's Anti-Corn Law Committee and after the defeat of Chartism in 1842 there was more positive backing from real working men. Yet generally they remained suspicious at what was offered as an automatic and autonomous benefit from the economic machine, for they were convinced that the masters would bring down wages as food prices fell. Some Tories also supported the agitation from the start, particularly in the business community – Swithin Anderton and Isaac Wright, for instance, and William Rand's accession to the movement in December 1840 was hailed with great delight by the *Bradford Observer*. Most of the other Tories kept aloof – the iron masters at Bowling and at Low Moor, most of the bankers, and the fervent Tories among the textile manufacturers. Thus the agitation was slow to gather momentum. The *Bradford Observer* complained from time to time that meetings were sometimes relatively sparsely attended. Its strength lay in the fact that its adherents included the wealthiest and most influential businessmen in the town. These men were, however, able to collect in their mills and warehouses 10,000 signatures for a petition to Parliament. The Garnett brothers raised 368, Titus Salt 192, Christopher Waud 178 and a number of others, including S. C. Lister, over 100. They gave generous annual subscriptions to the Anti-Corn Law League, organised the several meetings addressed by John Bright and Richard Cobden, supported the fairs and bazaars and kept together the local association which maintained this effort. The repeal of the Corn Laws in June 1846 was hailed as a great moral and ideological victory. An unjust privilege which the aristocracy exercised against the rest of society had been removed. The most serious impediment to the prosperity offered by industrialisation had been eliminated. The unhindered operation of economic law would show that the interests of capital and labour were identical. The moral and economic values of Liberalism had been accepted and the manufacturers' superiority in economic society had been recognised. Two months after repeal, 300 of the 'principal gentlemen' of Bradford held a celebratory dinner in the company of Cobden and Bright, the leaders of the League. As was customary, Salt spoke to one of the resolutions passed at the dinner. His was the shortest speech.[44]

The general election of 1847 was fought by a Liberal–Radical alliance with a joint committee. W. Busfeild stood for the Whig–Liberal section. The Radicals introduced Colonel Thomas Peronnet Thompson. He had had a long career in Radical politics and had recently been a leading advocate of the repeal of the Corn Laws – in which capacity he had been invited to Bradford. The Tories were in some trouble. Nationally, the party was in disarray after Disraeli's savage attack on Peel, the Prime Minister, for his repeal of the Corn Laws in 1846. Locally, John Hardy who had just had a stroke reluctantly gave up his seat and the party brought in two inexperienced newcomers – H. W. Wickham, one of the partners in the Low Moor Iron Works, and Hardy's son, Gathorne. Their opponents also had pre-election friction. Thompson's Radicalism was too extreme for many Whigs and Busfeild's Anglicanism made for uneasy relations with the Dissenters who dominated the Radical wing. But the strength of the Milligan–Forbes–Salt axis sustained the common front and the two candidates were returned with comfortable majorities.[45]

THE CONDITION OF THE WORKING CLASSES

Meanwhile, the working-class struggle which was interwoven with these events was becoming critical. For two years or so after the general strike of 1842 working people were principally concerned with wages and working conditions. The return of a sort of prosperity alleviated immediate fears and also led to a revival of trade-union activity and conventional industrial action. There were a number of strikes. One at Low Moor was defeated. One at Bowling Iron Works was successful, though fought with implacable bitterness. It was a strike of young colliers to which the management had responded by closing down two of the three furnaces in operation and so locking out most of the parents of the strikers. The Bradford Tailors' Union also took part in a national strike against low wages and deteriorating conditions of work. The principal complaint was against the development of the 'putting-out' system in the trade, and its most interesting activities, though unsuccessful, were the efforts to establish a tailors' co-operative.

The most dramatic activities were among the hand woolcombers, who despite the lack of an efficient alternative to their labour continued to face the deterioration of their position in the over-stocked labour market. In July 1843, the woolcombers held an open-air meeting to consider wages.

Although some master combers and spinners had given recent increases, others had refused to do so. Of these the most important was the firm of Wood and Walker, now, since the retirement of John Wood, directed by William Walker alone. The meeting decided to call a strike against the firm; it lasted a week after which Walker gave way since two thirds of his men had been able to find work with other establishments. Other recalcitrant firms followed Walker's example, although one of them at least, Addison and Co., demanded the services of an arbitration committee, composed of representatives of Garnett's, Waud's, Rand's, Pearson's and Walker's, before giving way. The strike was reported as having been very orderly; it was noticeable that it had taken great care to try to stay within the law, for during the strike, only men employed by Walker had voted or been allowed to negotiate. Still, such were the difficulties in interpreting the law that one speaker at least thought that, despite all precautions, they had probably acted illegally. At the end of August, the woolcombers renewed their efforts to get organised trade-union activity going, and met to form the Woolcombers' Protective Society to defend the interests of the 10,000 hand combers in the district.[46]

In the following year the working-class movement was invigorated when George White, already well known as a leading physical-force Chartist, and with several prison sentences behind him, came to work as a woolcomber in the town. In an assessment which at least does not err on the side of generosity R. C. Gammage, first historian of the Chartist movement, described him as 'a working man, a native of the sister isle', who 'had long taken an active part in Radical movements'.

He was noted for his inflexible perseverance, and determination in everything which he undertook to perform, he was ever ready for whatever kind of work fell to his lot; whether it was to address a meeting, write a report, or collect a subscription, he was equally clever in each transaction. In battering the head of a policeman he was quite at home, and if circumstances had favoured, he would just as readily have headed an insurrection, quite regardless we believe, of the danger to himself. George's chief talent as a speaker lay in his ready wit and poignant sarcasms, which were launched forth in

123

language anything but classical, and by no means agreeable to the polite circles though exceedingly well relished by men of a similar stamp to himself. George never did things by halves, but went the whole hog in everything which he undertook; and he never stooped to dissimulation. If he committed a wrong, he acknowledged the act, and defended it as frankly as though he had performed the most meritorious action. When accused by an opponent of having used unfair means to disparage him, he replied, 'Well, did not I tell you that I meant to put you down? and I have done it.' It is possible to charge George White with his almost utter want of courtesy; but his veriest enemy could never accuse him of anything approaching to cant, to which he always appeared an entire stranger.[47]

A rough character, but he had quick imagination and ready understanding and a comprehensive view of what Chartism was about; for he saw it as a part of a basic struggle between Capital and Labour for a just society rather than a simple campaign for the vote for working men.

George White joined Robert Mullen, John Clarke, John Smith and George Fletcher in the battle to strengthen the Woolcombers' Society. In 1845, when the trade-union world was reviving, the National Association of United Trades for the Protection of Labour, and its companion organisation, the National United Trades Association for the Employment of Labour, were formed. The first was to create a united society of separate unions engaged in the struggle to defend wage rates and to improve the legal position of trade unions. The second was to encourage the development of co-operative activities. Both Mullen and White pushed their claims among Bradford woolcombers. In August 1844, while preliminary discussions were still going on, they were explaining the ideas behind the renewed activity. The programme offered by the National Association was a comprehensive system of co-operative Socialism in which the woolcombers would become the 'proprietors of their own labour'. A joint stock company was to be established which would buy wool and combs, and build up a fund which would enable woolcombers to work on their own account. There was also to be a central provision store which would provide groceries at wholesale prices. In March 1845, C. Doyle of Manchester gave an address to the woolcombers on the purposes of the proposed 'amalgamation of trades' in the National Society. In the same week, the leaders of the woolcombers addressed a meeting of power-loom weavers to help the weavers to promote a union for themselves. It was a measure of the disintegration in the trade as a cohesive social organism that out of the 6,000 power-loom weavers in the district, only 300 came. Most of them were women – a fact noted with some surprise, although to be expected in a trade dominated by female labour, and in a district where women had always played their part in strikes and in the working-class political movement. A committee of four women and three men was elected to further the aims of a Weavers' Protective Association. Although these activities had some influence in Bradford as elsewhere on the development of Co-operation, little positive trade unionism seems to have emerged, for the trade depression which was to ruin woolcombers and weavers alike gathered strength towards the end of 1845 and made it impossible for them to sustain coherent organisations. Nothing was heard of the Weavers' Protective Association, and in August 1846, George White pronounced the epitaph of the Woolcombers' Society when he spoke of his disgust at their inability to combine in a union.[48]

Nevertheless, before the end of 1845 the Woolcombers' Society had two achievements to mark up. Its members had conducted a partially successful strike against the Rands. They had managed to obtain about half the increase they had demanded and had also prevented the threatened victimisation of machine combers employed at Rands by keeping the strike going for a week after the wage settlement had been agreed. It was a relatively quiet strike. There were very few reports of intimidation, though one man was burnt in effigy at his front door for 'blacklegging'. The second of the achievements was a devastating survey of the conditions in which Bradford woolcombers made their living, with which the Society hoped to stir the conscience of Bradford's well-to-do.[49]

As we have already noted, by 1845 the woolcombers were the most deplorably exploited of all the textile workers. George White defined the position when he said that 'their trade was a sort of common reservoir of all the poverty of England and

Ireland. It was constantly receiving new competitors from those who were poorer than themselves.'[50] Hence wages were very low and domestic conditions appalling. In the May, the Society set up a committee to bring out a report on housing conditions among the combers. With White as secretary, it issued a remarkable document. The preamble defined the general position:

We have upwards of Ten Thousand Woolcombers in this town and neighbourhood the major part of whom are compelled to make a workshop of their sleeping apartment; and as the nature of their occupation compels them to work over a charcoal fire, which is constantly burning in their apartment by day – and frequently left smouldering at night in order to expedite the labours of the following day – the most dangerous and deadly vapours are thus diffused through the confined and ill-ventilated room, and continually inhaled by the inmates, who unfortunately have no property save their health, and no means of providing for their families when their bodily vigour is impaired and broken down by the ravages of disease. Sufficient proof of these facts are exhibited in the emaciated appearance of the victims of this awful state of things; uniformly followed by premature death. . . .

Our dwellings are improperly constructed, and totally inadequate for the uses to which they are now subjected, and, as will be seen from the report, a most alarming state of physical and moral degradation is the inevitable result – our streets are filthy and in a most neglected condition – contagious and noxious vapours are hourly accumulating around us; even the common decencies of life appear to be disregarded; all of which circumstances might be avoided, if a proper system of sewerage and ventilation were adopted, and due attention paid to the other matters essential to health and common decency. . . .

It very firmly rejected criticisms that the situation sprang from the improvidence and immorality of the working classes and finished with a plea for the co-operation of the wealthy and educated: 'Let all unite and make this a labour of love. All may unite on this question.' It was compiled by George White as secretary to the committee and signed in addition by the president John Dewhirst, the treasurer Thomas Spurr, and the committee men William Dawson, George Flinn and John Carr, all of whom had helped with the collection of evidence. They had undertaken a wide survey of the houses occupied by hand woolcombers who had had to use their homes as workshops and reported on 333 of the worst cases they had seen. Among them were houses like those in *Cannon Street* where twelve people lived in two rooms measuring 13 ft 4 in. by 14 ft 4 in. each. There were five people working round a coal pot in one of the rooms, and all twelve including six females slept in the four beds in the other room. The house was situated in a passage 2 ft 10 in. wide. In *Eastbrook Terrace* another eight people lived in two rooms measuring 11 ft 8 in. by 10 ft. Two of them worked over coke fires and all, including the six females, slept in the two beds in 'the suffocating vapour of coke'. In *Regent Street* eight people lived and worked in a cellar 15 ft 6 in. by 13 ft 7 in. and 6 ft 3 in. below the ground. In rainy weather it was frequently flooded to 20 inches. Five children slept in one bed. A man, his wife and his mother in another.

The report also condemned the districts in which woolcombers lived. Examples of these were provided by places like:

Holgate Square – a miserable hole, surrounded by buildings on all sides. This place resembles a deep pit – no chance of ventilation; a number of men and women work in the cellars over charcoal fires, seven feet below the ground.

Nelson Court – a perfect nuisance. There are a number of cellars in it utterly unfit for human habitation. No drainage whatever. The visitors cannot find words to express their horror of the filth, stench and misery which abounds in this locality and were unable to bear the overpowering effluvia which emanates from a common sewer from the Unitarian Chapel beneath the houses.

Queen Street – One general description will suffice for this street and neighbourhood. It is a mass of filth – no drainage – the horse road unpaved and nearly a foot deep in mud, together with stagnant water.

The report was intended to take advantage of the growing national anxieties about conditions of public health, particularly in the large towns. Edwin Chadwick had already issued his famous *Report on the Sanitary Conditions of the Labouring Population of Great Britain*, described as 'the chief stimulus and starting point of the Victorian public health movement'. It had been followed in 1844 with the *First Report of the Royal Commission on the State of the Large Towns and Populous Places*. In 1845 also Chadwick started the Health of Towns Association, and three years later the first General Public Health Act became law. The woolcombers could claim an immediate though short-lived local success, for Scorsby and Pollard led the call for a town meeting to discuss the report. They were hoping to seize the initiative in the debate on municipalisation, but in fact the matter was not allowed to become a question of party division. Jonathan Glyde, the Horton Lane Congregational minister, William Glover, a member of his church, and B. Godwin, the Baptist minister, almost immediately associated themselves with Scoresby, and within a fortnight Robert Milligan and Titus Salt were members of the committee set up at the meeting.[51] The *Bradford Observer* had a sympathetic leader which pointed out that the working classes of Bradford occupied such 'pestilential dens as many of the narrow, crowded, ill-drained, ill-ventilated streets [were]', simply because they were poor. There was also at least one immediate positive consequence – subscriptions were raised for building a model lodging house for women and this was opened in 1847. For the rest, town meetings were not well attended, and the *Observer*'s plea for good will and good hearts awaited the resolution of the wider political conflict, within which Scoresby and Pollard had placed it.

The woolcombers themselves held a number of meetings at which practical suggestions were made. In a very eloquent speech, George White called on the master manufacturers, spinners and combers to build woolcombers' sheds so that work could be taken out of their homes. He pointed out that 'the present mode of woolcombers being compelled to work in their bedrooms causes the proprietors of cottages to disclaim accepting them as tenants; they are consequently compelled to occupy such filthy holes as I have endeavoured to describe'. He thought also that if the practice became properly widespread it would eliminate the sub-contracting which had proliferated in recent years to exploit the hardships and hazards of the woolcombers' lives. It was clear that by this time most combers were ready to welcome the introduction of machinery. They knew it was going to come, and the sooner the better. John

Howe, one of the leaders, expressed a general belief at one of the meetings. 'He was all', he said, 'for combing being done by machinery, if the masters could be suited as well, for it was so poor a job at best.' But he knew that the masters would not build shops for combing until all combing could be done mechanically, and that time was still some way in the future. George White's eloquence at the Odd Fellows' Hall – 'Is a man made in God's image worth less than a piece of stuff? Then go to Leeds Road end and see the palaces built to cloth' – might place the blame where it belonged.[52] It did not alter the disposition of the market or diminish in any way the profitability of a degraded 'putting out' system. Abraham Wildman's poem, written as part of this campaign, remained appropriate to their situation for at least another half a generation.

. . . The sweet breath of morning ne'er enters my dwelling
To clear the old fumes from the damp coloured ceiling
Which constantly oozing
Keep soul – body dozing
In this dismal hole;
Whatever the weather
We're huddled together
And breathe the slow poisons arising from coal.

Six children and wife, with self, number eight;
A bed of deal shavings our couch for the night;
We rise in the morning,
The same rags adorning,
To toil at the comb;
Like quarrymen digging
We're snatching and jigging
Our room is our workshop our bedroom and home. . .

It was not very good poetry, but it made the point for the readers of the *Bradford Observer* where it was published in March 1845.

Although the committee elected at the first town meeting organised one or two public meetings, little was heard about its activities after Major Jebb had rejected the Incorporation petition in August. The woolcombers also shifted the line of their campaign as the depression which was to deepen through 1847 pressed even more direct questions of bread and butter on them. For the next two years working-class meetings were concerned with questions of employment and the fundamental issue of the franchise, rather than the sanitary conditions of their homes, appalling as they were.

By March 1846, the *Bradford Observer* was registering concern about the level of unemployment. In a report of a meeting of unemployed operatives, it noted that 'sufficient had transpired at the meeting to prove . . . that there was very great and unexampled distress'. Nevertheless, as yet attempts to raise a public subscription for their relief met with little success. Indeed, through 1846 the question which aroused most concern was the Ten-Hour Bill which Lord Ashley was sponsoring. It was the culmination of a campaign for factory reform which had revived in the early forties and in which a reconstituted Short-Time Committee in Bradford had been very active. The campaign had been more formal than its predecessor for it was very largely a parliamentary campaign with none of the dramatic demonstrations of the thirties. It had remained a movement dominated by the Anglicans and Tories, but its public meetings were town occasions. Lord Ashley spoke at Bradford at the beginning of March and was supported not only by most of the well-known Tories, William Walker, the Rand brothers, William Cheeseborough, Rev. William Morgan and most of the local clergy, and Joshua Pollard, the West Riding magistrate, but by well-known Radicals like W. E. Forster and Edward Waud. The *Bradford Observer* also threw its weight behind the campaign.

The general body of manufacturers remained more chary. In May, Titus Salt chaired a meeting held in the Exchange Rooms to decide on their course of action. Explaining its purpose he said:

The spinners and mill-owners of Leeds, Halifax, Manchester and Lancashire generally had held similar meetings and had sent deputations to London to oppose the Bill: it was for the meeting to decide whether they would follow the example of other towns or adopt a different course. He had no doubt that the proposed Bill would be injurious to trade and to the working classes. How could the English manufacturer compete with foreigners who ran their mills fourteen hours a day and longer if need be? The difficulty of doing so was already apparent. Worsted goods were bought in the grey of foreign makers by Bradford merchants and brought home to dye: it was the same with yarns and it was self-evident that a limitation of the hours of Labour to ten would increase the difficulty. However, as a strong feeling existed among the working classes in favour of a reduction of the hours of labour, it might be advisable to endeavour to settle the question by agreeing to an Eleven Hour Bill.

It was a characteristic speech, expressing the common view of the manufacturing interest, short, lacking in any sort of speculative or general content, but intended to offer the basis for the containment of opposing interests. The meeting took his advice, though it can be supposed that general agreement had already been reached, otherwise, given his position by this time in the town, he would not have taken the chair at the meeting. The meeting agreed that 'the prolonged agitation of the question of hours of Labour in Factories tends to keep alive a spirit of jealousy and alienation between employer and workpeople'. Although a ten-hour day would undoubtedly be injurious both to trade and to the level of wages, the meeting was of the opinion that 'a middle course might be adopted which would heal divisions and settle the question upon a permanent basis: and would recommend an Eleven Hours Bill as likely to secure so desirable an object'. Christopher Waud, the brother of the E. Waud who had supported Ashley earlier in the year, and William Rouse, a leading Tory, but also a leading manufacturer opposed to the Bill, were appointed a deputation to London to watch the interest of the Bradford trade. Salt also chaired a sub-committee which included Daniel Illingworth and George Rogers, whose function was to be 'to take any other steps in opposition to Lord Ashley's Ten Hour Bill'.[53] The Bill, however, passed into law in 1847 and for several years the true ten-hour day – 56½ hour week – became a reality in Bradford factories.

Meanwhile, Bradford's working classes, both as 'unemployed operatives' and as Chartists, were holding well-attended public meetings through 1847. Nothing had been done so far to relieve the misery of the town. Manufacturers complained that the level of poor relief was too low. The Guardians suggested that wages ought to be raised. A quarrel broke out between George Fletcher, the militant Chartist, and William Rand, during which strong evidence was produced to show that Rand was paying some under-employed combers less than they might get on relief. In fact, these men had begged Rand, it was suggested, to give them the sack so that they could go on poor relief. On the other hand, Fletcher gave Salt one of the many acknowledgements he received during his career of his readiness to act generously in times of difficulty. Salt, of course, had the good fortune to be selling a new and fashionable commodity which had not suffered in the market in the same way as the general run of cloths. Fletcher, however, said of him that 'Mr Titus Salt, one of the best masters in the town, said he was paying his combers at full prices, and they were in full employ, (a fact which he, Fletcher, believed) and also expressed his willingness to pay increased rates besides'. The *Bradford Observer* kept up pressure with a leader which spoke firmly and precisely about the dangers of starvation among the poor in the town.

In October, masters and employees met once again to exchange views against the background of continuing misery. Fletcher said that wages had never been so low in twelve years. White, as always the principal speaker for the men, and with the knowledge, by this time well spread throughout the town, of the Lister–Holden machine-comb developments in his mind, declared that the hand comber no longer had a future. He appealed therefore to the manufacturers to support an allotments – small farm plan along the lines of O'Connor's Land Scheme. Salt, for once making a reasonably long speech, answered cautiously for the manufacturers. He could not speak about an allotments system as he had no experience of it, but he was prepared to support any reasonable scheme. On the other hand, he was certain that the best plan was for the hand combers themselves to run down their trade. Young men should be encouraged to look elsewhere for employment.[54] Before the end of the year a relief fund was established – Salt and six others started it off with £100 apiece – and a soup kitchen supplemented the woolcombers' own committee, which had been making regular collections of food from sympathetic shopkeepers. But the year closed amid a 'mass of physical misery, frightful to contemplate' with two-thirds of the worsted industry out of work and much worsted machinery not running more than two days a week.

The dramatic year of 1848 opened quietly enough. But the depression was never far from people's minds. The Guardians discussed the need to invoke the Settlement Laws against non-Bradfordians to reduce the rates and relieve the labour market. The Relief Committee gave out 10,246 lb of bread and 24,600 quarts of soup in one week and found that a suggestion to start a scheme of aided emigration attracted so much interest among woolcombers that the matter was referred to the Guardians who agreed to spend £2,000 on the scheme. George Fletcher made a moving appeal on behalf of the woolcombers – in the last two years the great majority had not had food enough to keep body and soul together. The following week a well-attended meeting of rate-payers vetoed any expenditure of funds on such a venture. The *Observer*'s Labour correspondent discussed the anomalies of the free market system with a frankness unusual in a paper of committed Liberal views.

How to find a profitable field of industry for every man who is able and willing to work, is the great problem of our times. It presses upon English society with ever more accumulating force; and self-interest and the instinct of self-preservation loudly call for its solution. Where ever we turn our eyes we find masses of men idle because there is no 'demand' for them in what is called the 'labour market'.[55]

By February, the political outlook was becoming more menacing, for the Chartists, encouraged by revolutionary events on the Continent, were once again preparing for direct political action. Through 1847 the National Association had been sending its speakers into the provinces to address the growing masses of under- and unemployed. In the July election there had been a significant Chartist participation, of which Thompson's candidature in Bradford could be seen as a symptom. More directly, Julian Harney had stood against Palmerston in Tiverton, Ernest Jones, who had joined the

Chartist ranks in 1846, fought Sir Charles Wood at Halifax, and Fergus O'Connor was elected at Nottingham. Contact with European Democratic Republicans and Socialists had grown through the forties as more and more came to live as exiles in London, and there can be little doubt that Giuseppe Mazzini, Frederick Engels, Karl Marx and others played a part in animating the events of 1848.

A month later, the same sort of social discontent as existed in the British Isles – a demand for popular government and a ferocious depression which revealed the contradictions of a capitalist system – had brought on revolutionary outbursts in every capital in Europe. A Socialist–Liberal coalition had seized the government in France, and a delegation of Chartists, Jones, Harney and McGrath, had conveyed fraternal greetings to them. Arrangements were made for a National Chartist Convention to be held in London in April and the work of organising a third petition to Parliament was accelerated.[56]

The first serious demonstration of excitement in Bradford took place on 16 March when a great open-air meeting was held at Peep Green, four miles from the town. The *Bradford Observer* described those who were walking to the meeting:

The greater portion of these pedestrians were cleanly attired and well dressed; but there were others who ... exhibited in their pallid countenances and their scanty clothing, signs of their poor and poverty stricken condition; there were many of this class who felt indeed – and well they might – that they had wrongs to be redressed, redress they who would, or how they could.

George White spoke to the first resolution which deplored the misery of the vast proportion of the people and called for changes in an unjust system of government as the only way to improve conditions. He said that he feared moral persuasion would never succeed on its own and made an uncompromising demand for revolutionary organisation. He finished with a reference to events in France where, he said, the Government was preparing both to fulfil its obligation to satisfy the 'right to work' and to introduce a form of old-age pension for men over sixty-five. John Smith, the Great Horton cobbler, was more conciliatory. Moving the resolution in favour of the People's

Charter, he found hope still in peaceful methods. Bradford had recently sent a friend of the Charter to Parliament; there were councillors and aldermen who supported its principles and so 'they would go, step by step, till the principles of the Charter were ratified by the House of Commons.

Upper and middle-class opinion in Bradford – never completely polarised against Chartism – spread from the outright hostility and fear which Tory magistrates like William Ferrand and Colonel Tempest felt to genuine sympathy for the victims of the misery which had helped to fire the agitation and with much of the political vision of the Charter. A few days after the Peep Green meeting, W. E. Forster chaired a Chartist meeting in the town, having agreed to take it because it was a properly constituted town assembly, which the Mayor (R. Milligan) could not, unavoidably, attend. Salt and Forbes headed the list of signatures to a poster issued in the town by the Reform Club, in which they expressed their sympathy with the objectives of the Charter and affirmed their readiness to work for its acceptance. At the same time, they asserted their disapproval of any disturbance of the public peace or violation of the law. It also seems that some of the better-placed among the male factory workers, overlookers, woolsorters, warehousemen and other beneficiaries of mechanisation, showed less enthusiasm for the Chartist cause expressed physically than representatives of the dying crafts. It has been impossible to identify any such employees among the reported members, and there is perhaps an implied criticism of these men in the condemnation of the 'coercive, tyrannical conduct of master manufacturers in inducing their workpeople to be sworn in as special constables'.[57]

The common denominator was the defence of law and order, and in fact by the beginning of April the public authorities had already begun to take precautionary measures. On the 1st of April, Milligan, as Mayor and chief magistrate for the town, asked the Home Office for the loan of side arms and accoutrements and began to swear in special constables. He reported to the Home Office on 6 April that although the town was still quiet the meetings of the Chartists grew in size daily and the violence of their language increased, and that he had therefore taken 1,525 specials under command.[58]

The angry enthusiasm of Chartists was not weakened by these measures. David Lightowler, like Ernest Jones a comparative newcomer to Chartist politics, was elected as Bradford representative to the National Committee, and on the day the petition was presented in London, a large procession, headed by William Angus, the secretary of the local Tailors' Union, and displaying the tricolour 'flag of liberty', paraded through the town. The delays and disappointments associated with the rejection of the petition in April did not halt recruitment in Bradford or in other parts of the Yorkshire and Lancashire textile area. Through May the political temperature rose sharply. As the impotence of conventional even if massive protest became clear, the men of Lancashire and Yorkshire, as in other parts of the country, including London, began to prepare, however inadequately, for some sort of armed rebellion. In Bradford Isaac Jefferson, a blacksmith living near George White in Adelaide Street, a powerful and intelligent man, was said to be doing a roaring trade in pikes and another report said that Bradford was becoming the best-organised district in the country with powerful sections in Great and Little Horton, New Leeds, Manningham and White Abbey. *The Times* also reported on the constant Chartist military activity in Bradford. Drilling took place openly in the streets; at Eccleshill on the north-eastern edge of the town Chartists were called on parade by bugle. Contact was also maintained with Ireland where the Government feared the possibility of an even more serious revolt and where many of the Bradford men had families and friends. It was this situation which led the Government to regard the Bradford situation as the most potent threat to public order in the country.

A meeting scheduled for 17 May was taken by the Bradford authorities as the first real challenge. The special constables were assembled, and strong bodies of police put to guard the Court House and the Borough Police Office. The Bradford and Halifax troops of yeomanry were placed in readiness in Rouse's mill yard on Canal Road. The embodied pensioners (who had been under arms for several weeks) and the regular military forces of infantry and cavalry waited at the barracks. In the event no breach of the peace occurred. Speakers were listened to quietly and the meeting dispersed in good order. A collection was taken for printing bills to be posted in shops friendly to the cause, and it was agreed to boycott those who did not display one. On this occasion, the women were the most militant, for the female Chartists – perhaps out of frustration – made their own gesture of defiance:

On one portion of the ground a meeting of females was assembled. One of the ladies declared that if the men could not get the Charter the women would and the party afterwards formed themselves into a procession and marched through the streets of the town.

A meeting of the unemployed held the following day was more aggressive. Although signs were beginning to appear that the long depression was coming to an end, unemployment remained high and still particularly affected the woolcombers who at last were also faced with technological obsolescence. The firm of Walker's (previously John Wood's), for instance, which at one time had employed 1,700 woolcombers, now employed, in this month, fewer than 400. The meeting assembled on Peckover Walk in the early evening and contacted the magistrates, who said they would consult with the employers. The meeting decided to do that for itself and sent messages to them inviting them to a discussion about the employment position. Only Titus Salt and William Walker turned up, as all the others, it was said, had already gone home for the evening. The crowd refused to disperse and speeches became more and more inflammatory as the evening went on. Joshua Pollard, the West Riding magistrate, who had been watching since the start from horseback at the edge of the crowd, intervened and gave a vehement warning against breaking the law of public order. A fierce exchange followed between Pollard and Joseph Holmes, a woolcomber from Horton:

Holmes: He states about this manufacturing of pikes. I say Go on with it. (loud cheers) Let every man arm to the teeth quickly. (renewed cheering) We are starving. (We are!) We've only 6d a head to live on.
Pollard: Be careful, my man, as to the advice you give.

Holmes: Mr. Pollard cautions me to be careful, but what I say, I say I am a starving man. (hear hear) Nay, I would sooner just now go to gaol than to my cottage. (hear hear) We are like the mass of my fellow men at this meeting – we have not a mouthful in the house. It has been said by an eminent writer that these were times to try men's souls, but I say these are times to try men's bodies. But if you let your bodies be tried you ought immediately attempt to put an end to it and specially to try other men's bodies by 16 inches of steel (immense cheers). Starving men! I am cautioned on every side [but] . . . I fear no gagging bill; nor do I fear any man; because in a worse position I cannot be placed. (No!) I shall be far superior in gaol. There I should have bread and water, but at my house there is nothing but water – there is no bread. I address you as brother guards; and I say – let every man beg from door to door for the means to get a pike and then let every man strike to force tyranny from its damnable throne. (immense cheering for several minutes)

Pollard repeated his warning and said that Holmes was doing the cause no good. Holmes replied, 'Mr Pollard, I am a starving man, I have not broken my fast today.'

A number of speakers maintained, despite Pollard's fierce denials, that the authorities were determined to hold them down by the bayonet. George Walton, another woolcomber, drew what the *Observer* described as 'a fearful and touching picture of the want and misery at his own dwelling', and Pollard, recovering control of his temper, became more conciliatory. He was afraid, he said, that there was a great deal of truth in the picture of suffering which George Walton had presented. However, he personally was doing all he could to mitigate it and proposed to arrange for a meeting with the magistrates within the next day or two. By this time the Mayor, Milligan, had also arrived and after he had spoken in much the same conciliatory manner, the meeting quietly broke up.

The outcome was nothing more than another town meeting at which further appeals were made for the support of charity. Salt, supported by the new vicar, Rev. J. Burnett, and Edward Hurley, a Chartist leader, introduced the principal resolution:

That this meeting regards with unfeigned sorrow the circumstances of destitution and misery into which so large a portion of the population of Bradford is plunged through want of employment, and expresses its hope that the distress will be met in a liberal and generous spirit by the inhabitants generally, and by the Guardians of the Poor especially and that if possible some means of employment will be found by which, for a season at least, until the ordinary trade of the town revives, the industrious labourer may be enabled to support himself and family by the labour of his own hand.

In his speech he said that he had been very pleased to be able to keep all his men – sorters, combers and mechanics – at work through the greater part of the depression. The outbreak of revolution on the Continent had, however, disrupted his markets, and as his export trade had fallen by £10,000 a month since February he had been obliged to put men on short time. Nevertheless, he was prepared to set on a hundred more woolcombers and stockpile their work. It could be a good speculation as the price of wool was low, and if not it would relieve the present situation a little. This was another characteristic intervention, not very profound, but practical and sincere, as far as it went, and it remained the only positive suggestion apart from subscriptions to the charitable collections. It did little to relieve the mounting tension.[59]

On 25 May the *Bradford Observer* reported that the town had been in a state of feverish excitement for a whole week. On the previous Monday, after a meeting near the bottom of Manchester Road, Chartists marched through the town in military formation, and in a type of quasi-military uniform, among them Isaac Jefferson whiskered and moustachioed and in a green velvet cap with the badge of rank of a commander. In the evening a meeting of the women Chartists paraded through the town at the conclusion of their meeting on Peckover Walk. The situation had reached such proportions that Dr M'Douall, one of the national leaders and one of those formulating similar plans elsewhere, came to the town to prevent a premature or partial outbreak for it seems that efforts were being made to co-ordinate local activities. His visit became the occasion of a meeting described as the largest ever held in Bradford. Chartist organisation sprang into activity and a huge meeting reported as 20,000 strong was organised with contingents from the surrounding districts as well as Bradford itself. The *Observer* gave a dramatic description of the event:

Before six o'clock in the evening, bodies of men came to the ground in military order; and the various cries of the commanders of these bodies, such as 'right wheel' and 'left wheel' as they took up their positions on the ground with mechanical regularity, had a strange effect . . . a stream of 'guardsmen' continued to swell up the numbers of the meeting till some time after six o'clock. There was a more than ordinary display of flags and banners, and there were several bands of music. . .

The Halifax contingent made a particular impression,

marching by sections each headed by officers wearing white blouses and black belts, the Chartist rosettes and green caps with red bands, which had a very imposing effect when the military bearing and steady march of the men was considered. On they came with music playing, banners flying and the glittering pikes flashing in the sun.

Hurley, Smith, Lightowler and White all spoke and M'Douall swore 'the people to keep the peace, to protect life and property; to avail themselves of the right of arming; to discountenance any premature outburst and never to cease agitating until the entire Charter became the law of the land'.

The authorities made no attempt to interfere, as yet, for, as they reported to the Home Office, they feared that an attempt to do so would lead to a serious and perhaps uncontrollable collision. In fact, as Milligan admitted in his report, several streets around Adelaide Street, where George White lived, were in the hands of the Chartists – the police not daring to go in. But informers kept both the Home Office and the local authorities well posted about events. Robert Emmet, an engine-tenter, and Michael Flinn, a woolcomber (and perhaps at one time a committee member of the Protective Society) were both eventually exposed and the identity of several others remained obscure. One of these reported that he had penetrated the movement completely and that nothing could happen without his knowledge as he was now secretary to his branch. A military headquarters was set up at the Northgate Hotel in the centre of the town, though troops were kept in barracks well out of sight.

During this week Milligan was criticised by a good many for his apparent inactivity. One Home Office correspondent, a Mr J. Binns – it is not clear that he was a spy – compared him to the Lord Mayor of London, who had proved so incompetent in the defence of London during the Gordon Riots of 1780, and whose inadequacy had been described by Dickens in *Barnaby Rudge*. He described the intimidation which shopkeepers had to face, and finished his letter with the demands 'Where were the authorities? Where was our Chartist Mayor to suffer such an act of injustice to go unpunished?' The West Riding magistrates were also ready with strictures on a political opponent, who was preparing on the new Bradford Bench to take over some of their old authority. What could happen, however, without careful preparation had been shown a day or two earlier. On his own initiative, one of the constables tried to arrest a drill sergeant of one of the sections of the guard. The rumour that David Lightowler was being arrested spread through the Manchester Road area like wildfire and a crowd of 2,000 appeared from nowhere to release the Chartist sergeant.[60]

During the following week the authorities took the initiative, for many of the national leaders had been arrested and it seemed time now to quell the Bradford rebellion. Bradford was described as a 'town under siege'. The Riot Act was read. Shops were shuttered up after midday. Police patrolled the town with cutlasses instead of staves, and there were as many troops on show as there had been, proportionately, in Paris. 'Bradford is in a state of military occupation' announced the editor of the *Bradford Observer* in some despair. A plan to attack the Manchester Road stronghold had been determined after a council of war where the magistrates Milligan, Colonel Tempest, H. W. Wickham, Joshua Pollard, Charles Hardy, John Rand, L. W. Wickham and T. G. Clayton conferred with the Lord Lieutenant, the Earl of Harewood, Major-General Thorn, Commanding Officer for the district, and the officers in command of the various detachments of troops. It was intended to arrest the Chartist leaders, orators, drill sergeants and armourers who were thought to congregate in and around Adelaide Street, where both White and Jefferson lived, and who in any case would be brought out by the attack. The operation was timed for midnight but owing to some misunderstanding took place about seven o'clock in the morning, when Mr Briggs, a superintendent of police, thought to be drunk at the time, took a force of 100 specials into Adelaide Street. It was repulsed ignominiously. *The Times* reported that the expedition

arrived at Adelaide Street about seven o'clock in the morning. It was surrounded immediately by a crowd of about 1,000, who poured on them from every avenue and completely hemmed them in the narrow street. [A hail of stones prevented them from retreating.] . . .

Immediately after the stones had been thrown the principal portion of the women and children, as if by concert, withdrew, and a ferocious attack was made upon the specials by hundreds of men armed with bludgeons, pokers and other missiles. The special constables fought bravely but were overpowered by the over whelming number of their assailants whose ranks were constantly receiving accessions, and whose object was to bar all means of retreat. After a severe conflict the specials were able to rescue themselves from their position, and when a little room had been gained heads were broken pretty freely on both sides. What damage the Chartists sustained is difficult to say, but the injuries of some of the special constables were very severe. One of them, Mr Buckley, a surgeon, was so dreadfully cut and wounded that his life was despaired of; but he has since somewhat rallied. Others of the body were more or less injured. They were followed for a considerable distance by the mob, who continued to shower bricks and stones after them like hail.[61]

Excited crowds flocked into the centre of the town and filled the streets around the Court House. From time to time, contingents of Chartists from outlying villages and townships marched through in military formation, and it began to look as if the boast made at recent Chartist meetings, that they could capture the town very quickly indeed, was to be fulfilled.

The magistrates were stung into more decisive action. At four o'clock in the afternoon a force of about 1,500 marched from the Court House in Hall Ings the short distance up Manchester Road towards the rebellious centre of the movement. They formed three divisions: police in front, specials in the centre and the cavalry and infantry in the rear. The Mayor, Robert Milligan, and the Chief West Riding

Magistrate, Joshua Pollard, led the attack. Once again the assault was confronted by a large force of Chartists and others, and the ranks of the police and specials were broken. This was not surprising, for an attack on Bradford's warren-like streets and courtyards was not an easy undertaking. The houses and alleys offered plenty of cover for the defence and it was relatively easy to break up an inexperienced force into small and vulnerable groups. They were saved by a somewhat tardy intervention of the dragoons. *The Times* report continued:

. . . the Chartists had assembled in great force, completely filling the street, and when the police attempted to force their way, a fearful onslaught took place. The police drew their cutlasses and the special constables their staves, and they were met by the Chartists with bludgeons and stones. Each side fought desperately for a short time but eventually the police and special constables were driven back, many of them dreadfully injured. The military, being in the rear, could not act at the onset, and the ranks of the civil power were thrown into confusion and disorder before the dragoons could be brought up. They galloped into the corner where the severest fighting had been and the Chartists began to waver . . . the dragoons having galloped into the thick of the fight very soon terminated the conflict, the Chartists beating a pretty general and very precipitate retreat. . . .

Seventeen men and one woman were arrested but few pikes were discovered during the house search which followed. *The Times* said that eighteen of the principal Chartists had been arrested but in fact only two of them were well-known. They were the woman, Mary Mortimer, a well-known member of the Female Chartists and William Sugden, a drill sergeant. Jefferson and Lightowler had been in Adelaide Street but escaped in the confusion.

The *Bradford Observer* did not conceal, either, the sympathy which at this stage it still had for the Chartists, or its amusement at the discomfiture of the police and the specials. It reminded its readers that Chartism was born of 'deep and heart-sickening' poverty and continued:

But the Chartist leaders are still at large; the mountain laboured and brought forth a mouse. Despite all the upheaval and the brave sight of the glistening bayonets of the infantry and the swords and helmets of the dragoons . . . few pikes and fewer Chartists were found.

Nevertheless there had been something of a crisis. *The Times* suggested that 'Bradford and its neighbourhood have been within an ace of falling into the hands of a revolutionary crew', and the *Observer*, commenting on the public concern aroused, said:

The whole empire has rung with reports of serious riots and revolutionary movements and collisions in Bradford. They have heard of you in Paris and Berlin and Vienna . . . you have become famous.

Milligan in his report to the Home Office claimed a substantial victory. He was certain that the display of force and the apprehension of drill sergeants had thrown the Chartists into confusion and that for the time being danger was past. Certainly, the Chartists became less regularly and openly active and there is some difficulty in determining what White and others were doing precisely. A large protest meeting took place in Wapping on the day after the events of Manchester Road, but all the speakers advised caution for the time being. There was a riot in White Abbey which had brought the military and the specials out again.

It is clear that the northern leaders, despite the many set-backs and the vigour of the authorities, continued to prepare for an armed revolt. There were plans in existence for an uprising at the end of May which had been postponed after the intervention of M'Douall. The development of the widespread conspiracy had nevertheless continued. Speeches which George White and George Webber of Halifax made, during June, made it clear that at some stage the plan for rebellion throughout Lancashire and Yorkshire – the heartland of the Industrial Revolution – included the establishment of a democratic republic. George White and George Webber seem to have been particularly active in making contact with other towns. After a ferocious attack on the Bradford magistrates at a huge meeting on Toftshaw Moor, White, accompanied by Webber, had gone into Lancashire. Speaking at Blackstone Edge on 15 June, White told his audience that 'the day for making long speeches had gone by – though he did not fear the gagging acts – at Bradford they were a dead letter for they had declared a republic there'. A fortnight later at Middleton just outside Manchester he repeated the call to action. The time had come, he said, when something more than speeches had to be delivered. 'The people, male and female, must organise and divide into sections and classes. At Bradford they had 15,000 organised up to the mark and they were not afraid of policemen and special constables.'

Through July and early August Chartist activity became more guarded. Meetings were held in private houses, drilling went on clandestinely, and contact was maintained with the Irish confederates, who were particularly strong in the area and who had been closely associated with the physical-force Chartists at least since April. The magistrates prevented a meeting in Bradford, reading the Riot Act and calling out the specials to disperse the crowd. On the other hand, the Manchester Road Chartists thwarted another attempt to arrest Isaac Jefferson, and White, speaking in Birmingham on 6 August, made a passionate plea for Irish liberty, and claimed to represent the United Committee of fifty men which represented 350,000 armed men in Ireland and the North. The rising was planned for 14 and 15 August. Lancashire was intended to start on the 14th and the Yorkshire towns to follow on the 15th (the same day as the London rising) after their leaders had returned from a final meeting in Manchester. Through the night of 14 August, hundreds of men, says the *Bradford Observer*, sat with pikes in hand awaiting the signal to move. It never came. The leaders, including White and Webber, had been arrested in Manchester, for the authorities had been constantly aware of what was going on. There followed a series of arrests, the most notable of which in Bradford was that of John Smith, and the movement disintegrated. Bradford remained quiet. At the beginning of September both Jefferson and Lightowler were finally captured. A number of Bradford men were given terms of imprisonment ranging from nine months to two years. White, who had charges to answer in Manchester, Birmingham and Liverpool, was given a year's imprisonment. A protest came from the *Bradford Observer*, which thought that Lightowler's arrest was an act of vindictive spite. He had, it was suggested, used his considerable talents with great irresponsibility, but had not broken the law. There was also one disturbance of public order. Rosemary Power and Sarah Linden, the wives of two of the men in prison, led a group of people to extract retribution from Robert Emmet, who had been revealed as an *agent provocateur* during the trials which took place at York.[62] As far as Bradford was concerned physical-force Chartism was finished by the end of September, though it held out a little longer in one or two parts of the country.

In Bradford, of course, the outburst had been as much as anything a measure of the exasperation of the woolcombers. Samuel Kydd, years later, was to describe the events of 1848 in Bradford as a 'revolution of the belly'.[63] But it was always more than this. There were other trades represented in the ranks of the Chartists – among those arrested were a tinner, a cobbler, a butcher and a printer – nothing like as badly pressed as the woolcombers, though it may well be that journeymen in a number of trades like building and tailoring were coming under the pressure of technical change. Chartists also were clear that their objective was a just society in which 'class legislation' had been abolished. It was also a more obviously working-class movement than it had been in 1839–40, and yet it revealed the continuing division in the ranks of the Bradford working class. Perhaps also White's rhetoric expressed a great deal of hope and concealed a good deal of inadequate preparation. Nevertheless, it was regarded as much more dangerous than any of the previous manifestations. The *Manchester Guardian* referred to the planned rising as an 'atrocious yet contemptible conspiracy' and gleefully reported its defeat: 'At least we know of no conspiracy at once so extensive in its ramifications and so numerous in its confederates which failed so signally and utterly in its objective'.[64]

There was more than an element of symbolism in the procession which went to the attack in Manchester Road. Joshua Pollard, one of the principal hereditary landowners in Bradford, coalmine owner and manager of Bowling Iron Works, an Anglican and a Tory, marched side by side with Robert Milligan, a Scotsman, cloth merchant, self-made man, Congregationalist and Liberal–Radical, and they were followed not only by the regular forces of 'law and order' but also by a large body of specials drawn from the middle, lower middle and better-off working classes. Here were the bases of the consensus, which was to dominate the mid-century, established in resistance to the demands of Chartism.

Though they had reluctantly accepted a new principle of order in the form of factory legislation, Dissenters and Liberals, the new men of an industrial gentry and middle class had won the outright victories of the period. The Corn Laws had been repealed; free trade was acknowledged as the intellectual inspiration of the economy. Efforts to maintain a general church rate had been defeated, as had attempts to strengthen the position of the Church in education. At the local level, local government had been taken from the hands of a magistrates' bench dominated by Tory 'county' families and a vestry dominated by local Anglicans. Conflict between Capital and Labour was to enter a quieter stage. Chartism, defeated with a good deal of political skill, had lost its impetus. Social institutions were already developing along lines suggested by the middle-class model, and these were to provide the bases of future stability. When White and Lightowler returned to Bradford from their imprisonment they were to find a very different political and social atmosphere.

IV

YEARS OF CONSENSUS: 1850–1868

THE STRUCTURE OF THE CONSENSUS IN BRADFORD

There is no doubt about the change in the climate of events and opinion in the 1850s. The revolutionary excitements which accompanied the twenty years of economic change gave way to a more orderly period of relatively stable economic prosperity and social consensus.[1] The *Bradford Observer* announced the arrival of 1850 in ecstatic terms. 1850, it said, had opened up the first year of the free-trade era; for with the disappearance of the Navigation Acts the last week of 1849 had seen freedom established in the commerce of the seas. 1849 had also been a year of great prosperity. A good harvest had been supplemented by the importation of twelve million quarters of grain and 'peace and plenty' had been brought to families which otherwise would have been scenes of want and discord; Bradford itself, the *Observer* continued, offered vivid proof of the importance of free trade beyond the specifically economic sphere, for there had been most encouraging signs of a new social harmony between the classes, upon which the complicated structure of the new industrial society depended. The English, it seemed, had emancipated themselves from the 'bad, man-made conventions of the past', and in the framework of the 'irreversible and perennial laws of nature and of human life' could begin the many environmental, social and moral reforms which industrial society needed. The hegemony of the Liberal middle classes was assured.[2]

Such sentiments were, of course, good Liberal journalism, but they sprang from the forward-looking convictions about progress which were central to Liberal thought. It was the same spirit which, at a facetious level, had persuaded railway engineers in 1846 to adorn the first train which arrived in Bradford with two placards bearing the messages 'Who'd have thought it' and 'See the conquering hero come', and at a higher level, informed the principle and the fact of the Great Exhibition of 1851. The optimism generated by technological development and economic success had been strengthened by the outcome of the events of the forties and the buoyancy of the economy in the early fifties. It now provided the basis for a broadly spread agreement about economic progress, social policy and a new social order, in which ends, roughly speaking, could be agreed and debate concentrated on means and timing. But anxiety also had to be kept at bay. Things had to appear better than – very often – they were. The readiness with which the press hailed every indication of the 'development of social harmony', the growth of what they called a proper understanding between the classes, hid a good deal of underlying tension.

The consensus offered, broadly speaking, the bases of common principle among the manufacturers and merchants who directed affairs in Bradford and who had reached a new unity. The alternative élite had reconstituted with the old élite a relatively homogeneous group bound by common economic interests and in broad agreement about major questions of social and political economy. There were disagreements and conflicts – taken seriously by the participants. Denominational connexions provided the most important, although they were not to be the subject of bitter political debate until the later sixties. The question of factory legislation re-evoked old alignments in 1850, in 1864 and again in the early seventies but produced only the pale shadows of the fights of the thirties and forties. When the National Association of Factory Occupiers was founded in 1855, with a good deal of Bradford support, including that of Salt, the articles of association excluded any attempt to attack existing legislation which limited the hours of work of women and children.[3] The problem of parliamentary reform aroused opinion ranging from the radical demand for manhood suffrage and the secret ballot – which was held eventually by men like S. C. and R. Kell and E. Kennion, and, probably, with less fervour by men like Salt and Milligan – via the household suffrage advocated by W. E. Forster and A. Illingworth through the fifties and sixties, to the belief that the 1832 Act needed little improvement, held by most Tories and, at bottom, old Whigs and 'moderate Liberals' like Jonathan Glyde, and Samuel Cunliffe Lister. In practice, most of them settled for some form of the 'cautious gradualism' which attended the extension of the franchise. It was unlikely that Tories such as John Rand and Alfred Harris took much pleasure in the highly successful visits which Kossuth, leader of the 1848 Revolution in Hungary against the Habsburg Empire, made to Bradford nor that they attended the entertainment given in his honour by Robert Milligan. At the same time, in European affairs, the formula of neutrality – benevolent or otherwise – satisfied most points of view. It was the minority of Unitarians and Quakers in Bradford – the Priestmans and the Kells – who dissented strongly from the aggressively expansionist policies being pursued on the frontiers of India and in China. Most important, although there were stirrings from time to time in the old Protectionist camp – Salt gave £1,000 on one such occasion towards the reconstruction of the Anti-Corn Law League – the directors of Bradford's economic life were by 1855 economic Liberals, free-traders almost to a man. All accepted without hesitation the prognostications of a glowing future for Bradford's merchants and manufacturers and listened with pride and approval to the panegyrics which came their way.

They had taken their production to the fertile plains of Hindustan – had taken them to the homesteads of their Saxon forefathers – had carried them where the golden orange glows in the midday sun – had decked with them the black-eyed damsels of Portugal and Spain – and even the iron-bound court of bleak Scandinavia did not check their enterprise. . .[4]

In local affairs, the Municipal Council spent some time easing out the growing pains. At first political sentiment ran high and elections were fought with great bitterness. The most serious dispute occurred in 1850 when the controlling Liberals brought forward a private parliamentary Bill for the extension of municipal power. It provoked Tories to a last stand which led in turn to a number of uncontrollable shouting matches in the Council Chamber. During one of them the Mayor, H. Forbes, withdrew plaintively complaining that they would be the laughing stock of the whole kingdom, if they went on like this. But this was almost the last serious strictly party dispute in the Council for many years. Response to national events also showed an even more obvious lack of clear political demarcation. By 1859 the *Bradford Observer* was complaining:

Once if you were not a Tory you were a Whig; the Radical being but a sub-division of the latter. In such a classification there was convenience, simplicity, comfort; but since these days how extensive the ramifications, how complicated the nomenclature.

William Rand, expressing the idea slightly differently, said that all political disputes had been resolved; they were now able to tackle problems of social and environmental reform.[5]

There were other indications of unity at this level. For the next twenty years men of Tory antecedents and tendency with political ambitions were not usually referred to as either Tory or (the new name) Conservative. At least they announced their conversion to free trade and a measure of parliamentary reform by being known as Liberal–Conservatives or Moderate Liberals. It was relatively easy to bestride the two camps. H. W. Wickham fought a parliamentary election in 1852 as a Tory, but in 1857 and 1859 stood as a moderate Liberal. William Rand, himself a leading manufacturer in the town, belonged to a family which had always played an important part in the activities of the local Anglican establishment. John, his brother, remained a Tory all his life, and such were the complexities of consensus that generally through the fifties he was supporting the Tory/Conservative in county elections and Wickham the Moderate Liberal in the borough. William became a Liberal—Moderate and was Mayor in 1854, leading a municipal council still dominated by the men who had carried the day against the old establishment. Two of Salt's sons also, it is worth recalling, abandoned the Dissenting Radicalism of their father for the Anglican Toryism of their wives, without any (known) breach in the family relations.

New institutions also reflected this unity. In 1849 a new club was started called appropriately the Union Club, non-political and areligious, a place where men of widely differing views could meet without embarrassment. Cultural experiments like the triennial music festivals, held in the newly opened St George's Hall for a number of years after 1853, postulated a broad élite audience ready to treat such events as town occasions. The Bradford High School founded in 1856 gave further proof. It was a non-denominational school which tried to combine the best in both English and German middle-class education. It offered both classical and modern subjects in its syllabus and was intended to serve the needs of those whose parents were alarmed at the inadequacies of the local grammar school but who did not want to send their sons to a public school. It was run by a committee which included Anglicans and Dissenters, Conservatives and Liberals.[6] But the most obvious symbol of a new coherence between the old factions was the Chamber of Commerce founded (as noted in Chapter II) almost immediately after the battles were concluded and now the most powerful institution in the town.

Working people shared many of the values of the consensus, for it was the offspring of a social culture rooted in those ideas of freedom and progress which accompanied the growth of capitalist society. It could be seen as offering opportunities in which men and women could organise their lives as independent and responsible people. It conceded that all responsible men were entitled to membership of the political nation, though what constituted 'responsible' was a source of bitter dispute. Overall it presented an ideal of industrial man in a continuum of values which spread from the concept of the clean and diligent worker through those of reliable and abstemious neighbour, caring spouse and parent to that of the good man and presented a framework within which courage and dignity could be supported. It also accepted a stereotype of working-class life which divided the working class into an élite of responsible and respectable people (in practice, the better-paid) and the mass of the working poor. Mistaking environmental deprivation for intellectual and moral inadequacy it thus regarded most working men and women as not much more than irrational, ignorant and immoral drunkards. The need for an 'intellectual, social and moral elevation of the working classes' was seen as the most important social problem of the time; education (in the rational values of industrial capitalism) as the principal means by which progress could be made. Yet for all the condescension with which the programme was presented, it offered outlets for working-class ambition and hope – the prospects of economic and social mobility and at another level, essential tools in the struggle for political democracy. Abraham Wildman's homely verse adds something to our understanding of the spirit behind it all, for working-class acceptance depended also on the endemic deference present in a society which did not easily tolerate a sense of the egalitarian.

There never were such times as these,
Progression rolls along.
Let ignorance die in its own bliss
As dies a feeble song.
The years are come, each household home
Will bless each friend and neighbour
And great men look with gladdened eye
On those who live by Labour.[7]

Here were the bases of a relationship within which the factory culture developed and which in general gave society a stability it had lacked in the days of intense industrialisation. It would be an oversimplification to suggest that only an 'upper' section of the working classes got any advantages from the relationship as it developed. But it was the case that (along with a lower-middle section of the population) it was this 'aristocracy of labour' which, because it was offered most, used most effectively the political and educative programme available. Thus, the most significant product was the alliance of middle-class Radical with the relatively prosperous and respectable working-class Radical, an alliance facilitated in Bradford as elsewhere by the emergence of a new generation of men who articulated the now dominant themes of working-class opinion.

Among Chartist leaders, George White retained his eloquence and some of his influence in the 1850s. Despite persistent rumours that he had misused Chartist funds, he was still the automatic choice of the Manchester Road woolcombers in their confrontations with employers in 1854 and 1857. But by the middle of 1858 he had conceded that without middle-class intervention there was little hope of social and political progress for the working classes. By this time his influence in Bradford was more or less exhausted. The quality of his life also seems to have deteriorated. He was reported in the press – admittedly never friendly towards 'the notorious Chartist' – as fighting brutally with his wife, and he was drinking very heavily. He died, a lonely man, in Sheffield workhouse in 1868.[8]

Of other Chartists and Chartist leaders the record is more fragmentary. Some of them, like William Angus (imprisoned in 1848), remained active in politics for many years as good left-wing Radicals prepared to collaborate with the middle classes. During the education controversy of the 1850s, David Lightowler was delighted to find himself on the same platform as the magistrate who had sent him to prison in 1848.[9] George Fletcher had helped to promote the candidature of the Chartist Julian Harney in the election of 1852 but thereafter was content to bring the Great Horton non-electors to the support of middle-class radicals. Isaac Jefferson, the Watt Tyler of 1848, made the occasional honorary appearance on a manhood suffrage platform through the sixties but in 1867 was actually enrolled as a special constable and for the rest lived quietly in Brownroyd with his sons and devoted his time to the Primitive Methodist Chapel.

But the defeat of Chartism and the final assault on hand combing shifted the weight of influence in the life of working-class Bradford. It moved away from the diminishing numbers of traditional textile craftsmen, the victims of industrial change, to its beneficiaries, the overlookers and warehousemen who exercised the skills of the new industrial world and to the artisans and tradesmen whose skills were not yet threatened. Many of them, particularly the younger ones, had not been committed to Chartism and had concerned themselves with developing those institutions which came to typify Victorian working-class society in its more acceptable forms. They were the men who with Alfred Illingworth's encouragement formed the Working Men's Reform Committee in 1860 and were described – predictably – in the *Bradford Review* as 'the most intelligent and judicious . . . men of integrity and character and who have the entire confidence of their fellow men.'[10]

It was to such men that George White had made an impassioned appeal in November 1855. He had maintained that 'the most important question of the day – the relative positions of Capital and Labour' was rapidly moving towards a solution. If working men hoped to face the encroachments of new machinery and the demands of a competitive society they would have to stand together:

We know that there has existed among the organised trades, a reluctance to make common cause with their fellow operatives; but the giant COMPETITION is marching forward with colossal strides and will level all those distinctions which have heretofore existed, therefore the trades of England will have to consider the question as a WHOLE and not in an isolated manner. Be it therefore known that the operatives of this country will have to stand or fall together.[11]

The men to whom such appeals were addressed were usually committed to manhood suffrage as a political goal and to this extent saw the problem of the working classes as a single general one. But they were prepared to exercise a good deal of caution in obtaining it and they did not think that a policy, like White's, of working-class solidarity offered a serious programme. Like middle-class commentators, they divided the working-class world into two – the intelligent and the 'uneducated', the respectable and the shiftless – and settled for an orderly and respectable, if relatively lowly, place in the hierarchy of Liberal capitalism.

Among them were men like Eli Carter, warehouse foreman, founder member of the Long Pledged Teetotal Society and the Bradford Band of Hope; Ben Wainwright, one of the few identifiable working men on the committee of the Bradford Mechanics' Institute, secretary of the YMCA; William Lobley, compositor and secretary of the Bradford Typographical Society, a master printer by the seventies; Malcolm Ross, lithographer and protagonist of the associative principles of James Hole; and W. S. Nichols, warehouse clerk and secretary of Titus Salt's Town Mission.

Several of them defined their position in published pamphlets and articles. Malcolm Ross spoke to the trade union section of the meeting of the National Association for the Promotion of Social Sciences in 1859, and published his lecture in a pamphlet. He condemned strikes as 'the most unjustifiable means which can be resorted to for the purpose of keeping the rate of wages at a high, or if you like it better, an equitable standard'. He thought they were bad because they were coercive; they inflicted irreparable damage on the morals and habits of workpeople; they injured the general trade of the country; they were 'naturally and logically' impotent to do what they set out to do, i.e. raise wages; they prevented the use of better means to elevate the people. He asserted that war between Capital and Labour was folly, 'for the great interests of both are identical, whatever people may say to the contrary. . . .' He did not, however, advocate the abandonment of the unions. He was, himself, a member of the highly exclusive Lithographers' Society. He saw them rather as the basis for the development of the principle of Association, which James Hole's *Lectures on the Social Sciences* could inspire, and which offered the way to 'manly independence rather than sycophancy and at the same time in no way promoted immoderate, unreasonable and over-reaching conduct'.[12]

Others entered the essay competitions which were fashionable as compelling working men to think about the problems of the day, and which in Bradford had been inspired through the local press by the meeting of the NAPSS. Both Joseph Kitchen, one of Salt's principal overlookers, and Eli Carter won prizes for their essays on the question of Wages – were they subject to any regular principle of law? Carter's essay – typical of almost all entries, including Kitchen's – contained a plea for mutual understanding between masters and workmen. Many men, he thought, had foolishly looked on their masters as tyrants and oppressors. Masters treated their employees as machines and looked down on them with silly pride and disdain. They should also remember that the merciless screwing down of wages was bound to cause ill-feeling, and they should distinguish more carefully between the good moral worker and the intemperate and immoral. He concluded:

But we hope sufficient has been advanced to prove that the grand fundamental law of supply and demand is the general law which regulates the price of labour, that it may, to some extent, be modified by combinations among either masters or workmen, although ultimately it will assert its power and province by the production of such evils as will be a punishment to those who interfere with its operations and that all kinds of labour generally, will command their real value if left free to be acted upon by this law. And lastly, that strikes and combinations have been generally detrimental to the interests of both masters and workmen.[13]

Carter also distinguished himself in 1864 by his attack on the Factory Acts Extension Bill, which was intended to cover potteries, collieries, match factories and warehouses. The *Bradford Observer* had taken the view that while Manchester warehouses might warrant the interference of law, Bradford warehouses needed no such protection. Carter agreed. At a meeting in St George's Hall he maintained that the warehousemen in Bradford would thank nobody for their help, and at another meeting suggested that the introduction of the factory legislation which laid down a statutory sixty-hour week would be detrimental, especially to the boys, since warehouses only rarely worked for sixty hours in a week. Ben Wainwright had taken much the same position in a letter to the *Observer*. He maintained that there were few branches of trade where working men were better fed, clothed, housed and educated than the stuff warehousemen. He contended that masters and workmen were able to settle their disputes without difficulty.

This apart, the changing composition of the textile labour force increased the authority of the factory masters and the prestige of the working-class factory élite. Continuing improvements in technology, the introduction of the machine comb and improvements in spinning machinery reduced the demand for labour among male adults and youngsters. Henceforward, women over twenty were to constitute the largest single group of workers in textiles. Men employed in the factories were to be privileged in a way which strengthened the structure of the factory culture, for men were never among the lowest paid; even when doing much the same work as women, they were always paid more.

Furthermore, by 1861, apart from the 2,000 or so hand combers still left and a handful of veteran hand-loom weavers, all *worsted* textile employment was within the factory. 45 per cent of all Bradford's working population, 63 per cent of the women and 33 per cent of all the men, obeyed the call of the factory 'buzzer' and the factory 'bell'.[14] Male textile workers, in particular, tended to be second- or third-generation town dwellers. More and more, the factory workers were men and women who, lacking the experience of a different way of life, faced the personal and social problems of their time in terms of what they knew – the factory world.

There was more opportunity for skilled work for men in Bradford textile mills than is often supposed, but they offered limited opportunities for trade-union activity. Craftsmen such as carpenters working in the mills were – often to the annoyance of their employers – usually members of a local organisation. Among textile workers, the stuff pressers and the most highly skilled of the woolsorters had their small and very exclusive societies. The makers up, also highly skilled, had a small association of 180 members. It had a fund of £7,000 in 1867 which it used for generous 'friendly society' benefits to its members. In twenty-seven years it had never had a quarrel with a master. There were a number of overlookers' organisations in the town, among them the Power Loom Overlookers' Society and the Amalgamated Overlookers. The president of this body, addressing an audience which included W. E. Forster, M. W. Thompson and S. C. Kell, assured them that

. . . their motto was 'United to help not combined to injure.' They had no connexion with strikes or trade unions. They were a class of men whose object was the benefit of each other in employment and to assist each other in sickness and death.

He was speaking in a year when most unions were anxious to present a picture of careful legality, but it is a fact that the overlookers were only ever militant about questions of working hours. As far as the basic occupations of the factory were concerned – spinning, weaving and woolcombing – these trades had to wait until the twentieth century for effective organisation.

This failure to organise properly was not due to the presence in itself of a large female element. Though it had some effect it is worth remembering that when there were disputes women were among the most aggressive. More was due perhaps to the fragmentation of the Bradford working classes between Irish Catholic and English Protestant. There was always tension here, and this gave the Orange Order (the largest in Yorkshire) and the employer-dominated Protestant Association plenty of scope for their unpleasant activities. There were two serious street battles – one along Otley Road to Undercliffe in 1844 provoked by the stupidity of the Orangemen, and one along Church Bank in 1862, the result of a visit of the notorious anti-papal propagandist, De Camin. But Irish and English workers had always got on together when questions of employment were in consideration, as they had in 1825 and between 1845 and 1848. It was the defeat of the weavers and woolcombers in 1825 and the undisguised hostility of masters which had weakened textile unionism beyond hope of quick recovery. In addition, the fragmentation of the industry as large numbers of commission firms came into existence broke up the cohesion of the labour force. It made the practical work of trade unions very difficult indeed, for since every firm, large and small, had its own practices, special products and appropriate wage lists, there could be no general approach to problems of negotiation. Nor could potential trade unionists exploit shortages of labour. Most of the work available was some form of machine minding requiring relatively little skill, though some of it, like weaving, could demand a high degree of concentration. Both spinning and weaving were principally women's occupations for which recruits continued to be available from the surrounding country areas, if they could not be found in Bradford.[15]

In most large mills a good deal of promotion came from within the factory itself. By the middle of the century, overlookers were frequently selected from long-serving employees; and young men in training for such posts were generally the sons of overlookers or other skilled workers within the firm. The factory school could also be a fruitful ground of recruitment, particularly for clerical staff – the numerate and the literate were marked out early for the commercial and administrative work of the industry.

The overlookers were of great importance in the factory culture. Their proportion to ordinary workers varied from process to process, but the average was of one to about thirty. They were responsible for the flow of production and thus controlled the distribution of work, the speed at which snags were overcome and the immediate discipline of the floor, from giving permission to go to the lavatory to a limited authority to hire and fire. They thus stood between the employer and the employed both in the productive process and in the social relations of work. Although wages enabled them to adopt the life-style of a lower-middle class and in some particulars – the education of their children, their religious affiliations – might lead them to do so, they were always regarded as working men. The mere fact that they worked factory hours obliged them to live very near if not actually among their fellow employees and thus kept them both geographically and socially in working-class society. At the same time at least the more senior of them had daily contact with managers and partners. Many of them had worked for one firm for a long time. They could have been responsible for the industrial training of younger members of the firm – sons and other relations of partners – working side by side with them at the sorting board or among the looms. They could form ties of obligation and affection of great importance for the bridging function they performed between the two worlds.

On several occasions W. E. Forster acknowledged the importance of the post. Giving evidence in 1856 to the Select Committee on Masters and Workmen, he referred to the difficulties of filling these posts owing to the common lack of education in the West Riding. In 1868, he spoke at the annual dinner of the Amalgamated Overlookers' Society. He suggested that the proper working of the factory system perhaps depended more on the influence of the overlookers than it did on that of the masters, and emphasised the moral influence they could bring to bear on the children and young people under their control. In a fanciful comparison which evoked much amusement, he likened them to the *episcopoi* of the early Christian Church; for, he suggested, it was not their task merely to help their employers to make money and thus provide employment, but also to enable their charges to live 'decent, comfortable, happy and virtuous lives'. He also reminded them of their political duties. 'A man who was an overlooker ought to be well qualified to form an opinion upon political questions.' Equally pertinent, however, in illustrating the influence of the overlooker was a case brought by the Worsted Committee against an overlooker who, on leaving one mill to take a position in another, had followed a practice said to be common – he had taken with him the best of the workpeople from the mill he had left.[16]

Workers generally identified easily with the factory, although this was a psychological process based as much on the cohesion of a social group with common experience as on respect for the authority of a master and the hierarchy which supported it. The factory was inevitably one of the principal points around which social organisation developed – eventually exploited by the formal creation of leisure institutions, works clubs and brass bands – and the factory culture was in one sense an expression of the way people saw themselves, as sharing a common fate. In the summer of 1850, the young men who worked for Waud and Co. fought a savage street battle with the young men who worked for Bottomleys, two firms standing side by side in Portland Street. It went on for a week, at every meal break and every evening, until finally the police got control. Like the soccer gangs of today, they could be dismissed as two gangs of hooligans enjoying themselves in their own peculiar way. It is unlikely that they were fighting for the honour of the firm, yet they were expressing a sense of group identity which was provided by the facts of common employment and which was not so easily offered elsewhere in the emotional aridity of a new conurbation. The incident clearly indicates sentiments of group loyalty which, through education, training and the organisation of leisure, could be harnessed to reinforce the development of a coherent social order.[17]

There was always a great deal of social homogeneity in the factory world and this could often extend as far as the employers. It was not because every successful business was a story of 'from rags to riches', although most of the successful entrepreneurs tried to maintain this pleasant fiction. It had more to do with the fact that, retaining the habits of a more coherent world, they did not obviously belong to a different order of beings. Many of them, at least in their early days, had lived like their workpeople, near the place of work and were familiar members of the local community. Some of them had acquired great wealth and great prestige as the creators of the industrial base of those communities. Yet, they still spoke the same language as their workpeople. Although their sons and daughters were in the process of assuming 'upper class' accents and manners, men like Salt and Ripley were still at home in the local dialect and spoke with ineradicable local accents. Illustrating the possibilities of a relatively 'open' society they enlarged the authority of the newly reconstituted élite.

But we must recall that the consensus rejected the essentially dialectical basis of the relationship of capitalists to working men. Its general purpose on this issue was to promote the view that the interests of Capital and Labour were always entirely identical. It left the essential of the argument – how was the dialectical process to be absorbed? – in dispute. In the last resort, therefore, the authority of the employer was sustained by legislation which was harshly class-oriented. The punitive incentives of the Poor Law Amendment Act formed part of nineteenth-century working-class consciousness, however flexible modern researchers may have shown its local administration to have been. The law on employment remained at best a harassment and at worst a ruthless impediment to trade-union activity. It found men guilty of conspiracy in restraint of trade if they met to agree on wages and hours of work, if they took into consideration men and women not present at the meeting; and it was conspiracy to agree not to work with any given person or to agree to try to persuade others to leave their employment. The truth was, said the *Daily News*, there was scarcely an act done by a trade union in regulation of its trade which was not conspiracy punishable by imprisonment, as at least one local trade-union organiser found to his cost when he tried to start a strike in the district. At the level of factory administration in Bradford the Master and Servant Act was reinforced by the old Worsted Act invoked frequently by the Worsted Committee on behalf of one or other of the employers. Under their operations, breaches of contract by workers and other acts of industrial indiscipline could be criminal offences subject to terms of imprisonment. The typical case brought before the courts was of a woman who had walked out of a factory without finishing the piece she had in effect contracted to weave. Almost invariably, the cause was a dispute with an overlooker about the distribution of good and bad pieces. The sentence usually offered the alternatives of either returning to finish the work, with payment of costs, or a month's hard labour in the House of Correction at Wakefield, although occasionally a woman was judged not to have merited the offer of freedom. The Bradford Bench was composed chiefly of textile manufacturers.[18] The search for the 'moral, social and intellectual improvement of the working classes' was after all the *carrot* of consensus politics. For all the undoubted virtues and opportunities for the exercise of virtue that this programme contained, the claims made on its behalf were always exaggerated and sometimes wholly unrealistic, and it hid beneath the condescensions of its terminology the anxieties of the upper and middle classes.

BRADFORD AND THE STRENGTHENING OF THE CONSENSUS

In Bradford in the fifties there were specific local circumstances which helped the development of easier social relations. By the middle fifties the period of really massive and prolonged immigration was over. After the stupendous increases of the previous four decades, authority was amazed to discover in 1861 that the town had only increased in population by 2·4 per cent from 103,771 to 106,218 in ten years. New machinery had diminished the immediate demand for labour. Population growth picked up again during the boom of the sixties, so that by 1871 the figure had reached 145,827, but by the mid-seventies it was clear that the real numerical expansion of Bradford was over. The considerable increases recorded for the next twenty years were due more than anything to the acquisition of outlying villages and the original area of the borough began to show a net loss of men by migration. (Indeed, by 1901 Bradford was one of the towns in England which had the highest numbers of native inhabitants.) Bradford's effective population growth peaked and began to slow down between 1850 and 1870, and during this period began to develop the element of stability which, until recently, has been its most marked feature for a hundred years.[19] Fewer immigrants meant fewer people making the first uneasy adjustments to urban life. From the fifties onwards the social habits of the urban world were institutionalised in a variety of organisations which furthered the development of coherent social identity.

The optimism which characterised the period was not shaken by the occasional economic set-backs. The recessions of 1854 and 1857 aroused none of the anxieties of the previous decade, although in some parts of the town they reached comparable levels of distress. Sam Kydd noted the relevance of the comparison. Writing in 1857 he remarked:

In 1848, I was in Bradford, when there was a 'rebellion of the belly'. I have seen the streets filled with children, women and men, hungry and angry; the shops closed and the government of the borough practically in the hands of General Thom and the soldiers under his command. I sincerely hope that such circumstances may never again occur.

He noted, however, that apart from the woolcombers, the complaints of the working men were not so much against low rates of earnings as against the irregularity and want of employment. For this reason, the approaching winter was viewed with great fear. Yet, in 1857 as in 1854, while expressions of good will and sympathy towards the unemployed were plentiful enough, genuine philanthropic and charitable activity was far less in evidence. The *Bradford Observer* lambasted 'those who had grown rich by the trade' and yet were content to ignore the difficulties of the recession, and asserted that in the depression of 1847, the manufacturers had been particularly generous, asking with some point 'Can it be that the Chartism of the day was the parent of the charity of the day?'[20]

The most unhappy feature of working-class life in Bradford homes was still the condition of the hand combers. In a town which took great pride in the splendour of its warehouses, many of them continued to live in putrid and unwholesome cellars, borne down by the hopelessness of the situation. 'There is a certain uniform misery expressed in the face of the woolcomber. It is not melancholy, it is not grief; it is the sinking of the whole system – body and mind. . .' wrote Kydd. Militant resentment at the destruction of the pride and dignity of the craft, which had taken men to the streets in 1848, had given way to resigned acceptance. Young men might change their work. Older men could do little to salvage the decencies of life. Thomas Dennison, a man of fifty-one, a close neighbour of Abraham Wildman in Adelaide Street, had started work as a woolcomber in Kidderminster, more than thirty years previously. Now, he thought with reason, he was too old to change. He was no longer fitted to outdoor work, and after thirty years at the combs knew nothing else. He had, he said, 'to comb to the end, and then – the workhouse and the – grave'. Their wages were as low as they had ever been, ranging between about eight shillings and four shillings a week. Salt and others made some effort to raise a charitable fund and T. T. Empsall, a young businessman not long in Bradford, tried to organise an Emigration Society, but little could be done in the face of the public apathy. Empsall was particularly bitter, for he saw it for what it was – a diminishing problem in which a little decent generosity would save needless suffering among the woolcombers.[21]

But if the woolcomber could be left to work out his own destiny on the tramp or the Poor Law test hill, the working-class problem as such still remained, for none could forget the terrors of 1842 and 1848. In the aftermath of Chartism what can best be described as a programme of reconciliation was developed in the interests of social harmony and 'the moral, social and intellectual elevation of the working classes'. It was one of the principal functions of the new employer élite to determine the pattern of such developments, and of all of its number Salt was for some ten years or so its leading advocate and exemplar.

Saltaire, conceived in 1850, was his outstanding but not his only contribution. In June 1849 he had taken the lead in

providing the initial financial backing for a local branch of the
Freehold Land Society and acted as its president with Forbes
and Forster as vice-presidents and Milligan, Brown and
Godwin as the trustees. The branch was in fact a building
society with a moral and political purpose, for it claimed to offer
the working man relatively cheaply a chance to obtain a
freehold property qualification which carried voting rights, the
opportunity to build a decent house and the occasion for
investment and saving. Indeed it made very lavish claims to
start with. Its first historian, J. E. Ritchie, wrote: '[It] is the
great fact of the age . . . it especially aims at the elevation of the
working man . . . it offers them independence, wealth and
political power.' It was closely linked with temperance and
claimed to be achieving a moral revolution by promoting habits
of sobriety and thrift among those who might otherwise waste
their time and money in the public house or the beer-shop.[22]

For a time, the affairs of the society seemed to prosper. A
number of men took shares which could be bought up to a
maximum of six at one shilling a share plus a weekly payment of
one shilling and sixpence per share, until land acquired
through the share had been paid for. In 1850 it acquired two
estates in Manningham, in 1852 another in Girlington and in
the following year three smaller sites. The two Manningham
estates and the Girlington were allocated to members and
developed, but by 1854 it was running into financial difficulties.
The depressions of 1854 and 1857 reduced subscriptions and the
practice of selling the land to members at cost price had left no
room for manoeuvre. The other estates were not developed and
the society was finally wound up in 1864.

How far it fulfilled its stated intention of getting the vote for
working men and giving them a steady investment is open to
question. Ordinary factory hands earning about fourteen
shillings a week could not afford a weekly subscription of one
shilling and sixpence. Few of those connected with it were
working men in the true sense. The Executive Committee was
made up of second-rank Radicals like Joseph Nutter, a
furniture maker, and E. H. Parratt, an ironmonger, all
comfortably placed. Among those allocated land in the
Girlington estate were Charles Stead, one of Salt's works
managers, soon to be taken into partnership, Frederick Rouse,

a member of the wealthy mill-owning family, W. Leveratt, the Chief Constable, Ben Preston, the local poet who had left the working classes well behind, and two of Salt's sons, George and William Henry.

The Bradford Society did not introduce many working men to the attractions of home ownership. What did happen was that the two Manningham developments – Salt Street and Northfield Place – contained some handsome terrace housing, much of which was owner-occupied, and the Girlington estate had a good deal of lower-middle-class/working-class housing of a superior type, much of which was rented to foremen, overlookers, clerks, schoolmasters and shopkeepers – a cross-section of Bradford's well-to-do working-class/lower-middle-class section of society. As such it was a significant contribution to the history of the suburban estate in Bradford; its stated intentions were always more grandiose than the practical achievement.[23]

In August Salt began what became a regular practice at his works – the works trip. Taking advantage of the railway developments which had recently opened up the West Riding, he entertained his employees to a day's outing at Malham and Gordale Scar in the Yorkshire Dales, one of the principal beauty spots in Northern England, and so began the practice of the works trip, a development of some importance in the history of labour relations. It was treated as a regional occasion. Four bands attended and 'played lively airs at intervals preceeding the starting of the trains and triumphant ones as the gay company passed by the chief stations on the line'. There were four trains in all and Salt, his eldest son William Henry, and a number of Salt's friends occupied a first-class carriage at the front. Crowds assembled to watch the departure and the unusual nature of the occurrence was emphasised by the appearance at Skipton of a number of 'respectable persons' including Sir Charles Tempest, to greet the party. The *Bradford Observer* reported:

It was a pleasant sight to see so many human beings so thoroughly happy . . . and the happiest of the whole company was the noble-hearted gentleman whose liberal soul had devised, and whose not less liberal generosity had supplied the means of diffusing so much enjoyment among his fellow creatures. . .

167

and concluded:

Thus ended the most unexceptional Factory turn-out Bradford has ever witnessed. It is, we believe, the first of its kind, we venture to say it will not be the last. The effect of such entertainment is good – permanently good. They tend to enlarge and refine the mind, and to cement the feelings of respect and attachment which must exist between the employer and his workpeople who participate in them.

Other employers took the hint and for several weeks similar events were recorded in the local press. Daniel Illingworth took 300 of his 'hands' on a walk through Allerton to Chellow Dene, one of the several retreats from urbanism which were still to be found in Bradford, and gave them tea afterwards at the Odd Fellows' Hall. Daniel Illingworth stayed on his own territory in West Bradford, but others were more adventurous. Tremell and Schlesinger took their workpeople to Fountains Abbey. Samuel Smith, the dyer, organised a trip to Liverpool and the Rand brothers took about 1,200 people, including sorters, woolcombers and handloom weavers, to Ripon. W. E. Forster and W. Fison took their workpeople from Burley-in-Wharfedale to Esholt, Apperley Bridge and Rawdon. The report of the excursion gave, in passing, one of those marginal sketches which illuminate a whole aspect of ordinary life. On the return journey, the train broke down at Thackley Tunnel – one of the dreaded spots of local Victorian railway travel – dark, dank and over a mile long. It stayed there with its austere carriages for more than an hour and the stranded passengers kept their spirits up by singing extracts from the *Messiah*.[24]

The *Bradford Observer* marked these events with a leader on 'Practical Christianity', which made the point that this was a better way than a military occupation to keep the peace:

It is a healthy condition of things when masters and servants, employers and employed are found working together in the hard but honourable paths of industry, with mutual understanding and satisfaction – the former in pursuit of gain, the latter of an honest livelihood: but far more so when, laying aside the master and putting on the friend, the Captains of Industry are found leading forth their armies in search of pleasure, into the bosom of nature, or mingling familiarly with them at the social board. We have often had occasion to complain of the barriers of wealth and feeling which separate the extremes of English society; and strongly convinced that this is not only unseemly but dangerous, we advert with the greatest satisfaction to the recent pleasure trips and festivities of our manufacturers and their workpeople.

We like the feeling which this indicates, and not less so the feeling which it is calculated to create. It shows that there are masters truly alive to the welfare of their workpeople; and when that feeling is declared in *deeds* the corresponding feeling of gratitude will not fail to spring up on the other side. We have tried to govern too exclusively by force or fear, at great expense, and not with the most satisfactory result: and now, though the experiment were doubtful, it were worthwhile to try to govern by love and kindness. But there is no fear of failure: – a railway trip to Skipton, and a good English dinner to the workpeople in any one of our great factories, is a better guarantee of the public peace than a regiment of soldiers.[25]

As an idea, it was not precisely new – the works dinner, for instance, was a well-established institution. What was new (apart from the use of the railway) was the sudden proliferation of such trips, the attention given to them in the press and the way in which they became a permanent aspect of factory life. Thus, while it is unnecessary to look for the touch of cynical manipulation, it can clearly be seen as part of the programme of social reconciliation which the new circumstances had made possible.

Salt also tried to stimulate a more general interest in the question of 'the moral and social condition of the people'. As Mayor and Chief Magistrate, in 1848–9, he had, he said, been shocked at the 'frequent evidence . . . of widespread immorality and vice, which appeared before him in court. He had also, he said, been made cognisant of the existence of scenes of wickedness of which he had had previously no conception.' He had spent a number of evenings making a tour, along with the Chief Constable, to see some of the more depressing scenes which the town offered. He had, accordingly, invited a number of the principal inhabitants of the town to a meeting to discuss the matter.[26] The committee of inquiry which was appointed at the meeting issued a report in the following year. It was, in effect, a plea for the organisation of disciplined and controlled leisure facilities. The committee was intended to uncover the occasions and opportunities for vice, and had found ample evidence of their existence. A great deal of the collected evidence, however, was thought unfit for general publication. The report merely noted that there were over 150 beer-shops in the town, the majority of which 'provided the means of dishonourable intercourse between the sexes'. Most of the public houses and hotels were little better and a number of high-class brothels, where 'vice loses a measure of its grossness though none of its guilt; the resort of many who would fain be classed with the virtuous and the respectable', disgraced certain parts of the town. It had nothing to say about the positive achievements of a working class which was beginning to make pattern and shape out of the urban coagulation of the previous twenty years – thus its findings were the accepted currency of the times, though expounded with intelligence and humanity. It found that the beer-shop system needed more effective control – it was useless to look for its abolition immediately. The means of religious instruction needed to be extended – even before the findings of the 1851 religious census had been published, it had been no surprise to find that most people in the town, 'far from being committed to any particular congregation, were either opposed or indifferent to the religion of Christ'. More provision for education was needed. The facilities of the Mechanics' and Church Institutes ought to be spread throughout the town and similar provision made for women. The reading habits of the working classes should be elevated by the provision of wholesome literature made available in libraries, and a concert hall was required where public amusement, divorced from a connexion with alcoholic liquors, was available. Above all, the report emphasised the need for the means of leisure which would lead men to 'substitute manly and open-air exercise for vicious and enervating pleasures'. It recommended that public parks should be provided and reported that one of the committee (Salt, in fact) was prepared to give £1,000 towards the cost of a park, if public subscriptions raised £10,000.[27]

The *Bradford Observer* noted sharply the weaknesses of the report. Except for a Town Mission which was intended to perform an evangelical function in the slums of Bradford, the proposals were unlikely to do much for the genuinely poor or the really depraved. The criticism suggested (without precisely stating) that the report was directed at the needs of the 'respectable' working man, the disciple of Samuel Smiles, and one who was very unlikely to confuse himself with the poor. The leader writer pointed out:

. . . a Music hall, a park, a library, the regulation of beerhouses, the suppression of brothels? Each is excellent. There will yet be a dense mass, a fearful stratum underlying the very basis of society, which neither music hall, park, nor library will frequently attract.

It also raised a more fundamental issue: 'the dark, uncleaned, unwatered and uncomfortable' homes of this dense mass – homes which prevented all semblance of decent life.[28]

Nevertheless the report was a serious exercise plainly related to a perceived need for social harmony, albeit like all such documents it assumed the need for condescension on the one hand and deference on the other. 'The more intelligent and wealthy class must contribute not only money but thought and time, personal influence and kindness while those below must place generous confidence in the desire of their superiors to serve them.' As a practical document, it was in its pages that the idea of Peel Park, the Female Educational Institute and the Town Mission – all of which were significant elements in the social pattern of Victorian Bradford – were first publicly mooted, and it stimulated a good deal of broadly educational activity which took place during the next decade.

The Town Mission held its first general public meeting shortly after the report was published. Salt was the principal force behind its foundation and acted as treasurer for several years. He remained its largest subscriber throughout his life and thought it the most important general charity he was connected with. Anglicans and Catholics held aloof for they saw it as a threat to the principle of the 'cure of souls' which provided the moral core of the parochial system. It had, however, a distinguished list of contributors in addition to Salt – among them Robert Milligan, William Murgatroyd, Henry Forbes, Edward Ripley, Daniel Illingworth, J. V. Godwin,

Henry Brown and Mrs Bacon – all either Baptists, Congregationalists or Methodists.

It employed four missionaries in the slums of Bradford where they were to 'combat the widespread contempt for divine things too frequently attended with a profligacy which corrupted the whole of society'. Their reports made gloomy reading, for they referred regularly to the casinos, dancing rooms, low theatres and beer-shops whose demoralising effect added, they said, to a sorrowful but not exaggerated picture, in which they saw little except brutal immorality. 'Intemperance and impurity are rife, the obligations of marriage disregarded . . . parental authority, filial respect and obedience are in many cases entirely destroyed.' But the language of the preacher tended to mask the performance of social work which offered a service based on professional commitment and personal conviction. The missionaries combined secular educational work with religious instruction. By 1852 a well-attended class for young women in White Abbey offered instruction in reading, writing, arithmetic and general subjects and another in Croft Street catered in the same way for 100 women and 40 men. By 1861, also, facilities for free medical consultation and free medicines had been arranged.[29]

A positive response to the plea for women's education was slower to take place. Then, in 1857, the Female Educational Institute opened its doors, and within five years had about 500 students attending its evening classes. They included 356 factory workers, 105 nursemaids and others living at home, 9 domestic servants and a handful from warehouses, shops and dyehouses. Of the 125 enrolled in the last year, 51 were totally illiterate, 19 could more or less read but could not write, 33 could read reasonably well and write a little, 14 could read well and write reasonably and only 8 could be regarded as able to read and write whatever they wished. About 20 could do simple sums. It was a minority of students who managed to sustain continuous attendance. Most of them were up shortly after 5 a.m. to get to work for 6 a.m, worked all day in the heat and racket of the factory until 6 p.m., then hurried through their domestic chores to get to classes which started at 7.30 p.m. and went on until 9.30. It attracted the services of a number of dedicated women like Mrs Fanny Hertz and must be regarded as one of the best manifestations of Victorian good works in Bradford.[30]

An informal approach to the problem of the 'moral, social and intellectual elevation of the working classes' stimulated by the report was the Sunday afternoon lecture usually given by a minister of religion. Rev. G. Condor delivered a series of six well-attended lectures on Christianity. Rev. W. Scott gave talks on 'Reading – its advantages and how to secure them'. Beyond question, the star in this field was Rev. J. P. Chown, a Baptist minister and a man of outstanding capacity in a town which took some pride in the intellectual stature of its preachers. He lectured for four successive years on a wide range of subjects and at the end of his last programme was presented with a testimonial by a 'Committee of the Working Classes of Bradford'. Altogether some 33,000 had attended the four series, which he had given, he said, with only the thought in mind of those 'who might be wasting their energies, abusing their talents, misspending their time'. It would, however, be impossible to estimate how many he drew from the beer-shop or the dogfight.[31]

The most obvious example of the concern for disciplined leisure was the public park which Salt had already offered to finance. As an idea, it was neither new nor unique. In 1834, E. C. Lister, giving evidence to the Select Committee on the Provision of Public Walks and Open Spaces, said that for many years he had opened his own grounds at Manningham to the public at holiday times. The *Bradford Observer*, which had had advance notice of the Salt Committee Report, took up the question after the Whitsuntide holiday in 1850. The holiday, it seems, had passed off with great *éclat* but, continued the paper, the use made of the Manningham Hall grounds had emphasised the value of a park to a town where the means of acceptable amusement were not readily available. The temperance interests had organised a gala. 30,000 had attended on the two days it opened. They had enjoyed the bands, and the natural beauties of the park; and had taken part with great enthusiasm in the dancing and the rural games, 'such as kiss-in-the-ring'. They had also, a correspondent to the paper pointed out, avoided the temptations of the public house and the vice of intemperance, and he concluded the account with the remarks that 'Mr. and the Hon. Mrs. Kay and friends condescended to walk through the grounds in the evening and were gratified that they did not notice a single instance of impropriety of conduct in the whole of the immense gathering.'

The paper continued to keep the idea at the forefront of opinion. In September 1850, it was maintaining 'the absolute necessity of securing the means of healthful recreation and innocent pleasure for the population', for 'a very general belief exists that cricket is better than cock-fighting, that bowls are better than a boxing-bout; and that all outdoor enjoyment is to be preferred to the tavern and beershop'. Most important, it was seen as leading to social unity. All classes would mix together in the pleasures of the park. Party feeling would diminish and fresh confidence between the classes would grow.

A committee negotiated the purchase of the Bolton House estate which lay towards the north-eastern side of the town. It agreed on a name – Peel Park – and set in motion the work on the natural and artifical amenities which the park was to offer. Enthusiasm cooled when those who could be expected to contribute were confronted with the need to find £8,000 to match the £1,000 offered by Titus Salt and a further £1,000 given by Robert Milligan. Progess in the collection of subscriptions went slowly and it was not until October 1856 that the committee cleared the debts it had incurred. In the event, the costs – £18,000 – were met by the sale for £6,500 of part of the estate which the committee had acquired, a government grant of £1,500, and public subscriptions of £10,000 including those of Salt and Milligan. It was taken over by the municipal authorities in 1863.[32]

Most advocates of the idea made the point that Bradford had little public ground to which the inhabitants had free access for sporting activities, and while this was true as far as it went, Bradford nevertheless had a good deal of open green space within its boundaries. Cricket was being played extensively by 1860 and within several years of that date well over a hundred matches were being played on any Saturday afternoon. By that date also the earliest of the great Bradford clubs had been founded. Working men were still finding places to hold their own unofficial athletic meetings, dog races and dog fights and to play the urban version of knurr and spell known as 'piggy'. Complaints in the press highlighted the significance of the park. One referred to an occasion when a footrace had been held in the fields near Peel Park, 'one of the competitors being positively naked and another practically so', and followed by an excited and noisy crowd of men, women and children.[33] A park added a great deal to the beauty and the amenities of the town. But its ultimate justification was the sort of use casual space could be put to. It was thought that social behaviour would improve through the use of a park. Men and women of all classes 'save the very lowest and abandoned, would find a refining and elevating influence, from the mingling of the classes, among pleasant scenes of recreation'. They would, said contemporaries, want to dress themselves and their children decently when they went to a park where they would encounter people from other walks of life.

If you want a population to be sensual, gross and unpolished, indifferent to the courtesies and insensible to the delicacies of social intercourse, you may abandon them to low, gross and brutal pleasures and associations, but give them the opportunities of higher enjoyment, appeal to those purer tastes which lie dormant in all and need only to be awakened – surround them with what is beautiful in nature and art – habituate them to associate with those more polished than themselves and you will gradually produce the elevation and refinement you seek; and as generations succeed one another, society will become virtuous and happy.

The Mayor, Samuel Smith, a liberal contributor to the fund, also emphasised the moral value of the park, when he presented the Committee's report in 1852. He hoped, he said, it would be well understood that all who went into the park would clean themselves up. No man ought to go dirty as a matter of public respect and decency, 'because the first step in raising the working man was to see him thoroughly clean'. He also proferred the advice that when, 'like Lord Harewood', they walked in their park, they should protect the property set aside for their enjoyment. 'Let their motto be "Touch not; handle not", and if they do that they will enjoy all the pleasure it is

175

possible to have without doing any harm whatsoever.'

The park quickly became an important addition to the amenities of the town. The central feature was a terrace which separated a large grassy space, intended at one time for use as a cricket field but used for casual games of all the respectable kinds, from a big natural amphitheatre which contained an ornamental lake and provided a vista of genuine beauty. (It also offered facilities for tobogganing in the winter.) There were bowling greens available, within a few years, and a band gave regular concerts on Saturday evenings through the summer of 1867. For many years the press carried regular seasonal descriptions of the progress of the gardens: '. . . the terrace is always beautiful . . . the shrubs have never looked better – the fine trimmed specimens of laurels of various kinds, ribes, posentillas now in beautiful bloom, cytissus with their delicate green foliage and other shrubs amply testify to the judgment and skill of the manager'. It also became the practice to hold an annual gala there on behalf of the voluntary hospital which had recently been erected. It was held on the Monday and Tuesday of Whit week, always the principal holiday of Bradford in the nineteenth century, and it became one of the few great corporate and communal occasions of the Bradford year. It was estimated in 1866 that almost 100,000 attended on the two days. Morris dancing, maypole dancing, acrobatics, the manoeuvres of the Bradford Company of the 2nd Rifle Volunteer Corps and a magnificent firework display were among the entertainments available. With great gusto, the press described the private picnics, the 'innocent rustic games and dancing' which went on to the accompaniment of one or other of the six bands playing in different areas of the park. How different it was, implied the report, from the raucous indiscipline of the traditional summer and winter fairs.

The final comment of the *Observer* was characteristic:

The myriads who spent Whit Tuesday in Peel Park . . . returned surcharged with fresh air, agreeably tired out and quite satisfied with their benefit, glad to go to bed, and ready for labour in the morning. It was remarkable that before midnight on Tuesday many of the leading streets were quieter than on ordinary nights and few idlers were visible yesterday. The fondness of our townspeople for trips and outdoor recreations is, when it can be gratified, a safeguard and preservative; and it goes far to account for the prevailing sobriety, good temper and order, which made the holiday no dissipation but an invigorating change.[34]

The park offered a great deal, but it was part of that re-ordering of social events of which the life of the factory and of the related urban area was the determinant. The tendency of the new society was to divide a geographical area by zonal function of work, domestic life and public leisure, where appropriate forms of conduct could be expected and if need be enforced. Thus a visit to the park was generally an event – albeit a minor one – an occasion for dressing up, for taking the family for a walk and ensuring that the children were clean and tidy. The park became the pleasure ground of middle and working class when they wanted or needed to be respectable and responsible members of society. Thus the imperceptible pressures which the environment of the park could create for those who used it, reinforced as they were by strict regulations, contributed to the controls on which the mid-century hegemony rested.

There is also the evidence of paternalism in action as between employer and employee. The big employers at least clearly exercised a good deal of political influence among their workers, and some of them expected to do so. Ripley in fact dismissed one of his senior employees, a chemist with more than thirty years' service in the firm, for voting against him. On the other hand, he had built a small industrial housing estate in Bowling – Ripleyville – ostensibly for his workers (though there were those reluctant to accept him as a landlord as well as an employer), had had a number of almshouses put up and had started a sick benefit club financed jointly by the workpeople and the firm. Berry's, an important textile engineering firm, and Christopher Waud's also had sick benefit clubs. The Priestmans, among the most generally charitable of the Bradford manufacturers, were probably the first Bradford firm to introduce a profit-sharing scheme, though it was restricted to their better-paid employees. One unnamed employer started a savings account for each of his young apprentices and a number provided factory land for use as allotments. Joseph Wilson, a small-scale employer and one of the early success stories of Primitive Methodism in Great Horton, left a record of his own views of the proper relationship between master and man:

> I tried to understand the worker's point of view and to lean to his side . . . I must try to serve them and do what I can for them so that my whole business life . . . would bear investigation on the basis of the highest standards.[35]

In the outlying villages where one or two masters could dominate the labour market it was very marked. W. Fison and W. E. Forster in Burley-in-Wharfedale, their reputation as enlightened employers well established, made facilities available for elementary and adult education and built up a famous factory choir. They also provided a library and a concert hall and ran a savings bank.[36] Much the same story could be related of the Fosters of Black Dyke, Queensbury and other firms in places like Denholme provided similar though less lavish facilities.

It is foolhardy to be too dogmatic about a purely local experience like this, when the evidence may well be simply not yet available. But the comparative paucity of evidence about Bradford itself does perhaps suggest that this way of mediating the acceptance of industrial capitalism was not – Saltaire apart – a powerful influence in Bradford in the third quarter of the century. The *Bradford Observer* criticised wealthy employers very sharply for their reluctance to follow Salt's example and contribute to resolving the acute housing problems of the period. It also compared Bradford very unfavourably with Halifax where Francis Crossley had recently founded an orphanage, donated a public park to the town and started a profit-sharing scheme for his workers, and where both he and Edward Akroyd were engaged in the building of 'model' industrial estates.[37]

There is plenty of evidence of a more specifically philanthropic activity, in addition to the spurt inspired by Salt in the aftermath of Chartism – the Female Refuge, the Tradesmen's Benevolent Institution and the Tradesmen's Homes, the ragged schools, facilities for the care of the dumb, deaf and blind, a cottage building society, the hospital network (an enlarged infirmary, an Eye and Ear and a Fever hospital) – which along with the Poor Law Hospital served the town until the twentieth century. But of a direct paternalism – the structure of industry had perhaps inhibited its more general development. The large number of small commission firms which had now appeared might sometimes promote a friendly 'face to face' atmosphere. They were unlikely to have the financial resources to offer the *quid pro quo* implicit in a paternalistic relationship. Then in Bradford there were no powerful unions whose existence might have stimulated a more positive response. And in any case, paternalism as an instrument of social change was being replaced by consciousness of civic need and a severer individualism was beginning to dominate in labour relations.[38]

WORKING-CLASS INSTITUTIONALISATION

At the same time, the cultural authority of the middle classes continued to find expression through those moral institutions which, whatever else they were, were always instruments of hegemony. Among these the ecclesiastical establishments were the most important, although some of the evidence does not immediately suggest this. The religious census of 1851 confirmed the worst fears of all perceptive church and chapel goers. The majority of English men and women were unlikely to be found in a church or chapel on a Sunday. Of those in Bradford who were not prevented through infirmity, illness, infancy, age or domestic duties, perhaps 30 per cent attended a religious service at some time during the day. Thirty years later, the *Bradford Observer* carried out a survey which showed no improvement in attendances, despite a massive programme of church and chapel building undertaken in the sixties and seventies. There were shifts in the relative importance of the various denominations. Anglicans had improved their position slightly, Methodists had just about held their own, and Old Dissent had lost quite heavily. The secular Sunday was becoming more attractive to the middle classes. On the other hand, a larger number of working-class people were going to church or – more obviously – chapel. Roman Catholic congregations had increased greatly. The Primitive Methodists had increased their numbers slightly, and a large number of smaller sects were attracting working-class people in numbers which became significant when added together. By thus accepting the obligations of religious attachment a greater number of working-class people were adapting to the social ethic of the community. To the extent that they were non-Anglican, they also provided a firmer base for the political alliance which had developed between middle-class and working-class Nonconformists.[39]

More generally this was still a non-secular world. It was a minority, but a very large one, which maintained the entrenched religious establishments, and it included almost all the recognised leaders of the community. A significant number of working-class people provided an element in the structure of middle-class hegemony around which the principles of consensus could be evolved. In Bradford about one in five of the population were committed to the life of church or chapel and saw themselves as the true defenders of Christian morality (which, of course, most of the others had not totally rejected). The church or chapel added a social dimension to the close-knit discipline of the family. It was not only the great political meetings on religious equality or the massive evangelical demonstrations at St George's Hall. Churches and chapels could be seen as associations of families offering in addition to spiritual guidance, friendships and marriage partners within the framework of a trusted organisation. Men's Bible discussion groups, mothers' meetings, young people's evening classes, choir and choir practices, bazaars and preparations for bazaars, Sunday school anniversaries, Sunday school treats, and increasingly more purely recreational activities left few evenings and holidays without some occupation for some members of a church or chapel-going family. The Mayor of Bradford was at least over-reacting in 1881 when he denounced the spread of the Continental Sunday and the 'conversion of the Sabbath into a day of sensual gratification'. The influence of the ecclesiastical establishments was still all-pervasive, the ethical debate still conducted in the terms they laid down.

The most important of the facilities provided was the Sunday school attached to almost every religious institution. A report of 1861 indicated that there were over 19,000 scholars enrolled in the seventy-six schools recorded in the Bradford Union, not far short of double the number who attended day schools. There were also about 3,700 teachers.[40] The Sunday school life was arduous. On Sundays classes ran from nine to twelve and again from two to four and homework was also sometimes given. Teachers were expected to take their duties seriously, attending preparation classes every week and visiting pupils in their homes. Impeccable standards of personal behaviour were demanded. School attendances around 66 per cent of total enrolments provoked regular complaints from pastors and other officials of 'backsliding' among teachers. But they still represented a massive contribution to moral education reaching well beyond the regular church and chapel communities, since parents frequently saw to it that their children went to Sunday school even if they were far from assiduous themselves. No other schools evoked anything like the zeal and general interest lavished on them.

By the 1860s, the Sunday school movement had become effectively institutionalised. The Bradford Sunday School Union provided an organisation for the dissemination of ideas and a forum for discussion which inevitably introduced a greater uniformity into the movement if only through the minor rivalries encouraged in the activities the Union promoted. Middle-class control had been confirmed. The categorical statement made by Baines that Sunday school teachers were drawn almost entirely from the middle classes was not true, at least in Bradford, but there were enough of them to ensure a preponderant influence and if nothing else the greater complexity of the movement's organisation gave key figures like Elias Thomas, the union secretary and a wool buyer employed by the Milligan enterprise, greater scope for the exercise of their activities.[41]

Day-time education was also dominated by the religious establishments. A number of dame schools where little – if anything – more than very basic reading and writing skills were taught and proprietary schools where religious instruction depended on the inclinations of the owner accounted for about

40 per cent of the school population. 60 per cent went to schools supported by public funds; either to one of the five factory schools run on the lines of the Church of England Society for Education or one of the public day schools under the control of one or other of the denominations. The number of day scholars always fell far short of the number of children of school age; of those on the register in the sixties between 50 and 60 per cent only were in regular attendance. On the other hand, hostility towards education was diminishing except, it was said, among 'those prohibited by poverty and profligacy'. Indeed there were artisans and shopkeepers who would pay between sixpence and a shilling a week to send their children to cheap proprietary schools where they would not mix with 'companions from a lower stratum of society'.[42]

The quality of education was at best variable. In 1870, only twenty-four out of fifty-five private schools were said to approach anything like efficiency. Of the publicly financed schools, inspectors criticised the brutality of the discipline and found little of value in the teaching, which was dominated by the techniques of rote learning. Only the Borough West School, supported by the Horton Lane Chapel congregation, came in for a modicum of praise. The headmaster, it was said, ran a well-organised timetable, in which weekly disruptions were avoided by his refusal to take in half-timers. In the other grant-aided day schools, inspectors claimed to have met practically no child who could read with comprehension or who had the most trivial elements of history and geography at command. But perhaps the sort of examination they gave was unfair. With a minimum age of employment still eight, the chances were that the cleverest children of the poor left school the earliest. Again, many of the children were first-generation day-school scholars discovering gingerly a world more or less alien to the world of the home. For them knowledge was a by-product of a process concerned primarily with introducing children to the discipline of an industrial society. Edward Akroyd, the Halifax millowner-philanthropist, expressed the idea differently. It was not, he said, the objective of education to bring up clever rogues, but to raise a body of orderly and loyal citizens.[43]

Provision for adult education was also firmly under middle-class control through the denominational organisations. The Church Institute moved into its own building in North Parade and continued to promote, as the syllabus said, 'general knowledge in subordination to religion' among its 700 members. Although it kept the Anglican flag flying it never challenged the Mechanics' Institute as an educational service. By the middle decades of the century the Mechanics' Institute offered an annual programme of day and evening classes, staffed by a number of highly skilled teachers. It had a library and a newspaper room for well over 1,000 members and every year organised a programme of public lectures by the most eminent scholars of the time. It also ran an art school, the first Bradford School of Design, started in 1848. So extensive did its work seem that its historian, C. A. Federer, claimed that in these years its committee was the unofficial school board to the borough.[44]

In 1859 J. V. Godwin defended the Bradford Institute from contemporary attacks which suggested that mechanics' institutes were irrelevant to the true needs of British society. Next to the Sunday schools, he said, it was the strongest power in the town in the work of popular education. He insisted that as an educational service for working men, working men rightly played a significant part in its administration. The evidence, however, suggests that its programmes of lectures were well attended but mainly by the already well-informed. The general education classes (including free classes in the literacy and numeracy skills) really served the needs of young men from artisan and lower middle-class families, except for a handful of the really able from the 'labouring masses'. Working men were elected to the committee regularly, but there were never more than one or two of them – Ben Wainwright was the one readily identifiable working man on the committee in the mid-century years. Godwin and his friends remained in control.[45]

It has been frequently noted that these were the great years of exhortation of the working classes. Men and women were requested and cajoled, threatened and implored to accept a definition of the good life which would maintain harmony and stability. Moreover, as we have already remarked, they were prepared to accept a good deal of it as making sense within the contemporary environment. Nevertheless, working-class life retained areas of independence both in activities which reflected the prevailing culture and even more obviously in those areas of experience where older values had not been obliterated by the norms of Liberal Capitalism. Middle-class reception of these activities ranged from qualified approval to downright hostility.

The purely working-class contribution to the anti-drink movement aroused in its early stages more suspicion than its protagonists had perhaps expected, and it was surrendered relatively quietly to consensus control. Working men had had a very forthright answer to the problem in teetotalism, total and unequivocal abstinence from all alcoholic drink whether in sickness or in health. In Bradford, they established in 1843 the Long Pledged Teetotal Society, which they claimed was the first of its kind in the world, and built in 1846 the first ever Teetotal Hall. Bradford's middle class treated the new venture with some reserve. When the hall was opened, leading temperance reformers like W. Morgan, H. Forbes and the two Rand brothers were absent, sending letters of apology. Only John Priestman turned up and he was very reluctant to act as chairman of the meeting. However praiseworthy an ideal for working men, teetotalism could be inconvenient at a practical level for members of the middle classes who might entertain a good deal and who perhaps shared Titus Salt's view that wine taken with meals was an enjoyable comfort. Then, the trustees were prepared to hire out the hall to working-class radicals like David Lightowler and so acquired a reputation of having too close a connexion with political extremism. In 1846 a new Total Abstinence Society (referred to in the parent body's minutes as the XX Society) drew away those who were disturbed by this reputation. Eventually, the expense of running the hall proved too costly for the rest; no wealthy and benevolent abstainer stepped in to ease the burden and by 1864 the hall was up for sale and the society ready for winding up. Working men and women continued to be active; indeed, according to Henry Hibbert, the temperance agent in Bradford, they were the backbone of the movement.[46] But by the late sixties the structure was very firmly linked to the religious establishments. Outside them, temperance/teetotal activity was small.

The most generously lauded working-class institutions were the friendly societies, after they had shed by the mid-forties their radical, 'secret society', connexions. Now, they were seen as the best embodiment of self-help in working-class life. In Bradford there were about thirty of these societies and perhaps 14,000 enrolled and subscribing members, about 10 per cent of the borough's population. The benefits they paid out came in the sixties to about £13,000 a year. Some of the societies were very large. The Bradford branch of the Manchester Unity of Odd Fellows, the richest in the West Riding, had 27 lodges and 3,382 members, and it paid out over £3,000 a year in death, sickness and medical benefits. Eight societies had over 500 members each and there were a number of local organisations like the Great Horton Friendly Society with 176 members and the Hunt Yard Benevolent Society with 109 members. The trade unions generally had their own friendly society systems. Most of the societies contributed to the local hospital and most of them supported a Medical Aid Institution organised by a few local doctors to supply treatment and medicines on a co-operative basis. It was acknowledged that friendly societies, like mechanics' institutes, were beyond the reach of the great mass of working people.[47]

The co-operative societies were more purely of the working class, though this movement also was never an affair of the masses. There was a Co-operative Store in Bradford in the thirties and in the next decade trade unionists and Chartists were trying to develop schemes of co-operative Socialism. But they had to free themselves from the ghosts of Owenism and Chartism before they achieved even a modified respectability – a process begun during the course of the 1850s. By this time there were in existence both a new Co-operative Store and a Flour Society. The Co-operative Store opened in May 1851. It had fifty members and did £20 worth of business in the first few weeks. A year later it had 100 members and averaged £45 of business a week. Five hundred 'well dressed people' – including a large number of women and several notables, W. E. Forster,

Dr Godwin and the prominent co-operators V. Neale, C. A. Fleming and L. Jones – attended the first anniversary celebration.[48] The Flour Society was started in 1849 and was relatively successful through the fifties and sixties. It had its own mill and in 1852 was said to be supplying 1,250 members with 'a good unadulterated flour at the lowest rates, with handsome bonuses on capital invested'. In 1854 its yearly turnover was £8,500 and in 1866 White's *Directory* reported it as 'one of the notable institutions in the town'. A typical member and one of the earliest of the directors was Sylvester Wilkinson, a millwright, in 1854 a married man of thirty-six. The son of a carpenter, he was brought up in Queen Street, one of the areas investigated by the Woolcombers' Committee in 1845, and was still living there in 1854 with a family of five children of which the two oldest girls worked as spinners in a local mill. In 1866 he became 'millwright and engineer' at Hollings Mill, and lived then in a new and improved back-to-back house along Whetley Lane.[49] By 1860 two new consumer co-operatives had also been established. These were the Bradford Industrial Co-operative Society and the Queensgate Society, both strictly consumer co-operatives. In 1866 they amalgamated and thus started the present-day Bradford Co-operative Society. Many of their early members had been connected with Radical politics. Howard, the first secretary of the Provident Society, was at one time a member of the Secular Society, but so respectable was the new amalgamation to become that the old connexion with Owenism and Chartism was forgotten when the time came in 1910 to write the jubilee history of co-operation in Bradford.

Over the years the movement had to face a good deal of criticism and obstruction. Some Chartists, Jones and White among others, criticised the ventures of the 1850s as encouraging competition rather than co-operation, but it was the Socialist-Chartist connexion which alarmed the middle classes. At one anniversary tea-party, Forster, who chaired the meeting, said that like most men of his class he considered Owenite Socialism a form of robbery but was happier with the co-operative principles of the Christian Socialists. He preferred co-operation for distribution rather than for production. What was more important, among the wholesalers and retailers in the town there was a long history of outright hostility. The Co-operative Movement – seen as a dangerous competitor – constantly faced disruptive tactics in getting supplies of goods, particularly basic commodities like coal and flour. Authority, however, eventually conferred its approval of a well-conceived experiment in self-help. Commenting on a tea-party attended by the Mayor, the Vicar and other local dignitaries, the historian of the Bradford Movement wrote: 'Co-operation, having now received the Mayoral blessing, the ecclesiatical benediction and a public recognition now and henceforth became a Bradford institution.'[50]

Among middle-class leaders of opinion, the independence of working-class people towards religion was more permanently disturbing. Roman Catholicism and Primitive Methodism had made some progress among them, but there were many – and not, as was frequently suggested, merely the profligate and depraved – who consciously rejected the ministrations of church and chapel. Many working men and women thought that religious leaders were divorced from the realities of working-class life, offering petty kill-joy sanctimoniousness for true moral worth, and for practical purposes they were little more than reliable supporters of the employing class. William Logan, the principal at Salt's Town Mission, summed the position up:

It is my firm and settled opinion that there are thousands of men and hundreds of women who would rather perish than enter our ordinary places of worship . . . with their present ideas of ministers as a class and the religious profession as a body they will not cross the threshold of our chapels and . . . the state churches . . . are out of the question. I refer more especially to what may be termed intelligent sober working men. Many of them read the Bible and speak in respectful terms of the principles propounded there, but it is impossible to prevail on them to enter our churches and chapels.

There was also a small but vigorous Secular Society in Bradford. Press notices of its activities were often facetious, but in fact the Society organised some very impressive meetings.

Through the summer the members held camp meetings on Shipley Glen or in 'hamlet dotted Airedale, richest and loveliest of Yorkshire's dales'. They adopted, it was said, Methodist tactics, stirring up veterans, arousing laggards and drawing together the latest and youngest recruits. On an appointed Sunday a large number of 'keen-witted men . . . all toilers and heretics, many with wives, sweethearts, children following in the train' would troop to the assembly where 'in rude dialect, with the ready common-sense logic of the workshop . . . homely orators criticize the Bible, are indignant at the immoralities of Calvinism, overturn the church's House of Cards, popularize the metaphysical disquisitions of Hume and pick flaws in the reasoning of Paley'. In 1864, the Society had a regular meeting-place at the Long Pledged Teetotal Hall where it kept a library and took in a number of periodical publications for its members.[51]

The principal stumbling-block in the way of harmony was the trade union. Trade unionists might say that their purpose was merely to ensure that their members were paid at a true market value, but their existence and activities were a decisive refutation of the consensus assumption that the interests of Capital and Labour were identical. Certainly in the textile trade the unions of skilled workers were little more than friendly societies, and most textile workers were not unionised at all. There were strikes, but they were spasmodic and ephemeral, confined usually when they occurred to a single firm. But in other areas of male employment, union organisation was more general. Engineers, blacksmiths, stokers, moulders, grinders, boiler-makers, masons, masons' labourers, joiners and carpenters, cabinet makers, plasterers, painters, tailors, coopers, chimney sweeps, lithographers, bookbinders, and printers all had their trade unions in the town.[52] They suffered the limitations imposed by common law on 'conspiracy in restraint of trade', by statute law through the 1825 amendment to the repeal of the Combination Laws, and the legislation regulating master and servant contracts contained no idle threat of imprisonment for servants. Of their local activities and strength we have little firm information, since practically none of their earliest records have survived.

Thus it is very difficult to judge the practical strength of a specific union. Plasterers, typographers and others had precise rules about non-union labour. But what was important was the extent to which a union could enforce its rules and here our only sources of information are the minutes and other papers of the Typographical Society, a continuous record from the mid-sixties onward. The picture which emerges is one of constant struggle to enforce the rules rather than one of their automatic and successful employment in the face of every infringement. The Bradford Society was formed in 1824 and joined the National Typographical Association in 1844. This collapsed in 1848 and was replaced in the north of England by the Provincial Typographical Association, which Bradford joined in 1859. In these years it was little more than a loose federation of local societies which used the Association for advice, information and moral support but nothing else.

The Bradford Society, like the others, conducted its own negotiations with employers. In 1866, the society contained between sixty and seventy journeymen compositors and pressmen. Its organisation was not as yet tight. Meetings were not held to a regular timetable and several in the year were declared inquorate and not held. Nor was the craft completely unionised. About three-quarters of those eligible within the borough were members but some of them were lax in paying their dues and the loyalty of others was not likely to withstand much pressure. Printing shops on the outskirts of the town had not been penetrated by the union and so provided a reserve of non-union labour for Bradford employers. In any case, the labour market was over-stocked. Young journeymen just out of apprenticeship and older men unable to maintain speed of work could usually only get the casual labour available during the busy part of the week when the *Bradford Observer* and the *Bradford Review* were going to press (and, in later years, in the busy part of the year when Bradford firms produced Christmas cards). A number of Bradford employers, including George Harrison, one of the larger firms, simply refused to recognise the union which in general felt the need to move with great circumspection. During the wage negotiations of 1866, the first in thirty years, they took care to assure the employers that 'your employees do not wish to press their claims arrogantly, nor do they intend to use anything but moral suasion to attain their object'. They also accepted that a number of firms would negotiate directly with their own employees rather than the union. On the other hand they were persistent. They applied the rules against non-union firms when they could. Through their efforts, a number of firms accepted the rules about apprenticeship and the exclusion of female labour. They also validated the work rules of many of the individual chapels and so moved gradually towards a systematisation of work practice in the town.

The printers' union may not have been typical of Bradford unionism in these years – stronger, perhaps, because of the accepted principle of chapel organisation within the firm, weaker because its central organisation may have been less tightly knit than those of other similar bodies. But, led by Tetley Hustler, described by his contemporaries as 'a great man who knew all the ways of the employer', the Bradford Society was always in the struggle, asserting the rights which working men had in their jobs and defending them against those trivial assumptions about economic man which ignore essential relationships between men and their work.[53]

Trade unions always faced great hostility. Although the textile industry was free from serious conflict, the other main branches of Bradford manufacturing – building and iron manufacturing – had serious conflicts. The stonemasons established some control of the use of stone-cutting machinery, after a protracted strike. The ironworkers were less successful. In 1864 they started a branch of the National Association of Puddlers which had been founded in the previous year. Hostile managements declared a lock-out when it became clear that the union men in their employment could not be broken by the traditional tactics of 'presenting the document', being required, that is, to make an affirmation not to belong to a union. The lock-out dragged on through the summer, militancy increasing and blacklegs and their families being subjected to some rough treatment. It ended when the workers accepted a formula which read: 'we agree that neither party shall henceforth object to the employment of any workman on the grounds that he does or does not belong to a trade union'. The ironworkers had gained something – the right to belong to a union, a right which the law was supposed to allow them, in any case. Discrimination against known unionists continued.[54]

The temper of Bradford's industrial élite was demonstrated in 1866. The Magistrates Court, in what is known as the *Hornby* v. *Close* Case, refused to entertain an action brought by the Leeds branch of the Boiler Makers' Union for the recovery of their funds from their treasurer, W. Close. The Boiler Makers, like most large unions, had assumed that their funds were protected under a recent Friendly Societies Act. The magistrates rejected this view and threw out the case on the grounds that a trade union as a 'conspiracy in restraint of trade' could have no existence in law. At the beginning of 1867, the Queen's Bench upheld the judgment.[55]

Among Radical merchants and manufacturers there were those who could express some sympathy with the difficulties trade unions and their members faced. S. C. Kell, older brother of the perhaps better-known Robert, wrote that he could envisage circumstances in which a strike would be justified. But his tolerance, like that of most middle-class observers, did not often extend to contemporary events. Trade unions fulfilled their true purpose, he thought, when they confined themselves substantially to keeping their members informed of the state of trade, facilitating mobility in the labour market, and educating their members in the principles of 'political economy'. What he had to say about the activities of trade unions was mere abuse; 'the annals of Trades Unions and strikes do present a sad spectacle of ignorance, folly and selfishness'.

On the other hand, the trade unions were reaching a period of liberation and expansion. The tone of local branch activity was less deferential, more militant. In the late sixties Professor E. S. Beesly was developing ideas about a Labour-Trade Union party with its own programme of social and political reform and he had some powerful support among Bradford unionists. In 1868, some unionists started a Trades Council which broke down after several months on a political issue. It was revived as a permanent institution in 1872.[56]

And we need to recall that important sectors of activity

outside the factory or the workshop continued to resist the pressures of the consensus. There was a well-publicised move towards team games and organised competition, but traditional pursuits – unhappily in some cases – were still there. The rat pit had gone, but cock-fighting, dog-fighting and dog-racing were still staged in the obscurer parts of the borough. Commercial provision for working-class entertainment – the music hall, the dance hall and the fairs – survived the self-righteous eloquence of respectable journalists and conscientious parsons. Young factory workers from all over the borough intimidated 'their betters' every Sunday evening with a regular and crowded promenade in Kirkgate, the principal thoroughfare in the town.[57] The public house also continued to fulfil its role as a focus of social activity. The *Bradford Social Reformer* might fulminate:

In the first mile of Manchester Road ... there are twenty-six beershops, six public houses and two dram shops. On Saturday nights the road is thronged with men, women and children, bent on pleasure ... hundreds call at the public houses and beershops ... working men of every grade from navvies and labourers to skilled artisans and their wives ... the din is so great as to stun those who are not accustomed to John Bull's convivial way of spending Saturday night.[58]

But most working people were neither regular chapel-goers nor confirmed drunkards, and some of them enjoyed good music and good reading; above all, many of them enjoyed the good singing often available most easily in the public house. The fact was that the public house was the most convenient place for meeting friends and dealing with minor matters of business. It offered facilities for social organisation like the funeral brief which operated from the Farmyard Inn in Bowling Old Lane. This was an unofficial mutual insurance group among those who used the public house. 220 of them subscribed a shilling, usually about ten times a year, whenever one of their number died, and paid a burial grant of £7 to the bereaved. Anything left over at the end of the year went to pay for an annual dinner. The trade unions used public houses as their headquarters until nearly the end of the century, for their regular meetings, as unofficial labour exchanges and as hostels for unemployed members on the tramp.[59] There is no need to romanticise, landlords no doubt did well and drunkenness was a real problem, but there was nothing in Victorian working-class experience which quite replaced the public house. The life of the streets also had its working-class flavour. It was the area of common space, in the sense that the middle-class street never was, where the children played and the adults gossiped, and where, despite the rancours and petty superiorities a working-class street could nurture, the sense of separate community could be confirmed.

POLITICS IN THE YEARS OF CONSENSUS

The political life of Bradford in the fifties and sixties reflected faithfully both the development of mid-century stability and something of the tensions which lay beneath. That parliamentary elections were actually contested on only two occasions out of a possible six between 1851 and 1865 is an indication of the existence of a broad consensus, and an examination particularly of the election of 1859 reveals something of its structure and development. That three contested elections took place out of a possible three between 1867 and 1869 is some indication of the degree to which tensions had built up through the period. At the start the victory of the 'new men' was confirmed by the unopposed return of Robert Milligan in 1851 to the seat which had become vacant on Busfeild's death. Milligan had acquired the reputation of a Radical by his careful treatment of the Chartists in 1848, but he was not prepared to commit himself on questions of parliamentary reform beyond a general acceptance of the principle. He fulfilled the sternest Liberal expectations on the question of his commitment to free trade. The most significant aspect of his election, however, was that he was a textile man, a Dissenter, and one of the middle-class immigrants who had helped to make Bradford the centre of the worsted textile trade. Proposing him for nomination, Salt said: 'I am glad to think that we have the prospect of sending to Parliament a gentleman who is one of ourselves, one who knows the interests and trade of the borough and whose honourable career is a pledge that he will attend to our interests faithfully.'

This was the first time that the textile interest and Dissent had been directly represented. For the next thirty years, except for two occasions – Peronnet Thompson (1857 to 1859) and Edward Miall (1869 to 1874) – Bradford's two parliamentary seats were held by local men closely connected with the local economy, usually a near-Tory and a careful Radical who together spanned the area of consensus.

In the general election which came in 1852, the situation was confirmed. The two sitting members, Milligan and Peronnet Thompson, were nominated by a united election committee of Liberals and Radicals. Non-electors also gave vociferous support. The Tories put up H. W. Wickham who made a bid for Moderate Liberal support on the grounds that he was a good free trader and had supported the 1832 Reform Act willingly. He was attacked constantly as a providential turncoat, and most commentators were surprised when he came second in the poll with Thompson out. Thompson and the Liberals blamed the handful of Catholic voters who normally voted Liberal but had switched their votes to Wickham because Thompson had supported the Ecclesiastical Titles Bill, a measure intended to inhibit the organisational development of the Catholic Church in England. Liberals were very, very angry:

Before 3 o'clock Colonel Thompson was at the head of the poll and not any effort on the part of the Tories could have dislodged him had not the Liberal Catholic electors come down in a body and voted for the Tory candidate . . . it was only by the addition of a few headstrong inconsiderate Catholic votes and a few drunken butchers that anything like an equality of votes was obtained.[60]

Thompson had lost by six votes, and eighteen Catholic voters had decided the issue at the end of the day. But, of course, if Advanced Radicalism had had more support in the electorate, Thompson would not have been in this dilemma. The fact is that in Bradford, a town where Radicalism was vociferous, there was a strong Tory–Whig–Liberal Moderate element which discouraged the election of Advanced Radicals.

This election also underlined the speed with which Chartism

was losing ground. George White had made a characteristic speech demanding full household suffrage instead of the £5 suffrage which was being discussed. His amendment was defeated and David Lightowler proposed a very woolly declaration about the franchise and the secret ballot, which had been first put forward earlier at the meeting by W. E. Byles. On election day, several Chartists nominated Julian Harney, but Chartist support was so meagre that he came last on the show of hands.[61]

The 1857 election was interesting in that it confirmed Wickham's move from Tory to Moderate Liberal and that it allowed the Advanced Radicals to elect Colonel Thompson, but it was the election which came somewhat unexpectedly in 1859 which provided the best example of a 'consensus' election.[62] The campaign began in January when Disraeli, as spokesman for the Tory Government, presented a Bill for the reform of the parliamentary franchise to the House of Commons. Its purpose was entirely practical; it was intended to strengthen the Tory hold on the county constituencies which had been threatened continuously since 1832, in the Tory view, by the spread of urban-industrialism. It might also appear, by the way, to concede something to popular interest in the matter of parliamentary reform. Disraeli saw it as expressing the fundamental difference between Toryism and Liberal–Radicalism. Toryism wanted to adapt the traditional structure of English constitutional government – its basis in the communities of the shire and the borough – to the century's development. Liberal–Radicalism was more closely concerned with the democratic principle – the equality of men within the constitution, the principle which Disraeli referred to disparagingly as the assertion of numerical superiority. It was, in any case, an exaggeration of the political position on the ground. Few Liberals showed much interest in the question of manhood suffrage and many Radicals settled in practice for household suffrage. The Bill contained no proposals for the extension of the borough franchise. On the other hand, it proposed to abolish the right of a forty shilling freeholder to vote in a county constituency if his holding lay within the boundaries of a borough constituency – a right which had been preserved under the 1832 Reform Act. It suggested a re-definition of borough constituency boundaries so that they included the urbanised and industrialised sectors of county constituencies. The county franchise was to be broadened. Non-Tories, inside and outside Parliament, could find little to recommend the Bill, seeing it generally as a measure of disenfranchisement rather than of constitutional progress. The heterogeneous collection of independent Liberals, Peelites, Irish and Radicals which had sustained the Derby Government – a minority Tory administration – for twelve months, in order to keep 'that greatest of all charlatans',[63] Palmerston, out of office, withdrew their support, and the Government was defeated. During the course of the debate, Russell had presented a series of resolutions in which he envisaged a £6 rental franchise for the boroughs, although he did not respond to the demand for a secret ballot (for Radicals, a necessary complement to any extension of the franchise). The writ for a general election was promulgated in Bradford on 23 April and the election was held the following Saturday.

The electoral qualification was, of course, the one established by the 1832 Reform Act – the £10 householder franchise in the borough. In Bradford, 3,599 male adults were entitled to vote – a minority of the adult population which included at most about 300 men who could in some way be classified as working men, albeit relatively well-to-do. At the same time a good many non-electors, lower-middle and working-class, were politically active and articulate. They formed a body of public opinion which could not be ignored, for there were well-established techniques -- the shop boycott, for instance – for bringing pressure to bear.

The most remarkable feature of the election was that it was one of the most decorous of all those in which a contest took place under the provisions of the two Reform Acts of 1832 and 1867. The candidates were all local men, well respected and wealthy. They were an impressive trio – Titus Salt, the Radical candidate, textile manufacturer of international fame, acclaimed in Great Britain, France and the USA as the instigator of what seemed to many the most forward-looking social experiment of his day; H. W. Wickham, the candidate of the centre, Liberal-Conservative, a partner in the world-famous Low Moor Iron Works and the representative of their political interests at local and national level; and Alfred Harris, the right-wing Conservative-Tory candidate, one of the partners in the principal Bradford Bank – the Bradford Old Bank. In general, they conducted their campaigns, as Salt had said he hoped they would, on the basis of public principle rather than in terms of personality. In any case they had only a week for campaigning. Each of the candidates toured the wards, addressing meetings in a number of public houses and occasionally disposing of electioneering largesse. Both on nomination day and on election day, the streets around the Court House in Hall Ings (where the hustings stood) were crowded, but no violence was recorded anywhere. There had been some personalised comment during the run-up but by Victorian standards it was very mild. Harris's supporters issued a scurrilous poster which poked fun at Salt's pronounced Yorkshire accent, lack of political education and inability to speak in public:

Mr. Chairman and Gentlemen

The District I come from want Reform. (Hear, Hear) They sent me here. (Cheers from the Opposition, Cries of "that's positive".) It isn't a sham they want. They want a *real* Reform. They've wanted, it or I shouldn't have been sent as their Representative to this "Honourable 'Ouse". (Sickly Smile from Mr. Horsman.) There's no Delusion'll go *down* with them. (A Voice, that's the reason they sent you *up*.) I employ Three Thousand Hands. (Vehement cheering) I've allus stuck to them theire (sic) Principles. (Faint cries 'which?') The whole country wants reform. (Hear, Hear.) The Church wants Reforming. (Question, Question.) I hope that Church Rates will be done away with. (Tremendous Uproar, Question.) My Fellow-Townsmen elected me as a fit and proper Person to represent them in your "Honourable 'Ouse", and they want Reform. So do I. (Cheers from Opposition and Cries of no doubt from others.) We're growing in intelligence. (Hear, Hear.) I know the Working Classes. The Working Classes know me. There's a lot of education going on. (Hear, Hear.) It's coming Brighter every day. (Vehement Cheers.) I'm on the side of Liberty of Conscience. (Question.) Bradford's a great Manufakterring Place. (Hear, Hear.) We make Stuff for all the World. (Cries of Stuff.) (Here the Honourable Gentleman will be nearly wound up, but will proceed to read the notes he has had prepared by Mr. Glyde.) Hope – "Honourable 'Ouse" – such measures – satisfy country – consolidate institutions – (Vehement Cheers On the Honourable Gentleman's getting successfully over the quadrisyllables.) [Shakes his Fist at the Speaker, and shouts *Reform* and *nowt but Reform!* Loud Cheers from all Sides when it's over.]

John Bright will follow the Honourable Member out, and *entreat him to give* SILENT *Votes in future.*[64]

Accusations and counter-accusations of undue pressure on the more vulnerable electors bounced backwards and forwards. Harris complained that Salt's canvassers were leaning heavily on local shopkeepers. Edward, Salt's son, replied that they were merely inquiring which way the shopkeepers intended to vote. The *Bradford Review*, the Radical paper, weighed in with a *tu quoque*, claiming that cashiers and managers employed by wealthy Conservative employers were intimidating those under them by inquiring what their views were. Members of the Orange Order were instructed to vote for Harris and one at least was expelled for his support of Salt and Wickham. It was the normal by-play of nineteenth-century elections. The election ended as quietly as it had been conducted. The only celebration of victory was a dinner organised by Alfred Illingworth and Edward Kennion for Salt's supporters in West Ward. Salt sent his apologies and did not attend. Some years later, when he came out of semi-retirement to throw his prestige as the Grand Old Man of Bradford Liberalism behind the pro-Miall campaign, he remarked on the bitterness which had come to envelop local political life. When he had fought in 1859, he said, they had fought a fair fight, and at the end of it, had shaken hands like English gentlemen and gone their several ways.

This lack of bitter controversy sprang in the first place from the fact that none of the candidates was heavily committed to political life as such. They were all local men, sharing the common life of the town and district, part of the same social and economic élite which dominated local affairs. Salt and Wickham were both magistrates. Salt and Harris were prominent members of the Chamber of Commerce, and Harris, as one of the partners in the Bradford Old Bank, was banker to the Salt family. They were bound by ties of common interest and mutual respect and saw themselves as representing the local community which it was to no one's benefit to tear apart.

In this election, foreign affairs was something of an issue, and towards the end of the campaign assumed some importance. Attitudes towards continental Liberalism and Nationalism reflected party attitudes and philosophies and the Italian crisis of 1858–9 – a crisis of Liberal–Nationalism which led to war between France and Austria – focused attention on the problem. The candidates were asked where they stood. Salt was for neutrality and strong defences – a populist view which fitted a national mood eager to applaud the formation of the Volunteer Rifles as a territorial defence force and matched Salt's own support of the Rifles. Harris was more aggressive. He stood for neutrality, but neutrality only if honour and interest were not threatened. Like most Tories, he attached great importance to the position of Austria as a conservative force in Europe and he was deeply suspicious of the French dictator, Napoleon III. Wickham was non-committal. Nobody pursued the matter deeply.

Religious controversy did not have the importance it was to assume later. The *Bradford Review* threw into the ring as a possible Radical candidate the name of Edward Miall, secretary to the Liberation Society and chief propagandist in the cause of Church disestablishment. But Bradford was not yet ready for Miall and the religious controversy which would accompany him and the idea was quickly dropped. Harris was forced to make a stand during the campaign and to confirm that he was utterly opposed to the separation of Church and State. The only question raised consistently was the matter of the Maynooth grant. Wickham saw no reason to interfere with the arrangements made by Peel. Salt replied tactfully, bearing in mind perhaps the impact of the Catholic vote in the election of 1852, that while he disapproved both of the principle and the fact of state grants for educational establishments, he had not considered the Maynooth question particularly and could not isolate it for discussion.[65]

So, in this election, the central issue was parliamentary reform, to which all parties were prepared to concede something, however unwillingly. It had of course rarely been out of public consideration for long. In the mid-fifties prosperity, sometimes, and the Crimean War, more specifically, had deflected some interest. One of David Urquhart's Foreign Affairs committees had been established in Bradford and had made some inroads into the already diminishing Chartist support. But, there had been Reform Bills in 1852 and in 1854, and 1857 saw the issue squarely back in the forefront of political activity. The *Bradford Review* started publication in 1857 as the principal outlet for Radical opinion in Bradford, and wealthy Radicals like Salt began to promote a new reform campaign, to parallel the national agitation which was getting under way. The ailing Bradford Reform Registration Society was resuscitated under the chairmanship of Titus Salt. John Bright, who spearheaded a national agitation, was invited to address a town meeting and in January 1859 at St George's Hall gave a survey of what he regarded as an acceptable programme: a ratepayer (rather than a household) suffrage, the secret ballot and some redistribution of seats. While the last flickers of organised Chartism were dying down (the last recorded public meeting in Bradford was in August 1858), middle-class Liberal–Radicalism was carefully easing into a position where the lowest common denominator between working-class political aspirations and the social trepidations of the middle classes could be established. With confidence, middle-class Liberals claimed the support of their erstwhile opponents. 'If they [the Chartists] are wise and really desire reform, they will not let the present opportunity slip, but will join the middle classes with all their strength to gain a sound and practical measure', wrote the Editor of the *Bradford Review* in April 1859.

By the time the campaign opened, there were three concrete proposals in view: the Disraeli Bill, Russell's counter-proposal of the £6 rental, and the John Bright programme. None of them met the working-class demand for manhood suffrage, although by 1859 this claim was being advanced consistently not only by Chartists and ex-Chartists but by the new generation of spokesmen for the working classes. The three proposals remained the framework within which the candidates were to make their appeal.

Titus Salt, backed by wealthy Radicals like Milligan and Godwin, came forward as the Radical candidate. His immense prestige as one of the founders of contemporary Bradford and one of the three or four wealthiest men in the town gave enormous strength to his political claim. He claimed the support of all Liberals on the grounds of his long-standing and impeccable record on reform. His father, Daniel, had been christened on one occasion 'the father of reform in Bradford' and Salt himself claimed to have been active since a young man in every activity directed against established privilege. He was preferred on this occasion to the much more politically oriented General Perronet Thompson, who had won the nomination against Salt in the general election of 1857, and was thus a sitting member. Salt wanted the seat. He was in no real sense politically ambitious, but his social ambitions had taken flight. He had been using the insignia of the gentry for some years on his carriage, and as a business advertisement – the heraldic crest and motto which he officially adopted as baronet in 1869. He had taken his sons from Huddersfield College and sent them to the more prestigious Mill Hill. He was engaged in the construction of Saltaire. His desire was to create an industrial dynasty, and he needed the parliamentary seat to confirm his prestige. He had been nursing the seat for some time. He had just completed a stint as president of the Chamber of Commerce. As chairman of the Registration Society, he was one of the three Bradford delegates to the West Riding Reform Association which had emerged as a by-product of the Bright campaign. Moreover, he was determined to stand and had the backing of the wealthiest section of the Liberal Party. The non-electors led by George Fletcher, old companion in battle of George White, also accepted him. There were those who deplored Salt's lack of political education and were confident that only his money had carried the day. *Reynolds's Newspaper* dismissed him as a 'breeches pocket' candidate.[66] In an age when local politics and local candidates were self-financing, Salt's money was never likely to be ignored. But there is no doubt that he had the genuine respect of many, including working men; and for the 'respectable classes', his Radical candidature was an insurance that nothing rash or extravagant was likely to happen. The spectrum of his support epitomised the alliance of Labour with the Radical/Liberal middle class; at the one end, Robert Milligan, wealthy Dissenter and merchant, ex-Mayor and ex-MP; at the other end, George Fletcher, ex-woolcomber and ex-Chartist; and somewhere towards the middle, E. P. Duggan, second-generation Irish Catholic and one of the first Irish Catholics to sit on the City Council, and comfortably placed artisans and men in commercial work.[67] In the circumstances, Salt asked for a sort of 'doctor's madate'. He was prepared to take the best that could be obtained. He hoped eventually for household suffrage, at the very least: But he was prepared to take Russell's £6 rental proposal as a useful instalment and hoped that Russell could be converted quickly to the secret ballot.

Wickham had been elected as MP for Bradford in 1852 on the Conservative programme and in spite of his persistent silence in the House had continued to hold the seat. Gradually he had moved politically towards the centre and was now quite acceptable to the majority of Moderate Liberals as a running partner for Salt. His most intimate supporters, however, were to be found among old Whigs like Edward Hailstone and Samuel Cunliffe Lister (who plumped for him) and among Liberal Conservatives like Isaac Wright, Bradford-born woolstapler and Anglican, and Alderman Beaumont, the Methodist sanitary reformer and teetotaller. He had offended most of the old Conservatives by his move to the centre and Advanced Radicals had little time for him. E. Kennion, for instance, referred to him sarcastically on nomination day as 'at best, an improving man'. It was not precisely clear where he stood on the reform issue – he was ill during the campaign and avoided some of the questioning. His voting record in the Commons indicated that Russell's proposals satisfied him. He had voted against the Disraeli Bill and had abstained on an amendment to introduce the secret ballot. In the subsequent Parliament, he was a loyal supporter of the Palmerston Administration.[68]

Alfred Harris was brought out as the Conservative candidate because of Conservative annoyance with Wickham. 'He had stood', he said, 'because otherwise the old Conservative interest was not represented.' His position was very clear. He accepted Disraeli's analysis of the position and would have accepted Disraeli's Bill without question. He was utterly opposed to both household and manhood suffrage. 'Whether they sent him to Parliament or not, he would ever stand up against such democratic ideas. He did not call that reform, it was revolution.' He continued that he wanted to see 'those moderate reforms which all loyal subjects were anxious to see which would include the honest intelligent working men of the country . . . and he was sure that that class did not want to see themselves swamped by household or manhood suffrage'. Under pressure towards the end of the campaign he appeared to concede the £6 rental. At his last meeting, in Manningham, he was subjected to close interrogation and some heckling from a group of non-electors, which included Eli Carter, Malcolm Ross and William Lobley. He responded acidly: 'Let those who are dissatisfied with this country while making their fortunes, let them go to America. He would go for progressive reforms but not for a democracy.' (Still, the meeting, we are told, broke up with 'good humoured cheers and counter-cheers from the two parties'.[69]) Although he was the principal banker in the town, he was probably the least well-known of the candidates, for he was not a large employer of labour. He was closely involved with the affairs of the Anglican Church and was better known for his connexion with the Bradford Infirmary than for his concern for politics. His strongest and most influential supporters came from well-established landowning families, Anglicans and the professions.[70]

The *Bradford Review* had a joke at the expense of the candidates:

In pieces, three sorts command great attention in the market just now. The first is a new sort called Bradford Twills, quite plain and stout of texture. The materials of which they are made consist of a good many alpacas and lustre English wools of approved toughness and such as have given entire satisfaction. The next sort is called *Iron de Chenes*. They are a fancy article consisting of a figure on a sheeny ground, which show colours which vary according to the light in which they are held. As this class of goods has been some time in the market they have been extensively tried by the weavers and we regret to say that many of the colours have proved washy and fugitive. It is remarkable that several shades of orange have become clearer and more distinct by usage. Owing to this and the absence of superior styles, this class of goods has been extensively purchased, though we have not met any who particularly like them. [There is also] Harriana Cloth, which is expected to be a favourite among elderly ladies and we have heard of one or two heavy orders in the agricultural districts.[71]

The election was won by the Liberal–Radical interest, Wickham heading the poll:

Wickham: plumpers, 87; Wickham–Salt, 1385; Wickham–Harris, 604 *Total* 2076
Salt: plumpers, 266; Salt–Wickham, 1385; Salt–Harris, 76 *Total* 1727
Harris: plumpers, 549; Harris–Wickham, 604; Harris–Salt, 76 *Total* 1229

The result was something of a surprise to the Salt camp which had expected Salt to head the poll. If election expenses were any indication, Salt was very anxious to do well, for he spent substantially more than the other candidates, £1,238 against the £960 spent by Harris and the £660 spent by Wickham.[72] It was suggested that Salt's failure to head the poll was due to the advice given to his supporters not to plump for him but to split with Wickham in order to keep Harris out of second place. In fact, there seems no doubt that the figures reflected the true feelings of the electorate. Bradford voters were happy with the consensus indicated in the Salt–Wickham–Harris splits.

The election has been considered as little more than an exercise in marking time, a point of view borne out by the fate of the Russell Bill which was allowed to die quietly amid general apathy. There can be no doubt that it was a victory for moderation. In the country the Tory vote went up and in Bradford it was after all a very moderate Radicalism which took a seat. Yet, in Bradford there was more in it than might appear at first sight. There were those who claimed Salt's victory as part of a general Nonconformist–Dissenter breakthrough in the West Riding, for five of the fifteen elected were non-Anglicans. The election confirmed the authority of the élite in the new industrial community, an authority first vindicated by the election of Robert Milligan in 1851. The candidates in this election represented, together, almost all the important resources of wealth of the community – textiles, iron manufacturing and banking. Thus, between them, they drew together all the principal strands of social and economic authority in the town, and stood for the dominant group operating within the framework of what were now commonly accepted institutions of local control.

One of the most important aspects of the election was the confirmation it gave that the alliance between Labour and the Radical Liberals had begun to work. As we have seen, after the dramatic confrontations of the 1840s, a good many middle-class employers developed an acute sense of the need for 'harmony between capital and labour'. Most of them also had an acute distaste for trade unions, especially if they threatened to touch the ordinary run of factory worker. Harmony, however, demanded concession; in practice, recognition that working-class aspirations as embodied in the Charter were important. Even if Chartism was dying, there had to be indications of progress towards the fulfilment of Chartist hopes. Here the concept of 'responsible citizenship', which was used to justify the emancipation of middle-class Dissent, could be adapted to the conciliation of the working class, or that part of it, at least, which it was thought important to conciliate. Thus Liberalism in the 1859 election moved cautiously towards the theme of household suffrage, the lowest common denominator which could guarantee working-class support and which by imposing a concept of 'responsibility and respectability' at the same time offered a safeguard against what seemed to many dangerous transfers of power. Working-class acceptance of a middle-class programme had to be explained in terms of acceptance of the consensus, for it involved the surrender of a basic principle of working-class politics – the right to manhood suffrage. It may well be that the battle for manhood suffrage was fought more strenuously than the local press, for instance, usually suggests, and in one sense working men settled for the best bargain they could get. However, the view persisted that the vote was something which attached to men whose acceptance of responsibility could be judged by their links with property.[73]

The Bradford MPs elected in the 1850s made little impression on the House of Commons, beyond fairly regular appearance in the division lobbies. None of them except Thompson intervened in a debate; they spoke only to fulfil the obligatory duties of presenting petitions. Their voting record was also fairly predictable. Salt voted on all the important stages of the Church Rates Abolition Bill, although, strangely for a man who had been so vociferous in the early days of that battle, he did not vote on the Third Reading. He voted on all the stages of Gladstone's Paper Duties Bill and the Customs Bill needed to implement the provisions of Cobden's French Treaty. He was in his place for the debates and votes on Russell's Representation of the People Bill. In fact, it looks as if he made a special trip to London to be present at the last of these he attended. It took place in August 1860 and was one of the two occasions when he voted from mid-July to the end of the session, for he was obviously withdrawing from parliamentary duty. His voting record in general displayed a common sense and tolerance, which occasionally took him into the lobby against orthodox Radical opinion, as, for instance, when he voted alongside diehard county squires like Edward Filmer to strengthen the Bleaching and Dyeworks Factory Bill. He also voted to keep income tax up and indirect taxation down, and supported the granting of a capital sum to the National Gallery for the purchase of pictures. He was opposed to flogging in the Navy. He was not against an occasional tactical abstention. He did not vote on a proposal to stop the grant to the Maynooth Catholic Seminary and so evaded this as he had in the election and for the same reason presumably: he did not wish to ruffle any Irish tempers.[74]

Of the men elected in these years, Salt's tenure was the shortest. Just before the start of the session in 1861, he announced that he would have to retire; he could not adapt to the demands of parliamentary life and his health was suffering. In his place a very different man was returned. This was W. E. Forster – able, energetic in many good causes and a fine speaker with the unifying characteristic of high ambition.[75] Forster was to become one of the outstanding politicians of the next twenty years, holding office in each of the Gladstone administrations of these decades. Although he claimed the designation of Radical and held the Bradford seat as the representative of the Left during the years that Wickham sat as a Moderate Liberal, he was never a conventional Radical. He was a Quaker who had married away from the sect and was the brother-in-law of Matthew Arnold, the author of *Culture and Anarchy*, whose view of men like most of Forster's Liberal business and political associates in Bradford was scathingly unflattering. He wanted a national system of education, and thought that the Church of England was the most suitable agency through which to organise it. He was no temperance man. He did not accept either of the two principles which had become articles of faith with many Bradford Radicals. Despite his early flirtation with Bradford Chartists, he rejected manhood suffrage. In one speech he explained carefully that few young men were fit to exercise the vote owing to their lack of education and went on to say that the objective of parliamentary reform was to split the 'respectable' from the 'dangerous' working classes by giving the vote to the better-off among the workers.[76] Nor did he support the cause of the disestablishment of the established Anglican Church. In time his political stance was to cause deep trouble in Bradford, and already in 1862 some Radicals like Kennion were beginning to reserve their judgement. For the most part, through the sixties Liberals and Radicals accepted him as standing for much of the best of contemporary Liberal — Radicalism. Conservatives, also, aware of the unity of Liberal and Radical on this score and perhaps recognising that he offered them unexpected benefits across the political boundary, did not challenge him. The *Bradford Observer*, having thanked Salt profusely for his services in the previous week's issue, greeted Forster's nomination in terms which implied sharp criticism of Salt's parliamentary performance.

Our future members should be men of proper qualifications and suitable training . . . wool spinning and iron smelting are not the best processes for educating statesmen . . . a seat in the House of Commons is not to be regarded as the fitting reward to a citizen that has been fortunate or successful in trade and is a large employer of labour. The sphere of such a one is indeed both honourable and highly important; and, verily, hath his reward in wealth – in respect, obedience, troops of friends. But we want a member of parliament for service and not for honours; for worth and not for ornament. . . For statesmanship we want men of wider views than a factory can produce; of broader and deeper insight into human wants and human rights than a mere business training can furnish.[77]

Both in 1861 and again in the general election of 1865 Forster was returned unopposed, and he did not have to fight the seat until the general election of 1868.

Nevertheless, political developments were such – despite the relative calm of the political scene – that there were to be three acrimonious elections between 1867 and 1868. The religious controversy which separated Anglican and Dissenter recovered in the sixties much of the bitterness it had had in the thirties and forties. This was partly due to the success as a pressure group of the Liberation Society which helped to harness to a common programme the various Nonconformist opponents of the Anglican Church, and thus helped to fashion the policies of the Liberal Party to which they belonged. It was the agitation mounted by the Society which stopped the proposals for a religious census in 1861; it made the abolition of church rates and the disestablishment of the Irish Church into important parliamentary questions. It did not represent the whole of Nonconformist opinion, and was never likely to come within sight of its central objective – disestablishment of the Anglican Church – but it was indefatigable in the pursuit of religious freedom, and focused opinion effectively among important minorities.[78]

In Bradford, its adherents seem to have been drawn principally but not exclusively from old Dissent. Elias Thomas was perhaps a typical supporter. He was of the comfortable but not wealthy middle classes, working as wool buyer for the Milligan and Forbes organisation. He was a director of the Yorkshire Investment and American Mortgage Company and of the Third Equitable Building Society. For some years he was secretary to the Bradford Sunday School Union and a member of the Home Mission and Lay Preachers' Association. He was also secretary to the Bradford Branch of the Liberation Society. There were others in humbler circumstances – Councillor Haley and Ben Wainwright, for instance. The Society's strength in Bradford, however, lay in the fact that, as in the West Riding generally, its supporters included some of the wealthiest and most influencial members of the community. Thus Titus Salt senior and Titus junior were among its most powerful supporters and contributed regularly and lavishly to its funds. The Kells and Illingworths were among its members; Alfred Illingworth in fact became the national treasurer of the movement.[79]

But this was not the only influence at work. The activities of the Church Building Society and the comparable efforts of Dissenters and Nonconformists were an indication both of positive commitment and of the rivalry which existed. The census of 1851 and other inquiries had clearly established the numerical weakness of the Anglicans in Bradford. The position was much the same in 1881 when the *Bradford Observer* noted:

If thoughtful Christians of the Reformation period had been told that for a population of nearly 200,000, the Church would provide 20,000 sittings and other religious bodies 60,000, they would perhaps have come to the conclusion that a really national establishment of religion was either impossible or must be conducted on very different principles.

It was this sort of threat that the Anglicans had been determined to resist; and Dissenters had not been reluctant to fight. A survey of 1872 showed that ten Anglican churches had been built since 1851. In the same time there had been twelve Congregational and Baptist and thirteen Methodist chapels erected. It is a reasonable assumption that the majority of Bradford's voting population, in one way or another, were caught up in this antagonism.[80]

Alongside the religious controversies, the agitation about parliamentary reform was also deepening. To some extent the two overlapped, for Nonconformists like Edward Miall saw religious equality and political equality as parts of the complete picture of the citizen, and many others saw, at least, that working men could provide welcome allies in the battle for religious equality. However, the press had noted, in the early years of the decade – and perhaps with some satisfaction, for Byles was losing a good deal of his Radical zeal as he grew older

– a good deal of apathy about political reform. James Wilkinson, a working man, was reported as complaining that

> when he contemplated the apathy of the class to which he belonged
> . . . he felt profoundly disgusted. If they did not look after themselves
> they might depend upon it no other class would. When they saw the
> interest taken in sporting matters and the apathy in political matters,
> he sometimes thought that disgrace and infamy ought to be heaped
> upon them.[81]

Yet, there was always some activity ready to burst into full-scale agitation when events offered the necessary encouragement. During the course of the debates around the Russell proposals in 1860–1, the Working Men's Reform Committee became the Bradford Political Union, through the addition of a number of middle-class members and/or subscribers. The main body remained working-class and included most of the best-publicised of them, W. H. Arnold, Benjamin Wainwright and Eli Carter, a few ex-Chartists like Willie Angus, Abraham Sharp and Henry Hodgson, and one or two with Chartist connexions like Cornelius Jefferson, the son of the great but aging Isaac. There were about twenty middle-class members, most of whom held positions which ensured that they could control the Union's affairs, who paid higher subscriptions and made special contributions ranging from £50 to £10. They included R. and S. C. Kell, J. V. Godwin, J. Law, H. Brown, S. Smith, A. Illingworth, W. Cannon, C. Turner, Joseph Farrar, and John Priestman. In addition, Titus Salt, Miles Illingworth, Nathaniel Briggs and W. D. Hertz gave subscriptions of £50 each. The one surviving list gives the names of 148 paid-up members. The union held a number of quiet but well-attended meetings between 1862 and 1864, though it was not until 1864 that they were able to boast of a meeting in St George's Hall, where Henry Vincent spoke to an audience of over 3,000.[82]

The meeting was held to promote interest in the reform proposals put forward by Edward Baines in 1864. These were based on a £6 rental suffrage and were unashamedly directed at 'the readers, thinkers, members of Mechanics Institutes, teachers in Sunday Schools and enrolled in clubs of mutual insurance or as depositors in Savings Banks'. Working class interest in reform had also been stimulated by the deep impression that foreign affairs had made during the preceding three or four years. Garibaldi in Italy, the American Civil War and the emancipation of the slaves, and the uprising in Poland had strengthened convictions about democracy. The trade unions – increasingly active – were beginning to take the immediate interest in political reform which led to the formation of the Reform League in the following year. In Bradford, working men showed in this year that they had an independent position to maintain and so came once again into the front line of the battle, as they had done in 1848 and were to do later in 1891. Henry Ripley, chairman of the Exchange Company, invited Lord Palmerston, the Prime Minister, to lay the foundation stone of the new Wool Exchange which was to be built in Market Street. It was an insult to working-class opinion, for Palmerston was widely regarded as the principal barrier to further parliamentary reform, and very quickly a Working Man's Committee was got together to organise an appropriate protest.

On the eve of the ceremony, which was to take place on 9 August, the committee presented a protest to Henry Ripley for handing over to Palmerston:

We, the unenfranchised working men of Bradford, in public meeting assembled, desire to welcome you to the town of Bradford as an aged nobleman and a stranger, but we deeply regret that in approaching your lordship we cannot accord you that cordial greeting which is our wont to do to all distinguished personages who visit our busy town.

Ripley refused to accept it and it was posted up in the town along with a dramatically coloured magenta poster asking all working men who attended the ceremony or watched the procession to do so only in order to 'maintain a dignified and significant silence.' Newspapers naturally gave conflicting reports of what in fact happened. The *Bradford Observer* concentrated on reporting the acclamations offered by other sections of society who did not want to be taken for vulgar working-class people.

Jostling and cheering in the streets was reinforced by the ladies and gentlemen from warehouse windows waving handkerchieves as if nothing could ever again reduce them to decent sober-ness. One of the stoppages took place in Peel Place and as the carriages halted, Lord Palmerston stood up, and amid renewed cheering, – bowed acknowledgements for his hearty reception.

The *Bradford Review* and *Reynolds's Newspaper* were more certain that Palmerston had had a very mixed reception, and perhaps most significant was the remark which Francis Crossley made at the dinner held in the evening. To the annoyance of a number of Liberals, he 'welcomed Palmerston but reminded the audience of the uneasy response of the working classes' and pointed out that if they received Palmerston with respect they had not forgotten that they wanted the vote. The working men in the crowds had obviously made their point. Some had turned their backs on the procession, and a good many had kept silent. The *Bradford Observer* carried a soporific leader:

How industry and commerce have bounded onwards since that time! till now, instead of Plug Riots – as twenty-two years ago, and instead of the agitation and consequent irritation and antagonism of classes – instead, moreover, of a deficient revenue, we have plenty of work and good wages, cheap bread, rather too little politics, some think, and a revenue increasing at the rate of a million a year . . . in this material prosperity we have reason to be thankful, but its value is enhanced by the good understanding which prevails among the various classes by whom it is produced and among whom it is shared.

It concluded that Palmerston was not really to blame for delays in parliamentary reform: one Bill at least had been defeated by the apathy of all Liberals – MPs and constituents; if Palmerston had not broken his heart over the failure of that Bill, neither had the classes which would have been enfranchised. National newspapers commented on Palmerston's discomfiture and suggested that he had enjoyed his visit to Saltaire more than his visit to Bradford.[83]

The countrywide agitation gathered momentum from 1864 onwards and its effects were as clear in Bradford as elsewhere. The Palmerston visit, which had had repercussions far beyond Bradford, in Bradford itself stung the reform agitation into life; it was to be pursued with great vigour (despite the accusations of working-class apathy made by the *Observer*) until the Disraeli

Bill which conceded the franchise to urban male householders became law in 1867. The first organisational developments came from the middle-class Radicals who had taken over from the old guard of Salt, Milligan and Forbes. They believed in the validity of parliamentary reform but they remained anxious about the independent working-class activity which the Palmerston incident, and developments in the trade-union world, suggested. In December 1864 a 'Grand Reform Demonstration' was held at St George's Hall. The *Daily Telegraph* reported it as the 'first signal of the forth-coming political campaign' for, designed as a purely local event, it had become a massive West Riding demonstration. Special trains brought supporters from all the neighbouring towns and villages to hear speeches by the leading local reformers, Francis Crossley, James Stansfield, Edward Baines, Kell and Illingworth.[84] It was organised by the 'friends of the National Reform Union'. This was the nucleus of the Bradford branch of the Union – a new Manchester-centred reform association. With G. Wilson as president it had picked up some of the old threads of the Anti-Corn Law League organisation, and made its primary appeal to the sort of men who had supported the anti-corn law agitation. But it was never exclusively middle-class. In Bradford it quickly extended its social range by incorporating the Bradford Political Union. Yet although its members were now drawn principally from the lower middle and 'respectable' working classes, it was never 'popular' in its appeal; at its strongest it had about 350 members, and control remained in the hands of the middle-class radicals. Though the committee included working men, the principal offices were held by the middle-class coterie – who also contributed most of the money. In 1865, 16 well-to-do Radicals, including Salt, together gave £540 to the Union to get it started. The normal subscription of ordinary members was one shilling, though several paid half a crown.[85]

The Reform Union helped to focus public opinion, but its function was not only to ensure that there would be a reform programme; it had also to impose a strong middle-class gloss on it. During the election of 1865, which followed several months after the death of Palmerston, Bradford middle-class Radicals made it clear that working-class initiatives were not welcomed.

The managers of the Liberal interest wanted to maintain the facade of Liberal unity, and to avoid a conflict with a local Conservatism which was beginning to develop in the shadow of the local branch of the Church Defence Association. It therefore proposed to run the sitting members, Wickham and Forster. Working-class Radicals were dissatisfied; Forster was quite moderate enough on the reform issue for their taste and Wickham had never convinced them that he was even a Liberal. In the hope of getting a more convincing reformer in the Commons, the old Chartist, Abraham Sharp, proposed Robert Kell as running mate for Forster and Wainwright put forward the name of Miall. Illingworth, good middle-class Radical and rabid anti-establishment man that he was, quickly put them in their place. Speaking to Wainwright's suggestion, he said that although Mr Miall was a right and proper person to represent Bradford, he did not think that anything would persuade him to split Bradford's Liberals. Forster and Wickham were returned.[86]

At the same time the middle-class Radicals accepted the emergence of a separate working-class organisation, the National Reform League. It had been founded in February 1865, with Edward Beales, a lawyer, as president and George Howell, a bricklayer by trade, as secretary. Its programme was manhood suffrage and the secret ballot. Thus it asserted the intrinsic dignity and worth of working men as individuals and as members of a class and rejected the middle-class view of reform as a concession made to individuals who had proved, in terms laid down by their 'betters', their ability to exercise the right of citizenship. Abraham Wildman, getting on in years now, found time and wit to greet its foundation with a verse:

Come, move along and let us pass,
You've long time been together.
You've branded us a rabble mass,
Bound minds and hands together.

We want not wealth by others gained;
We seek not titles nor applause.
But here we take our holy stand
To vote for those who make our laws.[87]

1. Portrait of Sir Titus Salt in old age

3. The Wool Exchange (c. 1870): Market Street and the bank area just being developed

4. Workmen's cottages, Saltaire, built in 1854

5. Workmen's cottages (back view)

6. Overlookers' houses, Saltaire, built in 1868

7. Executives' houses, Saltaire

8. The Institute, Victoria Road, Saltaire

9. Almshouses, Victoria Road, Saltaire

10. The Mill (viewed from the river bank)

11. The Congregational Church (viewed from the canal)

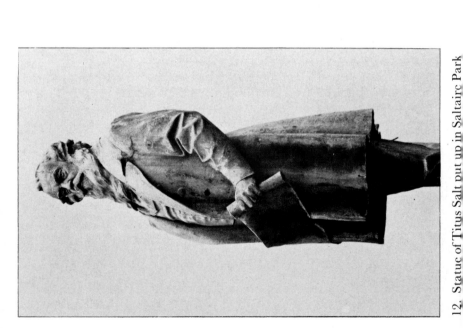

12. Statue of Titus Salt put up in Saltaire Park

13. Dinner served to the Prince and Princess of

Milner Field.

DINER DU 22 JUIN, 1882.

POTAGES.

Tortue Claire.   Purée d'Asperges, Princesse.

POISSONS.

Filets de Truite, Sauce Génevoise.
Turbot, Sauces Homard et Ravigotte.

ENTRÉES.

Croustades à la Victoria.   Ris d'Agneau à la St. Cloud.

RELEVÉS.

Rond de Bœuf à l'Anglaise.
Selle de Mouton rôtie.
Poulardes aux Nouilles.   Jambon, Sauce Madère.

RÔTS.

Paonnes et Canetons.
Pois à la Française.

Salade Russe.

ENTREMETS.

Gâteaux à la Montmorency.
Mousses glacées à la Cardinal.

RELEVÉS DE RÔTS.

Beignets à l'Allemande.
Terrine de Foie Gras à l'Aspic.

GLACES DE DESSERT.

Millefruits.

HENNINGHAM & HOLLIS, 5, MOUNT ST. W.

The League could not, however, avoid the embrace of middle-class Radicalism – financial constraints, if nothing else, compelled it to accept the assistance of men like Samuel Morley in Nottingham, and Kell, Illingworth and Titus Salt in Bradford, who, whatever opinions they occasionally expressed, were unlikely in practice to take their associates beyond household suffrage. Nevertheless, through 1866 and 1867, until the passing of Disraeli's Reform Bill, it exercised a powerful influence on events, for the rapid mobilisation of working-class opinion under its banner gave greater point to the ever-present memories of Chartism and the tacit threat of revolutionary activity, and stirred politicians to action.

The Bradford branch of the Reform League was started in September 1866. Robert Kell testified to the interest and goodwill of Union members by his presence at the inaugural meeting. Ernest Jones, representing the parent organisation, was received with deafening cheers. Edwin Smith confirmed for both the audience and the readers of the *Bradford Observer* that the Chartist tradition still lived:

Mr. Edwin Smith . . . expressed himself quite in raptures at the meeting, which betokened the revival of the old Chartist cause . . . he was the last secretary of the old defunct Chartist Association in the district, and possessed the empty money box, with three locks, on which he had a lien for money owing to him by the Society; but as another society was now established, he would gladly make them a present of the box. He added that he had been twice armed for the Charter, and now, with Mr. Jones he said, for the third time, they would have it.[88]

The branch recruited much more widely than the Reform Union had been able to do, for manhood suffrage was a much more compelling slogan than household or rental-based suffrage. Several weeks after its foundation the Great Horton Political Union, which had always preserved a strong Chartist tradition, joined, bringing with it the veteran moral-force man and founder member of the old United Reform Association, John Jackson. By the end of the year there were 1,000 members, by mid-1867, 2,500, and it had become one of the most influential branches in the country, a focus of political activism throughout the worsted textile area of the West Riding.

215

Some of its most important members held common membership of the Union and the League. In so far as they contributed to the funds of both, the Kells, Godwin, Illingworth and Salt could be taken as members of both organisations. Men like Ross, Wainwright, Lobley, Sharp, Angus and Arnold were more specifically so, Sharp in fact becoming president of the League, Lobley, treasurer and Arnold secretary. It was not surprising, therefore, that there was an unusual degree of joint activity between the two organisations in Bradford, on which the *Bradford Review* commented: 'the Reform Union and the Reform League are not trying to rival each other but assist each other in carrying out the good work'. The fact is that the threats embodied in the manhood suffrage programme were far from immediate. The working-class movement, unlike Chartism, was not a movement of social reform. It was a movement to gain legal and political rights within a society whose social framework most of its members accepted, and which they had no inclination to upset by violent action. For the Leaguers, manhood suffrage was not precisely the universal suffrage of the Chartists. It was a franchise for men who were properly 'residential and registered', a reservation which, as Karl Marx suspected, hinted at their aversion from what Forster had called the 'dangerous classes' – the mass of the labouring poor. Most of them would have endorsed Ross's letter to the *Bradford Observer*, even if they found him generally far too conciliatory:

The manhood suffrage movement . . . need not disturb the weak nerves of those who tremble at the bare idea of a physical force revolution. There will be nothing of the kind this time, that is most certain. The voice of the people will do all the work that is wanted, spoken as it is in a tone of high, deliberative authority.

In practice, Bradford working-class reformers accepted the gradualism of the middle-class programme; thus, early in 1866, they had agreed to support the Bill brought forward by Lord Russell for a £7 franchise in the towns, as a useful instalment. At the same time, men like Illingworth and Kell were unlikely to forget the latent threat of an independent working-class movement, particularly strong in Bradford as a result of

Beesly's activities. They were also very conscious that enfranchised working men could provide useful allies in the battle against Anglicanism. Considerations of this sort reinforced political conviction and led them towards occasional recognition of the possibilities of manhood suffrage and free and open acceptance of household suffrage.

The most dramatic contribution which the Reform League made to the campaign was the organisation of two spectacular demonstrations on Woodhouse Moor in Leeds, one in October 1866 and the other in April 1867. They were joint ventures with the Leeds reformers, organised on behalf of the whole of the West Riding reform movement. They were supported faithfully by the Reform Union, which on the first occasion passed a resolution affirming its willingness to collaborate and on the second occasion formed part of a joint sub-committee with the League to manage the demonstration for the Bradford district. They provided the occasion for the expression of a great deal of good will. Robert Kell thought that 'men and masters were in one boat in Bradford, and there was no fear of them falling out, whether the masters were Whig, Tory or Radical, on such an occasion as the present'. Godwin thought that

the working men were adopting a respectful, conciliatory, and constitutional course in the matter and one to which their employers could undoubtedly respond in a like spirit. The town of Bradford was indeed highly distinguished for the good feeling existing between the two classes – a feeling that enabled them to work together as they often did for the same great object.

And Councillor Haley said that 'he did not fear them [the working classes] . . . while desirous of gaining their rights they would know how to respect the rights of others'. The Midland Railway reminded them all that there was opposition as well as support, when it refused to run special day trips from Bradford to Leeds, and James King reminded the members of the Union that not all working men were as tolerant of their views as the Wainwrights and the Rosses. Though he supported the £7 franchise which Russell's Bill envisaged, he did so because he hoped that sooner or later 'the working men of Bradford would be able to "lick" all comers, and would not have to go down on their knees to the Whigs to ask them to accept their candidate, as they had in the case of General Thompson whom they had lost after all'.[89]

But there was no serious disruption of harmony. In 1866, at a preliminary meeting before the demonstration of that year, a resolution complaining that Russell's Bill did not go far enough took two votes – the proposer and the seconder. By 1867, the organised working-class movements were deeply involved, and friendly societies, trade unions, and co-operative societies decked out in the colourful regalia of their organisations all took part in the great procession from Bradford to Leeds for the second demonstration. Robert Kell, as President of the joint committee, signed the order for the procession along with W. H. Arnold, the secretary. William Byles, an opponent of manhood suffrage and the secret ballot, had had to admit in 1866 that he had been impressed both by the impeccable organisation of the October demonstration and by its size – the large number of men who had been prepared to sacrifice a day's pay and had walked to Leeds and back to show what they thought. He concluded: 'We had better come to a fair and moderate measure of Reform to the present agitation than thus conjure up an agitation which a moderate measure may not pacify.'[90]

By the beginning of 1867 Radical opinion had finally fastened on to household suffrage untrammelled by any modifications of levels of rent, rates or status, as the most generally acceptable solution. The Bill which Disraeli had introduced after the Derby Tory Administration had replaced that of Russell and Gladstone, contained provisions for a number of such 'fancy franchises' and it was in opposition to this Bill that the Woodhouse Moor demonstration of 1867 was called. It was one of the most important of a series of events which had taken place throughout the country (and which included the use by reform demonstrators of Hyde Park in defiance of the law) which persuaded Disraeli and others to accept the principle of household suffrage at least as a voting qualification in the borough constituencies. It may well be that the MPs who really desired change in the franchise were in a minority. But Disraeli was determined to have a Reform Bill, and it was clear that anything less than household suffrage would not satisfy a well-prepared working class in the towns. The combined voting strength of Gladstonian Liberal and Disraelian Tory saw the measure through the House.

Before the new Act could be brought into operation, Wickham died and a by-election had to be fought under the old provisions. The Advanced Liberals (as the Radicals were now in the habit of calling themselves) decided to bring forward Edward Miall, for they thought the time right to put Bradford in the forefront of the disestablishment battle by returning the principal figure in the Liberation Society. Salt telegraphed his support from Paris, where he was a guest of the French Government at the International Industrial Exhibition. Matthew W. Thompson came out as the representative of the Whig–Moderate Liberal interest. He had never been particularly active in Bradford politics and, like Harris, was better known for his support of the Anglican Church. He was also the chief brewer in the town and a director of the Midland Railway. He was supported by a heterogeneous collection of voters – Tories, Anglicans, Methodists who disliked Miall, Moderate Liberals and old Whigs and naturally other brewers, publicans and many others who disliked the idea of anti-drink legislation. Unlike the Salt election, this one had its share of violence. Election day itself was marked by a series of more or less pitched battles, the ground before the hustings presenting, said the *Observer*, 'such a scene [as] would have discredited the rottenest borough before the old Reform Bill'. Thompson won by a margin of 403 votes.[91]

Thompson's opponents had no difficulty in condemning the victory as the victory of the public house and the drinker, ignoring the views of those who saw the vote for Thompson as a vote against the sanctimonious kill-joy party. Bradford had never had a natural Radical majority on the 1832 electoral roll. As much as anything the Moderate–Radical alliance had guaranteed the Radical seat. Among manufacturers, for instance, Radicals were in a minority – many, like the Wauds and the Drummonds, preferred the Moderate ticket. A more clearly defined Conservatism was also beginning to take shape as men like Henry Mitchell, a leading textile merchant and years later the first freeman of the City of Bradford, began to emerge into public life. During the years of consensus the commercial and professional element which tended towards Conservatism had increased; and by the late sixties there were several very rich Conservatives – most notably Francis Sharp-Powell, a Lancashire landowner who had inherited the Sharp estate in Bradford – in and about the town, whose wealth allowed them to challenge the fortunes of the great Dissenter manufacturers. Paradoxically, Conservatism was also to benefit from the hostility which the idea of household suffrage ignited, for in many quarters it remained at best a 'leap in the dark' and at worst the harbinger of social revolution. Moreover, though it can be argued that Dissent was at its strongest in Bradford in the sixties, this did not give it an automatic majority over Anglican and Methodist. It is clear that there were the beginnings of a firmer polarisation of political forces, shown by the more tightly organised political life which was just about to begin.

In 1866 a Conservative Working Man's Association was begun. In the following year the Conservative Association started.[92] It had twenty members then, but within the next two or three years was to grow to over 2,000. The Liberals, starting from a better organised base, were more thorough. They recognised very quickly the value that an organisation based on the wards and spread throughout the town would have in dealing with the conditions under which elections would now be fought. In January 1868 a conference of all Liberals in the town was convened.[93] Representatives, elected on a ward basis, attended from all three Liberal organisations – the moderate Registration Society, the Reform Union and the Reform League. Robert Kell presided, although Wallbank, the President of the League, claimed the honour of originating the idea and moderate Liberal and advanced Liberal agreed in effect to form a single party pledged to support the same candidates and the same programme. There were some defections. S. C. Lister's withdrawal from Liberalism seems to date from this meeting and the German immigrant, Charles Semon, Mayor in 1864 and a good Liberal, spoke for several of his compatriots when he said that he could not conscientiously belong to the new society and refused to let his name go forward as a committee member. The new body superseded the old Registration Society and the Reform Union also disbanded in its favour. The League gradually declined and working men in their new role as voters accepted the idea of political reform through the programmes of the existing parties. In Bradford, therefore, Beesly's appeal for an independent working-class/ trade-union party was rejected and most of the League members joined the new Liberal Electoral Association. At the national level, the difficulties of the League became more and more acute. Howell was forced into solicitations for funds which became ever harder to raise. He met Isaac Holden in the lobby of the House of Commons and reminded him that his subscription was overdue. Holden paid for half a year. He wrote to the Bradford manufacturers who had supported him in the previous year and later visited the town. Their response was discouraging; even Salt did not offer any money when Howell saw him, although he relented after another personal appeal by letter and sent £100. The League was finally disbanded both nationally and locally in January 1869.[94]

The long struggle for political emancipation which Bradford men had fought along with others with such determination came so far to this. Some working men had obtained new status as members of the political nation and it was impossible for either party to ignore for long their claims to some sort of more direct representation. This was progress, but progress enveloped within the conventional social framework of the time. It ensured that – as Tawney would have said – the British working man would enter the constitutional process with cap in hand. In Bradford, Thompson's victory had emphasised the importance to Liberals of a Liberal–Labour alliance, and – though it had existed in practice for years – in 1868 a formal treaty of alliance was signed. The new Liberal Electoral Association had an executive committee of twenty-four. Only four of them were working men, though the electorate was now predominantly working-class. There were few if any revolutionaries about in these years. Yet deference was subsumed in the process at a variety of different levels and in different ways. Bradford does not seem in these years to have had men whose speeches had the ironic bite of Thomas Crowther's, a tape sizer of Todmorden, who, drawing an analogy between the Poor Law system and the way in which the reform issue had been obstructed, remarked: 'I have often noticed that if a man is poor he is expected to be perfect, and when some flaw or infirmity is found in his character, it is regarded as a sufficient reason for letting him starve.'[95] But Bradford men had shown that they could pursue an independent course both in the political and in the industrial world, defending old rights, entering new areas of activity and ready to make use of the new parliamentary weapon in the battle. There was no dramatic change in the climate of events as there had been in 1849–50; nevertheless it looked as if a new phase was about to begin in 1868.

THE MUNICIPAL CORPORATION AND THE ENVIRONMENT, 1848–1880

The administration of public space presented new problems of technological development and civic control and these were complicated by equally difficult questions of social and political behaviour.[1] In Bradford the pull of the old townships, the financial interests of property owners and other ratepayers (many of whom were relatively humble members of the lower middle and working classes), and the Canal Company, the privately owned public utility companies, the builders and the building speculators, and the still vigorously defended financial rights of the Ladies of the Manor in the town's fairs and markets all entered the equation. These had to be balanced against a desire for a town which gave some evidence of civilised control. Progress was inevitably slow. Some twenty years after 1847 there were still some who asked what were the substantial benefits of the change in administration.

In fact, by the early seventies, it was possible to discern a sense of Bradfordian civic consciousness. What this was in an industrial town of twenty-five years civic life and fifty years of effective growth, it is difficult to say. It was, I suppose, a mixture, varying from person to person in strength and composition, of pride in commercial achievement, one's own and that of the town's other successful inhabitants, a natural tendency to want to think well of the place one lives and works in, and decent humanity. At a practical level, a basic structure of urban engineering had just about been achieved. Building by-laws were becoming the instrument of positive, if limited, improvements in the quality of housing, development in the centre of the town was making for easier social intercourse and amenities like parks (and indeed cemeteries) were adding

223

something to the comforts of urban life. But it seems clear that such benefits as accrued in these years were exploited most effectively by the middle classes and their political associates in the lower-middle and upper working-class world. The labouring poor had less to be grateful for – as the persistence of high death rates among them indicated. Thus municipal activity – not always informed by the urgent pioneering zeal which swept all obstacles away – strengthened and sustained the political and social consensus of the mid-century.

While the confrontation between the new establishment and Chartism was being resolved in the streets, the newly elected Municipal Council was creating the institutions of the new administration. By the end of May 1849 the committee structure of the Corporation had been fixed. There were five committees: the Watch Committee, which included all members of the council, the Finance, General Purposes, Sanitary and Parliamentary Committees. Paid officials, the Town Clerk and the Inspector of Meat had been appointed with appropriate staffs, and a borough police force, eighty strong, under the command of a Mr Leveratt, was already engaged in its first and somewhat frightening exercise in the maintenance of public order. The Council also took over the duties of the Board of Commissioners but on grounds of expense rejected a proposal to apply for an extension of their powers. Thus its authority in matters of lighting and watching was still restricted to those areas of the Bradford and Little Horton townships covered by the Commissioners' Act. Indeed, ratepayers in Bowling, Manningham and Great Horton successfully resisted an offer to extend the authority of the police force throughout the whole borough. However, a series of by-laws were passed which dealt with the immediate and obvious problems of public morals, public health and public safety.

An analysis of their scope illuminates some of the day-to-day problems facing the inhabitants of an urban concentration on the way to becoming an urban community. Among them was a prohibition against keeping pigs in the houses or in sties along the front of a street – an attempt to limit for the sake of public cleanliness a widespread and centuries-old practice of supplementing a meagre protein diet. It clearly made some impact – for demonstrators through the stormy summer of 1848 began to carry slogans reading 'more pigs and less parsons'. Other by-laws concerned with the sanitary condition of the town tried to impose an obligation on local inhabitants to keep the streets clean, to control the slaughter of animals in the open street and to restrict the activities of the 'night soil' contractors to specific hours in the middle of the night. Those aimed at public safety tried to bring some regulation to the use of the public thoroughfares. Children were prohibited (with little success) from using the streets as playgrounds; hazards to pedestrians, like water or any other liquid falling from a house except through a pipe, unprotected cellars or other holes, outward opening doors, impediments to free passage along the streets, could all be subject to fines, and carriage and cart traffic was put under a fair amount of restraint. It is difficult to decide whether the prohibition on women standing outside a window, 'for the purpose of cleaning it', the sill being more than six feet above the ground, was for the defence of public safety or public morals. The prohibition on moving furniture between the hours of 8 p.m. and 6 a.m. offers its own insight into the development of an urban culture; 'moonlighting' to another parts of the town to avoid the payment of rent would have been to little purpose when Bradford had a population of about 10,000, some 2,000 families at the most, that is.[2]

The only by-law to invoke controversy – a controversy which was to endure in one way or another almost as long as the textile industry dominated the town's economy – was concerned with atmospheric pollution. A permanent layer of industrial smog which could turn in the winter months into the most terrifying of fogs was a constant reminder of the price paid for industrialisation. This was also a part of the price which many people thought could be reduced without too much difficulty precisely by those who benefited from it all. The forties therefore saw a resumption of the attack. It was one which Salt made particularly his own; when he became Mayor in 1848 he promised his utmost endeavours to try to free the town of the nuisance. As early as 1842 the *Bradford Observer* reported that a device called the Rodda Smoke Burner was in operation at his premises in Union Street. It continued:

If a stranger were to stand in Nelson Street and look at those before him, he would at once think that those belonging to Mr. Salt were connected with a mill in which the hands had 'turned out' and had not resumed work; for while the neighbouring flues are belching forth volumes of black smoke, those two emit no smoke at all: and, indeed, it is only occasionally, when the fire is renewed that so much as comes from a common house fire is perceptible. The contrivance is simple, inexpensive and realises a saving of 10% in fuel.

In the event, this device was nothing like as effective as the boast suggested. Other machines were tried by a number of people over the years and in 1848 the new Council passed a by-law stating that any manufacturer using a furnace or fire box in conjunction with a steam engine 'shall construct such fireplace or furnace in such a manner as effectively to prevent smoke or shall affix to such fireplace or furnace suitable apparatus to consume smoke'.

In 1848 Salt saw a machine in use at Crossleys' Works at Halifax which he considered effective and brought the matter up in Council. A number of councillors were prepared to support him in obtaining a resolution making the by-law immediately effective; for the mainly Liberal Council had been embarrassed through the summer by the attacks of the leading Tory, Pollard, who accused them of being ready to prosecute children for playing with hoops in the street but very unwilling to implement the law on smoking chimneys. But practically all the manufacturers on the Council objected. They claimed that the apparatus so far available caused loss of power and burnt out the boilers. One or two suggested that a lot of fuss was being made about nothing. All places, said one, had their disadvantages. 'Why! he knew a place on the coast where the inhabitants thought the sea the greatest hazard to health imaginable.' Further discussion was deferred to the next meeting – meanwhile Salt undertook to try out the machine in his own mills and report on its efficiency. Despite a favourable report, discussion meandered along until the by-law was modified in 1850 to give manufacturers the room for manoeuvre which they wanted. The penalty was increased from forty shillings a week to ten shillings a day, but manufacturers were now required only to prevent smoke to the extent that it was practicable 'according to such reasonable means as shall from time to time be available'.[3]

Salt's boast that he would rid the town of this plague was never fulfilled. There were few prosecutions under the by-law and Bradford remained until quite recently a town of black begrimed buildings and smoke-contaminated atmosphere, where bronchial and pneumonic illnesses were particularly insidious. It may well be, of course, that it was a problem only to be resolved when different sources of power and energy – a different fuel – became available. The Clean Air legislation of the 1960s revealed that domestic consumption of coal offered almost as much of a problem as its industrial use. But the pollution of the atmosphere was a matter of constant preoccupation; it was recognised in many quarters as one that ought to be faced more effectively and more vigorously and it was the failure to do this rather than the failure to find an answer which gave it a significance beyond the fact of its being one of the most unpleasant and unhealthy characteristics of the period.

The year 1849 also gave to those who wanted to learn a sharp and tragic insight into problems of public health. A second pandemic of Asiatic cholera which had started in Malacca in 1840 reached the British Isles at the beginning of 1849 and the first case in Bradford was diagnosed in March. Six of the local doctors agreed that an Irishman, Bernard Rice, living in Back Lane off Westgate had died of the disease. The Board of Guardians, the only effective sanitary authority, instituted a programme which included rapid burial, thorough cleansing of affected premises and the free issue of lime for disinfecting houses in threatened areas. The doctors and the Guardians also decided that they would give no publicity to the event in the hope that it might not spread. Although there was some reluctance to accept the fact and many preferred to think that there was an unusually bad epidemic of dysentery in the slums of the town, the increase in the number of deaths through spring and early summer inevitably brought the matter out into the open. In July the Coroner was compelled to hold an inquest on one victim and, reluctantly, to find cholera the cause of death. The *Bradford Observer* remarked that there was no wish to suppress the news that cholera was in the town, and as the epidemic developed the medical and sanitary authorities at last began to show some anxiety. The Board of Guardians began to receive daily reports from the doctors they employed and the Sanitary Committee of the municipality began to share the work of control and disinfection. The epidemic reached its height in August and early September. By 2 August there had been fifty-one cases and thirty-four deaths, principally located in the working-class areas – New Leeds, Wapping and Bradford Moor – in the eastern part of the town. On 9 August, the first of the few acknowledged victims from a middle-class area was notified – from Hanover Square, the new enclave in Manningham. By the time it had run its course 420 people had died, the great majority in the poor working-class districts of the town. Yet though there had been widespread fear of the epidemic there seems never to have been a sense of real urgency in the treatment of the victims. Publicity was given to the symptoms and to what were considered the best measures of immediate treatment. But suggestions for an emergency hospital were ignored and the number of doctors engaged by the Board of Guardians was not increased at all until the visitation was almost over. On the other hand, churches, chapels, banks and shops, but not mills and warehouses which remained open, collaborated in a Day of Public Worship and Humiliation.

A good deal of criticism was directed at the principal victims whose way of life was said to have contributed to their suffering. Of the first victim it was emphasised in the report of his death that he was a man of grossly intemperate habits who had been drunk the night before he fell ill. A little weak brandy taken every three or four hours was recommended as an immediate form of treatment, but the Board of Guardians issued a warning that 'the brandy will be of little service as a remedy to those who indulge in habitual spirit drinking or intemperance'. One of the medical officers, Mr Poppleton, complained sharply about the 'gross stupidity, shameful negligence and even dishonesty' of the poorer classes, for some of them given free brandy by the

Poor Law authorities drank it off instead of using it in the prescribed medicinal fashion. There were those who found it easier to think of the incident as a manifestation of the will of God, of which the tragic consequences were compounded by a lack of personal and domestic cleanliness, by immorality and intemperance, rather than as the product of uncontrolled public squalor.[4]

Reformers on the Council were, however, ready to seize the opportunity which the epidemic gave them to extend the powers of the municipality. In August, the Chairman of the Sanitary Committee, Farrar, opened the attack when he outlined the various inadequacies and deficiencies both in the provision of public services and in the maintenance of public controls. He believed, he said, that there could be no real improvement until the supply of water and gas, and provision of sewerage, drainage and paving were under the control of a municipality whose authority reached throughout the whole of the municipal borough, and he was supported by Alderman Beaumont, the distinguished local surgeon who added a denunciation of property speculators and jerry-builders who were prepared to inflict 'misery, disease and wretchedness' on their fellow citizens for the sake of the highest profit which the market offered, and whose activities could not be controlled through existing powers. The *Bradford Observer* became the almost weekly spokesman of the campaign to increase the powers of the municipal council to direct and control the development of the town:

Why cannot we have wider streets and dwelling houses better lighted and drained and ventilated? Why cannot we have that greatest of all boons pure water and in sufficient quantities?

The Editor and Farrar both linked the movement to the cholera which was just beginning to die down. The *Observer* spoke of man's Christian duty and suggested that 'The cholera most forcibly teaches us our mutual connection. Nothing shows us more powerfully the duty of looking every man upon the needs of another', and Farrar said that he was satisfied that within five years the savings made by the diminution of cholera and fever would have paid for the improvements which he had outlined.

229

Shortly afterwards a draft Bill was presented for the consideration of Parliament.[5]

The Bill was opposed by the Ladies of the Manor whose perquisites in Bradford – the fairs and the slaughter-houses which stood in the middle of the town – could be presented as intolerable nuisances, the Canal Company whose property had acquired the soubriquet of 'River Stink' very early in the battle, and property owners who did not take easily to the prospect of extensive drainage schemes which they might have to pay for. A straightforward political conflict developed between Tories christened by their opponents the 'Minority of Muck' and Liberal–Radicals seen by the Tories as the power-hungry servants of a group of manufacturers who wanted to pass on to the town the financial costs of the sanitary turmoil which they had created.[6]

Of course there were elements of truth in these polarisations; both views subsumed financial considerations of one sort and another. But there was always the central issue – how was industrialisation to be civilised at this level? Chadwick, whose work through the forties was the principal influence on the formation of intelligent public opinion, had no doubt. The inquiries into social conditions in the British Isles which he had carried out had provided plenty of evidence that private interest was unwilling, perhaps unable, to protect the public interest. No one could pretend that the free market operated effectively in such matters as drainage, sewerage, and the prevention of the preventable squalor and disease of urban centres. Thus, if men had acquired new freedoms to pursue their private ends, they had also to be restrained by new limitations which protected others, and these restraints could only be provided by public authority democratically elected and controlled. There was something to be said for the argument that the adoption of the General Public Health Act (1848) would have served all Bradford's purposes at less expense, and in fact the General Board of Health insisted on the inclusion of most of its provisions in the Bradford Act. But this argument was only used in the later stages of the controversy – the opposition really sprang from a reluctance to accept further extensions of municipal power.

The Bradford Improvement Act received the royal assent in July and came into operation in September 1850. The Council was now to be the local Board of Health for the whole of the borough with new powers to levy rates and deal with such matters as drainage, paving, lighting and cleansing throughout the whole of the borough; it also took over the work of the Board of Surveyors. Parts of the Town Police Clauses Act, dealing with recruitment, and the Streets Improvement Act, dealing with naming and numbering of streets, were also included in addition to the greater part of the General Public Health Act. The Act had a number of defects when compared with the original proposals of its supporters. Provisions which would have given the council authority to buy the Canal Company, author of one of the gravest environmental hazards in the town, and the Gas and Water Companies, heavily criticised for their inadequacies, were dropped, the Council deferring on the question of public utilities to the influence of wealthy institutions. On the other hand, the borough could be dealt with as a single unit for environmental purposes. Although Horton farmers might object to paying rates to improve a Bradford town centre, there were serious questions of sewerage, draining and paving for which nobody had responsibility, either in Horton or the other townships, not covered by the writ of the old Commissioners. In the longer term it was impossible to think of effective schemes of urban engineering restricted to part of the township of Bradford and a minute part of the township of Horton.[7]

In any case, within a year or two, the Council had renewed the campaign to buy out the Water Company and municipalise the water supply.[8] In 1842 an effort had been made to meet the enormously inflated demand for water caused by the explosion of the industrial economy. A new company took over from the old eighteenth-century institution. Its services were never even barely adequate and by 1848 criticism – to some extent of the principle but mainly of the failure in Bradford of a private monopoly in control of a public service – intensified. It started with the cholera epidemic, continued through the debate on the Improvement Act and reached a peak in the summer of 1852 when the droughts of the previous winter made it impossible for the Company to fulfil its responsibilities and revealed shortcomings in its programme of capital expenditure. At the height of the summer the position became very difficult indeed, and for six weeks domestic consumers had to purchase water from itinerant water sellers, or depend on the benevolence of millowners and others with private wells. This unhappy experience focused attention very sharply on the inadequacies of which Bradfordians, customers and non-customers alike, frequently complained.

There could be no doubt that the Company's supply facilities were overtaxed. There were three classes of customers – industrial users, domestic households and public institutions – and none could be entirely satisfied. Industrial customers were probably most efficiently served – the Company boasted of the excellence of the water supplies for wool washing and in another vein continued to supply the Lancashire and Yorkshire Railway with water when it was cut off from domestic users. But a good many of the manufacturers made use of wells and streams in their localities, and in any case the Company could only supply water for high-pressure boilers, not for condensing purposes. Above all, rapid industrial expansion was inhibited by the company's inadequacies. In the public sector the principal specific complaint was that the company, very conscious of its limitations, refused to accept a continuing responsibility for providing water to keep the streets clean. But it was of course the domestic customer who bore the main burden of the Company's inadequacies. Complaints about the quality of the water supplied to them were endemic. It was said to be too hard for domestic use, its colour was usually a disgusting dirty brown though occasionally it came out of the tap a violent red, and it could have a very unpleasant taste – one man, in fact, said that it had to be laced generously with treacle to make it fit to drink. There were more serious allegations. Bradford came out badly in comparison with other towns – Preston had 150 gallons per house per day, Wolverhampton 128 and Bradford 44½. The Company supplied more than half the population in 1851; but such evidence as there is suggests that far from extending its service it did not keep up with the demands of the building boom of the early fifties. The Company was reluctant to extend its services too far from the centre of Bradford. Applications from two households between seven and eight hundred yards along Manningham Lane were refused in 1852 and although most working-class districts were served by 1852 the service had only been extended to New Leeds, a little way from the centre of the town, in 1850 after the outbreak of cholera there had caused something of a public scandal. The *Bradford Observer* had commented then:

Even the boon of pure water which has been extended to most parts of Bradford inhabited by the poorer classes is at present denied to this locality and water of an inferior quality has to be brought in water butts and sold to the inhabitants. No wonder this place has been such a nursery of pauperism and disease when the commonest necessity has to be purchased by retail and therefore at an enhanced price.

The supply remained unsatisfactory. In the working-class districts tapped water, though available, was spasmodically distributed among households, since its provision was a decision of the landlord which depended more on the probability of higher rent than on anything else. This caused the Company a good deal of worry, for families without tapped water could make use of a friendly neighbour's tap at whatever financial arrangement they were prepared to make. The Company imposed a fine of £5 on such offences – rather more than the annual average rent of most of the properties involved. The *Bradford Observer* condemned 'this direct fraud on the water works company' and took the opportunity to suggest that the solution was to municipalise the supply and compel all inhabitants to have their houses connected to it. Alderman Beaumont expressed the commonly held view of the Company's activities, remarking that though it had barely provided a service in the early months of 1852, the shareholders had drawn dividends of 9 per cent.[9]

The dispute had political implications; Liberals like Beaumont and Radicals like Rawson were the principal opponents of the Company and Tories generally were prepared to defend it against municipal encroachments. But a neat political dividing line was avoided, for the fact was that among the directors and shareholders were wealthy Liberals and wellknown Radicals, some of whom were or had been members of the Council. A list which included Tory stalwarts like John Rand, John and Thomas Aked, Alfred Harris and Francis Simes included also William Byles, Henry Brown, Henry Forbes, Robert Milligan, Salt's two brothers-in-law, (William Haigh, and Charles Turner) and Christopher Wilkinson, once the epitome of working-class Radicals and now a prosperous bookseller and printer. In Council, the principal spokesman for the Company was William Rand, a Moderate Liberal, but as an Anglican and one-time Tory still nearer the Conservative position than most Liberals. Wilkinson, elected a councillor in 1853, supported the private enterprise case consistently, and Henry Brown, an alderman throughout the period, in three crucial divisions voted against the Council once, absented himself on a second occasion and abstained on a third. Clearly not all influential Liberals and Radicals were ready, for whatever reason, to espouse the cause of public monopoly.[10]

Early in 1853, both sides presented Bills to Parliament seeking extensions of their powers. The Water Company, stung into action by the controversy which had excited public opinion throughout the town, proposed to increase its supply to six and three quarter million gallons a day and to construct new collecting points in the Denholme and Hewenden areas. The Corporation Bill offered a plan which gave the prospect of ten million gallons a day to be obtained by adding to the existing plant reservoirs in the Harden, Oxenhope, and Stanbury areas. The Bill also contained a proposal to buy out and take over the functions of the Water Company.

Unexpectedly, both Bills were rejected at parliamentary committee stage. Though no clear reason was given, it was likely that the vigorous opposition of Keighley manufacturers, who were afraid that Bradford was proposing to take over Keighley sources, counted heavily against the Bradford Bill. The Company's Bill did not really propose a sufficient improvement and in any case ran against an enlightened area of public opinion which favoured public control of public utilities. But the most important fact was that the two sides were obviously drawing near to an agreement. Much to the annoyance of most Radicals, William Byles came out in his newspaper in favour of compromise, Henry Brown was pressing the same case in Council and both Forbes and Milligan, MP for Bradford in these years, threw in their influence behind the scenes. It seems that the committee was giving time for a settlement to be reached.[11]

Early in 1854 the Company and the Council reached agreement. The Council was to take over and operate the plant and other facilities of the Company, and it was to proceed with a scheme of improvement put forward by the Company. Two Acts of Parliament were needed to complete the statutory framework of the transaction, one to give legal sanction for the new developments which the Company's Bill had proposed in Wharfedale and the other to give the Bradford Corporation authority to buy out the company and go ahead with the Company's scheme. The new scheme met with some opposition. Reasonably enough, millowners along the line of development wanted their water rights to be safeguarded. Less reasonably, W. B. Ferrand, the Bingley squire, old factory reformer and a vociferous opponent of the Bradford municipality, attacked the scheme in order to protect a very small portion of his estate from minor spoliation, though he expressed his objections in terms of sympathy for Bradfordians who were going to be flooded with water and inundated with rates. Nevertheless the two Acts were confirmed in July 1854, and the final transfer took place in October 1855.[12]

The Water Company was generously treated. It got all it wanted. It shed great responsibilities which could only increase in complexity and volume. At the same time it was paid out at its own valuation and took £40 for each share of £20. At a winding-up meeting, each of the directors had also been awarded £1,000 by the shareholders as remuneration for their efforts, and these payments were presumably included in the liabilities which the Corporation took over. Altogether the transaction cost the Bradford ratepayers £237,963, of which £165,000 went to the Water Company, £61,194 to other liabilities, £10,351 to the Duke of Devonshire for an infringement of his property in Wharfedale and £1,420 in stamp duties.[13]

But in so far as the water problem was in issue, these were

only the preliminaries. It was to be years before the problem itself was under control, for while the town was not to grow as quickly in the future, industrial concerns, enjoying during the next twenty years a boom such as they were never to have again, made more and more demands on the system. It took five years to construct the plant of the new scheme and meanwhile there had been another serious drought in 1858 when rich men's servants were seen running to neighbours' houses to beg a drop of water to fill a kettle or to dampen the dough and when unfortunate teetotallers deprived of tea or coffee at breakfast had to make do with porter. Extensions to the original plan were added in 1859, 1862 and 1868, and a more effective system of supply at two separate levels was introduced. Nevertheless a report issued in 1872 was critical of the service. The various improvements had made it possible to extend greatly the provision of water to smaller towns and townships outside the borough, and thus recoup some of the outlays of capital expenditure. Mr J. Netten Radcliffe had investigated the sanitary condition of the town for the Local Government Board and had reported that this tendency had, he said, 'been pushed on somewhat at the cost of the borough itself for from the fluctuating nature of the sources from which the supply of water is obtained, and from the more rapid growth of the demand for water particularly for trade purposes than has been anticipated, this supply, in times of drought, has not proved sufficient to the due service of all the districts to which it is distributed'.[14]

Financial considerations thus affected the provision of services under a public authority as they had under the private one. Radcliffe reported that in 1870 the supply of water from waterworks which had cost £992,899 brought in an income of £41,380, though this was not the true margin of profit. Radcliffe also suggested optimistically that the new plant in course of building since 1868 should eliminate difficulties in the future; but although the very serious crises of 1852 and 1858 were not repeated, droughts still caused difficulties and the system of distribution was also imperfect. In the summer of 1874, for instance, residents in the newly opened area of Exeter Street were complaining that with an epidemic of measles and a hot summer to cope with they were getting water for about half an hour a day. In 1884 reserves were down to a week's supply and water had to be obtained from other adjacent water suppliers.[15] Yet progress had been made. Radcliffe commented on the good general quality of the water, in particular on its comparative freedom from excremental pollution, and thought that for this reason Bradford had rather less trouble with diarrhoea and dysentery than other towns in Yorkshire and Lancashire. In 1872 the authority could claim in normal times to supply over six million gallons a day, half of it to domestic consumers to whom the supply was intended to come at the rate of about twenty-two gallons per head per day. By the 1870s the authority felt in a position to insist that all new houses should be provided with a tapped water supply. The completed plant was expected to supply twelve million gallons a day. The creation of the plant itself was one of the great achievements of nineteenth-century urban engineering. James writes with commendable Victorian pride:

The result of these exertions . . . was the formation of the New Bradford Waterworks, which constitutes one of the mightiest triumphs of this engineering age and surpasses the greatest of the famous aqueducts which supplied Imperial Rome with water. From the chief feeder at Hebden near Grassington to Bradford the works extend twenty-four miles, intersecting deep glens, crossing high mountains, and piercing the hills by many miles of tunnel. Difficulties of no ordinary magnitude had to be surmounted in completing the work . . . on account of the rugged nature of the country and the porous quality of the strata on which the reservoirs rest.[16]

Nevertheless the problem of Bradford's water supply was not finally solved until the town and its industry stopped growing at the beginning of the twentieth century and the Nidd Valley waters were brought into use, in the Scar House Reservoir complex.

The other central issue – the provision of mains arterial sewerage as a preliminary to the effective draining and sewage control of the town – was tackled with noticeably less vigour. From time to time it was the subject of public discussion but meetings rarely attracted more than a handful of enthusiasts like Aldermen Beaumont and Farrar. Nothing practical was achieved until the late fifties and no progress in the building of main sewers until 1862, fifteen years after the borough had been incorporated. Its inadequacies were used in 1850 as evidence in support of the town's Improvement Bill. References were made to the official reports of the forties which had put in detail the sorry tale of narrow streets and yards without proper access to the main thoroughfares, no provisions for proper cleansing and drainage and no comprehensive authority to deal with them. Evidence was also called from Horton and Manningham to reinforce the municipal claim. Isaac Rowntree, the Horton surveyor, reported that there were very few drains in Horton and such as there were were poor. An owner might make his own and the surveyors might sometimes exceed their powers by making them; but they were never more than surface drains and sewers which discharged into the nearby fields. In Manningham it was much the same story.[17] In 1853 the borough surveyor put forward a plan for a system of sewers through the town; it was firmly shelved, for the Council took the view that the ratepayers were already overburdened by the great expense of buying out the Water Company.[18]

In 1858 and 1859 the town was flooded twice during heavy rain storms. Again during the summer of 1859 a frightening thunderstorm broke the feeble defences of the Beck and for some time the flood water ran through the Tyrrel Street, Market Street and Hall Ings area like a river, three feet deep. Damage was estimated at £40,000 and people with homes or business premises began to complain more seriously about the imperfections of the sewage system. Then in October the National Association for the Promotion of the Social Sciences held its annual meeting at Bradford. Public Health and Sanitation took up a fair share of the programme and the Town Clerk had read for him (he was indisposed) a lecture in which he chided his employers for dilatoriness and warned them against the false economy of trying to save money in a matter which so directly concerned the health of every person in the town.[19] Letters of complaint also began to appear in the press; recently erected houses were particularly singled out for criticism. The Girlington estate was simply discharging sewage on to the properties below them on Thornton Road. Salt Street inhabitants were accused of creating an 'abominable public nuisance'. Lacking all means for disposing of domestic waste and refuse, they had dug a trench sixty feet long to the drains in Southfield Square and so united the two new housing areas by means of a malodorous open sewer. The Borough Surveyor produced a new and more comprehensive plan, and the Council – after considerable delay and firm prodding both from the local press and from national organs like *The Builder* which reiterated the Town Clerk's accusations of 'penny wise, pound foolish parsimony' – finally sanctioned a programme for the building of the main arterial sewer system.[20] The first mile was completed in 1862; by 1864 another six miles had been added and by 1870 there were thirty miles completed.

More delay was caused by a dispute with a local landowner about the problem of disposal. The system discharged into the Beck and thus into the river Aire. In 1866, while the work itself was going on, W. R. C. Stansfield, who lived at Esholt on the Aire, laid an objection against the discharge of the sewage which he said was ruining his estate. In 1870 he obtained an injunction against the Bradford Corporation which prevented its officers from opening any additional mains or branch sewers or any house drains or sewers into the outfall sewer. Progress was halted until 1872 when, as Mr Stansfield accepted an agreement by which the Corporation undertook to 'take practical measures to purify the sewage before passing it into the river', the injunction became inoperative. A sewage works was erected at Frizinghall and then taken over by a private company which had accepted a contract to do the work. Private enterprise, however, found insufficient profit in it. In 1874, the Council took over and devised a process which was said (somewhat optimistically) to deliver all sewage into the Beck clear, tasteless, colourless, and in general free from harmful matter.[21]

Yet despite the creation of the tunnelled system and the resolution – though not as complete as claimed – of the problem of disposal, Bradford was to remain an unhealthy town for many years, owing to the deficiencies of its drains and sewers. Radcliffe in his report emphasised the need for secondary drainage in the older parts of the town where yards and ginnels and back alleys abounded. The *Bradford Observer* completed the tale of criticism:

He [Radcliffe] speaks of the drainage in the older part of the borough as 'most imperfect'; but we are not sure he knows the whole truth on this point. He may not be aware that the system of main drainage which the Corporation has at such great cost constructed throughout the borough is at this moment practically useless for a great part of its length, except for the carrying off of the flood water after heavy rains. The assertion may appear rash, but it is a notorious fact that only a small number of the houses in the borough are connected either directly or indirectly to the main sewers. The process of making the connections will under the most favourable circumstances be the work of years, and till it is completed, Bradford cannot be said to have an effective system of drainage.[22]

Radcliffe's most painful strictures, however, were directed at the methods employed to dispose of human excrement. In 1866, there were only 1,200 water closets in the whole borough (and not all were attached to the sewers); there were also between 12,000 and 14,000 privies and over 6,000 middensteads. These comprised the crude and simple method used for the disposal of human waste, perhaps still unobjectionable in rural surroundings; in a large town increasingly an indignity and a threat. The Bradford privy was usually a dry sanitary convenience, outside the house, and enclosed for the use of two or more families. It was attached to a large container known as the midden or middenstead which served the needs of a number of privies placed in a row raised above and alongside. The midden was partly sunk into the ground and by this time was generally covered, though open ones were not unknown. Other improvements were possible, but Bradford remained slow to respond. Radcliffe wrote of the system:

In the older parts of the borough the old-fashioned privy-with-middenstead exists in all its revolting abomination – a huge receptacle . . . sufficient to contain many weeks' or months' refuse, hollowed in the earth and lined with porous brick or sandstone. These receptacles are, for the most part, as offensive when empty as when full. In the newer parts of the town various attempts have been made to make the privy-with-middenstead less offensive; but the most successful of these attempts leaves the cardinal evils of the middenstead – its large size and permanent foulness – untouched.

Radcliffe recommended a change at least to the 'pail system' used in Rochdale. Medical opinion today would discount the foul smell as the source of disease, but the middens were the source of bacterial infection transmitted by flies and other insects and by the process of seepage into nearby water pipes. The fact also that the middensteads were emptied very rarely – perhaps at most twice a year – aggravated the problem, and at the same time the process of emptying was generally a further hazard to comfort and to health. An entry in Radcliffe's notes reads:

Keighley Street . . . the privies of three houses in this street have to be emptied through the house. Nos 10 and 11 have a small shut-in yard in rear common to both houses and measuring 28 feet by 7 feet. In this yard is an open middenstead with which two privies communicate, and which measures 9 feet by length and 4½ feet in depth, and probably has a depth of 6 feet from the door sill. This middenstead was filled with refuse to the sill of the door and *it had not been emptied so far as I could make out for eighteen months, probably two years.* Paving of yard broken and ground beneath sodden with filth. Stench considerable. When middenstead emptied, landlord allows tenant 1s. 6d. for cleansing yard and floor.

Cases like these were perhaps exceptional, but it was a minority of houses in Bradford at which the work of 'night soil' contractors and their men could be carried on without provoking serious discomfort, acute hygienic problems and heavy work for the inhabitants. Nor was relief to be quickly available. Radcliffe suggested that about 6 per cent of the houses in Bradford had water closets, in 1866. Thirty-five years later 27 per cent of the houses were provided with them. By-laws were in force which made obligatory the provision in new houses of an inferior type of WC. Domestic sanitation in the areas of older housing continued to be provided by the privy-midden. Its dangers were mitigated in many households as the value of hygienic discipline became clearer, but one visitor to Bradford could still in 1903 relate:

I have seen without enthusiasm, both earth closets and middens where pails were used, but this was my first acquaintance with the truly primitive arrangement in vogue in Bradford. The flies that bred in and swarmed about these filthy places, also settled thickly about the eyes of babies in the wretched little houses, whose front doors opened within a few feet of these 'insanitary' conveniences.[23]

Bradford landlords were perhaps understandably (though not excusably) reluctant to spend money on improving old and unwholesome property in the centre of the borough, but good properties also suffered, for the majority of landlords were small property owners with limited resources for modernisation programmes. Councillors also – themselves usually property owners – were reluctant to push too hard for vigorous action; it was frequently the case that results were well below the level of the advice which professional advisors recommended.

In these circumstances, housing conditions in Bradford could hardly be described as better than inadequate even for the times. In middle-class houses there were problems about the water supply, the inadequacies of drains and faulty water closets. Working class housing – and about 75 to 80 per cent fell into that category – provided one component of the constant threat of endemic disease. The Corporation, nevertheless, accepted its responsibilities within the constraints imposed on local government and was supported by enlightened public opinion in the town. The *Bradford Observer* had made an eloquent plea for action a year or two earlier:

Let the poor be extricated from their damp noisome courts and closes, give them houses fit for human beings to occupy, let them have plenty of light, suffer them to obtain a view of the sky from their dwellings; permit the light of heaven to penetrate every nook and corner of their abode and God's pure air to circulate about them, supply them with plenty of wholesome water for drinking and for the purpose of cleanliness. Afford them facilities for the speedy removal of ashes, garbage and all offensive matter. Home will then be sweet home.[24]

In 1853 the Corporation made a start with the publication of the first building by-laws. They were concerned with questions of easy access, all-round ventilation and the provision and siting of reasonable sanitary conveniences. Houses built in future, to be rented at over £8 a year, were to have their own sanitary accommodation. In property below that value, one privy or water closet was to be provided for every two houses. A report of the Building and Improvements Committee claimed a fair measure of immediate success within these limits but subsequent reports reiterated for some years the complaints expressed in the first Building Committee report of 1853. Despite its opposition, the Committee, which had demanded alterations in a large proportion of the plans laid before it for house building, had been obliged to sanction the continued building of back-to-back houses, often with cellar dwellings beneath, and courts where the houses surrounded the privies and ashpits and could not be properly ventilated. In 1858, however, a new Local Government Act gave Local Boards of Health increased powers to deal with housing problems of the time, and the opportunity was taken to give greater powers to the Committee. In 1860, a new by-law was passed which, since it provided that every house should have either at the back or the side a space of some 150 square feet exclusively belonging to it, forbade the further erection of back-to-back houses.[25]

The new regulation led immediately to cries of distress from builders in the town. The provisions, it was said, were too demanding; costs of house building would go up and rents would have to be higher in the new properties than working people could afford – the result would be a shortage of houses. There was in fact a severe shortage in the sixties, during which rents soared and some parts of the town became even more than usually overcrowded. But the causes were complex. Owing to the peculiarities of population growth in the fifties, a considerable surplus of houses had been left by 1861. Between 1851 and 1861, a population which had increased by 400 per cent in the previous thirty years grew by only 2·4 per cent from 103,771 to 106,218, for during that period a good many woolcombers and their families left the town, others who might have come if the labour market for woolcombers had survived went elsewhere, and a considerable number of Salt's employees moved to Saltaire. For several years, however, building activity remained high; in the successive years 1852, 1853 and 1854 the figures for dwelling houses completed were 1,358, 1,552 and 1,401. In 1851 there had been 108 unoccupied houses; in 1861 there were 1,772 and the average number of inhabitants per tenement in the township of Bradford was down to 4·7 from the 6·0 of 1851. Overcrowded slums remained, but the quick evacuation of Wapping, one of the principal centres of hand combing in the town, left the remaining occupants of that district to live amid abandoned and broken-down tenements more appropriate to a dying colony than a bustling, vigorous town. In these circumstances building activity declined sharply in 1855, reaching its lowest point in 1861 and not showing signs of real recovery until 1867. Building costs, labour and raw materials, were also high in the sixties.[26]

Investors, bearing in mind the severe losses which had followed the glut of the early fifties, remained timid for some years. It may well be that in 1864 and 1865 the by-law had some effect. James Drummond, the manufacturer, said that he had intended to build 200 cottages for his workpeople in Manningham but had abandoned the project as far too costly after the Building Committee had rejected his plans for back-to-back houses. But the lack of confidence in house investment was a product of the entire situation, not one aspect of it. The financial losses which followed the glut of the fifties were still being felt. The population figures published in 1861 confirmed the facts and figures and as the surplus continued until 1863 it was a year or two before the market recovered. Investors remained timid until the evidence suggested that the pattern of population growth had resumed a more normal pattern.

Populist sentiment fastened on the by-law as the sole cause of the shortage although the City Engineer showed that the increased cost was small and maintained stoutly that there was a market for better housing among working people, even at slightly higher rents. James Hanson, the Editor of the *Bradford Review*, threw the weight of his paper behind him and in 1865 the chairman of the Building Committee was still defying the massed opinion of the local building speculators. His report for that year held that the by-law worked well and that architects and builders were becoming familiar with it; the change would soon be apparent to everybody and 'the beneficial results produced in the improved character and convenience of small houses will be a matter beyond dispute'. But they had big guns against them; Dr Hunter's report *On the Housing of Poorer Parts of the Population,* published in 1866, reviewed the situation in Bradford and came down very firmly against the by-law, pointing to examples of what he considered adequate back-to-back houses in Cobden Street, Bright Street and Villiers Street, and assuming wrongly that the decline in building activity dated simply from the date of the by-law.[27] In 1865 the by-law was made the principal question of the local elections. The builders won and the chairman of the Building Committee lost his seat on the Council. The report for the year read:

Very important alterations have been made in the Bye-laws for the purpose of admitting the erection of houses on the Back-to-Back Arrangement, by the requiring a wide passage to be made between every two pairs of houses for the purpose of providing for ventilation by means of side doors or windows.

In the course of the next few years a compromise on the back-to-back was achieved. A separate privy had to be provided for each new house and regulations were established which fixed the minimum width of the street at forty-two feet. The open-ended street was insisted upon, so that the practice of building courts and alleys had to be abandoned and some light and air could find its way at last into working-class districts. Back-to-back houses were still permitted. The regulations were embodied in the Improvement Acts of 1871 and 1875 and provided a distinctive pattern of working-class housing in Bradford until it was superseded by the corporation housing estates of the 1920s. These houses were built in blocks divided into four. Each block was separated from its neighbours by a passage on each side six feet wide. Each of the four houses using the same passage shared a yard at the end of the passage where four privies and two ashpits were placed. Each house usually covered a ground space of between 32 and 35 square yards. It included a living-room, one large bedroom and usually a smaller one made by sharing the space above the passage between two flanking houses, and a cellar. Water was supplied to the cellar and a 'cellar-head' sink just outside the living room, and gas light was provided on all three levels. Slight variations on the basic pattern were developed. These included what were known as side sculleries – small kitchens at the head of the cellar steps on the opposite side of the door from the living-room, attics which could be used as bedrooms, small gardens and large cellars divided into coal cellar and wash cellar. Some houses of this type were often scattered in streets of ordinary houses. Generally, however, they were built together in different though neighbouring streets and provided a firm though minor differentiation within the working-class world.[28]

The Sanitary and Improvements Committee carried out a regular programme of improvements from 1850 onwards – though for years, sanitary control was far from stringent, the department being very small. Nevertheless, efforts were made to close down the worst of the many cellar dwellings, and to clear up some of the more offensive of public nuisances. After 1866 there was a new spirit abroad, not entirely the result of autonomous conversion. It followed government legislation which introduced a unified system of public health control throughout the country, and which established strong powers of central intervention against local health authorities who did not carry out statutory obligations. By making compulsory the appointment of medical officers of health and public analysts, legislation established a framework around which the great local public health departments could grow. The Sanitary Act of 1866 encouraged the appointment of a more complete range of nuisances inspectors and two Housing Acts (1868 and 1875) allowed local authorities to buy up, demolish and, for the first time, reconstruct sites where landlords refused to deal with houses unfit for human habitation.

The Medical Officer of Health for Bradford was appointed in 1872 after the Public Health Act had been passed – Bradford, like Birmingham and unlike Leeds, waited for the law – and the Public Analyst was appointed in 1875, following the passing of the Adulteration of Foods Act. Together with the Inspector of Meat and Slaughter Houses and the Nuisances Inspector they made the nucleus of a Public Health Department. The appointments had almost immediate effect in the volume of work done. In the 1860s, on average about 1,000 cases of nuisance were dealt with per year; by 1877 between 4 and 5,000 were being dealt with yearly.[29] The smoke question had already been taken up once again. In 1867 a sub-committee was given the work of re-investigating the matter, despite protests from manufacturers who claimed that 'the council wanted to kill the goose that laid the golden egg'. Somewhat naturally, they were let down lightly. In its report the Committee emphasised that 'while it was anxious that there should be no delay in the suppression of a nuisance of which the public had much reason to complain,' it felt obliged to note that fair consideration was due to owners, particularly of large works, who would have to incur serious expense in making their chimneys inoffensive.[30] On its recommendation a specialist Smoke Nuisances Inspector was appointed and prosecutions increased. Unfortunately, legislation passed in 1875 eased the rules in such a way as to make resolution of the problem very difficult since only black smoke was to be banned and penalties for breaches of the law were to be very light indeed. Nevertheless, the times were changing; Bradford, like most of the other great cities, was preparing to enter the modern world.

A sign of the changing times was the comparative ease with which the Gas Company was transferred to municipal ownership. There was some haggling over price but none of the public controversy which had surrounded the water supply question. The Gas Company became the property of the Town Council in 1871 at a cost of £210,000. During these years also the Council was able to enforce or undertake a series of physical improvements to tidy up some of the muddle and mess of industrialisation and to embellish (as far as that was possible) the centre of the town. By agreement with a newly formed Canal Company the section of the canal which ran into the centre and up to the parish church was drained and covered and one of the oldest of the 'public nuisances' thus eliminated. Draining and paving had gone on continuously since 1850, but was speeded up. Granite and other setts were introduced and although complaints about the noise were frequent, before long the Medical Officer of Health was boasting in his annual report that no town in Europe had such a large proportion of streets 'paved on such an admirable manner as Bradford with hard and practically impervious stone surfaces'. Important streets in the centre of the town were widened and new ones created to get rid of some of the confused tangle of traffic which industrial

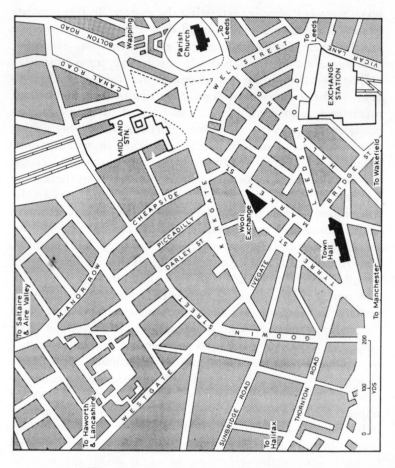

The improved centre of Bradford

prosperity brought. There was no direct route through the main part of Bradford from north to south. A great deal of through traffic – the great horse-drawn carts carrying wool, coal and iron goods – had to pass through the narrow, crowded streets along with the great amount of private transport. Market Street was widened and Godwin Street driven through a great deal of old and dilapidated property to link the southern roads more easily with the northern ones. Some years later Sunbridge Road was built to supplement the system.[31]

In 1866, the Corporation came to an agreement with the Lady of the Manor, Miss Rawson of Nidd Hall, to take a lease of the market and the fairs over which she still held feudal jurisdiction, in return for a payment of £5,000 a year. For a long time, the bi-annual fairs had been a particular cause of complaint. They were held on the open fair ground at the top of Darley Street and animals brought for sale were driven through the town, disrupting traffic, polluting the streets and jostling with pedestrians. 'Bucolicus' had tried gentle irony some years earlier:

Allow me therefore to express my admiration at the wise conservatism of our Corporation in perpetuating that most interesting and venerable monument of a departed age, the Street Cattle Market. How vividly it brings the past before us! How dull are all books of archeology in comparison with this living illustration of the fifteenth century![32]

At last something was being done; a more convenient site for the open market was established and by 1871 work was starting on the great covered market in Kirkgate and Darley Street, which was completed in 1878.

Old landmarks, the reminders of the semi-rural past, were fast disappearing. The old Manor House had gone to make room for the new market; the old soke mill in Aldermanbury, its owners bought out by the Corporation to extinguish another bit of feudalism in Bradford, and to make way for improvements in an area where new streets were being developed; the Bowling Green Hotel which had lost most of its special importance now that horse-drawn coaches no longer rolled down Ivegate. Old industrial sites like Cliff's Foundry were being demolished in the centre of the town which was quickly becoming exclusively the commercial and administrative zone. New buildings were going up continuously. Opposite the parish church merchants were creating a 'Little Germany' of superbly Victorian warehouses and the bankers were paying their obligations to a new civic consciousness with fine new buildings in Market Street, Bank Street, Hustlergate and Kirkgate. A new Mechanics' Institute (one of the best of the Victorian buildings in Bradford, now sadly demolished) was finished in 1871 and a new Church Institute Building in 1872. In 1873, to crown the building season, the new Town Hall was opened – legitimising the now established local authority, and demonstrating the emergence of a more general civic identity. James Burnley, a local reporter, was moved to extravagant praise of the new Bradford. Darley Street was taking on a 'classical character' and becoming with its vague hints of aristocratic connexion the fashionable town thoroughfare. Market Street, dominated by a Town Hall which copied parts of both the Palazzo Vecchio and Amiens Cathedral, and by the Venetian-Gothic-Victorian Wool Exchange, was 'so new and imposing as to seem like some Metropolitan thoroughfare'. When the dusk obscured the unreconstructed corners of the street, you might imagine yourself 'in some stately Continental town'.

For some twenty years now, other facilities, both publicly and privately funded, had been appearing in different parts of the town. On the initiative of Jacob Behrens, a new Eye and Ear Hospital was opened in 1865 to allow the work started in 1857 to expand; in 1864 the Infirmary had been modernised and enlarged and in 1873, after much controversy about its siting, a Fever Hospital paid for by Titus Salt and Alfred Harris was also opened. Peel Park was handed over to the Council, free of debt, in 1863. In 1873, the Council bought S. C. Lister's deer park in Manningham, opened it permanently as Lister Park, and was engaged in the construction of three other parks in Horton, Bowling and Bradford Moor. In the seventies *The Builder* was much impressed by the level of activity in Bradford:

At the present time an extraordinary number of town improvements are in progress in Bradford. Among these may be enumerated new sewage works, new Town Hall, new covered market and abattoir, extension of gas works and water works, a main artery from Sunbridge to Thornton Road, the widening of old thoroughfares and a more efficient system of paving.[33]

But this view of Bradford's progress needs to be evaluated in the light of Bradford's contemporary experience. We can say that within the limits imposed by the state of technical awareness, personal conviction and the willingness of ratepayers to foot the bill, the basic structure of urban engineering was eventually if somewhat tardily established. It was a very considerable achievement, making great imaginative demands on the men involved. It is also true that by the 1870s effective beginnings had been made in sanitary control and the regulation of house building. On the other hand, town development by its very nature led to an element of functional zoning which, while at one level an expression of urban efficiency, at another level, by promoting social divisiveness, imposed restrictions on the pace of improvement. In the forties Weerth noted how those who could afford to live at a distance from their work were moving away from the centre of the city, so that already there could be discerned several circles of occupation. The ordinary workers, he said, kept to the bottom of the valley in the midst of the factories and warehouses, and endured the full range of hygienic and sanitary horrors which the town could provide. The middle classes and those of the working classes whom fortune had favoured lived in the new suburbs which were springing up along the hills on the periphery of the town – in the new squares and crescents which were as 'attractive and charming as the valley bottom was disgusting'. The really well-to-do had established themselves over the hills in the rural villages beyond.[34]

The symmetry of Weerth's pattern was broken by the factories which had been built along the hillside, each of which attracted its quota of back-to-back housing, and by the social geography generated in each of the separate townships which made up the borough. But middle-class districts stood out clearly now along Little Horton Lane, Manningham Lane from Victoria Road to Apsley Crescent, and off Otley Road at Tennyson Place and Hillside Villas. Working-class districts were equally clear, in and around the bottoms of all the principal ways into the town – Westgate, Thornton Road, the Goitside, Manchester Road, Wakefield Road, Leeds Road, the High Street, Bolton Road and Manningham Lane. Differentiation within and between varieties of working-class and middle-class districts was also becoming more marked as changes in the by-laws and the ingenuity of builders introduced variations on the basic back-to-back or terraced house, and established social frontiers not easily breached.

Post-by-law back-to-backs were built around the edges of the built-up area in the interstices of the main thoroughfares, as between Otley Road and Barkerend Road, where a large working-class housing area grew up to take in Undercliffe Street, Ripon Street, Exeter Street, Maperton Road, Lonsdale Street and Wingfield Mount and in Manningham around the new Lister Mills. They contained examples of most variations of the back-to-back available, for in streets containing the basic type there were always a number of better type and higher rent and one or two streets contained only more expensive side-scullery back-to-backs. Throughout the nineteenth-century and beyond, however, a great deal of working-class housing in Bradford was of pre-1860 type. The worst parts of it had been regularly criticised since the 1840s, and during the 1860s the Silsbridge Lane area in particular came under very savage denunciation. In 1865, Dr J. H. Bell, Medical Officer of Health to the Poor Law Guardians, reporting to his employers wrote a frightening story of bad sanitation and overcrowding in this area. He said that the Silsbridge area was one example of a number of similar cases in the town and concluded: 'the worst nuisances and sanitary defects are those in which members and servants of the Corporation are most interested in their continuance.'[35] The substance of his report was quoted by Dr Hunter the following year in his *Report on the Housing of the Poorer Parts of the Population*. Some years later, the Corporation, using powers provided by the new Housing Act of 1875, had the worst parts of the Silsbridge Lane area demolished, replacing it by a new road (Grattan Road) and new warehouse and other commercial property. Slum property in the rest of the town remained more or less untouched until the end of the century except for the bits and pieces destroyed in the continual battle to close the most disgusting cellar dwellings and other uninhabitable houses. In particular, nothing was done about the disposal of household waste. In 1882, the Medical Officer was still complaining about the Corporation's unwillingness to introduce the 'pail' system used in Rochdale, for nothing, he said, was more prejudicial to the health of Bradfordians than the system of night scavenging which had to be used in Bradford to empty the privy middens.

Not all pre-1860 houses were slums. Their condition depended to some extent on the minor geography of their area and on the character and circumstances of the inhabitants. A description of a visit to one cellar dwelling off Westgate reads:

I came across an old woman supported by her daughter who is a weaver. They were evidently clean and house-proud, and their little home was comfortable and tidy withal. Things went tolerably smoothly with them, they told me, the girl earned fourteen shillings a week, out of which only two shillings and sixpence went on rent.[36]

But they were humble expectations which could find tolerable smoothness in such circumstances. Whatever the inhabitants, such properties carried – inevitably – the major social adversities of industrialisation. These were not purely the consequence of bad housing. There were still deficiencies of technical knowledge and skill. But they sprang primarily from the existence of poverty caused by a low-wage economy. The high mortality rates of these houses remained significant indicators of the real possibilities which urban industrial society offered.

As far as we can judge from statistics, which are not always adequate, the death rate in Bradford began to fall after 1850 and in the late seventies and eighties the improvement became dramatic. Infant mortality rates followed substantially the same pattern, though the improvement was not so marked, especially for children under the age of one.[37]

The critical years were between 1875 and 1881; the death rate fell below twenty-four in 1876 and below twenty by 1881. In 1871 the death rate for children under one was 220 per 1,000 births and by 1881 was down to 154 per 1,000; although these

The Great Paternalist

*Table 2 Average decennial death rate per 1,000 of population,
Bradford 1840–90*

1841-50	27
1851-60	26
1861-70	26
1871-80	25
1881-90	21.84

Sources PP Censuses of England and Wales, 1841-91
  Reports of Sanitary Committee to Bradford Municipal Council, 1859-70
  Reports of Medical Officer of Health for Bradford, 1876-90.

were not the worst in the country, they were substantially worse than the national average, and in any case what is most important is that they concealed wide differences in different parts of the town. Figures given in 1881 by registration districts do not separate areas of bad housing as sharply as later divisions into wards were to do. The 1891 figures which do so show obvious differences even within working-class districts. West Bowling, a ward with plenty of 'new housing', had a death rate of 21·9 per 1,000 and an infant mortality rate of 178 per 1,000 births. East Bowling, which contained a lot of pre-1860 houses, and South Ward, where the notorious New Leeds was located, had death rates of 24·5 and 25·3 and infant mortality rates of 198 and 211. The comparison between working-class and middle-class or rural areas is even more impressive. Infant mortality rates in Bolton and Heaton, two townships just incorporated on the edge of the borough, were 125 and 159 against South Ward's 211 and West Ward's 260. Between 1895 and 1897 the overall average annual death rate in the Longland area, the worst slum in Westgate, was 43·16. In the borough as a whole it was 17·93.[38] Earlier figures are less reliable and more spasmodically available, but there seems no reason to quarrel with Dr Bell's figures given in 1865:

The annual mortality for the whole of England is about 21·8 for every 1,000 persons living. Assuming the population of our borough to be 120,000 the death rate for the past year has been 29·1. For the townships of the borough it has been as follows: Bradford East, 30·9; Bradford West, 28·9; Bowling, 29·0; Horton 26·1; Manningham, 19·9. In the back streets I have described . . . it is 54·1 and in the Leys is

254

risen to 67·3 – the highest death rate under ordinary circumstances I have ever heard of.[39]

Clearly, in the middle seventies there set in a considerable improvement. It was due as much as anything to the appointment of properly trained public health officials with a professional commitment to excellence in their work, though this in itself reflected a higher and rising level of general public involvement. A concerted assault on public health problems started and a much improved water supply, the beginnings of more effective sewerage, the opening of the Fever Hospital and more comprehensive building regulations provided the weapons of the battle. Equally clearly, during the years with which this study is concerned – and beyond – many people lived in Bradford in conditions which ranged from inadequate to deplorable. A smoke-filled atmosphere deprived of sun and air conditioned them for the bronchial-pneumonic disease endemic in the town. The houses they occupied and the streets they walked in aggravated the constant menace of infectious diseases of all sorts. Of course, the lack of comprehensive technical and medical understanding made the complete resolution of some of these problems impossible at the time. But there was truth in the angry strictures of E. J. Smith, a friend (though a Liberal) of F. E. Jowett and a passionate reformer. The situation, he said, reflected an absence of ideas and ideals among men who 'had regarded it as their duty to facilitate the making of money whatever became of the loftier purpose of making men'.[40]

SALTAIRE

THE IDEA

> The moral character of a working family is almost without
> exception to be gauged by the character of their dwellings.
> *Dr Hector Gavin MD (1851)*[1]

Saltaire, built between 1850 and 1875, was one of several
industrial settlements developed by great employers of labour
in the mid-nineteenth century, and was undoubtedly the
largest and most comprehensive in the facilities it offered.
When completed it housed between four and five thousand
people, almost all the working population of which worked in
the great new mill opened by Salt in 1853, and around which
the settlement was built. Historians have usually described it as
an example of paternalistic philanthropy. But it was a company
village subject to the control of an employer/landlord and it is
primarily as an experiment in industrial relations that it ought
to be seen and was in fact seen by contemporaries. It was Salt's
personal response to the pressures urging peace and stability
between Capital and Labour which emerged in the aftermath of
Chartism. The point has been made that the core of this
problem was seen to lie in what men called 'the moral, social
and intellectual improvement of the working classes', and
improved housing was seen as offering one of the most
important contributions in this campaign. Thus Saltaire takes
its place – indeed an honoured place – among a number of
experiments in industrial township building and the housing of
workers.[2]

By the end of the eighteenth century, industrial settlements

256

associated with the development of new textile factories, ironworks and mines were becoming a relatively common sight. By the 1830s, the long list of their proprietors read, as Pollard suggests, 'like a roll call of the giants of the industrial revolution'. Panegyrists and critics were quick to appear. Andrew Ure, writing in 1835, found the houses which Mr T. Ashton had provided for his workers at Hyde commodious and more richly furnished than any he had seen before. They were built of stone, had each at least four apartments in two storeys and a small back yard. He was full of praise for the schools provided by Messrs Grant in their establishment at Bury and equally enthusiastic about the church which was 'elegantly designed and finely situated on a hill a little way from the works'.

Peter Gaskell, writing in 1836, acknowledged the truth in Ure's general view, as far as it went, but had many reservations. He equated the 'cottage' system, as he called it, with truck payment and in practice there were often close parallels since rents were frequently deducted from wages at the place of employment. He also considered that, far from providing a charitable subsidy to the housing of their workers – a commonly held opinion at the time – manufacturers made a handsome profit from their investment, receiving 'without risk or trouble or even collecting, 13 per cent while the common capitalist has very considerable difficulty in securing his 5 or 6 per cent and that has to be waited for and got together with great exertion'. It was, after all, he said, a safe investment. Rents were paid promptly, houses of this sort rarely stood empty long and proper maintenance could be insisted on. He perhaps exaggerated the financial rewards; undoubtedly employer/ landlords also exaggerated the extent to which they subsidised their tenants.[3]

It would, however, be wrong to equate the concept of the 'benevolent' or enlightened employer precisely with the notion of philanthropy. Motives, as always, were mixed. The first houses built in new or enlarged settlements were built to provide homes for employees who otherwise would not be available. Associated with the later expansion of such settlements there was a concern for industrial discipline which spilt over into concern for the moral and physical well-being of the whole man. Moral 'well-being' was nevertheless defined in terms acceptable to the employer both as an individual and as a member of a class which regarded itself as entitled to govern. It was concerned with the creation of attitudes appropriate to the day-to-day demands of the clock-dominated workplace – application, concentration and punctuality – and the continuing need for a deferential element in the new, as there had been in the old, society. Robert Owen's New Lanark was the only one which required a more revolutionary definition of its terms of reference, and even here there can be little doubt of the paternalism which lay behind it. This apart, employers needed good workers. If they could not, or would not, rely simply on the discipline of the wage, they had to provide conditions in which, within the limits of the social perceptions of the governing class, good men could remain good men. In this sense they may be honoured with the term 'enlightened'.

The 1830s and 1840s added a new intensity to the problems of society. The urban phenomenon reached crisis proportions and provoked a well-articulated reaction. Although men and women were making their own creative responses to the anonymity of the town at a level they could control, what was most obvious to the middle-class observer was the moral anarchy of these 'worlds of strangers'. The political dangers of the period sharpened this point of view, for everywhere the working classes in process of dissolution and re-formation threatened widespread political instability. The town was the principal arena for their struggles.

Social reformers concentrated their attention on the very obvious need to tackle the urban environment – to begin the task of providing the basic necessities of urban engineering – and on the political question of the working classes. It remained part of the general problem, as most of them saw it, of 'establishing harmony', of persuading working men that the interests of Capital and Labour were identical, and of promoting the good will needed on the part of all holders of capital – manufacturing and landowning – in the promotion of the 'moral elevation of the working classes'. Only Chartists and Owenite Socialists offered the possibility of fundamental changes in the social order, and most observers regarded them as the most frightening symptoms of the 'working class' problem.[4]

The programme of utopian settlement expounded by Owenite Socialism nevertheless contributed a great deal to contemporary ideas about ways of life appropriate to the new circumstances, despite the fact that its practical experiments – New Harmony, Orbiston and the others – failed. Ideas about non-socialist utopian settlement attracted a good deal of notice in the 1840s, and most of these ideas – directly or indirectly – took their inspiration from Owenism. Two of the best-known were those of John Minter Morgan and James S. Buckingham, both of whom had developed their ideas on social reform as followers of Owenite principles. Buckingham was lecturing throughout England in 1846 and, incidentally, included Bradford in his itinerary. In 1849, he brought together his ideas in the work *National Evils and Practical Remedies*. He had, he said, deplored for many years the lack of system in the management of both public and private affairs, and had been much impressed by the success of the 'co-operative communities of the Shakers and the Rappites' in the USA. The problem was to cure the social evils of the day by Organised Association, yet avoid the evils of Communism. His solution was a model town which he named Victoria – an architect's fantasy of a society of 10,000 houses located in the concentric squares of a town surrounded by the rural beauties of nature. In it would develop 'an association of masters and workmen as should give to each proportional interests in the results of all undertakings, according to the capital, skill and labour contributed by each to the profits made'.

John Minter Morgan had broken with Owen in 1840, for he considered that Owen's principles lacked the element of religion. He organised an association known as the Church of England Self-Supporting Village Society and published the *Christian Commonwealth* to give public expression to his views. There was little that was original in his ideas – his Christian community was to be a farming community of 300 families living in decent but not extravagant cottages around a great square dominated by the church. In addition to farming, handicraft industry was to be undertaken – all on a co-operative basis. The community was not, however, intended to have revolutionary character – it did not interfere with the distinctions of class or wealth. His work was widely known and received some praise. Like Buckingham he was an indefatigable lecturer and included Bradford in his 1850 tour.

The more prosaic findings of official inquiries and reports took up the theme when they pointed to the value of worker settlements provided by employers in improving the physical and moral condition of working people. Chadwick, reporting on the *Sanitary Condition of the Labouring Population*, was eloquent on the subject. The master prospered and the workmen benefited in a variety of ways. The example and the eye of the employer's wife encouraged habits of cleanliness and neatness, and the system of deducting rent before payment of wages saved time and prevented men from falling into debt. Riots and disturbance could be better avoided and discrimination applied to the selecting of tenants to make harmonious neighbourhoods. One witness is reported as observing:

... the proprietor acknowledged to me that although he made the improvements from motives of a desire to improve the condition of his workpeople ... he was surprised by a pecuniary gain found in the superior order and efficiency of his establishment, in the regularity and trustworthyness of his people, which gave pecuniary compensation for the outlay of capital and labour on them. He stated that he would not, for £7,000 change the entire set of workpeople on whom care had been bestowed for the promiscuous assemblage of workpeople engaged in the same description of manufactures.

The problem of working-class housing as such, the precise facilities which ought to be provided, the quality of the housing and its relationship to the 'moral well-being of the working classes' was brought into sharp focus during the forties and fifties by the establishment of several societies dedicated to the improvement of working-class housing. In 1844, the Society for Improving the Condition of the Labouring Classes and in the following year the Metropolitan Society for Improving the Dwellings of the Industrial Classes came into existence and within the next ten years some twenty such associations were to be found in different parts of the country. Henry Roberts, FSA, architect to the first of the societies, was a tireless propagandist. He wrote a number of pamphlets in which he discussed the practical questions of cost and size in considerable detail.[5] In the same cause, Frederick Pollock offered a design for the best and most economical method of building a pair of labourers' cottages. He made the point that 'it appears to be acknowledged by common consent that *three* bedrooms are essential to the well-being of the labourer's family. Without that number, there is neither the privacy nor the separation of the sexes which decency requires.'[6] The stamp of royal approval was given when the Prince Regent gave his name to a group of model cottages erected at the Great Exhibition.

Success was never to be as great as the reformers were inclined to claim nor as considerable as their efforts deserved. But the agitation did not wither away, nor was it confined to the metropolis alone. Throughout the country, it provided the climate of informed opinion which inspired the eloquent pleas of the *Bradford Observer* for decent houses for the poor,[7] which informed Charles Kingsley's lecture in Bristol in 1859 – 'You may breed a pig in a sty, ladies and gentlemen, and make a learned pig . . . but you cannot breed a man in a sty and make a learned man of him . . . in any true sense of the word a man at all'[8] – and promoted James Hole's exhaustive (though occasionally misleading) *Homes of the Working Classes with Suggestions for their Improvement.*[9] A principal of environmental order – the provision of decent housing – and a principle of moral reform – the 'elevation of the working classes' – had been brought together in a programme of social reform in which paternalism could be effectively focused.

Both in England and on the Continent there began in the forties and fifties a number of projects based on the needs of a particular industry or industrialist and embodying opportunities for a fresh start capable of manipulation and control. Perhaps the most successful of all was the project started at Guise in France by Jean Godin in 1853, for it survived as a co-operative the depredations of two wars.[10] In England Edward Akroyd built Copley on the outskirts of Halifax to protect himself 'against a sudden withdrawal of labour'. In

1846 John Grubb Richardson established Bessbrook near Newry in Northern Ireland to house employees in a linen factory which he and his partners were extending. The village was characterised by the generous allocation of open spaces – allotments and gardens, two public gardens and an area laid out for sport. The smallest houses contained only three to five rooms, but there was lavish provision for social amenities – school, dispensary and communal centre. Company shops, devoid of 'truck' abuses, provided for the needs of the villagers. The Quaker diarist, Caroline Fox, described Bessbrook as a 'happy and prosperous place with its immense linen factory, beautiful schools, model houses for workers, and lovely landscape, valley and waters'. Richardson was a member of the Society of Friends and a strong supporter of the temperance movement – indeed the village, like Saltaire, was frequently hailed by temperance enthusiasts as one of the triumphs of that movement. Richardson's explanation of his motives refers explicitly to a purposeful rejection of the large urban agglomeration.

I had a great aversion to be responsible for a factory population in a large town . . . so we fixed on a place near Newry . . . with water power . . . in a country district where flax was cultivated in considerable quantities . . . I was strongly impressed with the duty we owe to God in looking after the welfare of those around us . . . I had long resolved that he should have a temperance population in our colony.[11]

James Wilson, the managing director of Price's Patent Candle Company, was responsible for one of the most interesting of these experiments, the erection of Bromborough Pool on the Wirral when his firm moved north from Vauxhall in London. Wilson, who had, he said, been inspired by Dr Arnold of Rugby, had a laudable record in enlightened industrial relations. He was particularly concerned with the problem of dissociation in the new urban-factory world, and hoped to see the factory as a sort of surrogate village community.

Many a good family shuts itself up in itself, from not knowing where to find other families with which it can mix without fear of evil, and the young people . . . are charged by their parents to come straight home and to avoid forming any acquaintances in their work or elsewhere.

Unhappily the state of things . . . in every large town has generally been such as to make this care only wise and proper; but I hope we shall get into a different state here, and that all the good ones among you will be mixing more and more freely in each other's families, knowing each other's brothers and sisters and fathers and mothers, and finding among them true friends for life.

The new town was notable for its imaginative outlay and generous provision of open space and had been regarded by some as a true precursor of the garden village.[2]

Salt's motives in building Saltaire were as mixed as those of other improvers. His determination to move out of Bradford had sprung primarily from the needs of his business. Contemporaries often referred to it as a highly successful attempt to 'harmonise the interests of Capital and Labour'. In August 1870, *The Builder* ran an article on the 'Organisation of Labour' in which it referred to the dangers presented by an emerging working class without adequate links to society and the state, and called for industrial organisation which would unite providers of capital with providers of labour. One correspondent, taking up the argument, wrote in eulogistic terms about Saltaire: 'At Saltaire . . . we may see what can be done by properly organised industry. . . Surely this is an industrial organisation which is working a great social change. . .' Saltaire must be seen as designed to play its part in the 'conciliation of working classes' or at least that part of it which it seemed possible and worthwhile to conciliate, by proving the value of enlightened capitalism.

But, of course, the decision to build a model industrial village led into the greater problem – the problem presented by what seemed like the physical and moral anarchy of the industrial town and the frightening experience of Chartism. The answer seemed to lie in the development of a new social discipline – discipline in the use of space, in the relations of men as individuals with each other, and above all in the intercourse between master and man, and Saltaire may be seen as introducing this sort of discipline into the lives of its inhabitants. Salt did not articulate the idea in this way but had expressed something of its essence in very simple terms in his speech at the opening of the factory. He had he said been reluctant to add to the dirt and confusion of Bradford and he wanted to see a happy and contented people behind him. He had been very disappointed at the lukewarm response to his campaign against smoke pollution and he had been shocked by his experience as a magistrate and mayor of what seemed like the casual immorality of working-class town dwellers. Nobody whose factory stood in Union Street and had lived within five minutes' walk of Nelson Court could have been oblivious of the physical squalor in which some Bradfordians lived. Good houses were said to make good men. In a small village inhabited by people over whom he had authority there was a chance to create the sort of orderly and disciplined life which had defied the efforts of 'improvers' in the cities. It was a retreat from the real problem of the city, for it reduced the difficulties to easily manageable proportions. It was trying, however, to marry the social experience of the eighteenth-century village to the economic structure and technology of the nineteenth century. It exploited, that is, face-to-face relationships among people sharing the same loyalty or obligation to the common source of employment and authority, with the factory in place of the farm and the fields.

There were also both family and social ambitions which Salt hoped to fulfil. He suggested in his speech at the opening of the factory that he had rescinded an earlier intention to retire at the age of fifty because he wanted to 'leave something for his boys to do', and he had not bought a large estate and gone off to live in the country because he recognised that his roots were in industry. He felt at home amid the concerns which had occupied him all his life and would not have expected to fit into the world of the landed gentry. Thus it seems that he aimed at the creation of an industrial dynasty.[13] His social ambitions had undoubtedly taken off. He was a very rich man by the standards of the worsted industry and had been using a crest and coat of arms for some time – the one, in fact, which he eventually adopted when he was granted a baronetcy in 1869.[14] But he did not follow the common pattern and spread his fortune in a country estate. His wealth remained invested in industry and an experiment in industrial relations. There were limitations of time and class, the experiment took in business sense and personal ambitions, but it also represented a genuine desire to do well by his fellow men.

Balgarnie was mistaken when he suggested that the plan for Saltaire matured as the village developed. Correspondence which Lockwood the architect had with the General Board of Health in 1854 indicated that the original scheme was if anything slightly more grandiose than the completed village.

The plan for Saltaire deposited with your honourable board provided for a population of from 9000 to 10,000. It will be seen that sites are laid down for a church, baths and washhouses, a Mechanics Institute, Hotels, a covered market, schools and almshouses, an abattoir and Dining Hall and a Music Room.

It is also clear that Salt expected Saltaire to be made into a separate district and was very disappointed that the Local Government Board refused to move in the matter and left Saltaire subject to the control of the Shipley Board of Health obliged to pay the rates Shipley levied. He had clearly intended to be the only authority in his town.[15]

BUILDING SALTAIRE

The site which Salt chose for his new venture was about three miles from Bradford on a tranquil stretch of the river Aire where it leaves the lower slopes of the Pennines. It lay at the foot of Shipley Glen, part of the Baildon moorland which became a favoured spot for Bradford holiday crowds escaping from the sombre ugliness of the town. In 1850, the site still displayed a familiar West Riding rural pattern, a network of small fields enclosed in dry greystone walls and farmed for oats, hay and pasture. One lane, Dixon's Lane, ran through the site from south to north from the Bradford–Bingley Road down a slight slope to the river to an old mill standing on its bank. It crossed the Leeds–Keighley Turnpike, the Leeds–Keighley railway and the Leeds–Liverpool Canal, features of the site which had helped to determine Salt's choice. From Dixon's Lane, stepping-stones over the river led to another country lane and the moorland village of Baildon. One or two people had small market gardens in the site and about twelve families of farm labourers, quarrymen and domestic textile workers lived in cottages scattered along the lane. The principal landowner was W. R. C. Stansfield of Esholt Hall and smaller pieces were owned by Dr Outhwaite of Bradford, William Denby of Shipley and the Earl of Rosse, who had acquired considerable local property through his marriage to Miss Field of Heaton. Four years after the factory had been opened, Sam Kydd, the old Chartist journalist, visited Saltaire, and expressed his admiration of the position Salt had chosen:

The site chosen for Saltaire is, in many ways, desirable. The scenery in the immediate neighbourhood is romantic, rural and beautiful. From the streets of Saltaire may be seen the thatched cottage of the labourer in rustic simplicity and the quiet labours of the field surround those of the factory. . .[16]

Salt set in motion the arrangements for building the village immediately after the official opening of the factory. In October 1853, tenders were invited for the first cottages, a batch of fifty-three, and shortly afterwards the Shipley Board of Health accepted the plans presented to them by Lockwood and Mawson who had continued as architects to the project. When Alexander Redgrave, the local factory inspector, reported to the Home Office in October 1854, he was able to say that 14 shops were ready for occupation, 163 houses and boarding houses had been completed and about 1,000 people were already in residence.

The village was to develop around the spine provided by the principal thoroughfare from the Bradford–Keighley Road, a geometrical re-alignment of the old lane, called at the beginning Victoria Street but later renamed (as more suitable to its dignity) Victoria Road. On the opposite side of the road from the factory and above the railway which had passed through the factory yard, the development of the 'dormitory' area was begun. Fourteen shops were built along the line of the road, and behind them, house-building was started, in a series of rigidly defined parallelograms.

The houses constituted the first instalment of what could be called the 'Caroline Street' complex. It was flanked to the north and south by Caroline Street and Albert Terrace and took in William Henry Street, part of George Street, Amelia Street,

Edward Street, Fanny Street and Herbert Street. Three types of accommodation were made available, for Salt intended to provide a variety of houses to fit the needs of particular families – either for space, or in relation to family income, or to what status within the village and the factory seemed to indicate. Thus, at this stage, boarding-houses, and what were known respectively as overlookers' and workmen's cottages were provided.

Overlookers' houses were put up to make William Henry Street and George Street. Their general pattern was of a house with scullery, kitchen, sitting-room, cellar, three bedrooms and a small front garden. Variations of the pattern occurred in the middle of the rows, where several three-storey houses with four to six bedrooms were built. They all had decorative features in the form of the arched doorways and windows, typical of domestic architecture in this period. Hole put the building cost of these houses at £200. Amelia Street, Edward Street, Fanny Street and Herbert Street contained the so-called workmen's cottages. These had a living-room, a small kitchen and a cellarette but no true cellar and only two bedrooms. They had no garden and no decorative features, and according to Hole had cost £120 to erect. There was one variation in the workmen's terraces. At the ends of each terrace two houses were built on the back-to-back principle with slightly less floor space but greater height than the average. There were 53 overlookers' and 110 workmen's cottages.

The boarding-houses, built on the ends of William Henry, George and Amelia streets, formed part of Albert Terrace and Caroline Street. They were decorated in the Italianate Renaissance style used throughout the village and added to its visual attractiveness through the diversity of their design. They were a response to widespread concern about the appalling lodging-houses which people frequently had to use in the towns. Robert Baker, the factory inspector, described such accommodation which he had seen in Bradford in 1851: '. . . not four yards square . . . fifteen, sixteen and twenty persons preparing to pass the night, persons of both sexes, strangers to each other in the same room, in the same bed, on the same floor. . .'[17] In the event, except for two or three of them in the first few years, the boarding-houses were not used as such. Saltaire had a high proportion of lodgers in its population, but they tended to stay with friends or with members of their own families, and the boarding-houses were let out to multiple occupancies.

By the time the decennial parliamentary census was taken in 1861, the 'Caroline Street' complex had been completed. On the opposite side of the road from the boarding-houses in Caroline Street, rows of working men's cottages had been put up at right angles to Caroline Street to form Whitlam, Mary, Helen and Ada streets. Titus Street – a double row of workmen's cottages – which was planned eventually to run through the centre of the completed village, enclosed the complex along the southern edge. A memorial to the Salt family had been created in the form of a housing development in which the secondary streets stemming from both sides of Caroline Street (named after the mother) all bore the names of Salt's children, in order of birth from William Henry to Ada. With the building of Titus Street a modification in the workmen's cottages was also made. Salt and his architects decided that the reputation of the firm, if nothing else, required a better image than that provided by the rather dour accommodation being offered to the workmen, and they added the decorative features to the doors and windows which had previously been reserved for the better houses. All the workmen's cottages subsequently built were made to this plan, and some were now provided with three bedrooms. They were also laid parallel to Titus Street, across, rather than up and down the slopes of the hill. The village was now approaching the main roads to Leeds and Bradford, which ran in the same direction; the visual impact of pleasant houses running along the roadside was much better than one which would have been provided by a view of long and regular terraces stretching away down the hill, but the axis of building had to be turned at right angles to achieve the effect. By 1861, the village had been extended in this way by the addition of Constance Street and Shirley Street (named after William Henry's daughter and son). In the village, there were now 447 occupied houses and a population of 2,510. There were thirty-four unoccupied houses, principally in Shirley Street, which was just being taken into use.

During the flurry of general building which went on between 1866 and 1869, the housing programme was completed. Albert Road established the western boundary of the village. It consisted of twenty-two large and well-appointed houses, intended for senior executives and professional men associated with the firm, divided into two terraces by a row of eighteen overlookers' cottages. Facing the evening sun and the panorama of the Aire Valley, it offered a quite superb prospect for those who could afford its relatively modest rents. The space between Shirley Street and the Bradford Road, crossing the Leeds–Bramley Turnpike, was filled in with three rows of 'improved' workmen's cottages – Katherine, Jane and Dove streets (named after daughters-in-law) and by some good 'overlooker' and 'minor executive' houses in Daisy Place, Myrtle Place, Fern Street, Harold Place and Gordon Place. These embellished the public highways where they passed through the village.

Empty spaces had also been left after the erection of public buildings on both sides of Victoria Road. The residential area was therefore extended across the road; Titus Street and Caroline Street were extended and two rows of workmen's cottages, named after the architects Lockwood and Mawson, were put up. A few overlookers' houses of slightly different design were built on land still available in George Street and Victoria Road. In these, door lintels and windows were rectangular in shape, presumably to differentiate them more sharply from workmen's cottages decorated with the Italianate arch.

One house of particular interest was put up at the junction of George Street and Titus Street, near the central point of the village. It is a narrow-fronted house with a small glass-windowed tower on the roof. Its purpose has never been clearly established. The most popular explanation is that it was intended as a watch tower from which village activities could be surveyed and that it therefore expressed Salt's view of his relationship with the village – a view sustained by the fact that Sergeant Major Hill, the commissionaire and security officer at the mill, lived there in 1871. The difficulty is that much of the village cannot be seen at street level from the tower. It may well have been intended for use in time of public disorder; Salt, after all, had lived through the Chartist troubles. It would certainly have been of value if there had been a fire in the village. In practice, it was probably little more than a decorative feature marking the centre of the village.

A number of shops were included in the new streets. At the census of 1871, there were forty shops serving a population of 4,300 who occupied the 824 completed houses.

No precise list of rents is available. Hole suggested that they ran from 2s. 4d. per week to 7s. 6d. per week and a report in the *Practical Magazine* said that the standard two-bedroom houses cost from 3s. to 3s. 6d. a week inclusive of rates and taxes and larger three-bedroom houses with gardens 5s. a week. In 1883, the cheapest houses cost 3s. 3d. a week. The best indicator of their value, though not an exact statement of rent actually paid, is the annual assessment of gross rental value made for each house by the Shipley Board of Health for rating purposes. This is shown in Table 3. No attempt has been made to draw a comparison with rents in Bradford since the evidence for this period is fragmentary. During the sixties, however, when there was an acute shortage of housing in Bradford and Saltaire was just emerging, rents in Saltaire were lower, for in Bradford they rocketed and Saltaire remained unaffected by the market situation. According to Hole, the rent charged was an economic one calculated on the cost of building (excluding the costs of land and drainage) and a return of capital in twenty-five years.[18]

At all levels these houses compared very favourably with housing in Bradford. They were vastly superior to most of the houses built for working people before 1852, a good deal of which remained in the tenancy of 'respectable working people' until at least the late 1870s. The cheapest houses were rather small. Hole gives them a total floor space of between 34 and 35 square yards. Internal measurement of such a house in Mary Street gave between 31 and 32 square yards. The houses built after 1857 were bigger. Internal measurement of an 'improved workman's cottage' in Shirley Street gave a total floor space of between 36 and 37 square yards. For the total floor space of

Table 3 Housing in Saltaire, 1871

Street	Number of houses	Type and basic accommodation	Completed	Gross estimated rental, 1870
William Henry Street	22	Overlooker: parlour, kitchen, three bedrooms, cellar, garden	1854	£8 - £9. 10s.
George Street	76	As above, but several variations	1854–68	£7. 16s. - £9. 10s (one or two £12)
Amelia Street	22	Workman: living-room, scullery, two bedrooms, half cellar	1854	£6. 10s.
Edward Street	22	"	"	"
Fanny Street	27	"	"	"
Herbert Street	28	"	"	"
Whitlam Street	44	"	1857	"
Mary Street	44	"	"	"
Helen Street	44	"	"	"
Ada Street	44	"	"	"
Caroline Street	50	Decorated workman; Lodging houses	1854–68	£6. 10s., £10
Titus Street	61	Decorated workman; various	1854–68	£6. 10s., £7, £8
Albert Terrace	24	Lodging houses	1854–61	£10, £16. 10s.
Shirley Street	32	Improved workman: Living-room, kitchen, three bedrooms, half cellar	1861	£7, £8
Constance Street	32	"	"	"
Katherine Street	14	"	1868	£7. 16s.
Myrtle Place	4	Executive/overlooker: garden, three bedrooms, cellar	1868	£13. 4s., £9. 12s.
Daisy Place	5	"	"	"
Fern Place	4	"	"	"
Harold Place	6	"	"	"
Victoria Road	36	Improved overlooker and shops	1854–68	£9. 12s., £10. 16s., £12
Albert Road	42	Executive/improved overlooker	1868	No. 1 Albert Road (£18) the largest house in village. £13. 4s., £8. 10s., £10. 10s
Jane Street	23	Improved workman	"	£7. 16s.
Dove Street	24	"	"	"
Higher School Street	6	Improved; two bedroom	"	£7. 4s.
Lower School Street	7	"	"	"
Lockwood Street	10	"	"	£7. 16s.
Mawson Street	10	"	"	"
Gordon Terrace	12	Improved overlooker and shops	"	£8. 10s., £9. 15s., £13. 4s.

post-by-law back-to-back houses in Bradford, built after 1870 (and now pulled down), plans held in Bradford Central Library give between 35 and 36 square yards. Internal measurement of a similar house (also now destroyed) gave between 32 and 33 square yards.

The houses in Saltaire were supplied with gas direct to the home from the mill more cheaply than was available locally, and water until after 1860, after which date Salt agreed to take water from the Shipley Board of Health (except for the mill and Victoria Road). Apart from the executive-type houses in Albert Road, each of which had separate facilities, every two houses shared an ashpit. Each house had its own lavatory in the yard at the back of the house. This was more generous than the minimum requirements of the Shipley Board of Health which asked for one lavatory for every two houses. Except for a small number of houses built at the ends of the rows of workmen's cottages (and now converted), the houses in Saltaire were 'through' terrace houses, and thus fulfilled one of the progressive sanitary requirements of the day – the provision of a 'through' draught. Although some of the criticism of improved late nineteenth-century back-to-back housing may have been excessive, there can be little doubt that Saltaire's terrace houses were superior. What it meant was that every house was easily accessible from the back. The various parallelograms formed from the terraces were separated from one another by alley-ways which ran between the backs of each two rows of houses. From these, the lavatories could be conveniently and regularly cleared without the unpleasantness nor the constant danger to health which occurred in most back-to-back property where the middens were cleared at the front door of the 'back' houses, and where 'swilling out' was a constant necessity. The streets were swept weekly by scavengers employed by the firm.

The inhabitants did not suffer from the difficulties encountered by inhabitants of most new housing colonies. Streets were usually laid out and drained before the houses were built, and paved before they were occupied. A letter to the *Bradford Observer* in 1872, complaining about the disgraceful state of Mildred, Exeter, and Ripon streets, in a newly opened area of the Bradford Otley Road district, makes the point:

These streets are unpaved, completely impassable, and literally so many seas of mud. It is impossible for carts or cabs to get along them. Coals are delivered a barrow load at a time. . . . The water is turned off, a day at a time, without the slightest warning. . . . While I have pen in hand will you permit me to say the drainage of many of the cottages in these streets is very defective and in some of them the water is a foot deep in the cellars, and in others the smells which arise are very offensive indeed. . . .[19]

It is true that, apart from the principal thoroughfares, which were generously wide, the streets just fulfilled the minimum requirements of the local Board of Health for widths of nine yards before 1857, and ten yards afterwards. On the other hand, the houses did not exceed in height the width of the streets in which they stood. William Henry Street, the first erected in the village, was of quite lavish proportions. From house to house there was a distance of just over fifteen yards; from garden wall to garden wall, just over nine yards. The majority of the houses had a height of just over eight yards. Amelia Street, a street of workmen's cottages, with no gardens, and where the houses opened directly on to the pavement, measured eight yards two and three-quarter feet, but the height of the houses was seven yards two and a half feet. One contemporary observer criticised the narrowness of the streets, but they had the virtue of being open-ended. Thus they let in air, light and some sun, although the regularity of the building pattern must have created a mini-environment in each street, in which some houses, getting more light and sun than others, were healthier to live in. The inhabitants of Saltaire also avoided the worst effects of smoke pollution. The twenty-four furnaces of the mill were said to throw out no more smoke than the average kitchen fire. We have of course to allow for the hyperboles of Victorian enthusiasm. By the eighties, Titus junior himself was denouncing the firm in his capacity as a local Shipley councillor for its failure to burn up smoke effectively – but by mid-century standards, the smoke-consuming devices in use seem to have been very efficient.[20] More than anything, it was the austere regularity of the design which, years later, offended the romantic Yorkshire historian, J. S. Fletcher. He wrote:

Of Saltaire it is difficult to speak with any particular enthusiasm or appreciation, save from the purely utilitarian point of view. It is regarded by some people as the most wonderful place in Airedale and possibly in the world; and it is certainly worth a careful inspection if only for the sake of proving how very uninteresting and featureless a model village can be.[21]

This calls to mind the German historian's comment that the English thought soap was civilisation.[22] A good many people in the industrial towns of the north might have said that its use was proof that civilisation was beginning. Certainly, there were positive virtues in the relatively smoke-free, openended streets compared with the courts and yards which provided most of the domestic accommodation of working-class Bradford.

Although most of the public buildings in the village were erected during the final stages of development, some general amenities were provided from the beginning. A dining-room was put up opposite the factory to provide cheap meals for the many workers who had to come in from Bradford, Baildon, Bingley and Shipley. In practice, employees preferred to bring their own meals if they could not even with some difficulty return home for them. For the time being the dining-room became a utility building used for religious services, a school-room and a public meeting hall. As the population increased through the summer of 1854, those who wanted to attend a religious service began to hold weekly meetings in the open air. Salt provided a room and money to pay for a regular programme of speakers and when the dining-room was completed religious activities were transferred there. The meeting was treated as an offshoot of the Horton Lane Congregation until 1857 when a Congregational fellowship was formally established at Saltaire. In September 1856, a start was made with the building of a Congregational church, which was opened for worship on 15 April 1859. Its position directly opposite the factory had been determined when the village was first planned, and it is difficult not to read some element of symbolic reference in the siting. Church and factory stood closely juxtaposed on opposite sides of the road, for the business of God was the business of the world and the business of the world was the business of God. The church was the first public building to be completed, and on account of its position and the richness of its architecture remains the dominant visual image of the whole village.[23]

Salt also fulfilled his obligations as an employer under the 1833 Factory Act and provided schooling in the village. The Saltaire Factory School started life in the dining-room in 1854. A Mr Naden became headmaster, and Miss Wade was appointed mistress of the infants' department. (Coming from London, she had, apparently, found the sound of clogs unpleasant, the dialect used by the children uncouth and the boys under her care difficult to manage in the first month or so.) In 1865, the *Bradford Observer* reported that the room in use was 'beautiful and commodious' and the daily attendance over 500. Thomas Wright, the working-class scholar who later became Professor of Philology at the University of Oxford, was not, in retrospect, as impressed by the standard of education, though he remembered one of the young masters, George Morrell, with great affection. Clearly, the school suffered all the evils of the half-time system. Wright started work at Salt's Mill when he was seven – under the legal age – but he needed the work and being big and strong for his age was set on as a 'doffer'. His working week was from 6 a.m. to 12.30 one week and from 1.15 to 5.30 the following week, and he attended school on the alternate times. He said, 'when I left school I knew very little more than when I first went. I knew the alphabet and had a little smattering of elementary arithmetic, and I could recite parrot like, various scriptural passages and a few highly moral bits of verse; that was about precisely the extent of my educational equipment after three or four years of schooling. Reading and writing, for me, were as remote as any of the sciences. . . .' The vocabulary and sound-system of Standard English were also very unfamiliar and for many years afterwards he continued to speak 'nothing but the purest Bradford dialect'.[24] However, the factory inspectors found nothing to grumble about and the school was reported as one of the most successful in the district. George Morrell, who had come to Saltaire as assistant in 1860, survived into a more enlightened age, and had had a very distinguished career in local educational circles when he died in 1930.

The Saltaire Literary Society and Institute began on 8 November 1855, after a public meeting and a tea-party in the dining-room. For several years it used part of one of the boarding-houses in Albert Terrace as its regular premises, and housed there its newspapers and the library, the start of which had been financed by William Henry, when he married. Several years later the society moved into more ample premises on the third floor of one of the shops in Victoria Road. A reading room was opened every evening and several members took it in turn to read aloud every evening the more important articles of the daily newspapers. There was a debating and essay society which provided an occasional forum for Saltaire's poet, James Waddington, and the redoubtable Abraham Holroyd, the doyen of Bradford's literary circle. A regular programme of public lectures was arranged every year: the Rev. D. Fraser of the Independent College on the 'Female 'Poets of Great Britain'; the Rev. J. R. Campbell of Horton Lane Chapel on 'Mind maketh the man'; the Vicar of Methley, the Rev. Philip Yorke Saville, reading from Dickens, Sheridan and Scott; readings of their own works by the dialect poets, Edwin Waugh of Lancashire and Ben Preston of Eldwick. Men paid one shilling a year and women and boys eightpence. There were about 130 members in 1855.[25]

Salt provided one other much-praised amenity in the early years. In 1863, he had wash-houses and baths erected at the top of Amelia Street. The building itself has been described as 'vaguely Egyptian' in style. It contained two plunge baths, twenty-four baths and a Turkish bath, and the most up-to-date washing and drying facilities. The tradition says that Salt provided the wash-houses because he abhorred the untidiness of laundry strung on clothes lines across the streets, and was determined that his village should not appear in any way dishevelled. In fact, the practice was complained of much more generally. It was a nuisance to passing traffic and some men complained about the unseemliness of the habit, for women 'are not particular [wrote a correspondent to the *Observer*] as to what they hang there, but, if possible they will hang ladies' unmentionables right across the causeway as if they were afraid

people did not see them'. There was a conflict between two
different conceptions of efficiency and in this case the housewife
won. Reformers and philanthropists regarded the provision of
public wash-houses and baths as highly progressive.
Nevertheless, in Saltaire, as in other 'respectable' working-
class districts of northern England, they were not popular.
'Respectable' women preferred to make arrangements to take
their baths in their own homes and to do the weekly washing in
their own kitchens where they could be doing three or four other
things at the same time. The baths and wash-house, which had
been in disuse for several years, were demolished in 1894, soon
after the Salts had severed their connexion with the firm and
most of them with the village.[26]

Except for one building added to the plan later, the village
was completed between 1868 and 1872. In addition to the
housing already described, the layout of the principal
thoroughfare was improved and most of the public buildings
were erected. A correspondent to the *Bradford Observer*
described the new mill which had been put up at the bottom of
Victoria Road, on the site of the old Dixon's Mill, saying that,
to avoid spoiling the view along the main road of the village, it
had been provided with a chimney which was the exact replica
of the campanile of a celebrated church in Venice. He praised
the new factory school higher up Victoria Road, 'without doubt
equal if not superior to any other school in England'; and the
new post office, a 'splendid building' on the corner of Victoria
Road and Caroline Street.[27]

The erection of the public buildings began with one for which
Salt did not take direct responsibility. In the summer of 1866,
Salt gave the Wesleyan Methodists a site for a new chapel on
ground lying between Titus Street and the Bramley Turnpike
Road and later in the year put the foundation stone in place.
The chapel was ready for use in February 1868. It held 800 and
had cost £5,400. A bazaar in the dining-room, at which the Salt
women were the chief patrons, raised £650. The rest was raised
by public subscription.[28]

The new Factory Schools were opened on Whit Tuesday,
1868. As ever, the *Bradford Observer* was lavish in its praise:

... fitted up as they are for boys, girls and infants, they appear to be perfect. Whatever art could invent or money supply has been brought together here, and every aid has been lent to the sacred cause of education, that was possible to be obtained. The *ensemble* outside strongly reminded the beholder of some oriental temple, and the fittings in the interior and the accommodation are as noble as is the cause to which they are devoted.

J. G. Fitch, local Inspector of Schools and a severe critic of most West Riding scholastic establishments, was also full of praise after his examination of the work in 1870. Of the boys' school he wrote: 'this school is rapidly becoming one of the best, as it is already the handsomest in my district . . . the spirit and order of the school are excellent'; and of the girls' department: 'this department is well ordered and very efficient. Miss Walker is a methodical and painstaking teacher, and had brought the children to excellent habits of attention.' The schools together generally provided education for about 700; in September 1874, the number on the register was 806 half-timers and 454 day scholars, with an average attendance of 665.[29]

Later in the year on 23 September, forty-five almshouses were opened along the southern end of Victoria Road at the opposite end of the village from the factory. They were lavishly decorated in the style prevailing in the village, and were seen as resembling small Italian villas. They provided accommodation for sixty pensioners. Recipients of the charity had to be of good character, and had to continue circumspect in their behaviour. In addition to free accommodation, a married couple was given a weekly pension of ten shillings between the two and a single person seven shillings and sixpence. A cultivated area of flowers and lawn in front of the houses on the western side of the road was the only open green within the residential area of the village – significantly, the only part where a space was provided in which people could meet easily for a gossip. It was here that the poet of Bradford's working class, A. Wildman, spent his last years. By 1870 he was destitute and on the verge of entering the workhouse. Abraham Holroyd, now postmaster and stationer, and himself a beneficiary of Salt's generosity, brought the matter to Salt's notice and a place was found for Wildman overnight.

At the same time the Infirmary and dispensary was opened.

It had sprung from the need for a casualty ward for accidents in the mill and was developed into a small hospital and dispensary to serve the village as a whole. Its exuberant decoration, like that of the school and the almshouses, included the Salt family crest and the monograms of Titus and Caroline Salt.[30]

In the summer of 1869, Salt began the last stage of the programme, when he gave out an £18,000 contract to build an Institute which would fulfil both educational and social functions. It was to be both a college of further education and a social club and was intended to improve on the Mechanics' Institute concept which many people thought too austerely educational, and to offer a substitute for the public house which Salt did not provide in the village, but which in many places was still the only general meeting place for a whole variety of activities. The accommodation provided in the establishment included reading room, library, chess and draughts room, smoking room, billiard room with four tables, bagatelle room with three tables, a lecture hall holding 800, a lecture hall holding 200, two rooms for art, a number of classrooms, gymnasium and rifle drill room. Both a School of Art and a School of Science were established in accordance with the provisions of the Science and Art Department at South Kensington, and a broad curriculum of studies was provided for, both at advanced and elementary levels. The many different activities which had developed in the village were provided with accommodation, and the Literary Society along with its library was incorporated into the new institution. The fees for membership were small, ranging from two shillings for adult men and one shilling for boys between eighteen and thirteen to one shilling for adult women and sixpence for girls thirteen to eighteen. The hire of a room was to cost threepence per night. The administration was to be in the hands of a committee composed of eight people nominated by the firm and eight elected by the incorporated Literary Institute.

Although Pevsner, in our own day, has found little to praise in the building, most contemporary observers paid it the respect that they had given all the works of Saltaire. The building stood back from the road opposite the Factory Schools and so left a small square in Victoria Road, pointed at its corners by the four sculptured lions, War, Peace, Vigilance and Determination. Harper's *New Monthly Magazine* called it 'a rare tribute to learning and letters'. The interior decoration, which cost £7,000, was of 'a most gorgeous and elaborate description', and *The Practical Magazine* suggested in 1874 that 'a more magnificent or more complete educational establishment does not exist within the limits of the United Kingdom. Both in its external aspect and in its internal accessories the institute is almost unique.'[31]

To all intents and purpose, Salt finished the essentials of his work at Saltaire with the establishment of a park across the river, a short walk from the factory and the houses. He bought the land in 1870 and had it landscaped very attractively by Mr Gay of Bradford during the next twelve months. Gay altered the course of the river to make it more attractive and to make it more suitable both for boating and swimming. He created facilities for bowls, croquet, archery and a cricket ground which, many years later, the great Learie Constantine described as the prettiest in the north of England. About a third of the space was devoted to laid-out walks and flower beds. A promenade built along the rise of the terrain offered a view of the factory, merging comfortably into the rural background, which comes as a surprise to one more accustomed to the rigidities of most of Bradford's nineteenth-century mills. The rules and regulations laid down for the park, as in all Victorian parks, were strict – designed to foster 'the moral and social elevation of the working classes'. Drunks, dogs and unaccompanied children under eight were not permitted to enter. There was little space for casual play, though organised games could be played on the cricket field and the bowling green. Smoking was not allowed in the alcoves, and swearing, stone-throwing, and any form of 'indecorous conduct' led to immediate expulsion and sometimes a term of exclusion from the pleasures of the park. No kind of demonstration – religious or political – was to be allowed.

The opening ceremony was something of an occasion. Several thousands came to watch as the Saltaire Brass Band and the Rifle Volunteers marched down to the park to lead the Salt family to the pavilion on the promenade. Edward Salt, on behalf of his father, formally handed the park over to the assembled company; he hoped they would long enjoy it and drew their attention to the park regulations which had been freely distributed among them. Amelia Salt, in the absence of her mother, declared the park open.

... a *feu-de-joie* was then fired by the Volunteers, amid loud and prolonged cheers; the bells in the Church across the river rung out a loud and merry peal, and the band struck up and played the National Anthem. Sir Titus and his party then walked round the Park, and the memorable proceedings ended.[32]

The last building of all to be put up was the Congregational Sunday School, built at the corner of Caroline Street and Victoria Road, in 1875. Originally, the space had been reserved for an hotel, but the idea had been abandoned and the space re-allocated for use as allotment gardens. The Congregationalists decided that the basement of the church, which they had used as a Sunday school, was cramped and unsuitable and asked Salt for a site on which to place a new purpose-built structure. Salt agreed and gave in addition £7,000, provided they raised £500 towards the interior decorations. Like all Salt's buildings, it was lavishly decorated. The ceremony of laying the foundation stone was performed by Gordon Salt, one of the grandsons; Titus himself, suffering from an attack of gout, could not be present. The official opening took place in May 1876. Salt attended the ceremony performed by another grandson, Harold. He was already a sick man, with the developing illness from which he died, and had to leave before the ceremony was concluded.[33]

Whatever present-day judgement has decided, there is no doubt that Saltaire caught the imagination of Victorian observers. A visit there became an obligatory part of the itinerary of any well-known public figure who came to Bradford. When the British Association for the Advancement of Social Science met in 1859 and again when the British Association met in 1874, both in Bradford, Saltaire was inspected by most of the visitors. Lord Palmerston came after he had laid the foundation stone of the new Wool Exchange in 1864, and recorded that it was the most memorable experience of his visit. Edward Miall paid a visit after he had been elected MP for Bradford in 1869.

John Bright came in 1877 after he had unveiled the statue of Cobden in the Bradford Wool Exchange. A Mr Fox, lately Prime Minister of New Zealand, did a tour of inspection in 1876. He was laying out his own model village in New Zealand, and had visited villages in Ireland and England in search of ideas. He gave pride of place, he said, to Saltaire. In 1872, both the Burmese and Japanese ambassadors paid visits and caused a good deal of excitement. Visits like these seem to have been one of the perquisites of living in Saltaire. All who could turned out to see them.

Articles about the village appeared regularly in many newspapers and magazines between 1852 and the death of the founder in 1877, and there was a brief flurry of renewed interest (possibly encouraged for advertising purposes) when the whole concern changed hands in the 1890s. It fitted the pattern of Victorian industrial paternalism so exactly that little except adulation and flattery was ever printed, until fashions had changed. Mr Alexander Redgrave, who had been in Saltaire in the 1850s as an assistant factory inspector, caught the spirit of most commentators in his general report as Inspector of Factories for the six months ended 30 April 1871:

In one of his recent reports Mr. Assistant Inspector Walker describes the magnificent establishment of Saltaire, near Bradford, the result of the energy, judgment and benevolent views of Sir Titus Salt, Bart. Here are not only workrooms of unexceptional arrangement, and details of management economically and thoroughly carried, – not only is there one of the finest, and I believe longest work-rooms of the kind in the world, but the factory is made the centre around which a complete colony lives and thrives. Here is a town in the midst of the country, places of worship, market places, well built houses, well planned streets, a park, hill sides and woody dells for health and recreation, schools and industrial institutions for improvement.

In March 1856, the *Art Journal*, commenting on an etching which Abraham Holroyd had done of Saltaire, compared the factory and village to the 'strong baronial castle of feudal times, round which were clustered the humble abodes of those who found protection and support under the wing of the owner'.

Some years earlier, *The Nonconformist* had praised Salt for his disinterested vision in refusing to desecrate the environment further, and saw it also as the most fruitful step in industrial relations; happier 'moral relations' would have been established by the extension of the Saltaire principle – 'hayricks would be safe from the lucifer match, strikes would be as infrequent as earthquakes and the fire of patriotism would warmly glow in bosoms where it now lies damped and sullen'. *The Temperance Spectator* reprinted an article from the *Leeds Mercury* which thought there was more poetry in the history of Saltaire than in the exploits of feudal lords and suggested that, in moonlight, Saltaire might rival anything described in the *Arabian Nights*. It affirmed in conclusion the theme that most of them suggested in one way or another. Mr Salt had made great strides in resolving the labour question. He had shown that the care of his employees was perfectly compatible with success.[34]

A letter in *The Builder*, which recommended it as a model of how industrial relations should be conducted, has already been referred to. Rev. J. R. Stephens, speaking at a '10 Hour' meeting in October 1853, gave it the essentially Victorian gloss when, referring to the improvements which had taken place in master-man relations, impressed on the meeting 'the duty of aspiring to emulate the "model master" by endeavouring to become the "model man" – discharging the duties of his status in every respect with faithfulness and exemplifying by his conduct in all the relations of life that he was a good servant and a good citizen worthy of such a noble master as Mr. Salt'.[35]

Mr John Colebrook of Callander, Scotland, wrote, after a visit to Saltaire, to Mr B. Allsopp, the owner of the local paper, to encourage him to produce a new biography of Sir Titus Salt. He thought the evidence of his success would provide a sure refutation of the 'school of socialists' who insinuated that a man could not become rich honestly. It would give evidence to the working man that the improvement of his condition depended on the commercial success of the manufacturer and it ought to provide substantial encouragement to the statesmen, economists, philanthropists and social reformers who were seeking to resolve the problems of Capital and Labour and the rational and intelligent progress of the working class.[36]

There were more critical observers. Edwin Smith, who had published his *Voice of the People* in 1857, suggested in the one surviving number that Salt trapped a labour force at Saltaire by the promise of good wages and excellent conditions and having achieved the objective was now beginning to pull wages down. Samuel Kydd thought that Salt had done no more than was required of a good master, but paid tribute nevertheless to the achievement. *The Working Man* applauded the experiment but regretted the layout of the village which faced away from the natural beauties of the river and the valley, and so denied the inhabitants a 'priceless prospect' which would have gladdened 'the hearts of the occupants for ever'. 'Porcupine', one of the reporters on the *Bradford Observer*, thought that although Saltaire had much to recommend it, it had one very serious shortcoming. The individual rooms, he said, were too small either for comfort or health and some of the streets were unnecessarily narrow.[37]

It has frequently been suggested that John Ruskin, a more substantial critic, had the model village concept in mind when he spoke to Bradford's millocracy in 1864 about their new Wool Exchange. He had stayed in Bingley during his visit and must have passed Saltaire when he came to Bradford. He came nearer the bone than most, when he told Bradford's millowners that their ideal of human life was

that it should be passed in a pleasant undulating world, with iron and coal everywhere underneath it. On each pleasant bank of this world is to be a beautiful mansion, with two wings; and a stable, and coach-houses; and pleasant drives through the shrubberies. In this mansion are to live the favoured votaries of the Goddess [of the great art of 'getting-on'] . . . At the bottom of the hill is to be the mill; not less than a quarter of a mile long, with one steam engine at each end, and two in the middle and a chimney three hundred feet high. In this mill are to be in constant employment from eight hundred to a thousand workers, who never drink, never strike, always go to church on Sunday and always express themselves in respectful language.

Salt was invariably praised as the epitome of all that was best in Victorian capitalism; he had pointed the way to resolving the tension between Capital and Labour in 'a most ennobling way'. Ruskin put the other side of the question.[38]

As the years passed, the climate of public opinion changed, other experiments appeared to offer greater possibilities and planners and reformers began to look at Saltaire with a cooler, more appraising eye. In 1881, an article in Thomas Hughes's *A Manual for Co-operators* conceded Salt's benevolence but claimed that Guise, where the French co-operative village had been founded by J. J. Godin, was a far truer social experiment. Here, it asserted, men and women were successfully experimenting in a new type of social organisation based on the principles of 'Association'. Godin, in fact, was transferring the business around which the township lived to the control though not the ownership of a partnership of the workpeople, and had provided residential accommodation in the form of apartment blocks, where people could enjoy the advantages of separate dwellings and those of collective action at the same time. He concluded: 'The admirable results obtained by M. Godin . . . at Guise, call upon all who desire to see the homes of the working people what the homes of mankind ought to be. . .' Budgett Meakin could say in 1905 that Saltaire had fallen sadly behind the times. It should be approached, he thought, with feelings of respect and gratitude, for the nobility of the experiment. It still had, he thought, an air of solid comfort about it, but, compared, for instance, with the latest housing put up by Krupps in Germany, it seemed dismal and cramped. There was, he said, little beauty in the village and although a park of fourteen acres had been provided, the houses had been squeezed into twenty-six acres. He also thought that the institutions which Salt had provided had deteriorated very badly. S. D. Adshead, Professor of Town Planning at London University, was even more critical in a book, *Town Planning and Town Development*, written in 1923. His main observation also was that while public buildings and amenities, including the fourteen acres of park, had been lavishly provided, the houses were crowded together behind them, and concluded:

It is an example of the kind of philanthropy, which reflects credit on the promoter, but provides very little real happiness to the recipient. For at best it can only be said that it is a thirty to the acre congested scheme of terrace houses, surrounded by a park and an extravagance of public buildings.

But Adshead was talking about a different world, where paternalism as an instrument of social improvement aroused little enthusiasm. Contemporary social reformers, and others, generally accepted the validity of Dr Rhind's report to the Commissioners of the Paris Industrial Exhibition of 1867, in which he emphasised an unusual healthiness among people of Saltaire which he attributed to the superior sanitation, drainage and overall cleanliness of the village and the absence of drunkenness. Most people thought that it was a remarkable experiment in industrial and human relations and agreed that the award of the distinction of Chevalier of the Legion of Honour, granted by Napoleon III in recognition of Saltaire, had been well deserved.[39]

An anonymous visitor from the Isle of Man summed up in verse the spirit of deferential respect which the enterprise had aroused:

Closely contiguous to the factory stand
The pleasant homes of all the active band;
The newly-fashioned, open airy street,
Of cottages commodious, solid, neat,
Where all is order of a modern kind, [my italics]
With skill constructed and with thought designed.
Retreat for social joy, and homely rest;
Here, too, the object of paternal care,
(When Sabbaths on these glens and woodlands smile)
A sanctuary of peace, a house of prayer;
Where artisans forget their six days' toil,
And bend before their God in humble fear,
Rejoicing that their daily bread is sure.[40]

LIVING IN SALTAIRE

Although it has to be admitted that much of the village was visually drab and unexciting, it was not without some element of beauty. Of individual buildings, the church has been described as the finest built for free church worship in the north of England. There were pleasant streets like William Henry Street, not too large to swamp the effect of the characteristic

286

architectural decoration, small enough to give the impression of being actually lived in and enjoyed. Of course the settlement derived a great deal from its position. There is, for instance, the view along George Street which takes in the cupola of the Congregational church and the sweep of moorland behind. The harmonious grouping of the factory buildings along the river bank and the lower reaches of the southern slopes of the valley give a very different picture from that of the average run of Bradford mill, and it is worth comparing the Salt mill with the Lister mill a couple of miles away with this in mind.

But the village was conceived essentially as a utilitarian urban structure. In the streets of ordinary workmen's cottages no concession at all was made to the idea of visual excitement. Elsewhere use was made of the natural slope to vary the height of houses, windows and doors were decorated with the Italianate arch common in mid-Victorian building and several streets were provided with gardens. The basic pattern was one of a series of related parallelograms. The ordered regularity of the streets reflects the principle of order and control which had been a major part of its inspiration. Wherever they could, the architects obliterated the old geography, the straggling lane, the footpaths and the field patterns and developed a simple form of functional zoning. The factory, standing between river and canal, took up most of the north-eastern corner of the site. The church stood opposite the factory in an area defined by the railway, Victoria Road and a magnificent elm tree drive. The community lived along the southern (north-facing) slopes of the valley between the railway and the Bradford road. This area had its own micro-geographical pattern. The best houses were built on the outer edges of the principal dormitory area which lay to the west of Victoria Road, thus enclosing most of the workmen's cottages within a ring of more expensive housing. The public institutions which dominated the main thoroughfare locked in this area. What was missing in Saltaire was the village green, an uncontrolled and casual meeting place where men and women could congregate easily to gossip, grumble or have a bit of fun. At the bottom of the village there were allotment gardens and pig-sties. There was a cultivated area of lawn and flower bed in front of the almshouses. For the rest, five minutes' walk across the river was the disciplined leisure of a park which closed at sunset and on Sundays did not open until 2 p.m. Whatever the virtues of Saltaire, and no doubt they were many, it was primarily conceived more in terms of the industrial army than in terms of the village community.

The people who were to enjoy or struggle with the facilities which Saltaire provided were a relatively homogeneous group.[41] Of those living in the village in 1871, 75 per cent had been born in the West Riding textile area; 20 per cent of them were from the Shipley–Baildon–Bingley area and 23 per cent from Bradford and its adjacent villages. 13 per cent came from the rest of Yorkshire and the remaining 12 per cent from other parts of the British Isles and over and above these just twelve from abroad. In 1861 most of the inhabitants had come in from Bradford; by 1871 most came from the neighbouring villages and this was particularly true of the young people who came in after 1861. Between 1854 and 1858 key workers from the Bradford mills were being transferred to Saltaire. After that date the newcomers included many of the out-workers whom Salt had employed in large numbers in places like Allerton, Clayton and Baildon.

Those whose birthplaces lay outside the West Riding were usually craftsmen or employees of a particular kind, some of whom must have been specifically recruited as individuals. George Richards, the millwright, came from Norwich, Samuel Excell, a stone-mason, from Gloucester, and Alexander George, a tailor, from Scotland. Robert Lease, one of the office clerks, was born in Stepney, and the woman who took over the Infants' department of the school came from Bermondsey. The most interesting member of this group was the commissionaire, Thomas Hill, ex-Conductor of Ordnance in the Indian Army. He had served for twenty-one years and all the children living with him in Saltaire had been born in India. There was also a small group of about thirty families of textile workers, like the Sanctuarys and the Eastells, who came from the declining worsted textile areas of East Anglia and the South-west.

Since the experiment was not simply a charitable scheme for re-housing from the slums of Bradford, but an exercise in the establishment of an industrial village around a profit-making firm, there was always discrimination in the selection of inhabitants. The census enumerators' returns show how preference was given to key workers. Managers of departments and foremen in charge of the various operations could expect accommodation if they wanted it. Frederick Wood, the young Lightcliffe man recruited by Salt from the school there who had become chief cashier at the age of thirty, was given the best house in the village – No. 1 Albert Road at the south-western corner of the village. John Scriven, one of the wool-buyers, had a house in Fern Place, fronting the Leeds–Bramley Road. Charles Wormesley, the manager of the weaving shed, James Rushton, foreman in charge of woolsorting and James Dawson, the foreman of the wool warehouse, had all been living in George Street before 1861 and had all moved by 1871 to even better accommodation in either Albert Road or Victoria Road. The overlookers generally had been among the first to go to Saltaire; by 1861, all of them lived there and this was still the case in 1871. Almost all the warp-dressers whose work was crucial at an early stage in the textile process, were treated in the same way. Other groups moved in more slowly. In 1861, about half the main body of workers had obtained accommodation, and although a good many more were housed between 1861 and 1870, the total labour force was never completely absorbed. In peak periods, the mill employed about 3,200 of which the village when completed provided 2,500 and it is reasonable to assume that – for whatever reasons – tenancies were allocated to people with good hopes of permanent employment. The fact is that Saltaire had a selected population drawn from the 'respectable working classes'.

In this connexion, the fact that only a very small number of Irish-born people lived in Saltaire stands out sharply. It is possible that Irish people did not want to live there as it meant isolation from the main body of the immigrant community. On the other hand, Saltaire itself stands among streets where there was a high proportion of Irish people, some of whom may well have been employed at the Salt mill, and some of Salt's mills in Bradford had stood in the middle of Irish areas. This may, however, have reflected the prejudices of overlookers and other senior workers rather than a deliberate choice of company policy, for they formed an element in the so-called workers committee which was responsible for allocating tenancies in the village.[42]

As would be expected, it was a young population. Over 50 per cent in both 1861 and 1871 were under twenty. Women outnumbered men in almost all age groups in both census years and generally by considerable numbers in the groups of working age. Thus for the ages between eleven and forty there were 15 per cent more women than men in 1861 and 9 per cent more in 1871. The narrowing of the gap was accounted for by the settlement in the village of a large force of male maintenance workers – 47 joiners, 20 stonemasons, 10 gardeners, 7 blacksmiths and 64 labourers, and an office staff of 10 male clerks – and affected in particular the composition of the age group 21–30. It did not affect the balance within the mill itself; that is, the prospects of employment for young women who had outgrown the unskilled work of the spinning department. Thus the experience of young people was different from that of those who lived in a mining village. Girls tended to stay at home and work in the mill at least until they were married. Boys who could not take up the specialist work available, and were too old to work as doffers, reelers or 'bobbin liggers' tended to leave the village as they came through adolescence.

It was also to be expected that there would be a high proportion of unmarried women in the working age group within the village. 1,053 women between the ages of fifteen and forty-five were recorded in the census of 1871: 401 were married, 29 were widows and 623 were spinsters.[43]

Saltaire was a working-class village. Apart from a handful of families of professional men, and of a larger number of people engaged in the main commercial and other service activities of the village, all shared, to a greater or lesser degree, the common experience of the factory life, and the rhythm of its day. Work started at 6 a.m. and finished at 6 p.m. until 1872, after which work began and finished half an hour later. The day was broken by two intervals – one for breakfast between 8.0 and 8.30 a.m. and one for dinner between 12.30 and 1.30 p.m. On Saturdays the factory closed at first at 2 p.m. and later at 1.0 p.m. Over 2,000 people flocked along the streets six times a day – men, women and children whose lives were ordered to the signal of the factory 'buzzer'. The reporters of both *All the Year Round* and *Reynolds's Newspaper* were equally impressed by the sight of this industrial army. Charles Dickens junior wrote:

As I left Saltaire . . . the streets were filled with the 'hands' returning to their work; the women with their kerchiefs round their heads; the men dressed in long, light blue smock-frocks; the children running in and out amongst them and making the pavement echo with the rough music of their clogs. All looked prosperous and happy, and so properly do the colonists appreciate their good fortune that the policemen . . . are . . . necessarily the least employed of the community.

And Sam Kydd in similar vein:

At no factory can there be a better opportunity of seeing the 'hands' at meal times or at the close of the factory day than at Saltaire. All come up a flight of stone steps, leading from an open space in the works to the main street. At first may be seen six to eight men and women walking leisurely up the yard, converging as they approach the stone steps. Then follow some ten or twelve boys, who race each other to the top; next, a few 'hands' indiscriminately step rapidly along, as if wishful to be out of the way; gradually, the numbers increased, swelling rapidly, and filling the steps from side to side, from bottom to top. In a quarter of an hour thousands have passed before you; the clatter of clogs and the hum of voices has ceased; the streets look deserted. A better looking body of factory 'hands' than those at Saltaire I have not seen. They are far above the average of their class in Lancashire, and are considerably above the majority in Yorkshire.[44]

The factory created a structure of discipline, based on skill and experience, which could be expected to be carried on into a hierarchy of status within the village. The following table indicates its principal components.

Executive	Wool buyer, designer, engineer, managers and foremen of departments, chief cashier, overlookers.
Skilled	Wool sorters, warp dressers, craftsmen of maintenance staff, machine fitters, clerical staff, piece examiners and takers-in, finishers, weftmen/twisters.
Semi-skilled	Warehousemen, weavers, dye-house workers, engine minders, gas-house workers, time keeper, junior clerical staff.

Unskilled	Woolcombers, spinners, drawers and reelers, unspecified millhands, doffers, bobbin 'liggers', labourers and other unspecified maintenance work.

There were approximately 100 in the élite executive group, 600 skilled workers, 850 semi-skilled and 800 unskilled workers.

There were also about 250 inhabitants whose livelihood was not directly dependent on factory employment. In 1871, several men of professional status lived at the top of Albert Road and George Street – two civil servants, the Minister of the Congregational church, the Registrar of Births, Marriages and Deaths and two of the schoolteachers. There were another nineteen schoolteachers and the Wesleyan pastor in different parts of the village. This group included the apothecary in Victoria Road, the nurses at the hospital, the manager and matron of the baths, several coal merchants, the station master and his staff, the postmaster Abraham Holroyd who was also stationer and publisher, 69 shopkeepers and assistants, 52 dressmakers and milliners, 16 tailors, 9 bookmakers and cobblers, 5 cloggers and 2 photographers. There was also a policeman. The census of 1871 records in addition about 100 women engaged in domestic duties and another 615 adults, most of whom were wives looking after the home. There were 522 recorded simply as children. 515 were entered as scholars, although some of these must have been half-timers, since the census only records one specifically in that category.[45]

The outline of the social hierarchy in the village was confirmed by the wages paid for the various occupations. It is notoriously difficult to establish an accurate table of wages in the textile industry, even for the period when the difficulties caused by the various forms of minor sub-contracting had been eliminated by mechanisation. Kydd gave a list of wages which was, he believed, 'a close approximation to the actual wages paid per week to various classes of workmen' in Saltaire. Isaac Holden left some information about combing wages in his records and work memos. W. Cudworth supplied some figures in his work on the condition of the industrial classes in Bradford, which may be used with some circumspection; and more recently C. Richardson has compiled a table of wages from Board of Trade records. The information they provide is brought together in Table 4.

Table 4 Wage rates, worsted textile industry, Bradford, mid-nineteenth century

Designation	Kydd (1857)	Holden (1864)	Cudworth (1875-80)	Richardson (1857 and 1883)
Foremen			35s.–55s.	
Overlookers				
Mechanics		28s.		
Combing		32s.		
Spinning			30s.	
Weaving			30s.	
Warehouse		30s.		
Woolsorters (daymen)	28s.			
Takers in	28s.			
Mechanics and Craftsmen	26s.-28s.		25s.-30s.	
Warpdressers	20s.			
Woolsorters (not daymen)	20s.			
Sizers	18s.			
Carters			18s.	
Warehousemen	14s.-16s.	16s.	18s.-22s.	
Washers	14s.-16s.			
Machine combers (men)	from 9s.	16s.		10s. (1857) 15s. (1883)
Weavers, two loom (men)	15s.		15s.	
Turnsters	15s.			
Women				
Weavers				
one loom	9s.		8s. 6d.-10s. 6d.	
two loom			13s.-15s.	12s (1857) 15s (1883)
Spinners				8s.-10s. 6d. (1857)
Combing	9s.	9s.		
Boys and Girls				
Full-time			8s. 6d.-10s. 6d.	
Half-time			4s.	

Sources S. Kydd, *Reynolds's Newspaper*, 29 Nov 1857

I. Holden, Memo Book, personal papers (Bradford University Library)

W. Cudworth, *The Condition of the Industrial Working Classes of Bradford and District*, Bradford, 1887

C. Richardson, 'The Irish in Victorian Bradford', *The Bradford Antiquary*, New Series, Part XLV, June 1871.

Although the information provided in the table is inadequate, there is sufficient agreement nevertheless to give a reasonable approximation of actual wage rates. The table also clearly shows the two major general trends in nineteenth-century wages. As a matter of course, women earned less than men even if doing the same sort of work. Women weavers, even if they were good – and good weavers had a special place in the hierarchy of the textile factory – had the greatest difficulty in earning more than the unskilled male workers in the combing shed. Thus the values of a masculine society were maintained. The other trend which it illustrates is the wide difference in levels of wages between skilled and unskilled – a differential which varies between 40 and 60 per cent and provided the economic base for those differences in life-style which developed in a working-class community. To take an extreme example, the lives of James Rushton and Timothy Binns must have shown considerable dissimilarities. Rushton had worked for Salt from the start in 1834, and in 1861 was a woolsorter living with his wife and one daughter at 28 George Street. His wife's sister, who worked in the mill as a weaver, lived with them. The daughter was thirteen and worked as a boot-stitcher. In 1871, he was living in a newer and better house at 19 Victoria Road. He was now the manager of the woolsorting department. His wife had died and his daughter kept house. The sister-in-law continued to live with them and to work as a weaver. In 1884, the workpeople marked his completion of fifty years service to the firm with a presentation which commemorated his work for the village community, for he had always played an active part in its affairs. His income in 1861 was about thirty shillings a week and the household income was augmented by whatever his daughter and sister-in-law contributed from earnings respectively of four to five shillings and thirteen to fifteen shillings a week. In 1871, as working head of the woolsorting department, he was earning more than the fifty-five shillings given by Cudworth as the top wage of a foreman – a conservative estimate would be about £3. Timothy Binns was a woolcomber who had come to Saltaire from Bingley in the late fifties. He lived with a family of eleven children at 13 Shirley Street, a three-bedroomed house with no garden. He still lived there in 1871, by which time four of his children were married and three of them had left home; one still lived there with her husband and small son so that the house still accommodated twelve people. In 1861, seven of his children worked in semi-skilled or unskilled occupations, and in 1871 eight people contributed to the family budget. Family earnings came to between £4. 10s. and £5 a week in both years. The interests of these households touched – there were, for instance, weavers in both, and Timothy Binns was clearly a respected member of the community. He was a trustee of the Methodist Sunday School and vice-president of the community insurance club of which Rushton was president. But the average income per head was so much greater in the Rushton household that expectations and aspirations must have been greater.

There are a number of general points that can be made. Overlookers tended to have fewer children than others. The children of overlookers and craftsmen were likely to stay at school longer, rarely leaving before the age of twelve or thirteen. Their chances of better paid or at least more prestigious employment were always better than average. The sons of overlookers and craftsmen became overlookers and craftsmen themselves, the daughters, pupil teachers or apprentice milliners and dressmakers, although they often started working life in the spinning departments of the mill.

At the same time, the village was always more than the dormitory of an industrial battalion. A community reached beyond the fact of common employment to exploit that experience in the common habitation. It was facilitated by the fact of common origin – most of the population came from the West Riding and almost all of them from a textile background. As already noted, there were few Irish people to provide an element of cultural disassociation. The great majority of the population belonged to the same stratum of working-class life. Most of the householders were skilled or semi-skilled men who shared a common pattern of employment. Thus a large segment of working-class life – the mass of the labouring poor – where the social problems of industrial life were most fiercely encountered was under-represented. In Saltaire, the population was made up very largely of the 'respectable element' which might be expected to respond more amenably to the pressures the village created.

Thus, despite differences in men's occupations and their rewards, there were always more similarities than differences. Saltaire's population shared a common way of life to a degree that would have been difficult to establish in a naturally generated community. This was confirmed by an overall comparability of many family incomes. In 1871, Samuel Baldwin was a drawing-room overlooker living with his wife and three of his children in a newly built house at 28 Victoria Road. His two daughters worked with him in the drawing-room; his son was an overlooker. John Butterfield, a weaver, lived at 33 Titus Street with his wife, two sons – woolsorters – and two daughters – weavers like their father. The Baldwin family earned between them £3 to £3. 5s. a week, the Butterfield family about £4. The average income per head in each family was about 13s. per week.

In addition, people tended to stay in Saltaire. Of the 450 families there in 1861, at least 40 per cent were still there in 1871 – a high proportion, given the prevailing pattern of life expectancy and a working-class tendency to move house relatively frequently. In 1871, also, a large minority of families were related in some degree. The structure of discipline in the factory never corresponded exactly with the status structure of the village. Senior men like James Rushton and, in general, skilled men played a greater part than others in the administration of village facilities, but men like Timothy Binns in humbler occupations were not automatically excluded. And, most important, men not employed directly in the factory – Seth Bentley, manager of the baths and wash-house, and Alex George – were prepared to offer leadership when occasion demanded.

The majority of married women, whatever their husband's work, shared the common experience of life in the home, the shops and the streets, for most of them did not go out to work, at least if there were children to be looked after or if the total household income was augmented sufficiently by children, relatives or lodgers. The children also shared the common life of the factory school, the Sunday school, the streets and the surroundings, and, apart from a few, as the main body of unskilled workers in the mill.

Nor did the distribution of tenancies suggest a precisely regimented industrial village. The well-to-do lived in the most commodious houses in Albert Road. Overlookers' houses most frequently housed the better paid, but this was not the invariable rule. There were weavers and woolcombers scattered about William Henry Street, George Street and the middle section of Albert Road. There were also a number of overlookers living in the oldest and most inconvenient houses off Caroline Street. The new and improved workmen's cottages, like those on Katherine Street, were fairly evenly divided among unskilled, semi-skilled and skilled.

Housing provided scope for a good deal of neighbourly rivalry, a fact which led one inhabitant to remark that in Saltaire class started at your own doorstep. To live in a house with a garden was always in Saltaire an understandable housewifely ambition, and one informant suggested that corniced rooms also had special significance. Removals within the village were thus a persistent feature of village life. Of those who stayed between 1861 and 1871 over 50 per cent moved to better or newer houses as they were completed and left older property to the newcomers. One of the principal determinants of the pattern of tenancies was the fact that there were more overlookers and skilled craftsmen than 'overlookers' cottages' and a number of them had to live in the less expensive streets like Constance Street and Titus Street. And in the end, at any given time, family income and therefore family size was the decisive factor. A woolcomber with four or five other wage-earners could afford a house in William Henry Street. A young overlooker not long married and perhaps with a baby or two might prefer to live in the inexpensive accommodation of Herbert Street or Helen Street. Housing provided a significant demarcation at the top and to a lesser degree in the more unattractive houses. In the middle range there was a considerable social mix.[46]

The austere regularity of the village plan did not inhibit the development of a coherent and self-respecting community. Reporters commented on the 'well-cared-for' look of the houses

– the neat curtains, the flowers in the windows, the well 'swilled' and well swept yards and frontages, the window-sills and door-steps scoured with white or yellow stone. The local press, though ready to seize on any evidence of vice or lawlessness associated with Saltaire, could find little to offer. Three or four cases of theft were reported in the first twenty years. About twice a month a Saltaire man or woman was charged with being drunk and disorderly in the streets of Bradford or Shipley and there were several cases of wife-beating reported in the seventies when society was beginning to take this seriously. Nobody complained of Saltaire in the terms which one man used to describe an area of Bradford where an employer – as famous in some ways as Salt – had built houses for his workpeople between 1872 and 1874:

The population may be called migratory, their notions of the use of soap and water ambiguous, and their manner and conversation neither entertaining nor elevating. Truly, knowing Bradford well, I can safely say I have heard more swearing and lewd language in this place than in the whole of the rest of the borough . . . rows occur nightly . . . on Friday and Saturday evening the place is worse than Silsbridge Lane.[47]

The boys who congregated on the bridge and made rude comments about passers-by from outside Saltaire were a regular nuisance but caused only occasional protest, for this, after all, was the common hazard for any stranger passing through a West Riding mill town or village at this time.

Nor was there much evidence of the sort of tension (often associated with a newly established settlement) which generated complaints about facilities. William White, writing in 1857, said that one or two people thought the rents too high. One man had said that he could get a house in Shipley for £4 a year, with cellar and garden in which he kept a pig prohibited by the Saltaire tenancy agreement, but most of them 'expressed themselves well satisfied with their quarters'.[48]

Although Saltaire was not a slum clearance scheme as such, a sizeable proportion of its inhabitants had come from the inadequate and insanitary housing which surrounded Salt's mills in Bradford. Abraham Feather, engineman, had come from a house in Fawcett Court, the Bottomley, Hanson and Speight families from Hope Street; all lived in the shadow of three worsted mills and an iron foundry with a pump in the courtyard for water and dependent on the co-operation of neighbours for the use of such lavatory facilities as were available. In the first twenty years, Saltaire had an outbreak of smallpox, said by the local medical officer to have been confined to non-vaccinated families, though serious enough to close the Saltaire day and Sunday schools, an epidemic of scarlet fever and a number of cases of typhoid tracked down to defective drains. Precise statistical proof that Saltaire was a healthier place to live in than other industrial areas cannot be provided because Saltaire was not returned in official documents as a separate unit. It is, however, possible to draw some inferences from what is available. In 1906, for instance, the Medical Officer of Health for Shipley reported that death rates in the district of Shipley were as follows: North Ward 14·1; South Ward 10·6; East Ward 14·6; West Ward 10·2; Central Ward 14·3; Total 12·7. The population of Saltaire made up the greater part of the population of West Ward – about 4,300 out of 5,753. The proportion outside Saltaire contained a large well-to-do middle-class element; nevertheless, if they are disregarded and all deaths in West Ward attributed to Saltaire, the death rate for the year is still 14·2, just higher than North and lower than the working-class and industrial wards, East and Central. According to death-rate figures, Saltaire was also healthier than Bradford, for there the figure was 16·1 per 1,000 and only the townships Bolton, a farming area, and Heaton, where the boast was that it had more pounds sterling per square mile than any other part of the West Riding, both part of Bradford, were below Saltaire's 14·2.[49]

An investigation by Dr H. Jones, a Shipley medical officer in 1893, gives the same impression. He compared the through houses of Saltaire with an area of back-to-back housing nearby which, he claimed, was of comparable social composition, and established that death rates in Saltaire were invariably lower. He also divided the back-to-back area into three categories and obtained the following results:

		Death Rates	
Street A	25 yards wide		
	Density 160 persons per acre	open-ended	16.1 per 1,000
Street B	10 yards wide	cul-de-sacs	
	Density 300 persons per acre	and yards	28.1 per 1,000
Street C	15 yards wide		
	Density 207 persons per acre	"	22.5 per 1,000

Saltaire with a density of 197 persons per acre and with twice as many paupers as Street A had a death rate of 15·6 per 1,000. Of course, Dr Jones needed to look at death rates in the four basic types of through house in Saltaire – what was needed was proof that death rates in the least commodious houses there were lower than in Street A. Nevertheless, the investigation sustained the view that Saltaire generally was a much healthier place to live in than the run of working-class housing available even in the late nineteenth and early twentieth centuries. Even if the very best housing in Saltaire were to be eliminated, Saltaire compared well with housing of Street A type and was much superior to other types of housing pre-dating or contemporary with Saltaire. Jones had ignored the advantages of the Saltaire site in itself but there can be little doubt that by the standards of the day Saltaire was a healthy and coherent community.[50]

It was a natural development that the new settlement should have given rise rapidly to communal activities, both of a regular and a more casual nature. People in Saltaire usually gave generously to charitable collections, such as that for the emancipated slaves of the USA and the victims of the Chicago fire in 1871. There was a Saltaire Committee to provide financial help for the 'Oastler Statue Movement' and in 1865 the *Bradford Observer* drew attention to the generosity of Saltaire in contributing since 1862 from £12 to £8 weekly for the relief of the Lancashire cotton workers during the 'cotton famine' associated with the American Civil War. These activities were organised by the overlookers who collected in the mill. By 1857, a number of senior workmen had started the Saltaire Penny Savings Bank, Joseph Dawson, indefatigable as ever, and now the foreman of the wool warehouse, acting as secretary. About the same time, the Saltaire Funeral Brief Society was started.

This type of unregistered insurance society, intended to provide against the expenses of death and the Victorian funeral, was common in the West Riding. Their existence was often precarious, for there was no system of regular contributions, levies being made by house-to-house collection as deaths occurred. The danger was that a large number of the members would start to grow old together, and young people rather than meet regular and increasing expenses preferred to start new societies which did not demand the same outlay. The relatively stable and coherent situation in Saltaire seems to have given the Saltaire society an unusual strength. Certainly in 1879 it was still thriving with nearly 3,000 members, three-quarters of all those entitled under the rules to join. Children under seven were not accepted. For others, there was an entrance fee of threepence per adult and one and a half pence per child. The levy was twopence per adult and one penny per child on every occasion, collected by members paid 2s. 6d. for the work. In 1879, £180 was paid out in 'death' money, but little cash was held in hand and no regular balance sheet seems to have been published. An annual general meeting reported on the year's work. Like the savings bank, the society was run mainly by senior workers. In 1879, James Rushton was president, James Paley, a spinning overlooker, was secretary and the committee of fifteen was made up of overlookers, specialist mechanics, and warehousemen, with one only an ordinary 'millhand'. Among them were a number of men who, like Rushton, were constantly active in the affairs of the village – Sharp Varley, Samuel Baldwin, Edwin Cox and John Lambert.[51]

At a semi-official level, two sick benefit societies provided a system of communal health insurance. The society for men required a contribution of 6d. for young people (13–15) and 8d. for adults (15–50) each month and offered a benefit of 8s. a week during six months of illness, reduced to 4s. a week for the next six months and then 2s. a week. The women's society, founded in 1867, accepted all over sixteen on payment of 6d. a month and provided similar but smaller benefits. The firm supported both schemes, adding 4d. per month to each man's and 6d. a month to each woman's contribution. The schemes were still in operation in 1904, and presumably lasted until the inception of

National Insurance, several years later.[52]

Co-operative societies were also well supported in Saltaire. In the late sixties, three separate establishments were in operation, a branch of the Leeds Industrial Co-operative Society, the Saltaire Industrial Co-operative Society and the Saltaire Coal Industrial Society. Together, they claimed well over 600 members, three-quarters of the total number of families in Saltaire at the time. By 1878, the Saltaire Society was running into difficulty and was wound up. It was, however, reconstituted almost immediately under the leadership of Alex George, the tailor, and continued successfully for many years. It had food, drapery, clothing and boot and shoe departments and compensated for the no-credit rule by organising 'club' purchases for expensive items. Saltaire people, like many working people of the period, were committed to co-operative activity, not merely as a convenient and more inexpensive way of shopping. They showed their commitment by investing in the Cobden Memorial Mills enterprise started by E. S. Beesly and T. Hughes, and smaller sums in the co-operative initiatives of Henry Briggs in Methley and the Crossleys in Halifax. As elsewhere, co-operation also had a political flavour. Alex George was one of the most prominent Radicals in the village and he was supported by others like the Sanctuary brothers and Isaac Constantine.[53]

The entertainment of people in Saltaire was well organised on the serious and respectable lines which met with the approval of society. Indeed, there may be significance in the failure of an attempt to organise a Saltaire Fair and Feast in September 1865. In future those who wanted to have a bit of fun in this way had to go down to Shipley. The new Institute, however, provided scope for lecture programmes of a more ambitious type than had been previously available. The head of the Factory Schools gave a series of lectures on 'Science as applied to the trades of the district'. They were reported as well attended by the young men of the district 'who applauded quite enthusiastically the successful experiments'. Titus junior gave a lantern-slide lecture on a tour he had made through Turkey and Palestine. Katherine Salt and her sister, Miss Crossley, organised a series of 'cheap musical concerts'. Katherine Salt also started a series of classes in 'cottage cookery' – initially taken by a professional cook and then by some of the directors' wives and their servants and said to have attracted full houses. She had a similar success with a course for women on the laws of health. Housed in the Institute were the fife and drum band for the boys, a brass band which challenged the already famous Black Dyke Mills Band for pre-eminence in national competitions, and a gymnastics club which quickly became a leading club in northern England.[54]

Out-of-doors, the fishing club, with one of the woolsorters as secretary, provided sport for about 100 men. It was supported by Titus junior who established a trout farm at Milner Field and kept a stretch of the Aire inside the park stocked with fish. A company of the Thirty-ninth West Riding Rifle Volunteers was established in the summer of 1859, and sent on its way with a musical concert which raised £33 for the funds. Edward, George and Titus junior all held commissions in it for short periods and ninety young men in the village joined the ranks.[55] The most vigorous of the societies was the one begun in 1861, the Horticultural Society, renamed in 1876 the Horticultural, Pig, Dog, Poultry and Pigeon Society. Its regular members numbered about 100 and its annual show and exhibition was one of the highlights of the village's social life for many years. In 1863, the second exhibition was held on waste ground at the end of Titus Street. For the occasion the street was decorated with an avenue of firs and other trees, and garlands of flowers 'with suitable mottoes' were hung across the street. The band of the Rifle Volunteers entertained and games were organised for the children. The Head Gardener at Methley Park acted as judge of the produce on show. By 1870, a donkey show, horse jumping and a walking race had been added to the entertainment, and in 1876 it had grown beyond the resources of Titus Street and moved to a field close to the park. Here it added to its reputation by staging for a number of years an athletics meeting which attracted nationwide competition. In this society, also, the most prominent members and the most regular prize winners were skilled and long-serving employees – men like Eli Lambert, Isaac Constantine, John Hanson and James Ellis and, not unexpectedly, Sam Baldwin and James

303

Rushton. The point is, of course, that men of this type were more likely to be allocated and to keep the allotments which the firm provided, though they could not establish a total monopoly since there were 100 allotments and 38 piggeries along the canal-side.[56]

Organised games did not yet provide the established framework of Saturday afternoon leisure activity. Football as an organised pursuit in Saltaire was not reported systematically in the press for some years, although some must have been played. Cricket, however, was as well developed as it was in other parts of the West Riding. A number of minor teams based on the village were in existence for many years, teams like Saltaire Clarence, Saltaire Britannia, Saltaire White Rose and the teams associated with the Methodist and Congregational chapels. There was also the Saltaire Cricket Club, destined like the brass band and the gymnastics club to achieve national fame. It was founded in 1865 with 140 members and a promise from Salt to provide a playing area. It was reorganised in 1871 when the firm began to take a more positive interest in its affairs. The managing director, Charles Stead, became president, Titus junior sat on the committee and the firm gave both the ground in the new park and generous financial help. This club quickly entered the highly competitive structure of the best local cricket and became one of the major attractions of the park. The standard of the cricket available could be measured by the fact that the club staged a three-day match against the Nottinghamshire County side in 1877 and by the quality of the professional player engaged between 1873 and 1877. He was R. G. Barlow, of Lancashire and England, given a touch of immortality by the Edwardian poet L. Thompson in a nostalgic poem on Lancashire cricket which he wrote in 1907.

Oh! my Hornby and my Barlow long ago.[57]

The one limitation on relaxed enjoyment was the lack of a village public house. Few people writing in the nineteenth century about Saltaire failed to praise this omission, and the temperance movement never tired of claiming a famous victory. Mr Henry Hibbert, the temperance agent in Bradford, was shocked in 1887 to find that alcohol had been on sale at the Saltaire Exhibition associated with the opening of the new technical college. Saltaire had been looked to and spoken of with pride as the largest 'prohibitive' village in the country. When the village was built, Hibbert continued, Salt had intended that no alcohol at all should be sold there. He had yielded to great pressure and had allowed an off-licence shop to be opened, but after a short trial he had closed it down. In fact, there was always an off-licence shop after 1867, if not before. Mary Stallworthy, the tenant, was fined for selling beer outside licensed hours in 1868, and several months after Salt's death in 1877, G. H. Bailey, the apothecary in Victoria Road, was advertising his excellent stocks of ports, sherries, rum, Irish and Scotch whiskey, gin, brandy, claret and champagne. In 1875, eighteen months before Salt's death, Saltaire was caught in the dispute over the Permissive Bill which was intended to give local authorities greater powers to control the sale of liquor. Tired, apparently, of hearing of the temperance success of Saltaire, the opponents of the Bill sent an investigator to the village. He reported that the inhabitants of Saltaire drank beer and spirits like everybody else. They used the thirty public houses in Shipley as much as other local inhabitants, and, if they wanted to avoid being seen, went off to Bradford; and the village chemist sold as much liquor off-licence as was sold in some of the best public houses.[58]

Salt himself was not rigorous in his views or his personal use of alcohol. Indeed, one account states firmly that he was not a teetotaller. He served wine in his house and at the various public entertainments he gave to friends and colleagues, and provided beer for the Saltaire Rifle Volunteers when they held manoeuvres at Methley Park. In fact, during a speech on the importance of free trade he remarked while making a plea for the elimination of wine duties: 'that we at least ought not to be debarred by laws of our own making from the enjoyment of comforts denied to us by climate or other circumstances'.[59] It may well be that his attitude hardened as he grew older; his subscriptions to the various temperance and teetotal organisations were in his later years among the highest in Bradford, but like many moderately minded men he condemned the public house rather than what it sold. He thought that the public house presented unlimited opportunities for promiscuity and waste, and he saw no reason to encourage it. He was as much aware of the practical objections to a public house near the place of work as he was of the more broadly moral position of the temperance/teetotal man. Like many Victorian employers, Salt distrusted the employee who drank. Archibald Buchanan, for instance, giving evidence to Chadwick's commission of inquiry, said he would not engage a man who drank. It was not only that the public house offered a temptation to take time off work. In practical terms, the person who came to work in a factory after taking a drink or two could be at best a nuisance and at worst a danger. It was one thing to be working at home with comparatively uncomplicated machinery. It was another to be engaged in a large factory in the midst of the sophisticated engineering of the nineteenth century. According to Hibbert, Salt had once remarked that he could see no reason to build or allow to be built an establishment which could mar his success as a businessman. He would have agreed with the working man who said to H. Solly 'Ah, Mr Solly, what you've got to do is to get us to give up the public house. It's not what we get at home . . . it's what we drink when we get there . . . it's the company we keep.' Of course Saltaire had its sincere exponents of the temperance/teetotal position – men like George Morrell, the schoolmaster, who ran the very large Band of Hope in Saltaire. But very quickly the legend, though it was an exaggeration, of Saltaire as a model temperance village was born.[60]

Membership of a religious society was, as in most places, a minority interest albeit relatively strong and one which included many of the most influential of those connected with the village and the firm. In 1860, the Congregational Church had claimed a regular weekly congregation of over 400 and a full communicant membership of over 80. In 1875 the Sunday school claimed 110 on the register and 69 regular attenders, although about 400 could turn out for the annual bun-feast. The Congregational Church was the 'élite' church in Saltaire. Titus himself was never more than an occasional attender, preferring to attend a local church at either Methley or

Lightcliffe. W. E. Glyde, one of the partners and a brother of the Rev. Jonathan Glyde of the Horton Lane Chapel, was the effective leader of the congregation for a number of years. Titus junior and his wife took over the responsibilities which both diffidence and failing health prevented the head of the family from undertaking, and became principal benefactors and leaders after their marriage in 1866. George Morrell and Frederick Wood, the chief cashier, were among the deacons, and a number of well-to-do Shipley people also formed part of the communicant membership.[61] The Wesleyan Methodist Chapel had a substantial congregation and a Sunday school in the late seventies with eighty regular attenders. Its leaders were drawn from a wider social circle than those of the Congregational Church. They included at one time not only the manager of the wool warehouse, the mill engineer, and several of the overlookers, but several woolsorters and four or five woolcombers. Like the Congregational Church, the Wesleyan Chapel also served the district surrounding Saltaire, and by 1875 the Sunday school committee was composed of fifteen Saltaire men and fifteen from outside.[62] Of minor sects, the Swedenborgians were said to number, at full strength, about a hundred. They fulfilled their reputation as being drawn from the most intelligent of the working population by organising parties in their rooms as an alternative attraction to the traditional 5 November celebrations. There was also a small Christadelphian group which met regularly at a house in Victoria Road.[63]

It was to be expected in the middle years of the century that political activity would cause no trouble. Saltaire was seen as the visual proof of the Liberal–Labour alliance working at the social as well as at the political level. Few, if any, were enfranchised for parliamentary elections until after 1885, nor did local government elections play much part in the life of the village until the Shipley Urban District Council was established. The Liberal–Radical position of three of the Salt family, Titus himself, Titus junior and George, their active participation in the parliamentary reform agitation, and their defence of Nonconformist interests coincided with the position of many of their employees, while the minority of Conservative working men in Saltaire – men like the postmaster Abraham Holroyd, the warehouseman John Wood, and the printer William Berry, could be satisfied that views acceptable to them were heard in the Salt family when the heir to the baronetcy, William Henry, and the third son, Edward, became Tories in the mid-sixties. The population of Saltaire gave enthusiastic support to the reform agitations of the late fifties and sixties. In 1859, interest in Bright's speech was so great that Salt had it read out in all the rooms of the factory. Practically the whole of the adult population – male and female – attended a reform meeting in the dining-hall in 1861. In 1866, the working men of the Bradford and Shipley district held a demonstration on Shipley Glen, where Isaac Constantine the Saltaire woolsorter presided and urged their support for the government bill. By 1866 also there was a powerful branch of the National Reform League in Saltaire. Its secretary was Robert Power, an 'uncompromising radical', the son of the Edward Power who had been imprisoned in 1848 in Bradford for Chartist activity.[64] At the West Riding demonstrations on Woodhouse Moor in October 1866 and Easter Tuesday 1867 the Saltaire Manhood Suffrage Association turned out in force with the blessing of the firm, which closed for the 1866 occasion since it was not a public holiday. The Saltaire Brass Band played the accompaniment to the march from Saltaire to Leeds.

A picture of an industrious, respectable and socially energetic community emerges from what we know about Saltaire in the first twenty-odd years of its existence. At the same time it was not a community without problems of any sort. Depression, unemployment, short time and illness caused the same trouble as elsewhere. There was poverty in the village; for working-class life at almost any level was never all that far away from want. Though Titus Salt was a charitable man and usually made financial gifts to the poor at Christmas time he did not usurp the functions of the Board of Guardians. In 1871 there were said to be nine paupers in the village and Dr Jones indicated that in 1892 there were more paupers in Saltaire than in a nearby group of back-to-back houses of the superior type. From its inception in 1868, the Wesleyan Sunday School collected for its poor scholars and on a number of occasions made gifts of shoes and money to one or other of them. In 1879, a number of Saltaire men accepted invitations to emigrate to the USA, and during the same depression Katherine Salt supplied clothing to the school so that children without adequate clothing could come out in the cold weather to school. Individuals also had their problems with the firm, which had a reputation for not tolerating poor work. In 1868, Titus himself resumed activity for a time and, ignoring the evidence of a general turn-down in economic activity, dismissed one of the designers, whose work he thought unimaginative and the principal cause of the firm's trading difficulties at the time.[65]

Saltaire was never likely to become a prominent centre of crusading zeal. Nevertheless, individuals did challenge authority when the occasion demanded, although they were usually not directly employed by the firm when they did it. It was a Saltaire man who sustained the early agitation about what was known as 'woolsorters disease'. This was anthrax, the rapid fatal illness which sorters believed they contracted from working with foreign wools, particularly alpaca and mohair. (In fact, mohair was the usual source of infection, though the state of medical knowledge at the time prevented this from being known.) Within about fifteen years of the introduction of alpaca and mohair to the trade, sorters recognised that they were dealing with an industrial disease. Between 1866 and 1874 there were twenty-two deaths from it in Saltaire out of between 130 and 140 woolsorters. Agitation had begun as early as 1855. In January of that year the woolsorters at Queensbury, where Fosters of Black Dyke Mills used a great deal of alpaca and mohair, obtained a post-mortem examination of one of their colleagues. The surgeons reported that the examination had provided 'undeniable evidence that the mortality is attributable to the occupation of sorting the mohair and alpaca'.[66] Sam Kydd's report of November 1857 also referred to the matter:

The rate of mortality among woolsorters of alpaca and mohair is high. The dust rising from the material, when under manipulation affects the lungs; and instances have been frequent of men, apparently healthful, having become suddenly ill, and, within eight or ten days, dying. The facts are very well known at Saltaire, and are subjects of frequent conversations.

There was no more publicity for another ten years. Then in 1866 two sudden deaths in Saltaire opened up the question again. William Cawthra, the foreman woolsorter, died in late April and several weeks later Thomas Goldthorpe died at the age of forty-eight, leaving a wife and nine children. Both were much respected in the village, and Goldthorpe was particularly well-known as one of the enumerators for the 1861 census return. Thus the events caused a good deal of agitation. In the middle of 1867, Sutcliffe Rhodes, a highly literate and energetic working man who had recently been dismissed from the Saltaire mill, opened the question up in a letter to the *Bradford Observer*:

Much painful anxiety has of late been felt by a class of men who are employed in sorting of alpaca and mohair. It has by these men become a deep-rooted conviction that the clouds of dust and keenly penetrating hair which arise from these wools during the time of sorting must seriously affect the health, and endanger lives to an alarming extent. These foreign products have for a long time been looked upon as an underminer of the sorter's constitution. In some cases it is no doubt slow in its stealthy approach to the vital seat of health – but generally thought very sure. The sudden deaths of these men – thought to be its victims – have struck terror into the hearts of many of the same profession – men that in one week have been at their work, apparently strong and vigorous, have in the next been borne to the tomb. . . . In vain have weeping friends and acquaintances inquired into the nature of that which caused death. None can tell. It is no enviable position for a reflecting man to stand by the side of a vacant place, where but a few days ago he saw it occupied with perhaps a dear associate, now snatched away by some mysterious visitation, while he himself may fear a similar fate.[67]

He appealed to scientists to tackle the question. Six months later he reported that a 'philanthropic gentleman' (probably Titus junior) and 'an eminent physician', W. J. Ellis, both surgeon at Saltaire Hospital and Medical Officer for Shipley, were starting an investigation, and that a meeting of Saltaire woolsorters had been called to get volunteers for the investigation. Meanwhile a further series of deaths kept agitation alive. John Waddington's funeral received special publicity. As he was a member of the Saltaire Rifles, the

Commander accorded him the full honours of a military funeral. The passing of the cortege from Saltaire to the cemetery attracted an audience of several thousands from the village. In 1874, Ellis published as a result of his investigations an unhelpful pamphlet which managed to transfer most of the responsibility for the sickness to the sorters themselves. Shortly afterwards Rhodes wrote again to the *Observer* pointing out the weaknesses of the report. He agreed that the Salt firm had eventually come to place great emphasis on finding a solution but concluded that they had to take their share of responsibility for what had always been a tragedy:

It does not please me to make repeated references to these rooms [i.e. the sorting rooms at Saltaire] and I do so through no disrespect to masters at Saltaire, although much affliction might have been prevented had they paid closer attention to the due interests of their sorters.

Given the state of medical knowledge, the tragedy had to continue for a long time yet, but neither Salts nor anybody else was to know this, and the firm found the whole question an acute embarrassment.[68]

The most serious disagreement which occurred between the Salts and the local population concerned the Congregational Church. Shortly after the death of Sir Titus, the Congregational minister, Rev. R. Cowan, left after a disagreement with the trustees. The details were not recorded. It appears, however, that several of the wealthier members of the congregation, including Titus junior and his wife, had been dissatisfied with Cowan's preaching almost from the moment he had arrived. They had allowed the matter to rest because the majority of the congregation appeared satisfied. Recently, however, he had delivered a sermon which, wrote Titus junior, 'had so disgusted some of the ladies in the congregation' that a number of wealthy subscribers to the church threatened to withdraw. The deacons had taken it up and Mr Cowan had resigned although with great ill grace. Mr Cowan still had a good many supporters in the congregation. They organised a farewell presentation to which they invited among others the Mayor of Bradford. The intervention of Titus junior prevented the Mayor's attendance and Cowan's supporters, who included a number of local pastors, were angry. Rev. Dr Russell, a Presbyterian pastor, said that he 'would rather break stones by the road side at Saltaire than allow wealth to exercise an undue influence over his conscience'. The very distinguished Professor of Theology at the Yorkshire Congregational College, Dr Frazer, delivered some firm criticism of what he called 'high handed conduct' and Cowan, in his own defence, said that had the church been anywhere but in Saltaire he would probably be still there. The secretary made the presentation before an audience of about 450 and the *Shipley and Saltaire Times* reported that while he was speaking, 'there was scarcely a dry eye in the assembly, while many – and not all of them the younger portion – sobbed aloud. Such a sad scene at a presentation is seldom witnessed.' The lead in Cowan's defence was not taken by people who actually worked at the firm. The secretary was William London, a grocer in Daisy Place; the treasurer William Secker, the railway station master, and the chairman, William Ferrand, who had family connexions with Saltaire but did not live there himself. Nevertheless, an audience of 450 must have included some of the firm's employees.

Passion seemed to have died down, after Titus had indicated that he did not propose to enter the quarrel but, that if it persisted, he and his wife would stop their attendance and, naturally, withdraw their subscription, until it was healed. Sutcliffe Rhodes also wrote to the *Bradford Chronicle and Evening Mail* a letter critical of the Salt influence. He said that he was writing on behalf of people whose 'peculiar social position robbed them of an independent privilege of . . . freely speaking for themselves' and referred somewhat enigmatically to the 'black storms of party strife'. He added that a number of Cowan's supporters had defected as soon as the affair became public because they 'received their living from the magnates of the church' and that the people of the village had at last had the scales of delusion removed from their eyes by the discovery of 'false professions of religion, freedom and equality'. Titus claimed that he had always treated Cowan with the utmost kindness, and the *Bradford Observer* indicated that it had refused to publish Rhodes's letter because it considered that since his dismissal the writer had taken every opportunity to 'sully a name which will not suffer at his hands'. It is impossible to evaluate what happened since the nature of the quarrel remains a mystery. Nevertheless, it was a very instructive series of events.[69]

Many of the industrial villages of the West Riding shared some of the characteristics associated with the Saltaire pattern. In places like Denholme, west of Bradford, Calverley near Leeds, and Cowling and Sutton near Keighley, one or two firms dominated the life of the community, offering the only means of employment for most of the population, controlling at least some of the housing, and supporting the local institutions – cricket clubs, sick and benefit societies, chapels and educational establishments. On the outskirts of Bradford, Fosters of Black Dyke Mills dominated Queensbury, and Low Moor Iron Works had control of Wibsey Low Moor. In the borough of Bradford itself, Bowling was often referred to, with perhaps some exaggeration, as a feudal preserve shared between Bowling Iron Works Company and Ripleys, the dyers.

Saltaire offered a more complete authority, and there can be little doubt that in one way and another it was exercised. Salts held a superior position in the labour market. Sam Kydd's report on the village emphasised that only the best workpeople were employed, inferior 'hands' being dismissed after a trial period. According to one villager, a weaver had to be a 'good 'un' to work for Salt. The wages paid at Salts were no higher than those paid elsewhere and there is some evidence to suggest that they fell below the market price from time to time.

The tenancy of a good house was a considerable advantage – particularly in the sixties when there was a general local shortage – and a man might put up with a good deal to avoid losing it. The tenancy agreement does not give a clear indication of the relationship between employer-landlord and employee-tenant. The formal obligations placed on the tenant by it, beyond paying the rent, were to keep the house clean, not to keep pigs, poultry or rabbits in the backyard and not to overcrowd the house by taking in too many lodgers. Local inhabitants suggest that the rule about tenancy was that one member of the family had to work for Salt, but this seems to have been a later amendment. In Salt's lifetime the head of the family was expected to work for Salt or to have some necessary connexion with the village. If the connexion lapsed, for whatever reason, the family left the house and might be asked to pay a double rent until it did so. Though this rule was not always applied rigorously, the situation was usually serious. If a man lost his job, he was likely to lose his house. But since it was almost invariably the case that the working members of a family living in Saltaire all worked at the mill, a man in this situation knew that not only had he to find new work, but other members of his family also had to do so when the family resettled, owing to the difficulties of getting backward and forward to work.[70]

We know nothing of the financial structure of the firm in Salt's lifetime and suggestions that Salt was able to pay wages lower than the market rate owing to his social position as landlord-employer are no more than hints. It is therefore impossible to explore the possibility that he got any direct competitive advantage in this way. But there can be little doubt that, though the firm was not entirely free from labour troubles, it had the benefits which could be expected from a company village in terms of a steady and generally amenable labour force. Public evidence of the harmony assumed to exist between employer and employee, between landlord and tenant, was provided regularly after 1856. A feature of life for Salt's workers was the works outing. The first was in 1856, three years after the opening of the factory. The workpeople had subscribed to present Salt with his own sculptured bust. The ceremony was fixed for the anniversary of the opening, and the occasion made into a full day's festival. There was to be a *fete champêtre* at Crow Nest, Salt's country home, during the course of the day and, after the presentation of the bust in the evening, a concert in St George's Hall. The problem of transporting some 3,000 people from Bradford to Lightcliffe was resolved in military fashion and with proper deference to the hierarchy of the factory. The *Bradford Observer* advertised the orders of the day:

As early as half past eight o'clock in the morning of Saturday, the spinners, combing shed hands, warehousemen and hand loom weavers will assemble in the mill yard, Saltaire and proceed thence by special train to Bradford. On their arrival, they will form into procession, four deep, and headed by the drum and fife band, march to the Lancashire and Yorkshire railway station, and proceed by special train to Crow Nest. An hour later, the weavers, sorters, dressers, twisters and mechanics will assemble in the same place and be conveyed in the same manner. . . . The workpeople resident in Bradford will join their respective departments at the Midland Station.

The procession, headed by the girls and young women employees, marched across Bradford from the Midland Railway station to the Lancashire and Yorkshire station to the military music of the Saltaire band, carrying at the front two banners bearing the arms of Mr Salt and his motto *Quid non Deo juvante*. The procession attracted a very large audience and was saluted during the march by the ringing of the parish church bells. None, said the *Bradford Observer*, 'could fail to be gratified with the appearance of the honest and intelligent looking toilers. All were clean, tidy and well-dressed, some of the women being even elegantly attired.' At Crow Nest, they improvised 'harmless frolics of all kinds' and finished off that part of the day with an enormous tea. They were then transported back to St George's Hall for the presentation of the bust and the evening concert. This was a town occasion, Salt himself having an enormous list of personal guests – the Mayor of Manchester, the Mayor of Leicester, Francis Crossley, R. Milligan, H. Forbes, S. C. Lister, W. W. Rand, the officers of the 98th Regiment, and Mr Petrokokinos, the business associate from the Levant.

The next year, Salt took his workpeople to the Art Treasures Exhibition at Manchester on 19 September. Miss Burdett-Coutts and Mrs Gaskell were visiting the exhibition at the same time and took the opportunity to walk among the Salt contingent while it dined in the second-class room. They 'expressed themselves delighted with the appearance and conduct of the workpeople', particularly the large number of boys and girls who had marched to and from their places two abreast in the 'most orderly fashion'. The following year, the anniversary was celebrated in less ornate manner. The factory closed for half a day and outdoor dancing and food were provided on Shipley Glen. The family banner was displayed over the tables and the family attended the celebration. In 1859, after Salt had moved from Crow Nest and was installed at Methley Hall, he once again invited his workpeople to share the pleasures of his home. After that the anniversary was marked by a half-day holiday every year until 1864. In that year, he took his workpeople to Scarborough by train, where George Salt's elegant yacht the *Oithoma* was 'a special object of interest to the pleasure seekers'. The most lavish of these entertainments was one held in September 1873 to celebrate Sir Titus's seventieth birthday and the twentieth anniversary of the opening of the mill, when the employees and their families were entertained to a great feast in the grounds of Crow Nest, where the family had returned to live in 1867.[71]

It was inevitable that the Saltaire people should have a local reputation for subservience to their employers. There was, for instance, the incident connected with Disraeli's 1874 Factory Act, which conceded the fifty-six and a half hour week, the true ten-hour day at last. Charles Stead, who represented the Saltaire firm, consistently led the opposition to the Bill in the Bradford Chamber of Commerce and was extremely cantankerous when the time came to implement it. The question was relatively simple. One hour out of the three and a half to be saved would be gained by closing on Saturday at one o'clock. Half an hour had to be saved on each day from Monday to Friday. Someone had to decide whether the local mills should start work in future at 6.30 a.m. or finish at 6 p.m. The general feeling of the Bradford factory operatives was that in order to make things a little easier for the women and children, the mills should start in future at 6.30 a.m. Stead, for some reason, preferred the early start. He lost the case, but not before he had the Saltaire overlookers organise a ballot of their workpeople. His announcement that they had come down in favour of the early start was not convincing. Fison, W. E. Forster's partner at Burley-in-Wharfedale, remarked caustically that Saltaire must be the very greatest exception to the generality of factories, and one *Bradford Observer* correspondent said that any statement about the opinions of the

Saltaire people would have to be taken with a pinch of salt. A Saltaire man was stung to reply:

In conclusion allow me to say that there are not only a few good men and true at Saltaire, but there are a great many of the above named type, who would not sacrifice their opinions either religious, political or domestic, to suit either their employers or the individuals who threw out the insinuation at the meeting on Saturday last that the hands employed at Saltaire would be driven like a flock of sheep.[72]

In fact, just as from time to time there was protest in the village, the Salt management had its occasional labour problems also. There were two strikes during Salt's lifetime. One in 1868 concerned the weavers who said that they were not being paid up to the standard wage for the district. It took place as Salt was completing the final stages of the village and could not therefore expect to avoid the publicity which the national press gave it. Salt, who had been in semi-retirement for a number of years and had returned to take over control during a temporary crisis, is said to have dealt with the strike committee in an uncompromising fashion which gained the approval of his peers. He refused to meet the strike committee on the grounds that they were, by their own choice, no longer in his employment and said that he would consider the question of wages if they returned. The strike, which began on a Thursday, was over in time for work to be started on the following Monday. *Reynolds's Newspaper* reported, though no other paper did, that the junior partners, Salt's sons, had been booed and hissed by a large crowd of young men and women as they caught the train just outside the factory to go to the Bradford Wool Exchange. Otherwise the strike was conducted very tranquilly.[73]

Eight years later a more serious incident was more fully reported in the press. In the summer of 1876 the weavers, spinners and combers came out on strike again and the firm decided to lock out the rest. The West Riding textile firms were all feeling the effects of the depression which had steadily deepened since 1873; unemployment was running high, and short-time working was general. There had been a number of wage reductions in the industry and Salts had had several reductions in the previous eighteen months without a protest from the employees. It was the proposal for a further reduction of 1*s*. for those earning 10*s*.; 9*d*. for those on 7*s*. 6*d*. to 10*s*. 6*d*.; and 6*d*. for those earning less than 7*s*. 6*d*. a week, which caused the trouble. There was a special grievance among the two-loom weavers. Deductions imposed on one-loom weavers had been much lower and the result was that the differential between the two was almost eroded. The strike started on 23 June and ended a fortnight later on 4 July, during which time the firm took the opportunity to have some of the annual cleaning done and to begin a programme of re-tooling planned for later that year. A settlement was reached which restored 3*d*. a week to the spinners and in which the weavers had to accept a reduction of 2*s*. in the bonus rate.

There were a number of interesting aspects to the strike. For nearly a fortnight weavers, spinners and woolcombers with no trade union organisation to back them showed a good deal of solidarity, and flocked to the strike meetings which were held outside the village. At the same time, many of them were reluctant to take a lead, and in the event, Alexander George, the tailor, well-known as a capable Radical politician, presided as chairman over the meetings. Sutcliffe Rhodes, his reputation as a firebrand opponent of the firm well established, was invited to address the strikers by general approval of the meeting. He came and spoke to an audience of nearly two thousand. Unfortunately, none of the newspapers gave full reports of his speech on the grounds that to do so would have exposed themselves to actions for libel. He did, however, make a claim, not denied, that firms in Bradford and Shipley had been paying substantially more than the Saltaire firm. A committee of seven men – James Rawnsley, Ebor Armitage, Abraham Earnshaw, T. Allen, W. Atkinson, George Colbridge and James Tack – and seven women – Hannah Hudson, Emma Shackleton, Anice Shackleton, Amelia Marshall, Mary Ann Leach, Alice Naylor and Grace Spenser – were elected to conduct negotiations with the firm; most of them were either comparative newcomers to the village or did not live there. On the other side, Edwin Cox, a warehouseman who played a prominent part in many village activities, spoke up at the first meeting and recommended the strikers to make an immediate settlement. His words were drowned in the boos and hisses of the young women present, and one man suggested that Cox had been sent by the firm to get them all back to work. It remained a protest of the badly paid semi-skilled and unskilled workers, most of whom were women. None of the usual leaders from the ranks of the mill operatives – the Sanctuarys, Constantine, Tiffany, Holdworths or Copley – appear to have taken an active part. When the strike ended, there were immediate reports that those who had taken a prominent part in the strike were not being re-employed. A statement issued by the firm to allay suspicion was not entirely convincing. No instructions had been issued by the firm, it said. Overlookers had taken it upon themselves to dismiss a number of people, but the firm had every intention of finding work, as far as possible, for all who had worked previously at Saltaire.

It was a simple and far from dramatic protest. The strike remained extremely orderly. Meetings, despite the barracking which Cox received, were conducted with decorum. The strikers condemned the firm's dictatorial handling of the wage reduction but the issue was considered broadly and openly. One speaker referred to the difficulty of maintaining wages during a depression. Thomas Allen, one of the committee men, thought that they would have to be governed by those who had families, as to whether they stopped out or resumed work on the master's terms. Mrs Hudson pointed out that half-timers were losing 6*d.* out of about 4*s.* a week and that this was more than young families dependent on these earnings should have to accept. The committee faithfully reported, after they had had a meeting with Charles Stead, the managing director, and the one working partner not a member of the family, on the courtesy of their reception, although most of the strikers had blamed Stead both for the strike and the lock-out. During the first weekend of the strike the *Bradford Observer* reported, probably with truth (although it was playing down the whole incident in its reports): 'No one strolling through Saltaire on Saturday would have imagined that the entire population was out of employment. The cricketers, rowers, croquet players and others bent on recreation pursued their usual course.' Perhaps the semi and unskilled 'hands' had not done too badly. They had extracted some concessions. They had shown some talent for common action. There were spasmodic strikes against other firms, but a fortnight's strike in these years of depression was a good deal more than most of the other textile workers in the district could manage, for this was an industry which showed little capacity for coherent militancy. Yet once the lock-out was called off, the strike quickly collapsed, and further reductions of wages were imposed several months later with no protest at all from the workers.[74]

In matters which affected the trade the Salt firm took the conventional attitude of most employers. Salt himself had opposed the statutory limitation of hours of work, although he claimed at the time of his parliamentary campaign to have operated a ten-hour day in his factories before legislation came into force. He was one of the principal members of the employers' organisation formed in 1855 to put a brake on the reforming zeal of the new factory inspectors. In the deflection of the Nine Hours Movement from the textile industry the sons played a prominent part. George chaired the main protest meeting of Bradford manufacturers. Titus junior seconded the resolution which recorded the protest and Edward led the delegation which carried the protest to the Home Office.[75]

The attitude of the firm towards trade unionism is more difficult to define. Titus gave a donation to the trade-union paper, the *Beehive*, and Titus junior, the most intelligent and most radical of the sons, in a speech at St George's Hall defended very vigorously the rights of working men to form trade unions. But the late sixties and seventies saw the tentative reawakening of unionism in the textile trade. Salt's treatment of his workpeople in the strike of 1868 suggested that he would not have welcomed trade unions among the ordinary workpeople in his mill. In 1873 the Salt firm was one of the principal contributors to the National Federation of Associated Employers formed specifically to combat the menace, as employers saw it, of growing trade unionism. Like most politically Radical Bradford employers, Salt and his sons were at best ambivalent towards trade unions. They were acceptable as an idea, if they were weak and confined to the aristocratic crafts. They needed very careful watching if they invaded the world of weavers and woolcombers.[76]

Salt also showed some interest in a profit-sharing scheme but did not pursue it vigorously, and of course there was never a hint of interest in worker participation or control. There was no one of the calibre of a Jean Godin in Saltaire. Saltaire thus lacked the audacity of true originality, and was unable to absorb the pressure of changing times.

POSTSCRIPT

Saltaire, of course, was never insulated from the experience of society in general, as events in the seventies would demonstrate – if proof were needed. Attitudes to Saltaire also changed. Titus junior, 'lord of the manor' in Saltaire between 1877 and his death in 1887, treated the village nevertheless as a suburb – an important one – but a suburb of Shipley, rather than the unitary and separate town which his father's imagination had conceived. In the seventies alterations were made in the disposition of the resources which Salt had allocated both to charity and to education. It appeared that the operation of the almshouse system had allowed benevolence to be abused and had occasionally offered what was called 'a nursery for pauperism', a view which seems to match contemporary sentiment about both private charity and the poor law. A new system was introduced. The deserving poor living within three miles of Saltaire could be given a small weekly allowance in outdoor relief, thus ensuring that the recipient or the recipient's family maintained some responsibility. Twenty-two of the almshouses were used as Salt had intended, and the rest were rented out. Some of the money made available was used to improve medical care. Four nurses were employed as health visitors to improve standards of home care.[77]

In education, the Forster Act of 1870 opened up new possibilities since the duty of providing elementary education could be taken up by elected school boards using funds raised publicly. Accordingly, responsibility for elementary education in Saltaire was handed over to a newly elected Shipley School Board, and a system of secondary education covering a much wider area was financed in its place. Both Titus and his wife were involved in the development of the two grammar schools in Bradford, and they intended to make the same facilities available in the Shipley area. Limited facilities for secondary education were already available in the form of both day and evening classes. Now, more comprehensive arrangements were made. The Salts Schools, which included a Boys' and a Girls' High School and the educational facilities of the Institute, were established under a single Board of Governors, appointed in the first instance by the Salts and subsequently to be appointed by the Shipley School Board. The Boys' School was to offer an education for the universities, the professions and commerce, the Girls', a sound general education, and the Institute classes the technical and scientific education needed in industry. Although Saltaire children were in a considerable minority in the schools, it might be argued, as with the charities, that better use was being made of the allocated resources. But the village of Saltaire was no longer the geographical focus of activity.[78]

The impact of changing times, however, became very obvious towards the end of the century. The Saltaire of 1892 was a different place from the Saltaire of 1861. The Salt family was in the midst of the negotiations for its sale along with that of the mill. Physically it was no longer isolated but formed part of the built-up area which stretched along the axis of Manningham Lane–Keighley Road from Bradford to Bingley. Culturally part of Bradford, administratively it formed the main part of West Ward in Shipley Urban District Council. Saltaire itself remained a closely knit village community. But the social context in which the village had originated no longer existed. The paternalism which mediated the development of the factory culture had had its day. The deferential Radicalism which working men had contributed to the image of a harmonious society was no longer accepted by them. Working men were beginning to demand more real political authority, either through a Radical/Labour wing of the Liberal Party or in a new Independent Labour Movement.

In 1892, Saltaire men joined with Shipley working men to indicate that they were no longer willing to accept the political leadership of the local mill owners, and in particular the special authority of Salts. Together, they produced their own Liberal/ Labour candidate for the general election of 1892 to challenge the official candidate adopted by the Liberal Executive to fight the Northern Division, West Riding constituency. It is true that the man selected was a well-to-do member of the middle classes, W. P. Byles, owner of the *Bradford Observer*, but he was a very different man from the other candidate, A. E. Hutton, a right-wing Liberal and a member of an Eccleshill mill-owning family. Byles had consistently supported working men and women in their political aspirations and specifically had upset middle-class mill-owner opinion by backing the strikers at Manningham Mills, in 1890–91. Hutton withdrew from the election and Byles took the seat. Charles Stead, a Hutton man, whose authority as chairman of the Shipley Liberal Executive had thus been openly flouted, resigned. Byles's supporters took over the Shipley Liberal Party. As if to underline the narrative of events, Seth Bentley, the manager of Saltaire Baths and a regular critic of the Salt authority, took Stead's place. Among the Saltaire men who supported him on the Executive were vice-presidents Alex George, J. Cryer and Isaac Sanctuary, and all eight of the Saltaire delegation to the executive. The Independent Labour Party was also making progress in Saltaire as elsewhere. W. H. Drew, one of the founders of the Bradford Independent Labour Party, was dismissed from Saltaire Mills in 1891 'for not attending to his work and talking to other men'. Isaac Sanctuary joined the party in 1893, when a branch was formed in Shipley, and his place on the Liberal Executive was taken by his brother Jacob.[79]

With the death of Sir Titus in 1877, the inspiration behind the village disappeared, for none of the children, except perhaps Titus junior, shared his enthusiasm. Moreover, the community of interest between employer and employee implied in the experiment depended on the business success of the firm, and as the textile depression deepened through the eighties, matters went badly for the Salts. Writing in 1892, the German social commentator, G. von Shulze Gaevernitz, gave a depressing picture of an idea that had run out of steam. He suggested that while the benevolence of Sir Titus had prevented him from exploiting his favourable circumstances, his 'less high-minded' successors had not resisted the temptation. There had been labour troubles caused by reductions in wages during the depression and they had been dealt with by dismissing the leaders summarily. Some of the institutions were also in difficulty. The baths and wash-house were not in use and both the Congregational church and the Institute were in debt.[80] The firm changed hands several times between 1892 and 1923 and gradually the concept of the company village disintegrated. The firm began to sell off houses in 1896, the park was handed over to the Bradford City Council in 1921, and a new Salts' Sports and Social Club was opened shortly afterwards – a clear indication that the village no longer met the social expectations of the firm and its employees, though most of the inhabitants still worked in the mill. Then in 1933, the owners of the day, Salts (Saltaire) Ltd sold the house property to the Bradford Property Trust Ltd. It came as a shock to most of the inhabitants, many of whom returned from their summer holidays to hear the news. But the firm needed investment capital and thought that in the 1930s it was no part of their business to act as landlords as well as employees. The *Yorkshire Observer* provided a suitable epitaph:

Sir Titus was not only a great industrialist but he displayed the same excellent qualities in his housing policy, with the result that in construction these properties today are just as sound and solid as when they were built. All that is needed is improvements in sanitary facilities, fixtures and fittings, and the installation of electrical services to make the properties the finest type of workers' dwellings in the country.[81]

The venture brought Sir Titus great prestige and, I think, advantages in the running of his firm. The employees got healthy conditions in which a community could be built. Locally, it is frequently suggested that it was both unique and in advance of its times. Neither statement is true. As we have seen, there were a number of such experiments in the middle of the century and Saltaire was not the most successful, though it was probably the most comprehensive in the facilities it provided. It was the direct product of the 1840s and the sort of challenges and opportunities for immediate reform which the period offered. It was a retreat from the basic problem – the condition of the city. But it was perhaps the only way to bring about rapid and effective improvements in the circumstances of working people, albeit a small and selected number of them. When Salt died the concept was already edging towards the old-fashioned. Paternalism had fulfilled its function as mediating the arrival of industrial capitalism. More equitable ways forward, with less of the deferential, making use of the public institutions of an emergent democracy, were being explored. But this is not to disparage the achievement. Within the Liberal Capitalist ideology it reflected some of the best contemporary ideas on the relationship between the classes – or, to use the contemporary phrase, 'the social, moral and intellectual elevation of the working classes'.

VII

THE 'GRAND OLD MAN'
1868–1877

The Bradford of Salt's last year was a very different place from the township he had entered some fifty years previously. The change lay not only in the fact that the building of an industrial city had obliterated a good deal of the original geography. Bradford had come to the end of an era during which the preliminary fruits of industrialisation had been exploited. After an explosive boom in the early sixties trading conditions began to harden. Widespread competition challenged Bradford's supremacy in the worsted textile world as international customers started to exploit their own potentialities more effectively. By 1868 warnings were coming from the Universal Industrial Exhibition in Paris. Lord Frederick Cavendish, speaking at the Bradford Chamber of Commerce, said: 'there was no concealing the fact that as Englishmen they had cut a poor figure at the Paris Exhibition'. A little earlier a leader in the *Bradford Observer* carried a prophetic warning:

The time has gone by when England possessed so many political, geographical, natural and artificial advantages over other nations that she had only to ask for a clear field and no favours to be sure of easily distancing all competitors. . . .

Roubaiz attracts our buyers of fancy goods, and Belgium undersells us in worsteds abroad. It is neither wise nor right to deceive ourselves and we had better open our eyes to the fact that while some of our neighbours have advanced we have in some departments stood still and in others moved but slowly.[1]

These dangers caused at first no more than the tremors of alarm, for they were quickly masked by a powerful upsurge of demand brought on by the Franco-Prussian War. It was not until the end of 1873 that the trade began to worry. Then, the

Saltaire man, Charles Stead, giving a Christmas greeting from the Chamber of Commerce, said that the best he could think of was that 1873 was over: 1874 might be better. In fact the inflationary tendency of the previous two decades had been reversed, recession had set in, and weaknesses in the British manufacturing system had been exposed. For the local worsted trade, the situation was aggravated by a shift in fashion as the crinoline lost its pre-eminence to garments which hugged the female figure more closely; for this moved demand away from the relatively stiff mixed lustre cloths in which Bradford's principal strength lay to the softer all-wool cloths in which the French had always excelled. It was of course the beginning of the long deflationary period known traditionally (though, according to many historians, wrongly) as the 'Great Depression'. Whatever it was, the Bradford trade was to pass through a very uncomfortable period of adaptation to changed conditions. At the end of it it would no longer hold the position of unchallenged supremacy which it had had in the mid-Victorian years.[2]

The most obvious characteristic of the town was the development of urban stability. Population growth was slowing down. Between 1861 and 1871 the town increased in size by 31 per cent from 106,218 to 145,827, a much bigger increase than in the 'freak' decade of 1851-61, but substantially lower than in the peak period between 1831 and 1851. There was a further increase of 25 per cent to 183,032 by 1881, still greater than for the West Yorkshire conurbation where the increase was about 20 per cent. But the Bradford figures included the population of the township of Bolton, recently incorporated; and subsequent increases were to be accounted for almost entirely by this sort of colonisation. The figures also hid a small loss of young men by migration, the beginnings of a tendency which was to increase almost continuously in later decades. Bradford, now one of the great industrial cities of the world, was beginning to lose something of its magnetic quality. Stability was beginning to touch the structure of population. Within thirty years, Bradford would share with Halifax the distinction of having more native-born inhabitants than any of the other industrial centres of England and Wales.[3]

The formation of a class-divided society was also completed. Socio-geographical division within the town expressed this clearly, though the different areas were never as sharply defined as they were, for instance, in Leeds and Sheffield. It was confirmed by the development of a three-tiered system of education oriented to what authority thought suitable to the wishes or requirements of the various classes, and the emergence, as a sort of parallel to the Chamber of Commerce, of the Trades Council, a permanent body through which one form of working-class unity could be expressed.

Already in the late sixties the direction of Bradford's public affairs was passing into the hands of a new generation. Of the men who had controlled the early fortunes of the new parliamentary and municipal borough, Joshua Pollard lived to be a very old man, dying in 1886, but he had little influence on affairs after the mid-sixties. Joseph Farrar and Titus Salt died in 1876 and Henry Brown in 1877. Most of the others were already dead: Robert Milligan in 1862, his partner Henry Forbes in 1870, Edward Ripley and Christopher Waud in 1866, William Rand in 1868 and also in 1868 the Samuel Smith whose library formed the nucleus of the new Free Library. George Rogers died in 1870, Isaac Wright in 1872, the Samuel Smith who had built St George's Hall and John Rand in 1873. Of the younger men who had been associated with the great events of the past, W. E. Forster fulfilled his ambitious nature and reached distinguished Cabinet office, though on the way he split the Bradford Liberal Party. S. C. Lister and H. W. Ripley were still very active in local affairs, though their political allegiances were crystallising as pure Conservatism. In the nature of things, they shared their influence now with the Illingworths, the Holdens, Robert Kell, James Law, Briggs Priestley, Titus Salt junior, Charles Turner and James Hanson on the Liberal side and among the new Conservatives, men like M. W. Thompson, Henry Mitchell, J. H. Mitchell, George Waud and Francis Sharp-Powell. It is also worth noting that a new generation of working-class leaders was just beginning to assemble. Samuel Shaftoe, the most important of the late nineteenth-century Lib— Lab working men, arrived in Bradford in 1868 and had already begun to make his name in the trade-union world. James Bartley, one of the founder members of the Bradford Independent Labour Party, came in 1872.

These were the men who had to deal with the problems of the period in the new context of household suffrage. The Reform Act of 1867 had given the vote to householders living in towns and although the principle was to be extended to include rural householders seventeen years later, there was to be no basic change in the suffrage until 1918. The principle of manhood suffrage had not been completely surrendered but no great campaigns were to be fought about it. Nevertheless the extension of the electorate meant that the structure and the objectives of party politics would change. Party programmes would recognise more clearly the demands of a working-class electorate. At a national and a local level, questions of social amelioration took on a deeper import and the significance of both state and municipal initiative in these matters was more widely recognised. Political debate sharpened as the parties began to penetrate the ranks of the working-class voters. While the Act of 1867 led to the confirmation of the alliance of organised labour and the rest of the Liberal Party, it also provided the basis for a better organised Conservatism appealing directly for the working-class vote and eventually for the emergence of the Independent Labour Party. The consensus of the mid-century was beginning to disintegrate.

For several years Liberalism in Bradford at least was unstable, for the adjustments demanded of it were always more fundamental than those required in Conservatism. Defections among Moderate Liberals who rejected the Radicalism of what was in effect a new party, a bitter dispute about education, and a bid (even if ill-prepared) for more effective Labour representation, made for a very fluid situation. Conservatives were prepared to exploit the internecine struggle which developed – for it was in fact the Conservative battle which was being fought: what was to be the position of the Anglican Church? and how far was democracy to be allowed to go?

The split in the Liberal ranks opened up by the election of 1867 continued through three elections and was not really closed until several years after the 1874 election.[4] In the election of 1868, the first under the new Franchise Law, the

Liberal Electoral Association nominated Forster, the sitting member, and Edward Miall, with Titus Salt as chairman of a joint committee. They rested for the most part on the support of the Nonconformists and what they described as 'the thinking workingmen and intelligent Irish'. Although their views on the Anglican Church were poles apart they managed to run together partly because Forster's immense local and national reputation put his seat beyond jeopardy, partly because the question before the electorate was the disestablishment not of the English Church but of the Irish Church about which there was less controversy. H. W. Ripley, recently translated from Congregationalism to Anglicanism and with the fervour of the convert, came forward as an independent Liberal relying on the support of uneasy Liberals, of Anglican and Methodist Tories, and the personal support he could muster, particularly in Bowling where the Iron Works and his own dyeing establishment were located. The contrast was between Miall and Ripley; a good many Moderates split their votes between Forster and Ripley and it was in the end a question of where the new working-class vote would go.

Nobody was certain how the new electorate would vote; neither side was prepared to leave the test entirely to the democratic decision of individuals, preferring to support the new system with some of the more traditional practices of English electioneering. The Forster–Miall committee tried to minimise intimidation at work by persuading employers to put up notices that a man would not endanger his job by voting in accordance with his conscience. Ripley thought it unnecessary. In the event there was a good deal of 'extra-political' pressure from both sides, although election day passed off quietly enough except for one serious but limited battle in the Irish quarter of Silsbridge Lane.

The result came as a shock to the 'official' Liberals. Forster headed the poll; Elias Thomas and John Rawson might demur, but he was still seen as a very distinguished statesman who brought honour to the town as its representative. Miall was defeated with 8,768 votes against Ripley's 9,347. The Liberals had been confident that with the Liberal Electoral Association to organise the vote throughout the city they could control the flow of political events, and a national newspaper expressed a good deal of consternation at the result. Who would have thought, it said, 'that a great Liberal constituency where Toryism had not shown its head for years could not elect Miall?' But, as we have seen in previous elections, Toryism, though not well organised, was not dead, and under the stress of the new political dispensation could find bases for ready alliance with Moderate Liberal and Old Whig. The Radicals had another explanation. Immediately, they petitioned in the names of Titus Salt junior, Angus Holden, John Haley and Charles Hastings for Ripley to be unseated on charges of bribery. Ripley's supporters counter-petitioned against Forster in the names of Thomas Garnett, George Dawson, Samuel Storey and Thomas Ambler. The election campaign in fact had been in the best traditions of Eatanswill with plenty of refreshment in the various inns and public houses used by the candidates, and while some of it stood on the border of the convivial entertainment always available at election time there is little doubt that both sides had been guilty of more positive measures of persuasion. The conduct of a number of Forster's committee men was criticised, but the misdemeanour of Ripley's men, particularly among uncommitted and perhaps alienated Irish voters in the Silsbridge Lane area, had been not only excessive but blatant and he was accordingly unseated.[5]

The bitterness of this election continued during the subsequent by-election. Matthew William Thompson took Ripley's place as Independent Liberal against Miall, and although the opportunities for disorder and corruption were reduced when both sides agreed not to use public houses for committee rooms, nomination day (12 March 1869) saw one of the more violent spectacles of electoral rioting that Bradford had had. Polling, however, passed off very quietly.

This time the decision was reversed and Miall was elected by a majority of 1,500. It was the most gratifying triumph that Bradford Radicals had ever had, for they saw it as the victory of the righteous in the cause of the religious freedom of which Miall was the most important national protagonist. It was also hailed as the victory of the working man in alliance with his employer; this was the fruit of Liberal–Labour unity forged in the Liberal Electoral Association. Salt's comment was revealing:

This is a glorious day for Bradford. The working men have done their duty, they have proved themselves worthy of the franchise as I always knew they would. They only wanted to be trusted. You have done your duty and I thank you sincerely.

It is not easy to see just what the working man *qua* working man got out of Miall's victory. Miall had little knowledge of the world of Capital and Labour and his economics were of that unsullied Liberalism which the trade unions by their nature were intended to combat. But he had the reputation of being a friend to the working man; at least he was not an employer and might be expected to respond with an open mind to the demands of trade unionists for legal protection for their funds and the repeal of the conspiracy laws. Speaking during an election meeting, Connolly of the London Stone Masons' Union made the point during an attack on Neill, the biggest of the Bradford master builders, who had led the local employers during a recently concluded masons' strike: 'If he were a working man of Bradford and had to choose his side, he would say give him the side which was opposed to Neill and the employers associated with him.'

Nonconformists among working men could share Miall's position on religion and he offered all the dignity of a firm egalitarian Radicalism, but not all working men were Nonconformists, and Matthew Thompson could claim that he was as good a democrat as the next man and not a kill-joy into the bargain. The Trades Council did not endorse Miall's candidature, for some of its members wanted a form of 'pure and simple unionism' outside politics. But the veteran Chartists, William Angus, Isaac Jefferson and George Fletcher, spoke at meetings of his working-class supporters, Malcolm Ross made a number of sharp attacks on the Ripley–Thompson camp in the pages of the *Bradford Observer*, and men like Abraham Sharp, A. Kershaw, Ben Wainwright, and Henry Hibbert were prominent throughout the Miall campaign. The working-class vote went substantially to Miall.

The campaign also confirmed the re-emergence of Titus Salt

himself in a substantial political role. He had been in semi-retirement since his resignation from Parliament in 1861 but he now came forward once again and took his place as chairman of the joint Miall–Forster parliamentary committee. As always now, he was hailed with great enthusiasm whenever he appeared on a platform, but it was his reputation more than anything else that was needed. He was very nearly the last and certainly the most important of the great Bradford Radicals of the thirties and forties now left. His standing locally and nationally as one of the handful of men who had created the great industrial complex of Bradford was immense. No Radical campaigner wanted to be without his support now that the political conflict was properly resumed.[6]

During the lifetime of the Gladstone Administration elected in this general election, the Capital–Labour issue was always in the forefront of public concern. Union strength continued to grow and spread into new areas of labour activity. In 1872, the Bradford machine-combers tried to unite but with little success. More successful were those woolsorters who were ineligible to join the very exclusive Woolsorters' Society composed of highly skilled and highly paid artisans. They started a new Woolsorters' Association which was spreading into the outlying villages within twelve months and which absorbed the Society within twenty years. The Bradford miners became members of the West Yorkshire Miners' Association in 1872, and two years later felt strong enough to stage the union's annual gala in Peel Park. By 1871 the Dyers were beginning the organised activities which made them for many years the most militant of all the Bradford unions. The established unions were also becoming more aggressive. The printers, after the rise gained in 1866, pushed up minimum wages to 30*s.* a week and had negotiated a 55-hour week by 1874, and most craft unions had made similar progress.[7]

The employers, among whom were Titus and Titus junior, the Illingworths and the Halifax Crossleys, responded with predictable vigour and organised a new Employers' Association, the National Federation of Associated Employers of Labour. It was in origin a northern movement founded in 1873 with headquarters in Manchester and widespread support among West Riding employers. It was founded, the journal of the association, *Capital and Labour*, informed its readers, in consequence of 'the extraordinary development, oppressive actions, far-reaching but openly avowed designs and elaborate organisation of the Trade Unions'. Its objective, continued *Capital and Labour*, was 'by a defensive organisation of the employers of labour to resist these designs as far as they are hostile to the interests of the employers, the freedom of the non-unionist operatives and the well-being of the community'.

Debate about the Capital—Labour issue filled columns in the local press. Some of the material was of the predictable kind which men like Carter and Wainwright had been offering in the early sixties. Christopher Ellison, a veteran woolcomber, in an essay reprinted in the *Bradford Observer* made a plea for conciliation and understanding: 'We ought therefore . . . to look forward to the dawn of a better and brighter time, when labour and capital shall walk together in terms of friendship – yes of brotherhood.'

But generally the debate had taken on a new pungency indicative of the new confidence and consciousness which was spreading. In these years John Holmes, the old co-operator and associate of James Hole, sprang to the defence of labour in a series of letters in which he condemned the prevailing economic Liberalism as 'mere organised selfishness' and made a plea for high wages as a stimulus to consumption. He also offered a simple explanation of labour theory of value to a correspondent who had challenged Labour's claim to a share in such increased profits as might accrue to the employer:

My reply is that capital is but contributed and accumulated labour . . . I affirm that at first capital did not exist, and that it is men who by labour make capital; which capital of itself makes neither labour nor men. . . Capital is but accumulated labour and can but exist among a community of labourers.

A 'Factory Worker' also filled several columns of the *Bradford Observer* through 1872 with well-articulated attacks:

The English artisan who has nothing to do with . . . reckless speculation . . . is asked to lower his wages when the collapse comes, and patriotically starve while it continues, and if he does not meekly fall in with this, he is flouted and abused as a trade unionist who knows nothing whatever of the sublime and infallible laws of demand and supply.[8]

The unions were of course gratified at the government legislation passed in 1871 which finally legalised the position of the trade unions and so obliterated the injustice perpetrated by the Bradford magistrates and the judges of the Queen's Bench Division in the *Hornby* v. *Close* affair. On the other hand, they were appalled that the same government – the 'people's government, led by the people's William' – could pass the punitive Criminal Law Amendment Act which took away such protection as picketing had and which so defined the law on intimidation that any form of strike became a very hazardous occupation indeed. There were angry demonstrations throughout the country, and in Bradford the resentment produced a degree of permanent unity in the trade-union world which nothing else had so far achieved. Bradford men in fact had particular reason for anger, for Alfred Illingworth, the MP for Knaresborough in this Parliament, had voted, against the advice of the Minister, in favour of harsh amendments to the Bill introduced by the Lords, and Miall, the 'working man's MP', had been conspicuously absent at important divisions.[9]

Towards the end of May 1872, delegates of some thirty-two societies and branches met at the Black Bull Inn and arranged for a mass demonstration of protest against the Act. On Saturday afternoon, 8 June, some 4,000 men marched in procession through the principal streets of the town, each society dressed in the characteristic garments of its trade and displaying at its head a costly and elaborate banner. Representatives from the surrounding districts – Thornton, Eccleshill, Idle, Saltaire, Rawdon, Dewsbury, Bramley, Halifax and Leeds – attended and the whole procession was headed by a number of bands which included the Saltaire, the Valley Dyeworks, Third West Yorkshire Regiment Volunteer Fife and Drums, Third West Yorkshire Volunteer Brass, and a number of smaller units like the one associated with the Bowling Artillery Hotel. The only societies not represented were those associated with the textile overlookers and one or two of the highest-paid of the textile craftsmen.

The order of the procession was:

Skip and Basket Makers	Board and Case Makers
Twisters and Loomers	Iron Founders
Engineers (3 branches)	Core Makers
Tinplate Workers	Iron Dressers
Cloggers	Boiler Makers
Plumbers	Letterpress Printers
Hammerers	Coach Makers
Bricklayers	Warp Dressers
Stonemasons (2 branches)	Carpenters and Joiners
Stonemasons' Labourers	Dyers (4 branches)
Draymen	Plasterers
Tailors	Plasterers' Labourers

Although the demonstration was spoiled as a spectacle by the torrential rain which poured down throughout the afternoon, there was no doubt of its success in impressing onlookers with the seriousness of the men involved. It was certainly, wrote the *Observer*'s reporter, 'the most numerous and well ordered as well as the most imposing one of its kind which has ever been witnessed in Bradford ... the fact that the men were thoroughly in earnest in the cause which they have espoused of demanding the repeal of the Criminal Law Amendment Act, cannot be gainsaid.'

The demonstration ended with a public meeting, still in the pouring rain, on the old Fair Ground at the top of Darley Street. The Mayor, Matthew Thompson, presiding very unwillingly, made no secret of his lack of sympathy; but the meeting had been properly requisitioned as a town meeting, and he acted out of a sense of his proper duty to a large body of ratepayers who were, he said, aggrieved at what they considered an unjust law. Several national leaders spoke. Howell referred to the incredulity with which working men had greeted the Act, others spoke about the outrageous prosecutions which were already taking place, and a resolution was approved condemning the class legislation which had been passed. Despite its local success, like the many other demonstrations which took place, it did not change the thinking of this Government and it was left to the Disraeli Administration which followed to change the law.[10]

The positive gains of the Bradford demonstration came from the unity which had been achieved by the local unions. Out of it sprang the second and successful attempt to establish a permanent Trades Council. After several preliminary meetings to draw up a rule book, the Bradford and District Trades Council was formally declared in existence on 30 July 1872, with Samuel Shaftoe of the Skep and Basket Makers as president, Robert Scott of the Huddersfield Dyers as vice-president, William Scruton of the House Painters as treasurer and E. Riley as secretary. Although the secretary sent a letter to the *Bradford Observer* announcing that the new Council was in no sense a political body, it was in fact very quickly involved in political activity. By the end of 1873 a local Labour candidature had been promoted by members of the Trades Council. A meeting of 2,000 working men accepted a proposal to put up James Hardaker as a candidate at the next election, and to raise at least £1,500 to meet his expenses. An embryo ward organisation was also arranged.[11] As secretary of the Operative Stonemasons, during the protracted strikes and lock-out which had recently affected the Bradford building industry, Hardaker had acquired a considerable reputation as an eloquent speaker and able negotiator. He was a typical member of the 'labour aristocracy' of the late nineteenth century. He lived at 61 Villiers Street in a house in one of three streets (the others were Cobden Street and Bright Street) erected by working men in the 1850s under the auspices of the West End Building Society. They ensured the owner-occupier not only a comfortable home but also a vote in the county elections. He was a teetotaller active in the Bradford Working Men's Teetotal Society and secretary to the Girlington Baptists Band of Hope. He was also a Sunday school teacher at the same Sunday school. He was a firm Radical and if elected would have taken the Liberal whip. He was clearly not the stuff of which revolutions were made, but the implications of his presence on the hustings caused a good deal of discussion and concern and evoked a rapid and effective response from Illingworth and his friends.[12]

It is clear that the value of a Radical alliance was suspect for many months after the passing of the Criminal Law

Amendment Act. The validity of any sort of alliance with other political interests was challenged at the same time by the development of the Nine Hours Movement. This had begun as a movement among the engineers; it had been taken up by other craft unions and by 1872 had been more or less obtained by many of them. Textile workers had taken it up towards the end of 1871, and, led by the overlookers, it had become an aggressive movement in the West Riding towns. Mundella, the MP for Sheffield, with a reputation already established as an industrial reformer, brought a Bill before the House in 1872 to limit the working hours of women and children in factories to nine hours a day and consulted on a number of occasions with the Overlookers' Short Time Committees in Bradford and Leeds. A few employers like Fison, Forster's Burley partner, with antecedents in the short-time movement of the forties approved of the Bill, but the majority greeted it with their invariable hostility. The Bradford and Leeds employers had a joint meeting under George Salt's chairmanship to condemn the proposal. A nine-hour day, it was said, would give the foreigner a three-hour daily advantage. It was acknowledged that women and children now generally worked longer hours than most craftsmen, but suggested that nevertheless they did not work as hard in ten hours as men did in nine. A deputation of manufacturers which included Edward Salt, Henry Illingworth, Captain Shepherd, Henry Mason, M. Waud, James Tankard, and J. Craig of Holden and Son, a good cross-section of Radicals, Liberals and Conservatives, presented their views in a visit to the Home Office. They claimed that there was no widespread desire among workers for a reduction of hours, for many textile workers were on piece rates and the prospect only faced them with diminished earnings. It was, they said, the overlookers who had started the agitation not out of humanitarian concern but in order to bring their own hours into line with those of the mill craftsmen who had obtained the reduction through the unions. They claimed that they had recently granted an hour's reduction and might be prepared to grant another shortly, but they could see no case for the large reductions envisaged. They were referring to the fact that most of the large firms had recently agreed to close on Saturdays at

1 p.m. instead of 2 p.m. but since the concession had required three years' agitation, working men and women were sceptical of further generosity.[13] (Mundella's Bill did not pass the House and a less generous Bill, the Ten Hour Bill, was passed by the Disraeli Administration.)

There were, however, hints of a more aggressive mood in working-class politics. E. S. Beesly had put forward his programme in Bradford for a trade-union party and at a national level a Labour Representation League had appeared. *Reynolds's Newspaper* also published 'Northumbrian's' advice to the working classes: 'The working class should have *in fine* a creed of their own, and eschew all party distinctions between Liberal and Conservative for both parties are Conservative against Labour.'[14] But they were no more than hints. For the time being the working class remained in tutelage.

The question which was to lead to outright war in the Bradford Liberal Party was the provision of education by public authority. By the late sixties all parties were agreed that schools ought to be available for all the nation's children and that since the voluntary societies were unwilling or unable to make such comprehensive arrangements it had become an obligation on government to do so. Dissenters had dropped their opposition to state education as such and debate now centred on the precise obligation towards religious education which the state ought to accept. Dissenters generally favoured a completely free, compulsory and secular system of national education, financed by government grant and local rates, with which, it was hoped, the denominational schools would be unable to compete. The Act passed in 1870 paid scant regard to their views. It provided a back-up system of schools run by locally elected school boards out of government and local funds to be established where existing provisions were inadequate; attendance was not to be compulsory and fees would be charged. The Act also strengthened the position of the denominational schools by increasing the grants available to them and stretched Dissenter anger beyond breaking point with its twenty-fifth clause, which allowed school boards to pay fees out of local rates for poor parents who wanted their children to go to denominational schools.

The Act reflected a view shared by the Prime Minister, Gladstone, and the Vice-President of the Council, W. E. Forster, who piloted the Bill through the House and with whom it has always been associated. This was the view that the established church had been for centuries the most powerful instrument of social cohesion in the country and that it should therefore occupy a major position in any scheme of national education – a view Forster seems to have absorbed through his marriage connexion with the Arnold family. Many Dissenters were at least disturbed by the philosophical and educational implications of this view and at the level of everyday affairs angered at the thought of the advantages they thought the Act gave to the churches in the day-to-day battle for popular support. In all, they felt as much the victims of unexpected and unwarranted betrayal as the trade unionists had felt about the Criminal Law Amendment Act. It was, they proclaimed, indicative of the way in which the parliamentary party had always treated the Dissenters. 'The powerful Nonconformist section [of the Liberal Party] has never been treated with that respect and consideration which is its due', Titus junior protested on one occasion, and in many different parts of the country Dissenters began to lay down plans for exacting retribution.

In a constituency which had returned both Edward Miall and W. E. Forster running in tandem as prospective Members of Parliament, the civil war within Liberalism was inevitably harsh and unforgiving. There had been constant discussion at every level within the constituency from the moment the Bill was published and Forster came under direct attack as soon as it passed into law. At his first meeting with constituency members in January 1871 he had to face an adverse vote criticising his conduct. Charles Turner and Elias Thomas, Liberation Society men and always near opposition to Forster, moved and carried an amendment to the conventional resolution thanking Forster for his services:

That this meeting having heard Mr. Forster's account of his parliamentary experience during the past session of parliament, and fully recognising his previous services to the Liberal cause, regrets its inability to approve of the educational measures passed mainly by his exertions, and deplores deeply the ways resorted to [Tory votes] to secure its adoption in a Liberal House of Commons.[15]

Forster, however, considered that the opposition to the Education Act came from a comparatively narrow section of the party, composed of narrow-minded and dogmatic Baptists and Congregationalists led by Alfred Illingworth and his brother-in-law Angus Holden, with the help of Titus junior, all acting out of jealous sectarian spite. The Dissenters argued the matter as a question of equality. The position of the Church of England as the established church created an acute social division in English society, giving Anglicans a great advantage which followed them through life even 'to the grave itself', for cemeteries were divided into consecrated ground for Anglicans and unconsecrated ground for others. The Act exacerbated the division, for 'large additional endowment has been conferred upon the established church and new vested interests have been created which will have to be satisfied when [we] get a system of national education'.

The position within the Liberal Party had thus polarised. Forster ignored the suggestion, made to him by Titus junior, that he ought to find another seat and refused to compromise on any part of the Act. In November 1873 he made a particularly defiant defence of the Act in a speech at Liverpool, and Bradford began to prepare for the final battle. The leading Radicals had a private meeting at the beginning of January in the house of J. Wade, Forster's election agent, and voiced their demands for Forster's resignation. When Parliament dissolved later in the month, Forster had no hope of official Liberal support in the coming election but returned to Bradford ready to take on the Liberal establishment independently.

In the event, four candidates took the field. The Liberal establishment brought forward J. V. Godwin in place of Miall whose ill-health prevented him from standing. He was now an independent and wealthy wool merchant with a long record of public service in the town. The Liberal Association also took over James Hardaker's campaign and so re-established control of the public expression of working-class opinion. A joint committee was appointed to fight the dual campaign and Sir

Titus – 'one man who had been true to the party in all circumstances, one man who stood out pre-eminent among the Liberals of Bradford' – though now in failing health, continued as chairman of the campaign committee. H. W. Ripley, ambitious as ever and determined to wipe out the memory of his humiliation in 1869, came forward ostensibly as an Independent Liberal but with the backing of Conservatives whose ranks he was to join during the lifetime of the coming parliament. The result was a clear victory for the advocates of the Forster Education Act which had been at the centre of the battle. Forster won comfortably with 11,945 votes, Ripley came second with 10,223, Godwin third with 8,398 and Hardaker at the bottom with 8,115.[16]

Forster's chances were always better than they might seem at first sight. A good many simply thought the Act was a sensible measure of reform. Just over a quarter of his vote came from Liberals or Radicals who voted Forster–Godwin. Some of the most influential men in the Liberal ranks stood by him. James Law, leading member of the Horton Lane congregation, was the proposer of his nomination, and among his principal supporters were Henry Brown, the founder of the most famous departmental store in Bradford and treasurer of the Congregational Theological College; William Byles, of the *Bradford Observer*; and C. Semon, Jacob Behrens and A. Schlesinger, probably the most respected members of the German mercantile community. One Bradford Liberal complained bitterly of treachery in the ranks in the pages of *The Nonconformist*, naming Law and Brown and pointing out that the pastor, at least four deacons, and the most influential gentlemen of the oldest Congregational church in the town (Horton Lane), had voted for Forster. Forster could also rely on a good deal of Irish support, for although secular and committed Home Rulers voted Radical, since Hardaker had come out firmly for Home Rule, the Catholic Church was delighted with the Education Act. Good Catholics followed the priest's advice and rewarded Forster accordingly. E. P. Duggan, second-generation immigrant, for many years the semi-official Irish Catholic representative on such institutions as the Bradford Infirmary and the Charity Organisation

Society, and the first of nineteenth-century immigrant stock to win a seat on the municipal council, represented this area of support. Further, not all working men were prepared to follow Hardaker, for Forster's record on the trade-union issue was, if anything, better than that of Illingworth and his reputation as a great Radical still carried weight with men like Malcolm Ross, who publicly affirmed that he would be voting for Forster and Godwin.[17]

But the greatest part of Forster's support undoubtedly came from the Tories or near-Tories. M. W. Thompson seconded his nomination and S. C. Lister spoke up heartily on the platforms, wrote Forster. Both were soon to join the Tory Party. The Tory Party did not bother to present its own candidate, for although Forster insisted that he was a Liberal, since the passing of the Act they had tended to look on him as in a sense their man and they therefore threw their support behind him in defence of the education settlement. Sir Titus publicly repudiated Forster's Liberal claims and confirmed that much of his support came from the Conservatives.

As chairman of the Forster and Miall election committee of 1868 and also of that of the Liberal candidates at the present election, I trust you will allow me to remove some of the misapprehension which seems to exist on the part of a portion of the London press as to the relation of Mr. Forster to the Liberal Party here in the present contest. The two Liberal candidates unanimously adopted at a large representative meeting of that party, held last Tuesday night, are Messrs J. V. Godwin and James Hardaker. On the other hand, Mr. Forster is receiving the most ostentatious support of the Conservatives, who at their meeting determined not to bring out a candidate, feeling to use the words of their resolution, 'that their support ought to be generally given to secure the return of Messrs Forster and Ripley . . . and as his [Forster's] educational policy is one which has the cordial approval of the Conservatives, it has been resolved to adopt such a course as will not at least imperil Mr. Forster's seat.

If he be returned, it must be as the representative of the Tory Party.'[18]

Forster had some unusual company when he faced the Bradford electorate, for most of the leading Conservatives –

John Taylor, Henry Mitchell, Alfred and William Foster of Black Dyke Mills, W. Peel, Samuel Storey and Tom Garnett – came on the platform with him. The Conservative vote saved his seat, for the Ripley–Forster split, which must have been largely a Conservative vote, was sufficient in itself to beat either Godwin or Hardaker.

The education issue was of primary importance, but in view of the considerable agitation of the previous two years, some explanation is needed of the fact that the trade-union question was a relatively minor one in the election. Hardaker's programme put trade-union legislation seventh after the extension of manhood suffrage to county boroughs, disestablishment of the Anglican Church, compulsory school boards, abolition of Clause twenty-five of the Education Act, reform of the Licensing Laws and Home Rule. The simple explanation was the correct one. A specifically trade-union campaign was bound to be muted since Hardaker and his committee had acceped an alliance with the Radicals, among whom were men of the Illingworth–Holden stamp, who accepted trade unions – but on sufferance. Although Hardaker had announced at the beginning of the campaign that he would remain independent of all parties, the swift offer of financial support was too compelling for the Hardaker camp to ignore. They had made little progress towards the £1,500 they had set as a target for an election fund, for this was a formidable sum to raise among the 4,000 trade-union members Hardaker claimed to represent. Illingworth and his friends also offered to invest £6,000, the interest on which would be used to provide Hardaker with a salary if elected. Hardaker and his committee had not yet faced this problem. Hardaker also had close links with the Illingworth world. He was a Sunday school teacher and Band of Hope official at the Girlington Baptist Sunday School which was supported by the Illingworth family, and this may have made him readier to accept what was primarily an Illingworth offer.

Still, the surrender was a logical outcome of middle-class Radical policy which showed, as always, an anxiety to have 'the better sort of working man' behind it. Once the Beesly approach had been rejected, furthermore, working men had no philosophy or programme of their own to offer. What they had was the Radicalism which offered the sort of political equality that men like Hardaker had obtained already and a Nonconformist alliance in which a minority of working men were interested. The threat of independent action in Bradford proved for the time being to be ephemeral. Hardaker presented himself as a Radical candidate with special knowledge of trade-union matters and gave trade-union legislation a minor place in his platform programme. The deferential Radicalism which had taken hold of Bradford working-class politics in the mid-century continued to dominate until the young men of the Independent Labour Party presented their challenge towards the end of the century.

In 1874, no great Labour issues were raised from any platform. The election was a one-issue election fought on Forster's position that it was impossible to imagine a system of education which excluded the Bible from the classroom and the view (expressed by W. E. Glyde) that religious education should be left in the hands of parents and their chosen ministers of religion who had responsibilities which came from their training and education. Behind it lay the forty years of passionate politico-religious antagonism between Anglican and Dissenter. At the same time the debate, important as it was, drew on areas of social conflict beyond the question of religious education. The development of the local Liberal Party machine as an instrument of democratic control, through which debate and discussion could be channelled and converted into local party policy, was not really to the taste of men like Forster. It was one thing to concede a right to vote to all responsible men; it was another to concede rights of policy making as well, quite apart from the fear that the machine would become nothing more than an instrument of one or two powerful local leaders. Men who thought like Forster talked about a vulgarisation of politics. Some, as we have seen, were prepared to defect from Liberal–Radicalism with the passing of the 1867 Act. Among the defectors were those who supported Forster's stand on the Education Act and took a very hostile view of the recent developments in democratic politics. There had been a considerable upheaval in the ranks of Liberalism in these years. The *Bradford Observer*, marking the end of the election with the comment that 'the short, sharp, energetic battle of Liberal *versus* Liberal has come to an end', was optimistically anticipating events by some years. For the time being, there was a good deal of disarray.[19]

Strong Radicals in Bradford remained very angry. Titus junior expressed some of their impotence when he declared from the platform that Forster had treated the Bradford Liberals with utter contempt. They took some comfort from the fact that the Liberation Society began a new campaign for disestablishment which the Holden, Illingworth and Salt families backed very generously. They also reasserted their authority within the local party by tightening the party machinery and establishing as a rule the principle that a parliamentary candidate had to endorse the whole of the party programme as fixed through the party organisation. Forster refused to have anything to do with it. It was not until the approach of another general election that the voices of conciliation were completely noted. Then the rule was dropped and the great antagonists of 1874, Illingworth and Forster, standing together in 1880, took both seats.

It was, however, the development of a clearly structured system of education which signalled most effectively the end of the 'industrial revolution' years. In the sixties and early seventies Government placed English education in the class compartments into which English society was now divided. The Clarendon Report (1861) established the position of the growing number of public schools as the educational machinery of the very well-to-do. The Forster Education Act fixed the pattern of elementary education for the working classes. The Taunton (Schools Inquiry) Commission of 1864 and the Endowed Schools Act of 1869 fixed the pattern for the middle classes. Secondary schools already in existence were inspected by the Commissioners and placed in one of three categories: one for the sons of gentlemen, members of the higher professions and substantial manufacturers, which would prepare scholars for a university education; one for the children of members of the lower professions, farmers and small businessmen, where the leaving age would be sixteen, and one with a leaving age of fourteen for the children of well-paid artisans and shopkeepers.[20] The Commissioners, unimpressed by a Bradford Grammar School which displayed all the faults characteristic of schools of its kind and time, recommended that it should be placed in the second category. Local middle-class pride exploded. Behrens, whose High School was successful in educational terms but an increasing financial liability, led an immediate protest of local businessmen – Henry Mitchell, Henry Brown, Matthew Thompson and Sir Titus and his son – and negotiated the creation of a new school by an amalgamation of the Grammar School and the High School with a new charter, a new board of governors, a new building and a new curriculum. Formal connexion with the Church of England was broken, though the parish church retained the right to a seat on the board of governors. Religious instruction was limited to the teaching of the Bible, and children of any denomination were accepted. It was formally placed in the first category.[21]

There were substantial critics of the new arrangements. Although the new school spread in practice across the first two categories it nevertheless reflected faithfully the philosophy of the Commission and the Endowed Schools Act. The Editor of the *Bradford Observer* noted in a leader that the Bradford scheme had made a free Grammar School into the preserve, more or less, of the children of the professional, commercial and manufacturing élite. It pandered, he thought, to the snobbishness of those who did not want their children to mix with those from poorer homes and he dismissed as trivial the concessions made to the talent of the poor by way of examination and scholarship; for such scholarships were not to be their special allocation but open to anybody. Indeed, one of the first to win a scholarship was the eldest son of the Rev. Mr Cowan, the pastor at the Saltaire Congregational Church – not a rich man but neither poor nor a member of the working classes. The Rev. Mr Campbell of Horton Lane Chapel was more exact in his criticism:

The darkest cloud in England's horizon is the social separation of the people – the ever deepening and widening division in lines of caste. Can we find no better social nexus than cash and bash, flattery and terrorism, mutual ignorance and mistrust? Yea, verily, in a catholic system of education, we get the only stable foundation of a community of sentiments.

He went on to make a special plea for the working classes:

Let us then in the name of God endeavour to give the working classes an aristocracy of intellect and merit by fully recognising in our national system of education the republicanism of talent and the right of every man to an open career.[22]

Perhaps the Bradford School Board, which made – by the standards of the day – very generous provision for scholarships from the Board schools, thought that in thus trying to continue in education a sort of alliance of the middle classes with an aristocracy of labour, it was doing just this. Sir Titus had no doubts about the value of the new institution. Along with S. C. Lister and Henry Brown, he was one of its principal financial supporters, contributing to the cost of the new building and investing £6,000 to provide scholarships to the universities.

Since 1870, there had been an active Bradford Ladies' Educational Association with a committee of energetic women which included Sir Titus's daughter-in-law, Katherine, Mrs R. Kell, Mrs W. P. Byles, Mrs Schlesinger and Mrs Fanny Hertz, the driving force being the Female Educational Institute. They had been organising lectures of near-university standard for several years – a series in 1870 and 1871 on English Literature and one on the distribution of animal and vegetable life by C. Miall, soon to be Professor of Botany at the Yorkshire College of Science. In 1874, exploiting the growing interest in women's education, they presented a scheme to the town for a Bradford girls' grammar school and a year later were able to open it in the centre of the town, on much the same basis as the boys' school. It was always a good deal less self-conscious about its status as a middle-class institution. Mrs Salt served as a governor for many years and Sir Titus was among the most generous contributors, giving £500 of the first £6,000 needed to get the campaign for the school started, and as at the boys' school endowing five scholarships at the universities.

The establishment of the three-tiered system of education

confirmed the evolution of the class-structured society. Described in its simplest terms, in Bradford it consisted of an industrial gentry linked in a variety of ways to the political influence of the land, a middle class, professional, manufacturing and commercial, and a working class of artisans, factory workers and the very poor. Its symmetry was disrupted by the existence of a growing lower middle class – generally working-class in its dependent employment situation and middle-class in its aspirations – which was anxiously debating the relative merits of the cheaper private schools and the new higher-grade schools started by the Bradford School Board. Its stability was maintained through the overall unity of industrial gentry and middle class and through the degree of mobility at the interstices enjoyed in particular by the lower middle classes. It depended also on a working class slow to abandon its deferential posture and thus on the continuing alliance of organised labour and the Liberal Party.

Nevertheless the political consensus of the mid-century was crumbling. Within a year or two of Salt's death the new challenges of the seventies were clarified into firm political issues. Depression brought economic liberalism into question. The businessman's attack on free trade became a national issue in 1882 when S. C. Lister started his campaign for 'Fair Trade'. In 1886, with the defeat of the Home Rule Bill, the Irish question entered a new phase. The tentative beginnings of the working-class movement for political independence, led in Bradford by Fred Jowett and James Bartley, could be observed in the same year. It rejected the Radicalism of the Hardaker type and drew on the enduring record of autonomous action which had always upset the middle classes, the Chartist tradition, militant unionism, left-wing religious dissent, Secularism and the community of working-class life – in addition to the recent interpretations of Socialism which attracted others besides working-class people. The slums of towns like Bradford provided plenty of ammunition. The outlook for political consensus was poor. Salt's era was definitely over.

Salt continued in the intervals of painful attacks of gout to live a fairly active life until after the 1874 election. In addition to

349

his obligations as the 'Grand Old Man' he was occupied with the completion of Saltaire and became much more closely associated with the teetotal/temperance movement. He supported the new British Workmen's Non-alcoholic Public House movement and contributed substantially to the opening of the first house in Bradford. He also became one of Bradford's biggest subscribers to the United Alliance and a vice-president of the Licence Amendment League. His most important contribution to the development of late nineteenth-century Bradford was the £5,000 he gave to the new Fever Hospital. He continued his support of the Liberation Society and the cause of Congregationalism and was principally responsible for the rebuilding of Lightcliffe Congregational Church. He gave £1,000 to the Yorkshire College of Science which later became the University of Leeds. Much of his time was spent in administering the patronage in his gift as the result of his generosity to such institutions as the Bradford Infirmary, the Hull Seamen's Orphanage Home, the Northern Counties Lunatic Asylum and the Bradford Tradesmen's Homes.[23]

In the last few years of his life overt acclamation of his personal and public success, although always considerable, increased from every side. At one end of the scale, his arrival at a public or semi-public function was greeted with enthusiastic cheering and applause. The adults who lived in Saltaire presented him with his portrait and a highly laudatary address and the Saltaire children somehow managed to collect subscriptions for two breakfast dishes. His Lightcliffe neighbours presented him with a testimonial of goodwill and gratitude in 1871. At the other end of the scale Napoleon III in 1868 created him Chevalier de la Légion d'Honneur. He accepted the offer of a baronetcy in 1869, an award which promoted the comment that in a rationally constituted House of Lords his presence as a life peer would add dignity and authority to it. Though he was a Dissenter – the most influential in Bradford – the parish church bell rang its congratulations. In 1874, the statue which now stands at the Norman Arch entrance to Manningham Park was erected in Town Hall Square – one of the two Bradford men to be so honoured by their admirers the other being the very different S. C. Lister.[24]

By 1874, however, he was beginning to show clear signs of failing health. He attended the Godwin–Hardaker committee rooms during the 1874 election, but despite clamorous appeals from spectators outside he could not get up on to the platform to speak or show himself. By the beginning of 1875 he was living very quietly, and by the middle of 1876 a very positive decline set in. In October, he went to Scarborough, which had always been his favourite holiday resort, but returned to Crow Nest in no better health. From then on regular bulletins were issued in the local press and on 27 December the *Bradford Observer* reported:

From inquiries made at a late hour last night we learn that Sir Titus Salt is gradually growing weaker. He has been unable for four days to take the least nourishment. Up to yesterday he was always sensible but during the day he had several intervals of unconsciousness between which however he was able to recognise those who were around him. There is no doubt that the end is very near.

He died on 29 December 1876.

The family would have preferred a quiet and mainly private funeral, for they were on the whole reserved and, apart from Titus junior and his wife, not particularly appreciative of the public as opposed to the private position in which their father's wealth had placed them. In the event, the funeral which was arranged for 5 January 1877 was organised by the municipal authority as a civic event of first importance. The funeral was perhaps the greatest Victorian showpiece of the town's history – a display of civic consciousness and pride by men who were beginning to savour the achievements of Bradford's urban society and an indication of the esteem in which one of its greatest local exponents was held.

The day turned out to be reasonably bright and sunny, a relief for the organisers, since the weather had been bad, the streets covered in the ugly urban slush of a slow thaw, and snow-clearing operations along the route were just completed in time. The hearse, quietly decorated, accompanied by the family party, left Crow Nest, preceded by a detachment of mounted police, at 9.30 a.m. and arrived at Bradford at 10.45 where it was joined by the official procession assembled from

351

the Town Hall towards Manningham Lane. It started to move towards Saltaire at 11 a.m. A detachment of the Bradford Police, four abreast, followed the mounted police to the Congregational Church at Saltaire where they lined Victoria Road two abreast. They were followed by detachments of the West Yorkshire Rifle and Artillery Volunteers, whose band played the Dead March in *Saul*. They marched to the Emm Lane entrance of Manningham Park where they took up positions along the route. Representatives of local institutions with which Sir Titus was connected followed – the friendly societies, the Bradford Ragged School, Bradford Industrial Schools, the Eye and Ear Hospital, the Fever Hospital, Nurses' Training Institution, Infirmary, Chamber of Commerce, School Board, the Grammar Schools, Mechanics' Institute and the Seamen's Orphanage at Hull. The next group consisted of representatives of the merchants, manufacturers, traders and shopkeepers of the town, the Bradford Liberal Club, representatives of the county and borough justices, mayors of other towns and other gentlemen, the Mayor and Council of Bradford and MPs. All these took up positions along the route immediately after the military detachments, and waited for the hearse and private mourners to pass. The private carriages of those who were either too distinguished actually to line the route or wished to take part in a private capacity followed and representatives from West Riding institutions similarly lined the route as the cortège passed through Shipley into Saltaire. It was estimated that between 100,000 and 120,000 spectators watched the ceremony as it passed from Lightcliffe to Saltaire. In Saltaire, the mill was closed, house and shop blinds drawn and the streets of the village draped in black. Most of the employees were along Victoria Street, and the longer-serving men, like Rushton, Hanson, Baldwin, Naylor, Constantine and Feather, along the avenue leading to the church. Sir Titus was buried in the mausoleum he had had built inside the church, in 1861, after his retirement from Parliament, and the crowds who wanted to view the coffin and the tomb were so great that the mausoleum was kept open until 13 January and special trains were run from Bradford.[25]

Sir Titus Salt's career covered almost exactly the years of

Bradford's greatest urban growth and economic expansion, and since he was so closely involved in the events of the time reads like a comment on the Victorian idea of progress. Yet, notwithstanding his enormous success, not all his ambitions were fulfilled. He did not establish the industrial dynasty he had aimed at, for his sons (apart from Titus junior) appear to have lacked either the capacity or the interest to continue a successful textile business. Nor did he find an effective or durable solution to the problems of industrial relations. His strengths and limitations were the product of upbringing and experience. He was a Dissenter and a Radical and accepted the justice of the principle of political equality. On the other hand, he was unlikely to have taken Saltaire along the road on which his contemporary, Godin, took his industrial settlement. Yet, we, I think, must see him as a man of conscience and imagination, ready to use his wealth in more fruitful ways than the purchase of a landed estate. In his own day, he was seen as a heroic figure. On his death, every newspaper and journal of any importance carried an obituary praising his work. The Editor of the *Bradford Observer* wrote:

Sir Titus was perhaps the greatest captain of industry in England not only because he gathered thousands under him but also because, according to the light that was in him, he tried to care for all these thousands.

We do not say that he succeeded in realising all his views and wishes or that it is possible to harmonise at present all relations between Capital and Labour . . . but upright in business, admirable in his private relations he came without seeking the honour to be admittedly the best representative of the employer class in this part of the country if not the whole kingdom.[26]

NOTES

The following abbreviations have been used in the notes.

Advertiser	*Bradford Advertiser*
Balgarnie	R. Balgarnie, *Sir Titus Salt, Baronet, His Life and its Lessons*, London, 1887, reprinted Settle, 1970
BCL	Bradford Central Library
BL	British Library
Church Records	Bradford Parish Church Records
Cudworth *Bolton and Bowling*	W. Cudworth, *Histories of Bolton and Bowling*, Bradford, 1891
Cudworth, *Horton*	W. Cudworth, *Rambles round Horton*, Bradford, 1886
Cudworth, *Manningham*	W. Cudworth, *Manningham, Heaton and Allerton*, Bradford, 1896
Cudworth, *Notes*	W. Cudworth, *Historical Notes on the Bradford Corporation*, Bradford, 1881
Herald	*Bradford Herald*
James, *Continuation*	John James, *Continuations and Additions to the History of Bradford and its Parish*, Manchester and Bradford, 1866, reprinted Manchester, 1973
James, *History*	*The History and Topography of Bradford*, London and Bradford, 1851, reprinted Manchester, 1973
James, *Manufacture*	John James, *The History of the Worsted Manufacture in England*, Bradford, 1857
Jowitt and Taylor (eds)	J. A. Jowitt and R. K. S. Taylor (eds), *Nineteenth Century Bradford Elections*, Bradford, 1979
Obs	*Bradford Observer*
PP	*Parliamentary Papers*
PRO	Public Record Office
Review	*Bradford Review*
Reynolds's	*Reynolds's Newspaper*
Sigsworth, *Black Dyke*	E. M. Sigsworth, *Black Dyke Mills, A History, with Introductory Chapters on the Development of the Worsted Industry in the Nineteenth Century*, Liverpool, 1958

355

SST
Shipley and Saltaire Times

Trans NAPSS
Transactions of the National Association for the Promotion of Social Science

Victorian Bradford
D. G. Wright and J. A. Jowitt (eds), *Victorian Bradford, Essays in Honour of Jack Reynolds*, Bradford, 1982

I. Bradford in the first decade of industrialisation

1. John Nicholson, *Miscellaneous Poems*, ed. W. G. Hird, London and Bradford, 1876.
2. *The Voice of the People and Labour Advocate*, Bradford, 19 Dec. 1857.
3. Local detail has been taken from a large number of sources available in the Local History and Archives Departments of the Bradford Central Library. The most important printed sources are: John James, *The History and Topography of Bradford*, London and Bradford, 1851, reprinted Bradford, 1967; *Continuation and Additions to the History of Bradford and its Parish*, Manchester and Bradford, 1866, reprinted Manchester, 1973; William Cudworth, *Historical Notes on the Bradford Corporation*, Bradford, 1881; William Scruton, *Pen and Pencil Pictures of Old Bradford*, Bradford, 1889; the *Bradford Antiquary*, the *Journal of the Bradford Historical and Antiquarian Society*, Bradford, 1881 *et cont.*; the *Bradford Observer* 1834 *et seq.*, became *Yorkshire Observer* 1902 closed 1956.
4. Cudworth, *Notes*, pp. 1-93 *passim*; see also his 'Old Bradford Records, Bradford Glebe Lands', *Bradford Antiquary*, Vol. II, p. 185.
5. Acreage Returns, 1801, HO 67 (Public Record Office).
6. John James, *The History of the Worsted Manufacture in England*, Bradford, 1857; E. M. Sigsworth, Bradford on the eve of the Industrial Revolution, *Journal of the Bradford Textile Society*, 1953-4; *Black Dyke Mills, A History, with introductory Chapters on the Development of the Worsted Industry in the Nineteenth Century*, Liverpool, 1958; G. Firth, 'The Genesis of the Industrial Revolution in Bradford', unpublished PhD thesis, University of Bradford, 1974.
7. C. Richardson, *A Geography of Bradford*, Bradford, 1976; Bradford Parish Church Registers (Burials and Baptisms) 1710-1780 (Bradford Cathedral Archives).
8. *Parliamentary Papers* 1803 v p. 306, Report of a Select Committee on Yorkshire Woollen Petitions, evidence of Nathaniel Murgatroyd; *PP* 1806 iii p. 185, Report of a Select Committee on the Woollen Trade, evidence of Richard Fawcett.
9. H. Heaton, *The Yorkshire Woollen and Worsted Industry from the earliest times up to the Industrial Revolution*, Oxford, 1920, chaps 9-12 *passim*; Worsted Committee MSS (in Bradford University Library).
10. Parish Registers *loc cit*; Document, Numbers of Inhabitants in the street called Westgate and parts adjacent in Cudworth MSS Box No 6,

Notes

(Bradford Central Library), see also his The Bradford Soke, *Bradford Antiquary*, Vol. I, p. 74, Firth *op. cit.*, pp. 124-33.

11. James, *Manufacture*, p. 315; Sir F. M. Eden, *The State of the Poor*, 3 Vols. London, 1797.

12. W. Cudworth, *Histories of Bolton and Bowling*, Bradford, 1891; *Rambles round Horton*, Bradford, 1886; *Manningham, Heaton and Allerton*, Bradford, 1896; Scruton *op. cit., passim*; H. R. Hodgson, *The Society of Friends in Bradford*, Bradford, 1926; MSS Day Book of Abraham Balme (BCL).

13. W. Cudworth, Bradford in 1759, *Bradford Antiquary*, vol. II, pp. 216-17; G. F. Renton, The Water Supply of Bradford, MSS and pp. 21-24 (BCL) Heaton, *op. cit.*, p. 319; Eden, *op. cit.*

14. Eden, *op. cit.*; Hodgson, *op. cit.*; James, *History*, pp. 224-35; Visitation Return to Archbishop Herring 1743 (York Minster Archives).

15. *Obs*, 30 Oct. 1856.

16. James, *Continuation*, pp. 88-90; *Obs*, idem and 13 Jan. 1874.

17. Cudworth, *Notes* pp. 15-93 *passim*.

18. D. J. Jenkins, *The West Riding Wool Textile Industry 1770-1835 – A Study in Fixed Capital Formation*, Edington, 1975, pp. 224-250; James, *Manufacture* p. 606.

19. James, *Manufacture*, pp. 412, 387; *Leeds Mercury*, 8 Dec 1832.

20. Firth, *op. cit.*, Chap. 3, especially p. 190.

21. *PP* 1831, xviii, p. 318, Comparative Account of the Population of Great Britain in the years 1801, 1811, 1821, and 1831.

22. John Earnshaw, *The Records and Reminiscences of St. Patrick's Church*, Bradford, 1902, p. 115; *PP* 1836 xxiv, p. 499, 1st Report of an Inquiry into the Condition of the Poorer Classes in Ireland, App. G, Report on the State of the Irish Poor in Great Britain, p. 25.

23. W. Scruton, *Bradford Fifty Years Ago*, Bradford, 1891; also quoted in E. P. Thompson, *The Making of the English Working Class*, 1963 (Pelican, 1968, p. 312).

24. Cudworth, *Notes* p. 57; Abraham Holroyd, *Collectanea Bradfordiana*, Bradford, 1873, pp. 139-40.

25. *Obs*, 4 Mar. 1872; *Bradford and Huddersfield Courier*, 17 Nov. 1825.

26. *Leeds Mercury*, 27 Mar., 17 Apr. 1830.

27. W. Scruton, The Great Strike of 1825, *Bradford Antiquary*, 1888, Vol. I, pp. 67-73; J. T. Ward, A Great Bradford Dispute, *Journal of the Bradford Textile Society*, 1961-2, pp. 117-133.
    J. Smith, The Strike of 1825, (ed). D. G. Wright and J. A. Jowitt *Victorian Bradford – Essays in Honour of Jack Reynolds*, Bradford, 1981; see also Thompson *op. cit.*, pp. 312-14.

28. James, *Manufacture*, pp. 394-396; R. Balgarnie, *Sir Titus Salt, Baronet: His Life and Its Lessons*, London, 1877, reprinted Seatle, 1970.

29. James, *Manufacture*, p. 385.

30. Nicholson, *op. cit.*, pp. 263-64.

31. John Tester, *The History of the Commencement, Progress and Termination of the Bradford Contest*, Bradford, 1826.

32. Christopher Hill, Pottage for Freeborn Englishmen, ed C. H. Feinstein *Socialism, Capitalism and Economic Growth Essays presented to Maurice Dobb*, Cambridge, 1967.

33. The Committee of the Woolcombers and Stuff-weavers Association, *Addresses to the Mechanics, Artisans and Labourers of the Manufacturing Towns of Great Britain*, Leeds University Library; Tester *op. cit.*; Ward *op. cit.*

34. See for example letter of John Carter to Masters' Association in MSS Masters' Association (BCL).

35. James, *History*, pp. 168-9.

36. J. Reynolds, *The letter press printers of Bradford* published by the Bradford Branch of the National Graphical Association, 1972; *Leeds Intelligencer*, 3 Jan. 1832, 2 Nov. 1833.

37. *Ibid.*, 6 July 1832, 3 Jan. 1832.

38. James, *History*, pp. 224-237; Cudworth, *Bolton and Bowling*, pp. 283-4; *Leeds Mercury*, 6 Nov. 1830; Rev. W. Morgan, *The Pastoral Visitor*, Bradford, Sept. 1816, Vol. 2, No. 21, p. 129.

39. *Annual Report of the Bradford Mechanics' Institute*, 1834 (BCL); Charles Federer, 'The Bradford Mechanics' Institute, a History', 1906, Unpublished MSS (BCL).

40. James, *History*, pp. 169-170; *Leeds Mercury*, 6 Oct 1832.

41. *Bradford and Huddersfield Courier*, Statement of John Tester, 3 Nov. 1825.

42. J. T. Ward, Slavery in Yorkshire – Bradford and Factory Reform, *Journal of the Bradford Textile Society 1960-1961*; see also his *The Factory Movement 1831-1855*, London, 1962; *PP.* 1833, XXCI, Pt II, pp. 97-121, Factories Inquiry Commission Supplementary Report Employment of Children in Factories, Pt II; C. Driver, *Tory Radical The Life of Richard Oastler*, OUP, 1946, p.299.

43. For full discussion of Bradford nineteenth-century electoral history see D. G. Wright, 'Politics and Opinion in Nineteenth Century Bradford 1832-1880', 2 vols, PhD Thesis, Leeds University, 1966. See also his 'A Radical Borough; Parliamentary Politics in Bradford 1832-1841', *Northern History*, Vol. IV, 1969; *The Halifax Guardian and Huddersfield and Bradford Advertiser*, 8 Dec. 1831; *Leeds Intelligencer*, 3 Jan. 1832.

44. *Leeds Mercury*, 11 July 1831; J. Schofield, *Peter Bussey*, Bradford n.d.

45. Balgarnie, Chap. 2; William Smith, *Morley Ancient and Modern*, London, 1886.

46. West Riding Register of Deeds, HQ No 284, 334, HU No. 254, 278 IA 83 HR No. 263, 257 (in West Yorkshire County Record Office).

47. *Loc. cit.*, MG No. 638; *Obs*, 12 Mar. 1857.

48. Salt Family Bible in possession of Denys Salt Esq. (great-grandson of Sir Titus Salt).

49. *Obs*, 30 Dec. 1876.

50. Will of Daniel Salt (in Library of Borthwick Institute of Historical Research, York).

51. Will of Grace Salt – deeds of surrender of executor's power to Titus Salt (Borthwick); J. Ibbetson, *Directory of the Borough of Bradford 1845*.

Notes

52. Held by Denys Salt.
53. *Obs*, 7 May 1835.
54. Whitlam Family Bible in possession of Denys Salt. Census Enumerators' Returns – Townships of Bradford and Horton 1841.

II. The economy and the entrepreneur

1. James, *Manufacture*, Chaps 9–12; Sigsworth, *Black Dyke Mills*, Chap. 2. H. Forbes, Lecture: 'The Progress of the Worsted Industry', given to the Royal Society of Arts, 1851, printed in A. Holroyd, *Collectanea Bradfordiana*, Bradford, 1873, pp. 177-84.
2. Reprinted in *Obs*, 24 Dec. 1834.
3. James, *Manufacture*, p. 475.
4. *Ibid*, p. 456.
5. *Household Words*, ed. C. Dickens, 1852-3, Vol VI, pp. 250-3.
6. Day Book of Titus Salt held by Dr J. A. Iredale, Bradford University; J. A. Iredale, 'Titus Salt's Day Book 1834-1837', *Journal of Textile History*, Vol. I, No. 1, Dec. 1968.
7. James, *Manufacture*, p. 457.
8. *Ibid*, pp. 461, 584, 600.
9. Sigsworth, *op. cit.*, pp. 30-4.
10. *Obs*, 18 Sep. 1856; see also Report of Inquiry by H. S. Chapman on condition of handloom weavers, *Obs*, 27 Sep., 4 Oct. 1838; *West Riding Worsted Directory*, 1851, pp. 306, 317; Sigsworth, *op. cit.*, pp. 34-8.
11. For thorough discussion see J. M. Trickett, 'A Technological Appraisal of the Isaac Holden Papers', Unpublished M.Sc thesis, Bradford University, 1977; also J. Burnley, *History of Wool and Woolcombing*, London, 1889; S. C. Lister, *Lord Masham's Inventions*, London, 1905; Sigsworth, *op. cit.*, pp. 38-43.
12. J. Parry Lewis, *Building Cycles and Britain's Growth*, 1965, Appendix 5, pp. 319-22, p. 237; Sigsworth, *op. cit.*
13. James, *Manufacture*, Appendix pp. 17-21.
14. A. H. Robinson, 'Bradford's First Lord Mayor', *Bradford Bystander*, Vol. II, No. 83, July 1971.
15. Certificates of Naturalisation, *Index to Names* 1908 (in PRO); *Obs*, 22 Jul. 1870.
16. Richardson, *op. cit.*, Chap. 4.
17. *Annual Reports of the Bradford Chamber of Commerce*, Bradford (BCL).
18. J. Ayres, *Architecture in Bradford*, Bradford, 1972.
19. J. Ruskin, 'Traffic' – a lecture delivered in the Town Hall, Bradford, printed in *The Crown of Wild Olives*, London, 1866, 1906, pp. 72-114. H. Behrens (trans.), *Sir Jacob Behrens 1806-1889* – a translation of his unpublished memoirs, privately printed, Bradford, pp. 37-9 (BCL).
20. James, *Manufacture*, pp. 515, 543; *Obs*, 6 Feb. 1868.
21. Statement showing the gross amount of Property and Profits assessed to Income Tax and the amount of duty charged in Leeds, Bradford,

Manchester and Huddersfield for the year ending 5 April 1880 (document in BCL, Archives Section); *PP* Census of England and Wales 1871, Population Abstracts, Vol. III, pp. 482, 486.

22. J. W. Turner, 'Some Old Bradford Firms', MS lecture read to Bradford Historical and Antiquarian Society (BCL Archives Section); *Obs*, 20 May 1875.

23. W. D. Rubenstein, 'British Millionaires 1809-1949', *Bulletin of the Institute of Historical Research*, Vol XLVII, 1974, pp. 202-3.

24. 'The Bradford "Silk King",' reprinted from *Pall Mall Gazette*, *Obs*, 7 Mar. 1887.

25. Obituary, *Obs*, 14 Aug. 1897; E. Jennings, 'Sir Isaac Holden, First Comber of Europe', unpublished PhD thesis, Bradford University, 1982.

26. *Obs*, 6 Feb. 1889; *Bradford Observer Budget*, 10 Feb. 1906; Cudworth, *Manningham*, pp. 133-42.

27. Cudworth, *Bolton and Bowling*, pp. 244-50; H. W. Ripley, *What has Ripley done for Bradford and what has he done for education?* , Bradford 1868 (BCL); *Obs*, 7 Jan. 1883.

28. Balgarnie remains the principal source. See also Chap. 6, note 2, infra.

29. See note 10, *supra W. R. Worsted Directory, op. cit.*

30. *Obs*, 25 May 1848.

31. *Ibid*, 28 Oct. 1847, 7 May 1846.

32. *Ibid*, 21 Sep. 1843.

33. Salt's motives in building Saltaire have to be inferred. He provided only the vaguest of hints. See also Chap. 6, pp. 263-5.

34. *The Illustrated London News*, 1 Oct. 1853.

35. Lister, *op. cit.*, p.42.

36. B. Allsop, *The Late Sir Titus Salt, Bart, Founder of Saltaire, A Brief Resume of his Life and Works*, Saltaire, 1887, p. 23.

37. Cudworth, *Notes, passim*; *Obs*, 31 Oct. 1850.

38. *Ibid*, 17 Jul. 1856.

39. *Shipley and Saltaire Times*, 13 Jan. 1877.

40. Balgarnie, pp. 188, 238-40.

41. Compiled from lists of guests at dinners and other public occasions and printed in local press.

42. *Obs*, 27 Jun. 1844.

43. I should like to thank Mrs I. C. Carter, Assistant Secretary, Old Millhillians Club, for the information.

44. *Loughborough Herald and North Leicester Gazette*, 14 Jul. 1892.

45. *Bradford Observer Budget*, 26 Nov. 1887 – obituary of Titus Salt junior.

46. Brian and Dorothy Payne, Extracts from the Journal of John Deakin Heaton, *The Thoresby Miscellany*, Leeds, 1972, Vol. 15, p. 2.

47. *The Builder*, 15 Mar. 1873.

48. I should like to thank Denys Salt for the information.

49. *Bradford Evening Mail*, 2 Apr. 1873.

50. *Obs*, 26 Apr. 1893 – funeral of the Dowager Lady Salt.

Notes

III. Years of crisis: 1834-1850

1. George Weerth, *Sämtliche Werke*, Berlin, 1957, Vol. III, pp. 162-9. I should like to thank Alan Farmer and Janet Montgomerie (née Reynolds) for translating a number of extracts.
2. *PP* Census of Great Britain 1831, 1841, 1851.
3. A. Elliott, 'The Establishment of Municipal Government in Bradford 1837-1857', PhD thesis, Bradford University, 1976, for the whole of this controversial period; James, *History*, pp. 174-178.
4. *Obs* 19 Feb. 1835.
5. Proceedings of the Bradford Reform Society MSS (BCL).
6. *Obs*, 27 Feb., 13 Mar., 20 Mar., 10 Apr. 1834.
7. *Ibid*, 2 Jan. 1835, 12 Jan. 1837; Proceedings BRS d. 24 Feb. 1837.
8. *Obs*, 7 Sep., 31 Aug. 1837.
9. *Ibid*, 1 Mar. 1838.
10. For Scoresby see R. E. Scoresby-Jackson, *The Life of William Scoresby*, London, 1861; T. and C. Stamp, *William Scoresby Arctic Scientist*, Whitby, 1975.
11. *Obs*, 17 Aug. 1837.
12. *Ibid*, 26 Jan., 2 Feb., 16 Feb., 23 Nov. 1837; James, *History*, pp. 180, 181.
13. *Obs*, 1 Jun. 1837.
14. *Ibid*, 14 Jan. 1836.
15. *loc. cit.* Report of Inquiry into condition of Handloom weavers.
16. For Chartism see R. G. Gammage, *History of the Chartist Movement 1837–1854*, London, 1854, reprinted 1893, 1961; J. West, *A History of the Chartist Movement*, London, 1920; A. Briggs (ed.), *Chartist Studies*, London, 1967; A. J. Peacock, *Bradford Chartism 1838–1840*, Borthwick Institute of Historical Research, Borthwick Papers no. 36, 1969; J. T. Ward, *Chartism*, London, 1973.
17. *Obs*, 27 Mar. 1838.
18. *Ibid*, 15 Aug., 29 Aug. 1839, 30 Jun. 1840.
19. *Northern Star*, 15 Jun. 1839; Peacock, *op. cit.*
20. Samuel Bower, *Competition in Peril*, London, 1837; *A Sequel to the Peopling of Utopia*, Bradford, 1838; *The Peopling of Utopia*, Bradford, 1838.
21. *New Moral World*, 14 Mar. 1840, No. 73 n.s., p. 1173; *Obs*, 21 Nov. 1839, 28 Jul., 13 Oct. 1842.
22. *Obs*, 28 Apr. 1842.
23. Minute Book of the Bradford United Reform Club MSS (BCL).
24. James, *Continuation*, p. 101.
25. Proceedings of the Bradford United Reform Club *passim* (BCL).
26. Correspondence with the Home Office 15 Apr. 1841–27 Oct. 1842 (PRO HO 45/53).
27. *Obs*, 15 Aug., 12 Sep. 1844; *Herald*, 8 Sep. 1842.
28. *Obs*, 24 Nov. 1842.
29. *Herald*, 24 Feb. 1842.
30. James, *Continuation*, pp. 101, 102.
31. Rate Book for Bradford East 1841 (in Bradford Cathedral Archive).

32. For general discussion see M. Jenkins, *The General Strike of 1842*, London, 1980.
33. *Obs*, 4 Aug. 1842.
34. *Ibid*, 7 Jul., 28 Jul. 1842.
35. *Herald*, 18, 25 Aug. 1842; *Obs*, 25 Aug. 1842; James, *Continuation*, p. 104.
36. A. Elliott, 'The Establishment of Municipal Government in Bradford' *op. cit.*; 'The Incorporation of Bradford', *Northern History*, XV, 1979; see also D. Fraser, *Urban Politics in Victorian England*, Leicester, 1976.
37. Minutes BURC 27 Nov. 1843.
38. *Obs*, 7 Dec. 1843.
39. *PP* 1840, XI, pp. 388-9. Report of the Select Committee on the Health of Towns, Minutes of evidence by Mr Joseph Ellison; *PP* 1845, XVIII App. Pt II. Second Report of the Commission of Inquiry into the State of the Large Towns and Populous Districts, evidence of Mr James Smith pp. 314-16: evidence of Bradford Board of Surveyors pp. 335-48; Weerth, *op. cit.*
40. Elliott, *op. cit.*, Chap. 3; *Obs*, 14 Aug. 1845.
41. Cudworth, *Notes*, pp. 92-102; *Obs* 14 Aug. 1845.
42. Elliott, *op. cit.*; *Obs*, 8 Oct. 1846.
43. *Obs*, 19 Apr. 1847, 3 Aug. 1848.
44. *Ibid*, 28 May 1840, 30 Jul. 1844.
45. J. A. Jowitt, 'Dissenters Voluntaryism and Liberal Unity, the 1847 Election', J. A. Jowitt and R. K. S. Taylor (eds), *Nineteenth Century Bradford Elections*, Bradford, 1979.
46. *Obs*, 7 Feb., 3 Apr. 1844, 20 Jul., 14 Dec. 1843, 3 Apr. 1845.
47. Gammage, *op. cit.*, p. 154.
48. *Obs*, 1 Aug. 1844, 27 Mar. 1845.
49. *Ibid*, 10 Jul. 1845; *Report of the Bradford Sanatory [sic] Committee* appointed at a public meeting held 5 May 1845 (Hailstone MSS, York Minster Archive; copy also in BCL).
50. *Obs*, 10 Apr. 1846.
51. *Ibid*, 5 Jun., 12 Jun. 1845.
52. *Ibid*, 16 Oct., 6 Nov. 1845.
53. *Ibid*, 12 Mar., 7 May, 31 Dec. 1846.
54. *PP* 1848 Report of the Inspector of Factories d. 31 Oct. 1847 report of R. Baker; *Obs*, 20, 27 May, 3, 17 Jun., 28 Oct. 1847.
55. *Obs*, 6, 13 Jan., 3, 17 Feb. 1848.
56. J. West, *op. cit.*, p. 239; see also J. Burnley, *Looking for the Dawn, a Tale of the West Riding*, London, 1874, a novel about Bradford-1848. It provides good local colour but otherwise has little merit except as demonstrating a middle-class inability to come to terms with working-class aspirations.
57. *Obs*, 16 Mar., 13 Apr. 1848.
58. Correspondence with the Home Office Apr. – Sep. 1848 (PRO HO 45/2410).
59. *Obs*, 13 Apr., 4, 18, 25 May 1848. Verbatim Report accepted on its face value – it was probably conducted in local dialect.

60. Correspondence with the Home Office *loc. cit.*; *Obs*, 25 May 1848.
61. *The Times*, 31 May 1848.
62. *Obs*, 1, 8, 15, 29 Jun., 13, 20 Jul., 17, 24 Aug., 13 Sep. 1848.
63. *Reynolds's*, 1 Nov. 1857.
64. Reprinted *Obs*, 13 Sep. 1848.

IV. Years of consensus: 1850-1868

1. For general discussion see A. Briggs, *The Age of Improvement*, London, 1959; *Victorian People*, London, 1954, Pelican 1965; *Victorian Cities*, London, 1963, Pelican 1970; W. L. Burn, *The Age of Equipoise, A Study of the Mid-Victorian Generation*, London, 1964; H. Perkin, *The Origins of Modern English Society 1780–1880*, London, 1969; T. R. Tholfsen, *Working Class Radicalism in Mid-Victorian England*, London, 1976; John Foster, *Class Struggle and the Industrial Revolution*, London, 1974.
2. *Obs*, 3 Jan. 1850.
3. National Association of Factory Occupiers, *Special Report of Executive Committee*, 1855 (BL).
4. *Obs*, 7 Jun. 1855.
5. *Ibid*, 13 Jan. 1859.
6. *Prospectus of Bradford High School*, Jul. 1868 (Yorkshire Hailstone Collection, BL).
7. Abraham Wildman, 'Stanzas', *Obs* 19 Aug. 1852.
8. *Reynolds's Newspaper*, 9 Aug. 1868.
9. *Obs*, 2 May 1850.
10. *Bradford Review*, 28 Jul. 1860.
11. *The Democrat and Labour Advocate*, 3 Nov. 1855.
12. M. Ross, *An Address to Trade Unionists on the Question of Strikes*, Bradford, n.d. (BCL).
13. *Review*, 15 Jan. 1859.
14. *PP* Census of England and Wales 1861.
15. *Obs*, 31 Jan. 1870, 6 Feb. 1868; for the Irish disturbances see *Obs*, 30 May, 6 Jun. 1844, 18, 25 Sep. 1862.
16. *Ibid*, 29 Feb. 1872.
17. *Ibid*, 14 Mar. 1850.
18. *Ibid*, extract reprinted 29 Sep. 1859; see also *Ibid*, 22 Aug. 1850, 9 Aug. 1866; for contemporary criticism of Worsted Act see *Advertiser*, 28 Jul. 1855 – remarks of the magistrate, W. Murgatroyd.
19. *PP* Census of England and Wales 1851, 1861, 1871, 1901.
20. *Reynolds's*, 1 Nov. 1857; *Obs*, 9 Feb. 1853.
21. *Reynolds's, loc. cit.*; *Obs*, 22 Mar. 1849.
22. E. Naylor, *Bradford Building Societies from 1823*, Bradford, 1910; J. F. Ritchie, *Freehold Land Societies*, London, 1853.
23. *Obs*, 31 Jan., 6 Jun. 1850; S. M. Gaskell, 'Yorkshire Estate Development and the Freehold Land Societies in the 19th Century', *The Yorkshire Archaeological Journal*, Vol. 43, 1971; Bradford Freehold Land Society MSS (BCL).

24. *Obs*, 23 Aug., 6 Sep. 1849.
25. *Ibid*, 20 Sep. 1849.
26. *Ibid*, 28 Jun. 1849.
27. *Report on the Moral Condition of the Town* – see *Obs*, 7 Mar. 1850.
28. *Obs, loc. cit.*
29. Bradford Town Mission Minutes and other documents (BCL); *Obs*, 11 Apr. 1850, 22 Mar. 1855.
30. F. Hertz, 'Mechanics Institutes for Working Women with special reference to the manufacturing districts of Yorkshire', *Transactions of the National Association for the Promotion of Social Science*, 1858, pp. 347-54; *Obs*, 7 Mar. 1867.
31. *Obs*, 24 Jan. 1856.
32. Cudworth, *Notes*, p. 153.
33. *Obs*, 1 Jun. 1872.
34. *Ibid*, 15 Aug. 1850, 8 May 1851, 10 Feb. 1853, 3 Jun. 1868, 24 May 1866.
35. J. Wilson, *Joseph Wilson, His Life and Work*, Bradford, n.d., p. 29 (BCL); see also *Obs*, 28 Mar. 1870.
36. M. Warwick, 'W. E. Forster's Work in Burley-in-Wharfedale', *The Yorkshire Archaeological Journal*, Vol. 43, 1971, pp. 166-73.
37. *Obs*, 17 Aug. 1865.
38. See P. Joyce, *Work Society and Politics, the Culture of the Factory in Later Victorian England*, Brighton, 1980, Chap. 4, for useful discussion.
39. *PP* 1851, Vol LXXXLX, p. ccliii, Census of Great Britain, Report and Tables on Religious Worship; *Census of Public Worship in Bradford* being statistics of the Attendance at Religious Services in the Borough on December 11 and December 18 1881, Bradford, 1882.
40. *PP* 1861, Vol XXI, Part II, pp. 175-242, Report of the Assistant Comm., J. S. Winder Esq., on the state of Popular Education in Rochdale and Bradford; see also G. W. Fenn, 'The Development of Education in an Industrial Town (Bradford) in the Nineteenth Century', *University of Leeds Institute of Education Researches and Studies*, Jan. 1952–Jan. 1953.
41. *Obs*, 12 Feb. 63 – report by Rev. W. Kinglake.
42. Winder, *loc. cit.*
43. E. Ackroyd, *The Present Attitude of Political Parties*, London, 1874.
44. C. A. Federer, *op. cit.*
45. J. V. Godwin, 'The Bradford Mechanics' Institute', *Trans NAPSS*, 1859; *West Riding Worsted Directory*, 1857; *Review*, 2 Feb. 61 – Abraham Holroyd, 'The Education and Self Culture of Working Men and Women'.
46. MSS, The Bradford Long Pledged Teetotal Society (BCL); *Obs*, 2 Sep. 1874.
47. W. Cudworth, *The Condition of the Industrial Working Classes of Bradford and District*, Bradford, 1887, pp. 70-3; *PP* 1874, XX, III, Pt II, pp. 206-7, Report of Hon. E. L. Stanley.
48. *Obs*, 1, 8 Jan. 1852.
49. A Bradford Carpenter's Family during the Industrial Revolution – Information compiled by Mr D. Ellison from documents held at

Teachers' Resource Centre, Bradford.

50. J. Bennett and J. Baldwin, *The City of Bradford Co-operative Society Jubilee History*, Bradford, 1910.
51. *Obs*, 9 Jan. 1862; *The Non Conformist*, Vol. XIII, New Series No. 373 d. 12 Jan. 1853; see also E. Royle, *Victorian Infidels*, Manchester, 1974.
52. Cudworth, *Industrial Working Classes*, pp. 79-83.
53. J. Reynolds, *The letter press printers of Bradford*, Bradford, 1972, *passim*.
54. D. F. Garne, 'Bradford – Radical City in the Liberal Age', unpublished MA thesis, Bradford University, 1976.
55. *Obs*, 24 Jan. 1867.
56. M. Ashraf, *Bradford Trades Council 1872 – 1972*, published by Bradford Trades Council, 1972; R. Harrison, *Before the Socialists*, London, 1965, pp. 138, 139; S. C. Kell, *The Political Attitudes of our Law Making Classes towards the Unenfranchised and the Duties of Working Men under the Present Political Circumstances*, Bradford, 1861.
57. J. Burnley, 'The Streets of Bradford' – Extracts from *Obs*, 1883 (BCL).
58. *Bradford Social Reformer*, 14 Sep. 1867.
59. Ellison, *op. cit.*, Reynolds, *op. cit.*
60. *Obs*, 23 Oct. 1851, 7 Jul. 1852.
61. James, *Continuation*, pp. 115-18; Garne, *op. cit.*, pp. 40-2.
62. J. Reynolds, 'The General Election of 1859', J. A. Jowitt and R. K. S. Taylor (eds), *Nineteenth Century Bradford Elections*, Bradford, 1979, pp. 35-49; W. L. Guttsman, 'The General Election of 1859 in the cities of Yorkshire', *International Review of Social History*, Vol. II, Part 2, 1957, pp. 231-67; F. E. Gillespie, *Labour and the Politics of England 1850-67*, Chicago, 1927, London, 1966; F. B. Smith, *The Making of the Second Reform Bill*, Cambridge, 1966; Wright, *op. cit.*; Garne, *op. cit.*
63. So referred to by R. Kell in a letter to R. Cobden, 29 Mar. 1857 (BL Add. MSS 43689).
64. Nineteenth Century Election Posters (collection in BCL).
65. *Obs, Review, Advertiser, passim*, Mar.–May 1859, particularly 23, 30 Apr.
66. *Reynolds's*, 1 May 1859.
67. *The Poll Book The General Election*, Bradford, 1859.
68. House of Commons Division Lists, Sessions 1859–61 (House of Lords Library).
69. *Obs*, 30 Apr. 1859.
70. For biographical sketch of Alfred Harris see W. Cudworth, *Manningham, Heaton and Allerton*, Bradford, 1896, pp. 213-15.
71. *Review*, 23 Apr. 1859.
72. *Obs*, 22 Sep. 1859.
73. J. Reynolds, 'The General Election of 1859', in Jowitt and Taylor (eds) from which this account of the 1859 election is taken.
74. Division lists *loc. cit.*
75. For Forster's career see W. Wemyss Reid, *The Life of William Edward Forster*, London, 1888; see also G. J. Holyoake, *Sixty Years of an Agitator's Life*, London, 1882, Vol. II, p. 126.

76. *Obs*, 24 Jan. 1867; *Parliamentary Debates*, 3 S CLXXVIII p. 1644, Speech
     – Borough Franchise Extension Bill, 8 May 1865.
77. *Obs*, 21 Feb. 1862.
78. D. M. Thompson, 'The Liberation Society 1844 – 1868', in Patricia
     Hollis (ed.), *Pressure from Without*, London, 1974.
79. For Thomas see J. R. Beckett (ed.), *Bradford Portraits*, Bradford, 1892,
     p.55; for Bradford activity in general see *The Liberator* e.g. Vol XXI
     (New Series, Vol. 1), Jan. 1875; Records of the Liberation Society MSS
     (Greater London Record Office).
80. *Loc. cit.* See also *Obs*, 25 Oct. 1872, reprinted from *Non-Conformist
     Supplement*, 23 Oct. 1872, State of Religious Accommodation in large
     towns.
81. *Obs*, 4 Feb. 1864.
82. The Bradford Political Union MSS – list of members (BCL).
83. 21 Jul., 4, 11, 18 Aug. 1864; *Reynolds's*, 14 Aug. 1864.
84. *Obs*, 15 Dec. 1864.
85. Political Union *loc. cit.*; Minutes of a meeting of delegates to a conference
     at Manchester and other friends of the National Reform Union; Bradford
     Branch of the National Reform Union MSS (BCL).
86. *Obs*, 6 Jul. 1865.
87. A. Wildman, 'A Poem – the Obstructors and the Obstructed', *Obs*, 2
     Feb. 1865.
88. *Obs*, 6 Sep. 1866.
89. *Ibid*, 12 Apr., 4, 11 Oct. 1866.
90. *Ibid*, 11 Oct. 1866.
91. *Ibid*, 4, 7 Oct. 1867.
92. *Ibid*, 4 Oct. 1866.
93. *Ibid*, 16 Jan. 1868.
94. Reform League Letter Book 7 Oct. 1866 and Jul. 1867 to Apr. 1868
     passim (Microfilm, Bradford University Library, originals in Bishopsgate
     Institute, London).
95. *The Working Man*, 21 Apr. 1868.

V. The Municipal Corporation and the environment, 1848-1880

1. For general discussion see W. M. Frazer, *A History of Public Health 1834-
    1939*, London, 1950; Barbara Thompson, 'Public Provision and Private
    Neglect' in *Victorian Bradford*, for the only comprehensive study of
    Bradford. See also Elliott, *op. cit.*
2. Garne, *op. cit.*, pp. 158-74; Cudworth, *Notes*, p. 95 *et seq*; *Borough of
    Bradford – By-Laws*, 27 May 1848.
3. *Obs*, 15 Sep. 1842, Feb 1849 – May 1850 *passim*.
4. *Ibid*, 1 Mar. – 23 Sep. 1848 *passim*.
5. *Ibid*, 18 Oct. 1849.
6. Elliott, *op. cit.*, pp. 133-45.
7. Cudworth, Notes, pp. 121-22; *Obs*, 14 Mar., 9 May 1850.

8. R. West, 'Worstedopolis and the Waterworks', unpublished BA dissertation, Bradford University, 1980, (BCL); G. F. Renton, 'The Watersupply of Bradford', MSS (BCL); Elliott, *op. cit.*, pp. 168-98 *passim*.

9. *Obs*, 28 Feb. 1850.

10. West, *op. cit.*, Appendix 1 for list of shareholders.

11. West, *op. cit.*; Renton, *op. cit.*; Elliott, *op. cit.*

12. Cudworth, *Notes*, pp. 130-3.

13. *Ibid*; Renton, *op. cit.*, p. 104.

14. Reports to the Local Government Board 1869-1908. Harvester Card 16. Report by J. Netten Radcliffe on Certain Defects in the Sanitary Administration of Bradford (Yorkshire) and on the recent prevalence of Enteric Fever and other Diarrhoeal Diseases 17 Jul. 1872, (BCL).

15. *Obs*, 11 Jun. 1874; Renton, *op. cit.*, p. 138.

16. James, *Continuation*, p. 118.

17. *Obs*, 11 Dec. 1852, Report of a meeting on Sanitary Reform; see also 2 and 9 May 1850, report of parliamentary committee stage of Improvement Bill.

18. City of Bradford pamphlet, *Work of the Sewage Department with some Historical Notes 1870-1831*, 3rd edition, 1931.

19. *Obs*, 13 Oct. 1850, Report of the proceedings of the meeting of the National Association for the Promotion of Social Sciences held at St George's Hall Bradford in Oct. 1859; see also *Ibid*, 17 Feb. 1859.

20. *Ibid*, 24 Mar., 22 Dec. 1859; Charles Gott, *Report of the Borough Surveyor on the Arterial and Main Sewers required for the Sewerage of Bradford*, Bradford, 1859.

21. Work of the Sewage Department, *op. cit.*

22. *Obs*, 19 Aug. 1872.

23. Reports of Female Sanitary Inspectors to Bradford Health Committee, Sept. 1903, quoted from *Sanitary Record*, 23 July 1903.

24. *Obs*, 7 Mar. 1850.

25. *Report of the Sub-Committee on the Operation of the Building Bye Laws*, Bradford, 7 Mar. 1864.

26. J. Parry Lewis, *Building Cycles and Britain's Growth*, London, 1965 Appendix 5; The Censuses of England and Wales 1851, 1861, 1871; *Reynolds's*, 25 Oct. 1857.

27. J. Hanson, *Why are Houses so scarce and Rents so High?*, reprinted as pamphlet from *Review* 9, 16 Sep. 1865; *PP* 1866, Vol. XXXIII, 8th Report of the Medical Officer of Health to the Privy Council, Report by Dr H. T. Hunter on the Housing of the Poorer Parts of the Population in Towns, pp. 498-513 App. 2.

28. There are plenty of examples of this type of housing to be seen. Pre-by-law back-to-back houses have almost entirely disappeared.

29. *Annual Reports of Committees to Council* Reports of the Sanitary Committee 1859-1870; Annual Reports of the Medical Officer of Health for Bradford 1876 *et seq.*

30. *Report of the Smoke Prevention Sub-Committee*, Bradford, 1867 (BCL).

31. Cudworth, *Notes*, pp. 152, 167, 193; Reports of MOH, 1885.
32. *Obs*, 11 Dec. 1856, 18 May 1878, 14 Mar. 1872.
33. Cudworth, *Notes*, pp. 158-9, 163-193 *passim*; J. Ayers, *Architecture in Bradford*, Bradford, 1972; Cudworth, *Manningham*, p. 142; *The Architect*, 8 Oct. 1870; *The Builder*, 8 Mar. 1873; *Obs*, 1866; *Bradford Chronicle*, 9 Sep. 1873.
34. Weerth, *op. cit.*
35. *Obs*, 6 Sep. 1866 – report of Dr J. H. Bell to the Board of Guardians.
36. H. Fieldhouse and H. Cragg, '"Poverty Corners" in Bradford', *The Yorkshireman*, 1886, p. 248.
37. I wish to thank Mrs Barbara Thompson for her help with these figures.
38. *Reports of MOH*, 1876-1892.
39. *Obs*, 20 Sep. 1865 – letter from Dr J. H. Bell on the sanitary condition of Bradford.
40. E. J. Smith, *Race Regeneration*, London, 1918, p. 22.

VI. Saltaire

1. Hector Garvie, M.D. F.R.C.S.E., *The Habitations of the Industrial Classes, Their Influence on the Social and Moral Condition of these Classes*, published by the Society for Improving the Condition of the Labouring Classes of London, 1851.
2. For Saltaire see B. Allsopp, *The Late Sir Titus Salt Bart, Founder of Saltaire, a Brief Resumé of His Life and Works*, Saltaire, 1887; R. Balgarnie, *Sir Titus Salt Baronet His Life and Its Lessons*, London, 1878, reprinted Settle, 1970; W. Cudworth, *Saltaire Yorkshire England a sketch history*, Saltaire, 1895; *Round about Bradford*, Bradford, 1878; A. Holroyd, *Saltaire and Its Founder Sir Titus Salt Bart*, Bradford, 1873; Local Studies Department, Bradford Central Library, *Saltaire the origins of a model industrial community*, published by Bradford Metropolitan Council Libraries Division; J. Reynolds, *Saltaire – an introduction to the village of Sir Titus Salt*, published by Bradford Metropolitan Council Arts Galleries and Museums; R. W. Suddards (ed.), *Titus of Salts*, Bradford, 1976; J. Horsfall Turner, *Shipley, Idle and District*, Shipley, 1901; R. K. Dewhirst, 'Saltaire', *The Town Planning Review*, Vol XXXI, 1960, pp. 133-144; R. Driuff, 'Saltaire, pioneer factory village', *Town and Country Planning*, May 1965; J. M. Richards, 'Sir Titus Salt', *Architectural Review*, Vol. LXXX, 1936, pp. 213-18. See also W. Ashworth, *The Genesis of Modern British Town Planning*, London, 1954; 'British Industrial Villages in the Nineteenth Century', *Economic History Review*, Second Series, Vol. III., 1951; W. H. G. Armytage, *Utopian Experiments in England 1560-1960*, London, 1961; Leonardo Benevolo, *Le Origine dell'urbanistica moderna*, Bari, 1963, Eng. trans. Judith Landry, London, 1967; F. Choay, *The Modern City: Planning in the Nineteenth Century*, trans. from French by M. Hugo and G. R. Collins, London, 1969; W. L. Creese, *The Search for Environment; the garden city before and after*, Yale, 1966; J. S. Curle, *Victorian Architecture, Its Practical Aspects*, Newton

Abbot, 1973; A. Briggs, *Victorian Cities*, London, 1963, Pelican 1970; B. Disraeli, *Sybil or the Two Nations*, London, 1845 *et seq*; J. Hole, *The Homes of the Working Classes with suggestions for their improvement*, London, 1866; L. Mumford, *The Culture of Cities*, London, 1938, *The City in History*, London, 1961, Pelican 1966; S. Pollard, *The Genesis of Modern Management*, London, 1965, Pelican 1968, 'The Factory Village in the Industrial Revolution', *English Historical Review*, No. 79, 1964; C. Stewart, *A Prospect of Cities*, London, 1958; J. N. Tarn, *Five Per cent Philanthropy – An Account of Housing in Urban Areas between 1840 and 1914*, London, 1973.

3.   Pollard, *Management*, p. 234; A. Ure, *The Philosophy of Manufactures*, London, 1835, 2nd impression 1967; P. Gaskell, *Artisans and Machinery. The Moral and Physical Condition of the Manufacturing Population*, London, 1836. See also D. W. Smith, 'Textile Factory Settlement in the Early Industrial Revolution', PhD thesis, Aston University, 1976, pp. 108-94.

4.   Choay, *op. cit.*, pp. 27-32, 97-9.

5.   See, for example, H. Roberts, F.S.A., *The Dwellings of the Labouring Poor*, London, 1850, 4th ed. 1867; Cheyne Brady, *The Practicability of Improving the Dwellings of the Labouring Class*, London, 1859.

6.   Frederick Pollard, *Essay and Design for the best and most economical method of building a pair of labourers' cottages*, London, 1851; *The Working Man*, 3 Mar. 1866.

7.   *Obs*, 7 Mar. 1850.

8.   C. Kingsley, 'Great Cities and their Influence for Good and Evil', *Miscellanies*, Vol II., London, 1857.

9.   The suggestion, for instance, that all houses in Saltaire were built with three bedrooms. He was probably unaware when he completed his manuscript that the Bradford building by-laws had been altered once again. The building of back-to-back houses could be resumed after 1864 though they were to be of an improved type.

10.   J. Godin, *Solutions Socials*, Paris, Brussels, 1871; R. H. Guerrand, *Les Origins du Logement Social en France*, Paris, 1967.

11.   G. Camblin, *The Town in Ulster*, Belfast, 1951; *Illustrated London News*, 3 May 1890; E. Akroyd, 'On the relations betwixt Employers and Employees', *Trans. NAPSS*, 1857.

12.   J. N. Tarn, 'The Model Village at Bromborough Pool', *The Town Planning Review*, Vol XXXV, 1964-5, pp. 329-36; J. P. Wilson, *Letters to the boys and men of Price's Patent Candle Company*, London, 1854 (BL; see particularly letter d. Easter Day 1852).

13.   Balgarnie, pp. 121-2.

14.   *Obs*, 3 Apr. 1851.

15.   Balgarnie, p. 114; Correspondence with the General Board of Health, 5 Dec. 1851-23 Nov. 1854 *passim* (MH 13/166 PRO).

16.   *Reynolds's*, 29 Nov. 1857; *Obs*, 9 Apr. 1874 – Shipley Glen.

17.   R. Baker, *The Present Condition of the Working Classes*, Bradford, 1851.

18.   Tenancy Agreement, Ada Street 1883 – in Saltaire Library; *Practical Magazine*, Vol. 3, No 15, 1874, p. 165; Hole, *op. cit.*, p. 68; Shipley Local

Board of Health, District Rate Book 1871 (BCL).

19. *Obs*, 20 Feb. 1872.
20. *Ibid*, 21 Dec. 1859, 17 Oct. 1872.
21. J. S. Fletcher, *A Picturesque History of Yorkshire*, Vol II., London, pp. 159-61.
22. Quoted in G. M. Young, *Victorian England, Portrait of an Age*, London, 1936, p. 24.
23. *The Congregational Register of the West Riding of Yorkshire*, Vol. VI, London and Leeds, 1860, pp. 26-39.
24. E. M. Wright, *The Life of Joseph Wright*, Vol. I, London, 1932, pp. 30-2.
25. *Obs*, 8 Nov. 1855; for Holroyd, see *Souvenir of the Unveiling of the Holroyd Memorial in Clayton Church yard*, Bradford, 1893, and M. Vicinius, *The Industrial Muse*, New York, 1974; for Waddington, C. Green (ed.), *Flowers from the Glen. The Poetical Remains of J. W. of Saltaire*, Bradford, 1862.
26. Holroyd, *op. cit.*, pp. 38-9; Balgarnie, p. 144; *Obs*, 8 Nov. 1869.
27. *Obs*, 7 Oct. 1868.
28. *Ibid*, 11 Oct. 1866, 15, 29 Aug. 1867.
29. *Ibid*, 10 Mar. 1870; Shipley School Board, *Report of the First Three Years' Work* ending 29 Sep. 1877.
30. Holroyd, *op. cit.*, pp. 43-50; *Obs*, 31 Jul. 1869; for Wildman, see *Obs*, 24 Mar. 1870.
31. *Obs*, 14 Apr., 7 May 1871; Balgarnie, pp. 228-33.
32. *Obs*, 23 Mar. 1871.
33. *Ibid*, 1 May 1875.
34. *The Non Conformist*, Vol. XIII, New Series, No. 411, 28 Sep. 1853, p. 779; *The Temperance Spectator*, 1 Apr. 1865.
35. *Obs*, 6 Oct. 1853.
36. In possession of Mr B. H. Allsopp of Shipley.
37. *The Working Man*, 19 May 1866; *Obs*, 29 Jan. 1870; *Reynolds's*, 29 Nov. 1857.
38. J. Ruskin, *The Crown of Wild Olives*, London, 1866 (1906 edn), pp. 105-6.
39. Balgarnie, pp. 218-26; *Obs*, 14 Sep. 1869 on the award of a baronetcy.
40. Poem – 'A Visit to Saltaire, Christmas 1857', *Obs*, 21 Jan. 1858.
41. Census Enumerators' Returns – Saltaire 1861, 1871.
42. Queensbury, dominated by Fosters of Black Dyke, also claimed to have no Irish families. *Obs*, 25 Jul. 74.
43. Enumerators' Returns, *loc. cit.*
44. *Reynolds's*, 29 Nov. 1857; *All the Year Round*, 21 Jan. 1871.
45. Enumerators' Returns, *loc. cit.*
46. *Idem*; I should like to thank Stephen Daniel for a valuable exchange of ideas and information; for discussion of the textile village community – R. Blauer, *Alienation and Freedom*, Chicago, 1964, pp. 58-85.
47. *Obs*, 9 Nov. 1874.
48. W. White, *A Month in Yorkshire*, London, 1858.
49. Medical Officer of Health for Shipley, *Sanitary Report for the Year 1906*; *Annual Report of the Medical Officer of Health for Bradford*, 1906.
50. Dr H. Jones, 'Relative Mortality Back to Back/Through Houses Shipley/

Notes

Saltaire', *Public Health*, Vol. 5, 1892-3.

51. *PP* 1874, Vol. XXIII, Part I, Royal Commission on Friendly and Benefit Building Societies Fourth Report of the Friendly Societies Committee; *SST*, 15 Mar. 1879; Holroyd, *op. cit.*, p. 88.

52. *Rules of the Saltaire Women's Sick Benefit Society*, Shipley; Holroyd, *op. cit.*, p. 89.

53. *PP*, Accounts and Papers 1874, Vol. LXII, p. 403, Return of Industrial and Provident (Co-operative) Societies; *Obs*, 29 Nov. 1866, 3 Jun. 1867, 13 Mar. 1871, 16 Nov. 1874; *SST*, 16 Jul. 1876, 10 Feb. 1877, 10 Aug. 1878; Saltaire Co-operative Society Ltd, 18th Report and Balance Sheet, 30 Jan. 1877.

54. *Obs*, 14 Apr. 1871; *SST*, 8 Dec. 1877.

55. *Obs*, 13 Nov. 1869, 28 Jun. 1870, 28 Dec. 1872.

56. *Ibid*, 27 Aug. 1863.

57. *Ibid*, 29 Jan. 1865, 9 Mar. 1871; *SST*, 21 Oct. 1876; R. G. Barlow, *Forty Years of First Class Cricket. His Career and Reminiscences*, Manchester, 1908.

58. *Obs*, 3 Oct. 1877, 19 Mar. 1868, 23 Jun. 1877, 16 Jan. 1875, 3 Oct. 1877.

59. *Ibid*, 17 Jul. 1856; *The Practical Magazine*, Vol. 3, No. 15.

60. *Working Man*, 16 Jun. 1866; F. M. Herrington, *The Lions of Saltaire and other pieces*, Huddersfield, 1871.

61. Saltaire Congregational Church Records – held at the United Reformed Church, Saltaire. I should like to thank the Rev. T. J. Harwood, for permission to use these.

62. *Saltaire Methodist Church 1865-1968*, Souvenir Centenary Handbook; Minutes of the Wesleyan Methodist Sunday School, Saltaire 1869-1878, 1878-1890 (held in Saltaire Library).

63. Holroyd, *op. cit.*, p. 85.

64. *Shipley Times and Express* (previously *Shipley and Saltaire Times*), 30 Jun. 1914; *Obs*, 5 Apr. 1866.

65. Methodist Sunday School Minutes, *loc. cit.*: *Obs*, 16 Jan. 1868.

66. *Obs*, 4 Jan. 1855.

67. *Ibid*, 3 May, 12 Apr. 1866, 24 Jul. 1867, 12 Mar. 1868.

68. William Henry Ellis, *A Few Observations on so-called Sorters' Disease*, Bradford, 1874; *Obs*, 25 Mar., 21 Dec. 1874, 7 Jan. 1875.

69. *SST, Obs*, Feb.–Mar. 1876 *passim*; *Bradford Chronicle and Mail*, 16 Mar. 1877.

70. *Obs*, 16 Mar. 1865.

71. *Ibid*, (18, 25 Sep. 1856, 24 Sep. 1857, 23 Sep. 1858, 29 Sep. 1859, 22 Sep. 1864, 27 Sep. 1873.

72. *Ibid*, 30 Nov., 1 Dec., 3 Dec. 1874.

73. *Reynolds's*, 22 Mar. 1868; Balgarnie, p. 44; *Obs*, 16 Mar. 1868.

74. *Obs, SST*, Jun.–Jul. 1876, *passim*; *Capital and Labour*, 24, 31 May 1876.

75. *Obs*, 14 Aug. 1872.

76. *Capital and Labour*, 31 Dec. 1873; *Obs*, 20 May 1874.

77. *SST*, 5 Apr. 1879.

78. Deed of Endowment – the Salts Schools, 1877; see also *SST*, 29 Sep., 6

Oct. 1877 and 8 Oct. 1879 – speech by W. E. Forster.

79. *Obs*, *SST*, Jan.–Jul. 1892, *passim*; *SST*, 5 Aug. 1893.
80. G. von Schulze Gaevernitz, *Social Peace* (trans. from German by C. M. Wicksteed), London, 1892, pp. 58-9.
81. *Yorkshire Observer* (previously *Bradford Observer*), 1 Aug. 1933.

VII. The 'Grand Old Man', 1868-1877

1. *Obs*, 6 Jan. 1867, 23 Jan. 1868.
2. Sigsworth, *Black Dyke*, Chap. 3, pp. 72-134.
3. *PP*, The Censuses of England and Wales, 1861, 1871, 1881, 1901; see also T. Welton, *England's Recent Progress, 1881-1901*, London, 1911.
4. For politics of the period, see D. G. Wright, 'Politics and Opinion in Nineteenth Century Bradford 1832-1880', 2 vols, PhD thesis, Leeds University, 1966, and his 'The Bradford Election of 1874' in Jowitt and Taylor (eds); Tholfsen, *op. cit.*, Chap. 10.
5. *Obs*, Nov.–Dec. 1868, *passim*.
6. *Obs*, Feb.–12 Mar. 1869, *passim*; *The Liberator*, Vol. XV., 1 Apr. 1869.
7. K. Laybourn, 'The Attitude of Yorkshire Trade Unions to the Economic and Social Problems of the Great Depression 1873-1896', Chap. 3, unpublished PhD, thesis, Lancaster University, 1972; J. Reynolds, *Letterpress printers*; see also W. Hamish Fraser, *Trade Unions and Society, the Struggle for Acceptance*, London, 1874.
8. *Obs*, 4 Jul., 12 Dec., 30 May 1874.
9. Fraser, *op. cit.*, p. 160.
10. *Obs*, 10 Jun. 1872.
11. Ashraf, *op. cit.*, pp. 24-6; *Reynolds's*, 28 Dec. 1873; *Obs*, 23 Jan. 1874; *Bradford Observer Budget*, 27 Dec. 1873.
12. See pp. 341, 344, 345, infra.
13. *Obs*, 25 Mar. 1872.
14. *Reynolds's*, 18 Feb. 1872.
15. *Obs*, 17 Jan. 1871; *Reynolds's*, 22 Jan. 1871.
16. Wright, 'Election of 1874', *op. cit.*; *Obs*; *Bradford Chronicle and Mail*, *passim*, Feb. 1874.
17. *The Non Conformist*, Vol XXXV, New Series, No. 1473, London, 1874.
18. *The Times*, *The Daily News*, 2 Feb. 1874; *Obs*, 3 Feb. 1874.
19. *Obs*, *Bradford Chronicle and Mail*, *loc. cit.*
20. Perkin, *op. cit.*, pp. 299-302; B. Simon; *Studies in the History of Education, 1780-1870*, London, 1960, Chaps 6 and 7.
21. A. E. Busby, *History of the Bradford Grammar School*, Bradford, 1969; *Obs*, 25 May 1878.
22. *Bradford Observer Budget*, 11 Jun. 1870; *Obs*, 19 Aug. 1870.
23. M. F. Ellison, *A Short History of the Bradford Girls' Grammar School 1875-1965*, Bradford, 1965.
24. Balgarnie, Chap. XVI; *Obs*, 14 Sep. 1869, 22, 24 Apr. 1871.
25. *Obs*, Dec. 1876–14 Jan. 1877, *passim*; *SST*, 6, 13 Jan. 1877.
26. *Ibid*, 6 Jan 1877; *The Times*, 30 Dec. 1876.

Index of People

Index

Index

375

General Index

Index

Index

Smoke Pollution 24, 25, 88, 225-7, 247-8
Social Geography 251-2, 328
Socialists (Owenite) 93, 102, 124, 185-6, 259
Societies for the improvement of working class housing 260
Spinning 10, 12, 19-20, 28, 54
State of Trade 21, 33, 62-3, 97-8, 109-10, 117, 122, 130, 148, 164, 326-7
Street Improvement 241-7
Strike of 1825 24, 28-33, 159
Sub-contracting 12, 30
Suffrage, *see* Franchise
Sunday Afternoon Lectures 173
Sunday School 35, 180-81
    Union 181
Surveys of Attendance and Accommodation, Ecclesiastical 71, 179-80, 209

Taunton (Schools Inquiry) Commission 346
Teetotalism, *see* Temperance
Teetotal Hall 184, 188
Temperance 24, 28, 43, 173, 184, 304-6, 350
Textile fortunes 66-75
Tops 10, 29, 109
Tories 26-7, 37-8, 96, 98, 110, 116-17, 119, 130, 151, 195, 230, 233, 331
    see also Conservatives
Town Mission 155, 170-72, 187
Trade Unions 16, 122-5, 155-6, 158-9, 168, 185, 188-91, 333, 335, 335-9
    Bradford Union of Weavers and Woolcombers 30-34
    Demonstration 335-6
    Leeds Union of Clothworkers 33
    Operative Carpenters 32, 37
    Operative Stonemasons 337
Turnpike Roads 11

Universal Suffrage, *see* Franchise

Victoria 259
Voice of the People 5, 284

Wages 30, 98, 156-7, 165
Warehousemen 154, 157-8
Water Company 16, 231-7
Weavers 12, 28-9, 54-5, 90, 98-9, 109, 125, 295
    Protective Association 125
Weaving 10, 20, 54-5
Whitsuntide Gala 173, 176
Window Tax 13
Women in Public Activities 103, 125, 137, 139, 143, 146, 159, 172-3, 185, 318-19, 348
Wool 49-50, 53
    see also Alpaca, *Donskoi*, Mohair
Woolcombers 10, 12, 16, 24, 28-33, 90, 99, 109-10, 122, 125-30, 137, 164-5
    Protective Society 33, 123-5
    Report on Housing 126-9
Woolcombing 10, 20, 30-31, 55-6
    Machines 55-6, 74
Woollen manufacture 10
Wool Market 18
Woolsorters 32, 34, 52, 158, 294
    see also Anthrax
Wool Staplers 11-12, 41-2, 44
Working class(es) 15, 28-36, 96-8, 110, 122-46, 152-92, 201, 205, 210-22, 331, 333-8, 341, 344-5, 348-9
    and Consensus 152-63
    and the factory 158-62
    Religion 35-6, 187-8
    Sub-culture 34-5, 184-93
    see also Saltaire
Worsted Act 162-3
Worsted Committee 13, 21, 71, 162, 171
Worsted Industry 10-11, 18-22, 49-60, 326-7

Yeomanry 34, 106, 136